Computer Engineering

Data Storage, Networking and Security

Nikola Zlatanov

To my friend Steve
with best wishes for life!

7/3/2020

CONTENTS

CHAPTER 1: BOOTING AN INTEL SYSTEM ARCHITECTURE 1

OVERVIEW 1
NON-HOST–BASED SUBSYSTEM STARTUP...2
STARTING AT THE HOST RESET VECTOR 3
MODE SELECTION 3

EARLY INITIALIZATION 7

SINGLE-THREADED OPERATION 7
SIMPLE DEVICE INITIALIZATION 8

CPU INITIALIZATION 9

MICROCODE UPDATE 9
LOCAL APIC 9
SWITCH TO PROTECTED MODE 10
CACHE AS RAM AND NO EVICTION MODE 11
PROCESSOR SPEED CORRECTION 11

MEMORY CONFIGURATION 11

POST-MEMORY..13
   Memory Testing..*13*
SHADOWING 14
EXIT FROM NO-EVICTION MODE AND TRANSFER TO DRAM 14
TRANSFER TO DRAM 15
MEMORY TRANSACTION RE-DIRECTION 16
APPLICATION PROCESSOR (AP) INITIALIZATION...17
CPUID—THREADS AND CORES 17
   Thread:...*17*
   Core:..*17*
   Package:...*17*
   Startup Inter-Processor Interrupt (SIPI)...*18*
   AP Wakeup State *18*
   Wakeup Vector Alignment *18*
   Caching Considerations...*19*
   AP Idle State *19*

ADVANCED INITIALIZATION 19

GENERAL PURPOSE I/O (GPIO) CONFIGURATION 20
INTERRUPT CONTROLLERS 20
   Programmable Interrupt Controller (PIC)...*21*
   Local Advanced Programmable Interrupt Controller(LAPIC)...*22*
   I/O Advanced Programmable Interrupt Controller (IOxAPIC) *22*
   Message Signaled Interrupt (MSI)...*22*
INTERRUPT VECTOR TABLE (IVT) 23
INTERRUPT DESCRIPTOR TABLE (IDT) 23

Exceptions 23
Real Mode Interrupt Service Routines (ISRs) 23
TIMERS 23
Programmable Interrupt Timer (PIT) 23
High Precision Event Timer (HPET) 24
Real Time Clock (RTC) 24
System Management TCO Timer 24
Local APIC (LAPIC) Timer 24
MEMORY CACHING CONTROL 24
SERIAL PORTS 25
Console In/Console Out 25
CLOCK AND OVERCLOCK PROGRAMMING 25
PCI DEVICE ENUMERATION 26
GRAPHICS INITIALIZATION 26
Input Devices 27
USB INITIALIZATION 27
SATA INITIALIZATION 27
SATA CONTROLLER INITIALIZATION 28
Setting the SATA Controller Mode 28

MEMORY MAP 30
REGION TYPES 30
REGION LOCATIONS 30
LOADING THE OPERATING SYSTEM 31

CHAPTER 2 - COMPUTER MEMORY, APPLICATIONS AND MANAGEMENT 32
OVERVIEW 32

COMPUTER MEMORY BASICS 33

TYPES OF COMPUTER MEMORY 35
Framework RAM 36
Store and Registers 38
volatility,primary classification 39

TYPES OF MEMORY 40
VOLATILE MEMORY 40
NON-VOLATILE MEMORY 40
MEMORY MANAGEMENT 40
MEMORY ADMINISTRATION BUGS 41
EARLY COMPUTER FRAMEWORKS 41
VIRTUAL MEMORY 42
MEMORY ASSURANCE 42
MEMORY HIERARCHY 43
THE NEW GENERATION OF MEMORY 47
The Third Dimension 47
A Real Need For Speed 48

CHAPTER 3:COMPUTER BUSSES, PORTS AND PERIPHERAL DEVICES 49

   OVERVIEW 49
   FOUNDATION AND TERMINOLOGY 49
   INTERNAL BUS 51
   EXTERNAL BUS 51
   USAGE POINTS OF INTEREST 52

HISTORY 53

   1ST GENERATION COMPUTER BUSSES 53
      Single framework bus 54
      Minis and Micros 55
   2ND GENERATION COMPUTER BUSSES 56
   3RD GENERATION COMPUTER BUSSES 57
      Examples of internal computer buses: 57
      Examples of external computer buses: 59
   PERIPHERAL DEVICE DEFINITION 60
   SORTS OF PERIPHERAL DEVICES 62
   CASES OF PERIPHERAL DEVICES 63

INTRODUCTION 64

   BUSSES 64
   INTERNAL TYPES OF SLOTS 64
   PCI EXPRESS 65
   PCMCIA 65
   AGP 65

SORTS OF CARDS 65

   VIDEO CARD 65
   SOUND CARD 66

EXTERNAL TYPES OF CONNECTIONS 66

   USB 66
   FIREWIRE 67
   PS/2 67

DEVICES 67

   REMOVABLE STORAGE 67
   NON-REMOVABLE STORAGE 68
   INPUT 68
   OUTPUT 68

CHAPTER 4: HARD DISK DRIVE AND DISK ENCRYPTION 69

   INTRODUCTION 69
   HISTORY 70
   MAGNETIC RECORDING 73
   SEGMENTS 76

Error rates and handling...78

Capacity 82

Estimation 82

System use...83

Units..84

Form factors 84

Value advancement...85

    8-inch 86

    5.25-inch 86

    3.5-inch 87

    2.5-inch 87

    1.8-inch 88

    1-inch 88

    0.85-inch 88

EXECUTION QUALITIES...89

Time to get to data..89

Defragmentation 89

Time to access 89

Look for time 90

Latency 90

Data exchange rate 91

DIFFERENT CONTEMPLATIONS..92

Interfaces and access 92

Integrity and failure 94

SHOWCASE FRAGMENTS 96

Desktop HDDs 96

Portable (tablet) HDDs 96

Endeavor HDDs 97

Customer gadgets HDDs 97

MANUFACTURERS AND SALES 98

Outer hard disk drives..98

Visual portrayal 99

Disk encryption 100

Straightforward encryption..100

Disk encryption versus Filesystem-level encryption 101

Disk encryption and Trusted Platform Module 102

Usage...102

Password/data recovery mechanism 103

Challenge/reaction secret word recuperation instrument...103

ERI document watchword recuperation component 103

Security concerns 104

FULL DISK ENCRYPTION 104

BENEFITS 105
THE BOOT KEY ISSUE 105

CHAPTER 5: SCSI DRIVES AND RAID ARRAYS FUNCTIONALITY 107

INTRODUCTION 107
SCSI BASICS 107
   SCSI connector...*107*
SCSI TYPES 108
   SCSI-1 ....*109*
   SCSI-2: *109*
   SCSI-3: *109*
SCSI CONTROLLER 110
CONTROLLERS, DEVICES, AND CABLES...110
   Inward layer:...*111*
   Media layer:..*111*
   External layer: *111*
SCSI TERMINATION 111
SIGNALING 112
   Single-ended (SE) *112*
   High-voltage differential (HVD) *112*
   Low-voltage differential (LVD) *112*
AN ACTIVE TERMINATOR 112
SCSI COMMAND PROTOCOL..113

RAID 115

WHAT IS RAID?...115
DATA STRIPING 116
THE DIFFERENT RAID LEVELS 117
   RAID-0..*117*
   RAID-1 ....*117*
   RAID-2 ....*118*
   RAID-3 ....*118*
   RAID-4 ....*118*
   RAID-5 ....*118*
   Synopsis *119*
HOW TO DEAL WITH RAID 119
   Hardware RAID *119*
   Programming RAID *120*
HARDWARE VERSUS PROGRAMMING RAID 121
FRONT-END AND BACK-END SIDE..122
VENTURE CONTROLLERS 122
BASIC CONTROLLERS...123

CONCLUSION 123

CHAPTER 6:INSIDE OF AN OPEN-SOURCE SATA CORE...125

SATA OVERVIEW 125

NOTES ON TERMINOLOGY 127

DWORD: 127

CORE, HOST BUS ADAPTER (HBA): 128

HOST: 128

DISK, DEVICE: 128

OUTLINE INFORMATION STRUCTURE (FIS): 128

SATA DETAILS **128**

PHYSICAL LAYER 128

OUT-OF-BAND SIGNALING 129

THE OOB SEQUENCE 130

8B/10B ENCODING 131

THE COMMA AND THE ALIGN PRIMITIVE 133

SPREAD-SPECTRUM CLOCKING 134

LINK LAYER 134

  ALIGN *135*

  SYNC: *136*

  X_RDY *136*

  SOF *136*

  R_IP *136*

  HOLD *136*

  HOLD_ACK *136*

  EOF *137*

  WTRM *137*

  R_OK *137*

  R_ERR *137*

  CONT *137*

  PMREQ_P/PMREQ_S/PMACK/PMNAK *138*

FLOW CONTROL 138

CRC 140

SCRAMBLING 140

TRANSPORT LAYER 140

SATA CONCLUSION **142**

CHAPTER 7: CUDA AND GPU ACCELERATION OF IMAGE PROCESSING **143**

OVERVIEW 143

MULTICORE CPU AND GPU 144

CUDA IS JUST APPROPRIATE FOR PROFOUNDLY PARALLEL CALCULATIONS 144

CUDA IS TO A GREAT DEGREE APPROPRIATE FOR CALCULATING 144

CUDA IS APPROPRIATE FOR HUGE DATASETS 145

COMPOSING A KERNEL IN CUDA 145

COMPOSING PROGRAMS WITH CUDA 146

CUDA WITHOUT A GRAPHICS CARD 146

DEVICE ARCHITECTURE: STREAMING MULTIPROCESSOR (SM) **146**

TRANSPARENT SCALABILITY 148

SM Warp Scheduling 148

Computational capacities 149

GPU quickened video translating 149

Video decoding processes that can be accelerated 150

Acceleration 150

GPU FRAMES **150**

graphics cards 150

Integrated graphics solutions 151

Hybrid solutions 152

Stream Processing and General Purpose GPUs (GPGPU) 153

External GPU (eGPU) 154

Applications 155

GPU organizations 155

CHAPTER 8: ARCHITECTURE AND OPERATION OF A WATCHDOG TIMER **156**

Overview 156

Architecture and operation 156

Watchdog restart 156

Single-stage watchdog 157

Multistage watchdog 157

Time intervals 158

Corrective actions 158

Fault detection 159

errors we caught 161

First aid 162

Sanity checks 163

Picking the timeout interim 165

Duplicating the interim 166

SELF-TEST **167**

Multitasking 167

The way of the undertakings 168

Waiting assignments 170

Concurrent access 172

Monitor interval 172

Debugging 172

Need of monitoring undertaking 173

Debilitating the Watchdog Timer 174

CONCLUSION **174**

CHAPTER 9:THE KERNEL BOOT PROCESS **175**

Introduction 175

Elements of the Kernel 176

The central processing unit (CPU) 176

Arbitrary access memory (RAM) 176

Input/output (I/O) devices 176
Device management 177

CHAPTER 10: ARM ARCHITECTURE AND RISC APPLICATIONS 185

Overview 185
ARM's Basics 186
ARM's Business Is Different 187
What Does ARM Mean For Consumers 188
Will ARM Be In Your PC 188

OAK SEED RISC MACHINE: ARM2 189

Market share 190
Core license 191
Structural permit 193
Cores 193

ARM CORTEX APPLICATION PROCESSORS 193

Cortex-A Series - High performance processors for feature rich Operating Systems 193
Applications include 193
Cortex-R Series - Exceptional performance for ongoing applications 194
Applications include 194
Cortex-M Series - Cost-touchy answers for deterministic microcontroller applications 194
Applications include 195
SecurCore™ 195
FPGA Cores 195

RUNDOWN OF APPLICATIONS OF ARM CORES 196

32-bit architecture 196
CPU modes 197
Client mode: 197
FIQ mode: 197
IRQ mode: 197
Manager (svc) mode: 197
Prematurely end mode: 197
Indistinct mode: 198
Framework mode (ARMv4 or more): 198
Screen mode (ARMv6 and ARMv7 Security Extensions, ARMv8 EL3): 198
Hyp mode (ARMv7 Virtualization Extensions, ARMv8 EL2): 198

INSTRUCTION SET 198

Stack/store architecture 198
Additional Design Features 199
Number-crunching instructions 199
Registers 200
Aliases: 200
Conditional execution 201
Different elements 203

PIPELINES AND OTHER USAGE ISSUES...204
COPROCESSORS..204
DEBUGGING..204
DSP ENHANCEMENT INSTRUCTIONS..205
SIMD AUGMENTATIONS FOR SIGHT AND SOUND...205
THUMB..206
THUMB-2...207
THUMB EXECUTION ENVIRONMENT (THUMBEE)...208
FLOATING-POINT (VFP)..208
    VFPv1 Or VFPv2...209
    VFPv3 or VFPv3-D32...209
    VFPv3-D16...209
    VFPv3-F16..209
    VFPv4 or VFPv4-D32...209
    VFPv4-D16..210
    VFPv5-D16-M..210
PROGRESSED SIMD (NEON)...210
SECURITY EXPANSIONS (TRUSTZONE)...211
NO-EXECUTE PAGE INSURANCE..212
EXPANSIVE PHYSICAL ADDRESS EXTENSION...212
    ARMv8-R...212
64/32-BIT ARCHITECTURE...212
    ARMv8-A...212
    ARMv8.1-A...213
    AArch64 highlights..213
RECORDED WORKING FRAMEWORKS...214
INSTALLED WORKING FRAMEWORKS...214
CONSTANT WORKING FRAMEWORKS..214
CELL PHONE WORKING FRAMEWORKS..214
DESKTOP/SERVER WORKING FRAMEWORKS...214
    64-bit working frameworks...215
DESKTOP/SERVER WORKING FRAMEWORKS...215
PORTING TO 32-OR 64-BIT ARM WORKING FRAMEWORKS...215

CHAPTER 11ARDUINO AND OPEN SOURCE HARDWARE AND SOFTWARE.......................................216

PHILOSOPHY...216
WHY ARDUINO..216
HISTORY..218
HARDWARE...219
OFFICIAL BOARDS...221
SHIELDS...222
SOFTWARE...222
TEST PROGRAM..223
DEVELOPMENT...224
APPLICATIONS...224
ACKNOWLEDGMENTS...225

LEGAL QUESTION 225

CHAPTER 12:CHANNEL MULTIPLEXING, BANDWIDTH, DATA RATE AND CAPACITY **227**

INTRODUCTION 227

CHANNEL MULTIPLEXING 227

TIME DIVISION MULTIPLEXING (TDM) 227

FREQUENCY DIVISION MULTIPLEXING (FDM) 230

Variations of FDM 232

SPACE DIVISION MULTIPLEXING (SDM) 234

MIX OF FDM,TDM AND SDM 234

CONNECTION BETWEEN BANDWIDTH, DATA RATE AND CHANNEL CAPACITY 235

Flag Bandwidth 235

Channel Bandwidth 235

Channel Capacity or Maximum Data rate 235

NYQUIST CRITERIA FOR MOST EXTREME DATA RATE FOR SILENT CHANNELS 236

SHANNON'S CHANNEL CAPACITY CRITERIA FOR LOUD CHANNELS 238

CHAPTER 13: CPU VS. SOC – THE BATTLE FOR THE FUTURE OF COMPUTING **240**

CENTRAL PROCESSING UNIT 240

LITTLE SCALE JOINING CPUS... 243

VAST SCALE MIX CPUS.. 243

MICROPROCESSORS...**244**

OPERATION 246

FETCH 247

DECODE... 247

EXECUTE 248

STRUCTURE AND EXECUTION 248

CONTROL UNIT **250**

ARITHMETIC LOGIC UNIT... 250

MEMORY MANAGEMENT UNIT 250

INTEGER RANGE 251

CLOCK RATE 252

PARALLELISM 254

Instruction-level parallelism (ILP) 255

task-level parallelism (TLP) 255

INSTRUCTION-LEVEL PARALLELISM 256

TASK-LEVEL PARALLELISM 258

DATA PARALLELISM 260

PERFORMANCE 261

SYSTEM ON A CHIP **262**

STRUCTURE 264

CONFIGURATION STREAM.. 266

FABRICATION 267

THE DISTINCTION BETWEEN A SOC AND CPU 269

ARE CPUS IN TRANSIT OUT 270

CHAPTER 14: DIGITAL SIGNAL PROCESSING USING ADC AND DAC **274**

OVERVIEW 274
QUANTIZATION 274
DITHERING 278
THE SAMPLING THEOREM 279
DIGITAL-TO-ANALOG CONVERSION 286
ANALOG FILTERS FOR DATA CONVERSION 290
CHOOSING THE ANTIALIAS FILTER 299
MULTIRATE DATA CONVERSION 303
SINGLE BIT DATA CONVERSION 306

CHAPTER 15: DYNAMIC MEMORY ALLOCATION AND FRAGMENTATION **314**

INTRODUCTION 314
C/C++ MEMORY SPACES 314
    Static memory...314
    Automatic variables 315
    The heap 315
DYNAMIC MEMORY IN C 316
    The malloc() 316
    The free() 316
    The calloc() 317
    The realloc() 318
DYNAMIC MEMORY IN C++ 318
ISSUES AND PROBLEMS 319
    Sufficiency 319
    Garbage administration...319
    Fragmentation 319
    Timeliness 319
STACKS 320
UTILIZATION OF MALLOC() 320
MEMORY FRAGMENTATION 321
MEMORY WITH A RTOS...323
CORE RTOS BLOCK/PARTITION MEMORY ALLOCATION 323
MEMORY LEAK DETECTION 325
REAL-TIME MEMORY SOLUTIONS 326
STACKS 326
DYNAMIC MEMORY 327
CONCLUSION 328

CHAPTER 16: PROGRAMMABLE LOGIC DEVICES AND EMBEDDED SYSTEMS **329**

INTRODUCTION 329
DIFFERENT TYPES OF PROGRAMMABLE LOGIC 330
    PLDs 330
    CPLDs 331

FPGAs *333*

EQUIPMENT PLAN AND ADVANCEMENT 334

DEVICE PROGRAMMING 337

APPLICATIONS 337

PROTOTYPING 338

EMBEDDED CORES 338

HALF BREED CHIPS 339

RECONFIGURABLE COMPUTING 339

POINTS TO KEEP IN MIND FOR PROGRAMMABLE LOGIC (PL) SELECTION 339

    1.   *Entryway Count* *339*

    2.   *Number of I/O Pins* *340*

    3.   *Cost per Chip* *340*

    4.   *Accessible Tools* *340*

    5.   *Performance* *340*

    6.   *Power Consumption* *341*

    7.   *Packaging* *341*

USING PROGRAMMABLE LOGICDEVICES 341

PLDAPPLICATIONS 343

WHYPLDS ? 344

    Increased Integration *344*

    Lower Power *344*

    Improved Reliability *344*

    Easier To Use! *344*

    Easier to Change *344*

ILLUSTRATION DESIGN 345

    Example ABEL-HDL DescriptionFile *347*

    Example VHDL Description File *348*

    Example Verilog Description File *348*

CHAPTER 17: THE DATA CENTER EVOLUTION FROM MAINFRAME TO CLOUD **349**

MAINFRAME 349

DIFFERENCES FROM SUPERCOMPUTERS 350

CLOUD 351

WHAT IS A MAINFRAME COMPUTER? 352

IS THE MAINFRAME DIED? 353

THE MAINFRAME IS' N DEAD 353

THE MAINFRAME'S PLACE IN THE CUTTING EDGE CLOUD WORLD 354

CLOUD COMPUTING 357

RELATIVE CONCEPTS 359

    Mode, Client–server *361*

    Framework computing *361*

    Haze computing *361*

    Dew computing *361*

    Mainframe computer *361*

    Utility computing *362*

    Shared *362*

ATTRIBUTES 362
    Performance *363*
    Efficiency *363*
    Reliability *363*
    Scalability and elasticity *363*
    Security *363*
FIVE FUNDAMENTAL ATTRIBUTES 364
    On-demand self-service *364*
    Broad network access *364*
    Asset pooling *364*
    Quick versatility *364*
    Measured service *365*
SERVICE MODELS 365
INFRASTRUCTURE AS A SERVICE (IAAS) 366
PLATFORM AS A SERVICE (PAAS) 366
SOFTWARE AS A SERVICE (SAAS) 367
CLOUD CUSTOMERS 368
DEPLOYMENT MODELS 369
PRIVATE CLOUD 369
PUBLIC CLOUD 370
HYBRID CLOUD 370
OTHERS 371
    Community cloud *371*
    Distributed cloud *372*
    Intercloud *372*
    Multicloud *373*
ARCHITECTURE 373
CLOUD ENGINEERING 374
SECURITY AND PROTECTION 374
LIMITATIONS 375
WHAT'S TO COME 376
CONCLUSION 376
SHORTAGE VERSUS WEALTH, RATIONAL VERSUS COUPLED ARE SIMILARLY AS CRITICAL 377
THE TRIUMPH OF SW OVER HW 378

CHAPTER 18: COMPUTER SECURITY AND MOBILE SECURITY CHALLENGES 379

PREFACE 379
VULNERABILITIES AND ATTACKS 379
BACKDOORS 379
DISSENT OF-SERVICE ATTACK 380
DIRECT-ACCESS ATTACKS 381
EAVESDROPPING 381
SPOOFING 381
TAMPERING 381
PRIVILEGE ESCALATION 381
PHISHING 382

CLICKJACKING 382

SOCIAL BUILDING AND TROJANS...382

SYSTEMS AT HAZARD 382

BUDGETARY SYSTEMS 383

UTILITIES AND MECHANICAL HARDWARE 383

AVIONICS 383

PURCHASER DEVICES 384

SUBSTANTIAL ENTERPRISES 384

AUTOMOBILES 384

GOVERNMENT 385

EFFECT OF SECURITY RUPTURES..385

ATTACKER INSPIRATION..386

COMPUTER INSURANCE (COUNTERMEASURES)..386

SECURITY MEASURES 386

LESSENING VULNERABILITIES 388

SECURITY BY OUTLINE 388

SECURITY ENGINEERING 389

HARDWARE INSURANCE MECHANISMS 390

    USB dongles *390*

    TPMs *390*

    Computer case interruption detection *391*

    Drive locks *391*

    Incapacitating USB ports..*391*

    Mobile-empowered access devices *391*

SECURE WORKING SYSTEMS 391

SECURE CODING 392

ABILITIES AND ACCESS CONTROL LISTS 392

REACTION TO RUPTURES 393

    Identifying attackers *393*

    pursuing each attacker *393*

    Law enforcement officers..*393*

PROMINENT COMPUTER SECURITY ATTACKS AND RUPTURES 394

    Robert Morris and the principal computer worm *394*

    Rome Laboratory *394*

    TJX loses 45.7m client Visa subtle elements...*394*

    Stuxnet attack *395*

    Worldwide observation revelations *395*

    Target and Home Depot breaks...*395*

    Ashley Madison rupture *395*

LEGAL ISSUES AND GLOBAL REGULATION 396

GOVERNMENT 396

ACTIONS AND TEAMS IN THE US...397

    Enactment..*397*

AGENCIES...398

    Nation Security *398*

    Federal Bureau of Investigation *398*

Division of Justice 398

USCYBERCOM 398

role of FCC 399

Computer Emergency Readiness Team 399

INTERNATIONAL ACTIVITIES 399

FIRST 399

Council of Europe 399

Europe 400

National groups 400

Canada 400

China 401

Germany 401

India 402

Pakistan 402

South Korea 403

Different nations 403

NEW ERA OF WARFARE 403

The cyber security work showcase 404

Security Analyst 404

Security Engineer 404

Security Architect 405

Security Administrator 405

Boss Information Security Officer (CISO) 405

Boss Security Officer (CSO) 405

Security Consultant/Specialist/Intelligence 405

PHRASING 406

authorization 406

Anti-virus software 406

Applications 406

Verification systems 406

Robotized hypothesis demonstrating 406

Backups 407

access control list 407

Chain of trust 407

Secrecy 408

Cryptographic 408

Cyberwarfare 408

Data Integrity 408

Cryptographic systems 408

Mobile security 410

CHALLENGES OF MOBILE SECURITY 411

Threats 411

Outcomes 413

ATTACKS IN LIGHT OF CORRESPONDENCE 414

Attack in light of SMS and MMS 414

ATTACKS IN LIGHT OF CORRESPONDENCE NETWORKS 415

Attacks in light of the GSM networks...*415*

Access Point spoofing...*416*

Rule of Bluetooth-based attacks...*417*

Attacks in view of vulnerabilities in software applications *418*

Working system *418*

Attacks in light of hardware vulnerabilities *419*

Cases of malware...*423*

Ransomware *424*

Spyware *425*

NUMBER OF MALWARE 425

EFFECTS OF MALWARE 426

Conveyability of malware crosswise over stages *426*

Countermeasures...*426*

Security in operating systems *426*

Rootkit Detectors...*427*

Process detachment...*428*

File authorizations...*428*

Memory Protection *428*

Improvement through runtime situations..*428*

Security software *429*

ANTIVIRUS AND FIREWALL 429

VISUAL NOTIFICATIONS 429

TURING TEST..429

BIOMETRIC RECOGNIZABLE PROOF..429

ASSET OBSERVING IN THE SMARTPHONE 430

BATTERY 430

MEMORY USE 430

SYSTEM ACTIVITY 430

SERVICES...431

SYSTEM RECONNAISSANCE 431

SPAM CHANNELS 431

ENCRYPTION OF PUT AWAY OR TRANSMITTED DATA 431

TELECOM ARRANGE OBSERVING 432

MAKER OBSERVATION 432

EVACUATE INVESTIGATE MODE 432

DEFAULT SETTINGS..432

SECURITY REVIEW OF APPLICATIONS..433

IDENTIFY SUSPICIOUS APPLICATIONS REQUESTING RIGHTS..433

DISAVOWAL METHODOLOGY 433

MAINTAIN A STRATEGIC DISTANCE FROM INTENSELY ALTERED SYSTEMS 433

ENHANCE SOFTWARE FIX FORMS 434

USER MINDFULNESS 434

BEING DOUBTFUL 435

AUTHORIZATIONS GIVEN TO APPLICATIONS...435

BE WATCHFUL 435

ENSURE DATA 435

INCORPORATED STORAGE OF INSTANT MESSAGES 436

RESTRICTIONS OF CERTAIN SECURITY MEASURES 436

    Single-assignment system..436

    Vitality self-governance 437

    System Directly...437

UP AND COMING GENERATION OF MOBILE SECURITY 437

RICH OPERATING SYSTEM 437

SECURE OPERATING SYSTEM (SECURE OS) 437

TRUSTED EXECUTION ENVIRONMENT (TEE)...438

SECURE ELEMENT (SE) 438

CHAPTER 1: BOOTING AN INTEL SYSTEM ARCHITECTURE

OVERVIEW

The hardware platform needs to conduct multiple tasks after the external power is connected to the platform for the first time before the processor can be brought out of reset. First, the power supply should be brought to its nominal state; after that, there are a lot of derived voltage levels needed on the settled platform. For instance, the input supply consists of a 12-volt source on the Intel architecture reference platform, but the platform and processor, both require some different voltage rails like 1.5 V, 3.3 V, 5 V, and 12 V. They both also require that the provided voltages are in a certain sequence. This process is known as power sequencing.

This power sequencing is controlled by analog switches, which are typically field effect transistors. A complex program logic device (CPLD) is what usually drives the sequence. A minute number of the input clock and oscillator sources are what the platform clock are derived from too. To produce the derived clocks required for the platform, the devices use a phase locked looped circuitry. These clocks furthermore take the time to unite. The reset line to the processor is de-asserted by the power sequencing CPLD after all of these steps have taken place. A general idea of the platform blocks described is shown in figure 1. Liable on the integration of silicon features, starting before the main processor, about a part of this logic might be controlled by microcontroller firmware on the chip.

Figure 1: **POWER SEQUENCING OVERVIEW**

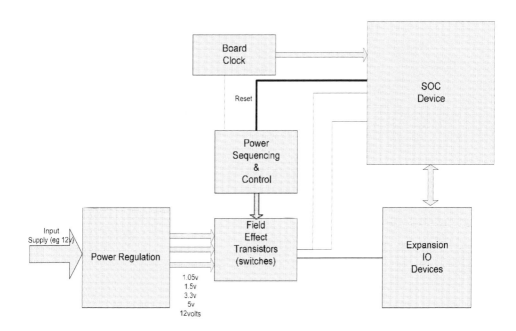

NON-HOST–BASED SUBSYSTEM STARTUP

As a fragment of the Intel architecture, before the core host system starts, a range of subsystems may begin earlier.

One such component is The Intel Manageability Engine (ME) which is available on some mainstream, desktop, and server derived chips. The main system firmware does not initialize these devices; however, there is a chance for some level of interactions that should be considered in the firmware settings, or for the clocks to be able to work properly, or of the flash component in the descriptors for the ME to start up. The main system firmware can make calls to the ME and vice versa.

2

Another example is the micro-engines. In the embedded market sections is the part of telecommunications section mechanisms, which are known as the micro-engines. These engines have their firmware that has the ability of start independently of the BIOS system, but there have to be allowances for this made in the ACPI memory map by the host system BIOS to allow proper interaction to occur between the micro engine subsystem and the host drivers.

STARTING AT THE HOST RESET VECTOR

The processor starts fetching commands once the processor reset line has been de-asserted. The location of these early processor commands are recognized as the reset vector. In the flash memory, the reset vector may comprehend instructions or an indicator to the real staring instruction sequence. The vector location is architecture-specific and mostly depending on the processor is in a fixed location. It is important for the initial address to be a physical address since the MMU (if it exists) has not yet been enabled. The first fetching instructions for Intel architecture begin from 0xFFF, FFF0. To the top of memory, only 16 bytes and these must contain a far jump to the remaining the initialization code. Since there is no software stack or cache as RAM available to date, this initialization code is always written in assembly.

It is pretty common to flush the cache in this step with a WBINV instruction because default does not enable the processor cache. Newer processors do not need the WBINV instruction, but it does not have any harm.

MODE SELECTION

Three operating modes and one quasi-operating mode is supported by IA-32:

• Protected mode offers flexibility, great performance, a wide set of architectural features and backward compatibility with the current software base that exists. It is like the processor's innate operating mode.

• Real-address mode also called "real mode" is an operating mode which gives the programming environment of the Intel 8086 processor a few extensions. These methods have the capability to shift to the system or protected management mode. The system transitions back to Real-address mode after every reset or power turn on.

• System management mode (SMM) provides a transparent mechanism operating system that is used for applying power management as well as OEM differentiation features. This mode is a standard architectural feature in all IA-32 processors, starting with the Intel386 SL processor.SMM is entered with the activation of an external system interrupt pin (SMI#), this produces a system management interrupt (SMI). The processor shifts to a distinct address space in SMM while it saves the context of the program or task that is running currently. Then, the SMM-specific code can be executed transparently. When the processor returns from SMM, it is put back into the state it was in before the SMI.

• The system firmware makes an SMI handler in normal conditions, which may take over the system from the host OS over time. There are usually valid workarounds that are performed in the SMI handle. Managing and logging-off faults may happen at the system level. This brings forward a potential security issue; there is also a lock bit that does not interfere with this mechanism.

• It is usually suggested by Real-time OS vendors to disable this feature because it has a possibility of undermining the nature of the OS environment. In a situation like this, the additional work of the SMI handler has to be merged into the RTOS for that platform, or otherwise, there is a risk of missing out on important information while responding to errors or workarounds. If the SMI handler and RTOS development work together fine, the feature has some benefits.

• The virtual-8086 mode is a quasi-operating mode. Even in protected mode, the processor supports it.

This mode enables the processor to execute 8086 software in a manner that is safe and can perform multiple tasks at one time.

Intel® 64 architecture works well with all operating modes of IA-32 architecture and IA-32e modes:

• IA-32e mode—in this mode, compatibility mode and 64-bit mode are supported by the processor

• 64-bit mode allows 64-bit linear addressing. It works for spaces larger than 64 GB of a physical address as well.

• Compatibility mode lets applications with legacy protected-mode to be run without any changes.

Figure 2: Illustrates how the processor moves between operating modes.

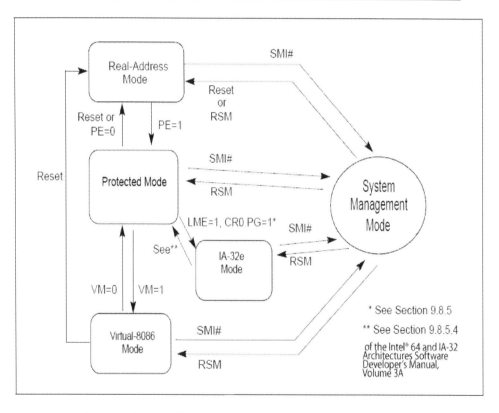

Figure 2 Switching Processor Operating Modes

When switched on for the first time, the processor will be in a special mode which is similar to real mode. However, the top 12 addresses lines will be asserted high. The boot code can be directly retrieved from NVRAM, which has the physical address of 0xFFFxxxxx, with the help of this aliasing.

These top 12 address lines will be run following the instructions provided by the firmware during the execution of the first long jump. If prior to the first long jump, one of the protected modes is not entered, the processor, with 1 MB of addressability, will go into real mode. The chipset will have to alias a range of memory that must be under 1 MB in a range that is equal to 4 GB for the real mode to work without the memory and to continue to access NVRAM. If the chipset does not alias, it will need to be switched to normal mode before the first long jump is performed. Under such circumstances, the internal caches and translation lookaside buffers (TLBs) are also invalidated by the processor. The processor is still able to run in real mode. While some venture it is to make sure that the platform can boot legacy code (example DOS OS) written several years before, it is more an issue of presenting and needing to authenticate the modification into a broad ecosystem of players and developers, and backward compatibility concerns it would generate in test and manufacturing environments, and other usual upgrade hurdles that will remain to maintain the boot mode, as well as Intel, reset vector "real."

A special subsection of the real mode is the initial power-on mode. To allow aliasing, the top 12 address lines are held high where the processor can perform code from the nonvolatile storage, for example, flash, situated within lowest one megabyte as if from the top of memory. The firmware's normal operation (such as BIOS) allows the modes to switch to protected mode quickly in the boost sequence. After the processor gets into protected mode, switching back to real mode is not necessary except during a legacy option ROM is being executed which causes a legacy software interrupt calls. 32-bit code is run by the flat mode. Then the logical address is mapped to the physical address (paging off). The Interrupt Descriptor Table is used for interrupt handling. This mode is suggested to be used to operate all BIOS/boot loaders. The segmented protected mode serves no use in the BIOS sequence for the initialization code.

Intel produces BIOS specifications or BIOS writer's guides. These provide details about different initialization sequences like chip-specific and technology-specific. These manuals provide in-depth details on all parts that need to be set but how to set them is not described in there. From a hardware architecture point of view, the following set up outlines of early initialization and advanced initialization.

EARLY INITIALIZATION

To initialize the processor core and memory, least will be done during the early phase of BIOs/boot loader.

In a system, BIOS built using the Unified Extensible Firmware Interface (UEFI) 2.0 framework, the Security (SEC) and the pre-EFI initialization (PEI) stages are normally identical with "early initialization." It does not trouble if legacy or UEFI BIOS is used; the early initialization sequence is alike for a specified system from a hardware opinion.

SINGLE-THREADED OPERATION

The normally single threaded system firmware is booted by the CPU core or thread. The CPU core/thread is also the bootstrap processor in the multi-core system. A semaphore flag bit in the chipset is what the processors run at RESET. The first processor to get there sets the flag. The proceeding processors find it and mark a WAIT or SIPI or halt state. The first processor initializes the main memory. Application processors (APs) continue with the rest of the boot. For a multiprocessor (MP) system to truly enter MP operation 6, the OS must take over. Though it is feasible to do a partial parallel processing throughout the UEFI boot phase, for instance during memory starting with numerous socket designs, any correct multi thread action would need variations to be made to the DXE phase of the UEFI solutions to permit for this. Visible benefits need to arise for broad adoption.

SIMPLE DEVICE INITIALIZATION

The bootstrap processor (BSP) and I/O peripherals" base address registers are required for the configuration of the memory controller. These are prepared in the early initialization stage.

In the Intel architecture memory map, the device-specific portion is highly configurable. Although some devices are memory-mapped and have mechanisms that are part-specific, a logical PCI bus hierarchy is used to access and see most devices.

I/O or MMIO space is predefined. Device control registers are mapped to these. These can be set up before the memory map is configured. By this process, the early initialization firmware is enabled to configure the memory map of the device that is required to set up DRAM. The firmware must establish the configuring of DRAM that is on the board before configuration of DRAM itself. SOC devices that are based on the architecture of other processors can provide a static address map which is valid for internal peripherals while the external devices are linked with a bus interface. The bus-based devices are plotted to a memory range that is in the SOC address space. A configurable chip select register is provided by these SOC devices that can specify not only the base address but also the size of the chip select enable memory range. The SOC devices that are based on Intel architecture are based on the logical PCI infrastructure for inner and outer devices.

The position of the device in the host memory address space is explained by the PCI base address register (BAR) for individually of the devices. The device initialization naturally allows all the BAR registers for the devices needed as a part of the system boot path. All devices are assigned with a PCI base address by the BIOS by the writing of relevant BAR registers while the PCI enumeration. Formerly full PCI details, the BIOS must allow PCIe BAR and the PCH RCBA BAR for memory, I/O and MMIO dealings during the initial phase of boot.

Reliant on the chipset, some pre-fetchers can be empowered at this stage to speed up the documents transference from the flash device. For ideal performance, attuning of certain DMI link settings might be required.

CPU INITIALIZATION

CPU startup consists of easy configuring of processor and machine registers, enabling the Local APIC and loading a microcode update.

MICROCODE UPDATE

Microcode is involved in the application of machine-defined architecture. It is a hardware layer of instructions. It is most prevalent in CISC-based processors. Microcode is developed by the CPU7 dealer and is united into an internal CPU ROM during production. Since the ill-famed "Pentium flaw," Intel processor architecture lets the microcode to be well-run in the field by a BIOS update or through an OS update of "configuration data."

Nowadays an Intel processor must be requisite the latest microcode update to be measured as an acceptable CPU. Intel delivers microcode updates that are written to the writable microcode store in the CPU. The microcode update can only be loaded and authenticated by the processor for which it was designed due to the way Intel has encrypted these updates. Depending on how many processors are supported, BIOS may have to carry multiple microcode updates on socketed systems. To limit any known errata's exposure in the silicon, the microcode updates should be initialized early in the boot sequence. In case certain events are reset, some microcode updates may have to be reapplied to the CPU.

It is important to load the BSP microcode update before the processor gets in the No-Eviction mode.

LOCAL APIC

It is necessary to enable the Local APIC so it can handle any interference that occurs before protected mode is enabled.

SWITCH TO PROTECTED MODE

Previously the processor can be swapped to protected mode; the software-initialization code must need to load a least amount of protected mode data structures and code modules into memory to support the dependable operation of the processor in protected mode. The following data structures are a part of it:

- An IDT
- A GDT
- A TSS
- (Optional) An LDT

Minimum of one-page directory and one-page table in case paging is used.

A code segment which consists of the code that has to be implemented when the processor enters protected mode

One or more code modules that have the required interrupt and exception handlers

Initialization code must also initialize the following system registers before the processor can be switched to protected mode:

- The GDTR
- Optionally the IDTR. This register can be initialized instantly after protected mode in enabled, but must be done previously interrupts are enabled.
- Control registers CR1 through CR4
- The memory type range registers (MTRRs)

With these code modules, data structures, and system registers initialized, the processor can be swapped to protected mode by 8 loading control register CR0 with values such that set the PE flag (bit 0). It is possible that after this the system will be unable to enter 16b real mode. Until the next hardware reset in done, Legacy Option ROMs and Legacy OS/BIOS interface cannot be entered.

CACHE AS RAM AND NO EVICTION MODE

Since no DRAM is available, the code primarily functions in a stackless atmosphere. Most of the latest processors have an internal cache that can be formed as RAM (Cache as RAM or CAR) to offer a software stack. Developers must write tremendously tight code when 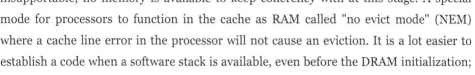 using CAR because, at this point in the boot sequence, an eviction would be insupportable; no memory is available to keep coherency with at this stage. A special mode for processors to function in the cache as RAM called "no evict mode" (NEM) where a cache line error in the processor will not cause an eviction. It is a lot easier to establish a code when a software stack is available, even before the DRAM initialization; least amount of setup is performed by the initialization code to use a stack.

PROCESSOR SPEED CORRECTION

Due to many reasons, a processor may give a sluggish boot performance than its capability. It may be a smaller amount risk to run in a slower mode, or it may be done to save additional power. For a faster boost, it will be substantial for the BIOS to strengthen the speed to something faster. It also may need to initialize the processor's speed step technology. However, this optimization is not compulsory since it is expected that OS is going to have drivers to tackle the issues when it loads.

MEMORY CONFIGURATION

The technology of DRAM and capabilities of memory controller can cause changes in the start-up of the memory controller.

The data on the DRAM controller is exclusive for SOC devices, and in these types of cases, the SOC vendor provides the initialization memory reference code (MRC). Direct contact with Intel is requisite to get access to information at a low level. Deprived of the MRC, developers can comprehend that for a specified DRAM technology, they must trail a JEDEC initialization sequence. It is probable that it will be a single point of entry and exit code, which has multiple boot  paths confined within it and will be a 32-bit protected mode code. The settings for different bit fields such as loading for a given number of banks of memory and buffer strengths is something that is chipset-specific. Memory tests are conducted to make sure memory configuration has good timing. The phenomenon of these tests is an extra difficulty which is hard to duplicate with deficiency of a genuine code which originates from the memory controller vendor. Workarounds for errata and interfaces with some other subsystems like the Manageability Engine can simply not be reinvented, 9 yet can be reverse-engineered. The latter is of course not supported very much.

DRAM configuration parameters include 8-bit, 16-bit, varying memory sizes, power management, add-in module or soldered down (DIMM) configurations, and page closing policy. Considering that soldered down DRAM is usually populated by embedded systems, the configuration at boot time might not have to be discovered by the firmware. These configurations are known as memory-down. The firmware is specifically built for the target configuration. The Embedded Computing Group lays this case forward for Intel preference platform. At current DRAM speeds, the wires among the memory controllers work like transmission lines; the SOC may deliver automatic adjustment and runtime control of resistive compensation (RCOMP) and delay locked look (DLL) competences. These abilities permit the memory controller to alter elements like the drive strength to confirm error-free process with time and temperature differences. Numerous factors and add-in modules that are reliable for this memory are allowed by this platform.

Some forms of factors are often located on embedded systems, and small outline dual in-line memory module (SODIMM) is one of them. The DIMMs provide a serial EPROM. The serial EPROM devices comprehend the DRAM configuration data known as a serial presence detects data (SPD data). The firmware reads the SDP data to recognize the device configuration and successively configures the device. The serial EPROM is connected through SMBUS, due to which the device must be accessible in this early initialization phase so that the software can launch the memory devices on board. It is probable for memory-down motherboards to join serial presence detect EEPROMs to allow for multiple, updatable memory configurations to be controlled proficiently by a single BIOS algorithm. To allow for an EEPROM-less design, it is likely to offer a hard-coded table in one of the MRC files. See Appendix A for the deriving of SPD table.

POST-MEMORY

Multiple cleanup events happen after the completion of initialization of the memory controller.

Memory Testing

 Memory testing has become a part of the MRC. However, it is probable to improve more tests should the design merit it. On a cold boot, the BIOs dealers typically run a memory test. Writing custom firmware needs the writers to select equilibrium between thoroughness and quickness, as greatly embedded/mobile devices necessitate swift boot times and memory testing can take up significant time.

If testing is merited for a design, testing the memory straight after initialization is the time to do it. As the system and the subsystems are not active, and the OS has not chosen the side of the host on the platform. A lot of errors manifest themselves randomly, at times inconsistently. Many hardware features, during boot as well as during runtime, can contribute in this testing. At first, such features were considered to be server features but eventually they have come more into the reach of the client and embedded market.

One of the most occurring is ECC. About some embedded devices use error correction codes (ECC) memory, which could require extra initialization. After power up, the contents may not show due to the position of the correction codes. All memory must be written to since it guarantees that the ECC bits are effective and arranges the ECC bits to the suitable contents. Sometimes, BIOS has to zero the memory manually to prevent any security issues. Occasionally memory controller directly relates the feature into hardware to be more time effective.

The system may not be able to-do a memory wipe or ECC initialization if it is liable on the base of reset and security needs. On a warm reset sequence, memory context can be conserved.

If any memory timing changes happened or other configuration changes occurred that require a reset to take effect, this is the time to accomplish a warm reset. The early initialization starts over with the warm reset but affected registers have to be refurbished then.

SHADOWING

Executing starts off directly from the nonvolatile flash storage (NVRAM) from the reset vector. This operating mode is called execute in place (XIP). The read performance of DRAM is faster as compared to nonvolatile storage. Mostly the early firmware copies from the slower nonvolatile storage into RAM because code running is much slower from flash. A RAM copy is run by the firmware. This is called shadowing. With same contents in RAM and flash, address decoders in the RAM copy are different in shadow, with the RAM copy in front of flash copy. The program execution begins from RAM. The chip is able to pick ranges that can shift from flash to RAM execution, on other embedded systems. Most computing systems run minimal in place. But, some embedded platforms that are limited Ram-wise have to perform all the application in place. This option is usually available for embedded devices that are small. As for Intel architecture, only early boot steps are executed in place, before the configuration of the memory. Instead of a simple copy, sometimes firmware is compressed to minimize the requirements of NVRAM for the firmware. The execution of a compressed image can now be done by the processor in unable to execute. The firmware copy is located below 1 MB on Intel architecture platform.

The act of decompression and data size has both come to a compromise. A decompressed image loads slower than an uncompressed image. If prefetchers are enabled in the processor, then they may quicken up in place execution. In pipelining the data from flash to processor, certain SOCs with internal NVRAM cache buffers offer assistance.

EXIT FROM NO-EVICTION MODE AND TRANSFER TO DRAM

The data and code stacks were held in the processor cache before initializing of memory. The cache must be flushed, and the special temporary cache mode must be left after the memory initialization. The stack will be relocated in system main memory and cache will be reconfigured as part of AP initialization.

Before jumping into this part where the stack should be set up, the shadowed portion of BIOS should be in memory. A memory location for stack space should be selected. The top of the stack should be entered, and the stack will count downwards. Make sure enough memory is provided for the maximum stack.

The SS: SP ratio should be set up properly in real mode. In MRC execution, protected mode is more likely to be used. In this case SS: ESP value is set about memory location.

TRANSFER TO DRAM

This is where the code jumps into memory. The jump will be of no use if this point does not conduct a memory test. A system failure is shown by a POST code between "end of memory initialization" and the first following POST code mostly indicates a catastrophic memory initialization problem. The hardware may require a detailed debug if a new design is present in the hardware.

Figure 3   Intel® Architecture Memory Map at Power On

Reset Vector

0xFFFFFFF0	EIP (last 16 bytes of memory)	4 GB – 16bytes
0xFFFFF	Unaddressable memory in real mode	
	ResetAliased	Reset vector read from oxffff:ffff0 aliased from 0xFFFF0
0xF0000	BIOS/Firmware	960KB
	ExtendedSystem BIOS	896KB
	Expansion area (maps ROMs for old peripheral cards)	768KB
	Legacy video card memory	640KB
0x0000,0000	Accessible RAM memory	

Figure 3   Intel® Architecture Memory Map at Power On

15

MEMORY TRANSACTION RE-DIRECTION

Intel chipsets, for legacy option ROMs and BIOs memory range, typically come with memory aliasing abilities that permit reads and writes to segments of memory lower than 1 MB to be either routed to/from DRAM or nonvolatile storage found just below 4 GB. Aliasing is controlled by certain registers which are called programmable attribute maps (PAMs). During, before and after firmware shadowing, these registers are required to be altered. The redirection of memory access is not the same for all chipsets. For example, a chipset's read and writes could be controlled, while some other chipset would only permit control over the reads.

All FWH entrees to E and F segments (E_0000–F_FFFFh) will be focused to the flash component downstream if PAM registers remain at default values (all 0s) for shadowing.

This will function to boot the system but is very slow. Shadowing, as we know, enhances the speed of boot. E and F segments (E_0000–F_FFFFh) can be shadowed by using PAM registers. Changing the enables (HIENABLE[], LOENABLE[]) to be 10 (write only) will do so. This directs the reads towards the flash device and writes towards memory. First reading and then writing the same address will shadow the data in memory. Memory reads are directed to memory after the BIOS code has been shadowed into memory, and can be changed to '01(read only).

This also prevents accidental overwriting of the image in memory. See the example in Table1.

PAMRegisters	RegisterAddress
PAM0	0F0000–0FFFFFh
PAM1	0C0000–0C7FFFh
PAM2	0C8000–0CFFFFh
PAM3	0D0000–0D7FFFh
PAM4	0D8000–0DFFFFh
PAM5	0E0000–0E7FFFh
PAM6	0E8000–0EFFFFh

Table 1 Address Ranges of the Programmable Attribute Map

16

The chipset datasheet should be consulted for specifics on the memory redirection feature controls valid for the target platform.

APPLICATION PROCESSOR (AP) INITIALIZATION

Even in SOCs, there is a high chance of having more than one CPU cores, which are considered BSP + AP to system initialization. The BSP is responsible for starting and initializing the system, but application processors (APS) also have to be initialized with similar features as BSP. Before memory, the APs are left uninitialized. After initializing, processors are put in WAIT for SIPI state after the memory has already started. To do this the system firmware must:

- Find microcode and then copy it to memory
- Search the CPU code in SPI and copy it to the memory— it is a vital step to prevent XIP for the remaining sequence
- Send Startup IPIs to all processors
- Disable all NEM settings, if this already has not been done
- Load microcode updates on all processors
- Enable Cache On for all processors

Intel® 64 and IA-32 Architectures Software Developer's Manual provides some specifics of this sequence, but more in depth details are given in the BIOS Writer's Guide for that specific processor or on CPU reference code that might be found from Intel. According to UEFI viewpoint, the AP initialization could be either a part of the boot flow's PEI or the DXE phase and could be either in the early or advanced initialization. At the time of this printing, there is some debate as the final location.

CPUID—THREADS AND CORES

Intel processors have different packaging configurations. This is why some terms must be made clear for processor initializing:

THREAD: It is a logical processor that dividends resources with a logical processor present within the same physical package.

CORE: It is a processor that exists with another processor in the same physical package but does not share any resources with it.

PACKAGE: A "chip" that has various cores and threads.

Note: On one package, Threads and cores are noticeable by implementing the CPUID instruction.

Intel® 64 and IA-32 Architectures Software Developer's Manual, Volume 2A provides details of CPUID instructions for various processor families.

Additional packages must be looked for "blindly." BSP should provide enough time for all APs to 'log in' to make sure more than one physical package can be adjusted in the design. After maximum processors "log in," it can be assumed that there are no more processors in the system.

STARTUP INTER-PROCESSOR INTERRUPT (SIPI)

BSP sends an SIPI to all threads and cores for activating secondary threads or cores. SIPI is then sent by using the BSP's LAPIC, indicating the physical address from which the application processor (AP) should start executing. This address should be below 1 MB memory but should be lined up with 4 KB boundary.

AP WAKEUP STATE

The AP begins executing the code on receiving the SIPI, pointed by the SIPI message. Contrary to BSP, AP starts code execution in real mode. This requires that the location of the code that the AP starts executing is located below 1 MB.

WAKEUP VECTOR ALIGNMENT

There is another important architectural restriction in the AP execution starting that is usually not paid attention to. AP initialization's entry point code has to be lined up on a 4-KB boundary. Intel® 64 and IA-32 Architectures Software Developer's Manual, Volume 3A section "MP Initialization Protocol Algorithm for Intel Xeon Processors" can be referred to for this.

The Intel® 64 and IA-32 Architectures Software Developer's Manual, Volume 3A section "Typical AP Initialization Sequence" illustrates what is typically done in by the APs after receiving the SIPI.

CACHING CONSIDERATIONS

To prevent caching conflicts, it should be made sure that caching layouts stay same in the whole system since processors have combinations and attributes regarding shared processing registers between threads.

The Intel® 64 and IA-32 Architectures Software Developer's Manual, Volume 3A section "MTRR Considerations in MP Systems" outlines a safe mechanism for changing the cache configuration in systems containing more than one processor. This can be used for systems with one or more processors.

AP IDLE STATE

How APs behave during firmware initialization depends on the implementation of firmware, but is mostly limited to short initialization interval, after which they enter a halt state with an HLT instruction, and then wait for BSP to order some other operation.

AP processors should be put in the power-on state (WAIT for SIPI) after the OS is ready to perform OS boot. It can be achieved if BSP sends all APs instructions of INIT ASSERT IPI followed by an INIT DEASSERT IPI.

ADVANCED INITIALIZATION

Advanced device initialization follows the early initialization. The advanced initialization makes sure that the DRAM is initialized. This phase is mainly fixated to device-specific initialization. Advanced initialization tasks are also known as Dynamic Execute Environment (DXE) and Boot Device Selection (BDS) phases in a UEFIobased BIOS solution. These devices have to be initialized for enabling embedded systems. The following list is particular to a SOC with Intel architecture but is not suitable for all embedded systems.

- General-purpose I/O (GPIO)
- Interrupt controller
- Timers
- Cache initialization (could be done during early initialization as well)
- Serial ports, Console In/Out
- Clocking and overclocking
- PCI bus initialization
- Graphics (optional)
- USB
- SATA

GENERAL PURPOSE I/O (GPIO) CONFIGURATION

GPIOs are a vital part of the extensibility of the platform. As suggested by the name, GPIOs can be configured for input as well as output. They can also be configured for an innate functionality Some GPIOs can work like strapping pins depending upon pull-up or pull-down resistors. At boot and runtime, these may have a second meaning. These are also sampled by chipset at RESET. They serve as sideband signals for system wake-ups. Most mainstream platforms use GPIO 27.

System-on-chip devices are capable for use in many configurations. The devices that have more capabilities can reveal the I/O pins simultaneously. This happens because many functions are multiplexed to one I/O pin. The pins should be configured before they are used. The configurations allow these pins to be used for a specific function or for general use, under which they can be used as input or output pins. These pins can be used on devices for controlling logic or behavior of the device. GPIO control registers provide control as well as status.

To make sure the feature is properly used, system firmware developer should work between 64 and 256 GPIOs. Separate options between the board designers on each platform should also be worked on.

INTERRUPT CONTROLLERS

There are various ways of handling the interrupt in Intel architecture. The following or their combination can be used to handle interrupts:

- Programmable Interrupt Controller (PIC) or 8259
- Local Advanced Programmable Interrupt Controller (APIC)
- Input/Output Advanced Programmable Interrupt Controller (IOxAPIC)
- Messaged Signaled Interrupt (MSI)

PROGRAMMABLE INTERRUPT CONTROLLER (PIC)

If PIC is the only enabled interrupt device, it is called as PIC Mode. Among modes where PIC takes care of all interrupts, this is the simplest. The system by use of LINT0 operates in single-thread mode. All APIC components are sidestepped.

For every PCI device that is onboard, integrated, and add-in, IRQs should be set by BIOS per board configuration.

Fifteen IRQs are available with two cascaded 8259s in the PIC. IRQ2 is used to link the 8259s, so it is unavailable. There are 8 PIRQ pins supported in PCH on mainstream components. These are named PIRQ[A# :H#], and they route PCI interrupts to IRQs of the 8259 PIC. PIRQ Routing Registers 60h–63h (D31:F0:Reg 60- 63h) controls the PIRQ[A#:D#] routing. The PIRQ[E# : H#] routing is controlled by PIRQ Routing Registers 68h–6Bh (D31:F0:Reg 68 – 6Bh). See Figure 4 below.

The PCH also connects the 8 PIRQ[A# : H#] to 8 individualIOxAPIC input pins, as shown in Table2.

PIRQ#Pin	Interrupt Router Register for PIC	Connected to IOxAPICPin
PIRQA#	D31:F0:Reg60h	INTIN16
PIRQB#	D31:F0:Reg61h	INTIN17
PIRQC#	D31:F0:Reg62h	INTIN18
PIRQD#	D31:F0:Reg63h	INTIN19
PIRQE#	D31:F0:Reg68h	INTIN20
PIRQF#	D31:F0:Reg69h	INTIN21
PIRQG#	D31:F0:Reg6Ah	INTIN22
PIRQH#	D31:F0:Reg6Bh	INTIN23

Table 2 Platform Controller Hub (PCH) PIRQ Routing Table

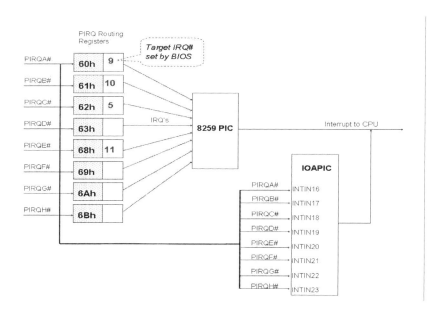

Figure 4 Platform Controller Hubs (PCH) PIRQ to IRQ Router

LOCAL ADVANCED PROGRAMMABLE INTERRUPT CONTROLLER(LAPIC)

The local APIC is present inside the processor. It is responsible for controlling the interrupt delivery to the processor. Every local APIC consists of its set of connected registers along with a Local Vector Table (LVT). The LVT provides specifics of how each interrupt should be delivered to each processor core.

I/O ADVANCED PROGRAMMABLE INTERRUPT CONTROLLER (IOXAPIC)

The ICH/IOH contains the IOxAPIC which increases the number of IRQs accessible to 24. EveryIRQ has a related redirection table entry that can be enabled or disabled. It chooses the IDT vector for the associated IRQ. It is only available in protected mode, however. For more information on initializing the IOxPIC, use Chipset BIOS Writer's Guide.

MESSAGE SIGNALED INTERRUPT (MSI)

MSI is normally not used by the boot loader for handling interrupt.

INTERRUPT VECTOR TABLE (IVT)

The Interrupt Vector Table (IVT) can be found at memory location 0p. It consists of 256 interrupt vectors. The IVT is used in real mode. Every vector address is 32 bits and contains the CS:IP for the interrupt vector. Intel® 64 and IA-32 Architectures Software Developer's Manual, Volume 3A section "Exception and Interrupt Reference" provides a list of real mode interrupts and exceptions.

INTERRUPT DESCRIPTOR TABLE (IDT)

The exception and interrupts required in protected mode are available in the Interrupt Descriptor Table (IDT). These interrupts and exception are present in the same location as IVT. Around 256 interrupt vectors are available in the IDT. Intel® 64 and IA-32 Architectures Software Developer's Manual, Volume 3A give thorough explanation of the IDT.

EXCEPTIONS

Exceptions run to handle error situations. For example exception handle page fault and general protection fault. For every exception handler, placeholders/dummy functions should be used at least. If this isn't done and an exception is met that can't be handled, the system could behave strangely.

REAL MODE INTERRUPT SERVICE ROUTINES (ISRS)

The boot loader and OS communicate with the help of real mode ISRs. For example INT10h is used for video services such as changing video modes and resolution. Sometimes legacy programs and drivers would call INT routine directly considering that the real mode ISRs are be available.

TIMERS

There are numerous timers that can work with latest Intel Architecture system.

PROGRAMMABLE INTERRUPT TIMER (PIT)

The PIT (8254) is located in the IOH/ICH. The system timer IRQ0 is present in the PIT. Refer to the chipset datasheet for more details.

HIGH PRECISION EVENT TIMER (HPET)

HPET contains three timers. It exists in the IOH/ICH. Initializing the HPET is not usually needed by the bootloader. It is only used by OS. Chipset BIOS Writer's Guide offers more details.

REAL TIME CLOCK (RTC)

The system time (seconds/minutes/hours/and so on) is found inside the RTC which can be found in the IOH/ICH. These values are given in CMOS, which is discussed ahead. There is a timer in the RTC that the firmware uses. Look into the appropriate chipset datasheet for further details.

SYSTEM MANAGEMENT TCO TIMER

IOH/ICH contains the TCO timers in which reside the Watch Dog Timer (WDT). Systems hangs can be detected by WDT, and it can reset the system.

Note: It is important for any firmware's debugging on Intel architecture chipsets that use a TCO Watch Dog Timer to be disabled by firmware as quickly as it can be after it is reset. The system resets result when the system is halted for debug before WDT is disabled. WDT powers on the chipset and the firmware debug is not allowed. Watch Dog Timer is re-enabled by OS if it wants. The chipset datasheet can be used as it provides a detailed implementation of the TCO Watch Dog Timer. Refer to the Chipset BIOS Writer's Guide for more details.

LOCAL APIC (LAPIC) TIMER

There is a timer in the Local APIC which the firmware can use. The Intel® 64 and IA-32 Architectures Software Developer's Manual, Volume 3A should be referred to find in depth specifics of the Local APIC timer.

MEMORY CACHING CONTROL

Memory regions having unique caching behaviors applied differ among different designs. If detailed caching requirements are not available for a platform, this guideline will give a "safe" caching environment for the usual systems:

- Default Cache Rule – Uncached.
- 00000000-0009FFFF – Write Back.
- 000A0000-000BFFFF – Write Combined / Uncached
- 000C0000-000FFFFF – Write Back / Write Protect
- 00100000-TopOfMemory – Write Back.
- TSEG – Cached on newer processors.
- Graphics Memory – Write Combined or Uncached.
- Hardware Memory-Mapped I/O – Uncached.

BIOS programs the MTTRS, but Page Attribute Tables (PATs) are used mostly to control caching down to page level with OS.

SERIAL PORTS

Initializing of RS-232 serial port or UART 16550 is done for runtime or debug solutions. USB ports require substantial initialization as well as a huge software stack, but on the contrary, serial ports have a low register-level interface. Even during early POST, a serial port can be enabled to give serial output support.

CONSOLE IN/CONSOLE OUT

Boot service during the DXE phase, comprises console in and console out protocols.

CLOCK AND OVERCLOCK PROGRAMMING

The BIOS sometimes has to activate the system's clocking depending on what solution for clocking the platform has. A subsystem like a Manageability Engine or baseboard management controller (BMC) is likely to have this duty in server platforms. It is likewise conceivable that past the basic clock programming, there might be extended setup choices for over clocking, for example: Enable/disable clock output enables depending on enumeration.

- Clock spread settings are adjusted. The amount is enabled/disabled and altered.
- Settings are given as fixed register values which are decided from expected usages.
- For adaptive clocking support, under-clock the CPU. The BIOS needs to do the adjustment with ramp algorithm if under-clocking is done directly.
- Lock out clock registers before moving on to host OS.

PCI DEVICE ENUMERATION

Peripheral Connect Interface (PCI) device enumeration is a general term that denotes the detecting and assigning of resources to PCI-compliant devices in the system. Resources that are needed by every device are assigned by the discovery process including the following:

- Memory, prefetchable memory, I/O space
- Memory-mapped I/O (MMIO) space
- IRQ assignment
- Expansion ROM detection and execution

PCI device discovery can be used with all the newer (non-legacy) interfaces, for example, PCI Express (PCIe) root ports, USB controllers, SATA controllers, audio controllers, LAN controllers, and many add-in devices. All these newer interfaces work perfectly with the PCI specification.

PCI Specification provides more details. References section provides a list of all possible specifications that can be applied.

The DXE phase does not execute most of the drivers in the UEFI system which is strange. However, theBDS Phase allows most of the needed drivers in UEFI to execute to allow system boot.

GRAPHICS INITIALIZATION

For a platform with a head, the first option to be typically implemented in the string is the video BIOS or Graphics Output Protocol UEFI driver. The console can be configured after the main console out is up and running.

INPUT DEVICES

The board schematics can be referred to determine the I/O devices in the system. A system normally consists of one or more of the following devices:

EMBEDDED CONTROLLER (EC)

In mobile or low power systems normally an embedded controller is used. There is a separate firmware in EC that has control over the power management functions for the system along with PS/2 keyboard functionality. EC datasheet provides more specific details.

SUPER I/O (SIO)

The PS/2, serial, and parallel interfaces are usually controlled by SIO. Instead of implementing a legacy-free system, many of the systems continue to support some of the legacy interfaces. The specific SIO datasheet can be used for details on programming information.

LEGACY-FREE SYSTEMS

USB is used as the input device is by legacy-free systems. In case support for the pre-OS keyboard is mandatory, the legacy keyboard interfaces should be 22 trapped. IOH/ICH BIOS Specification gives more details.

USB INITIALIZATION

Both EHCI and now XHCI are supported by USB controllers. It is comparatively easier to enable the host controller for standard PCI resources. It can be done that USB is not enabled before the OS drivers take over after having a good system. If EHCI or XHCI require pre-OS support, the tasks related to USB subsystem can become relatively complex. An SMI handler has to be used to ploy port 60/64 admissions to I/O space in legacy USB to change these to the correct keyboard or mouse commands. If booting is preferred to USB, then this pre-OS USB support is compulsory

SATA INITIALIZATION

The ATA/IDE programming interface is supported by an SATA controller which also supports the Advanced Host Controller Interface (AHCI) (that is not obtainable on all SKUs). The term "ATA-IDE Mode" in the following discussion denotes ATA/IDE programming interface that brings standard task file I/O registers in use or PCI IDE Bus Master I/O block registers. The AHCI programming interface is mentioned as "AHCI mode," and memory-mapped register/buffer space is used by it. Also, it is a command-list-based model.

RS – Intel® I/O Controller Hub 6 (ICH6) Serial ATA Advanced Host Controller Interface (SATA-AHCI) Hardware Programming Specification (HPS) is a specific document that contains details on SATA software configuration and considerations.

SATA CONTROLLER INITIALIZATION

The following provide the general guidelines for initializing the SATA controller under POST and S3 resume. It is the duty of system BIOS to restore the registers that are initialized during POST after resuming from S3,

SETTING THE SATA CONTROLLER MODE

SATA controller has to be programmed by BIOS before starting other initializing steps. Programming the SATA Mode Select (SMS) field of the Port Mapping Register (D31:F2:Reg 90h[7:6]) sets the SATA controller mode on. During runtime, the SATA controller mode may never be changed by BIOS. It should be noted that the following modes' availability is based on the use of SKU of PCH.

When AHCI Mode or RAID Mode is being enabled by BIOS, D31:F5 should be disabled by setting the SAD2 bit, RCBA + 3418h[25]. It should be made sure by BIOS that memory space, I/O space, or interrupts are not enabled for this device before the device itself is disabled.

IDE MODE

Programming the SMS field, D31:F2:Reg 90h[7:6] to 00 can set the IDE mode. SATA controller is set up to use the ATA/IDE programming interface in this mode. In this mode, 6/4 SATA ports are controlled by two SATA functions. One of these routes up to four SATA ports, D31:F2, and the second one routes up to two SATA ports, D31:F5 (Desktop SKUs only). The Sub-Class Code, D31:F2:Reg 0Ah and D31:F5:Reg 0Ah will be set to 01h in IDE mode. Since there are no special requirements of OS, this mode is also called compatibility mode.

AHCI MODE

By programming the SMS field, D31:F2:Reg 90h[7:6], to 01h the AHCI mode can be selected. SATA controller is set up to use the AHCI programming interface in this mode. One SATA functions D31:F2 controls the six SATA ports. Sub Class Code, D31:F2:Reg 0Ah, will be set to 06h in this mode. No specific OS driver support is needed by this mode.

RAID MODE

By programming the SMS field,D31:F2:Reg 90h[7:6] to 10b, the RAID mode is selected. This mode allows the SATA controller to use the AHCI programming interface. The 6/4 SATA ports are controlled by one SATA function, D31:F2. The Sub Class Code in RAID mode, D31:F2:Reg 0Ah, will be set to 04h. OS driver support is not needed in this mode.

For ROM to be able to access all 6/4 SATA ports, the RAID mode provides the option for ROM to enable and use the AHCI programming interface with the setting of AE bit, ABAR + 04h[31]. There is a chance that all register settings set by the BIOS that can be applied to AHCI mode will also have to be set in RAID. Another possibility is thatto provide AHCI support to ATAPI SATA devices, the BIOS are required, which is not handled by the RAID option ROM.

PCH supports stable image-compatible ID. When the alternative ID enable, D31 :F2 :Reg 9Ch is not set, the PCH SATA controller will report Device ID as 2822h for a desktop SKU.

ENABLE PORTS

Few SATA drives do not start spin-up unless the controller enables the SATA port. To minimize drive detection time, and as a result, the complete boot time, system BIOS should permit the SATA port initially while POST (for instance, immediately after memory initialization) by setting the Port x Enable (PxE) bits of the Port Control and Status register, D31:F2:Reg 92h and D31:F5:Reg 92h. The requirement, to start spin-up of such drive(s).

MEMORY MAP

Firmware not just defines the caching behavior of diverse memory regions for OS consumption, but also provides system memory's "map" to guide the OS which regions are available consumption. Real mode interrupt service 15h, function E8h, sub function 20h (INT15'E820), applied by the firmware, is the mechanism used most widely to load boot and determine the system's memory map.

REGION TYPES

There are many general types of memory regions that the interface defines:

- Memory (1) – General DRAM provided for consumption by OS.
- Reserved (2) – DRAM address that is not for the consumption of OS.
- ACPI Reclaim (3) – Memory that has ACPI tables for which runtime access is not required by firmware.
- Refer to the applicable ACPI specification for specifics.
- ACPI NVS (4) – Memory that consists of all ACPI tables for which runtime access is required by firmware. Seethe appropriate ACPI specification for details.
- ROM (5) – Memory that decodes to nonvolatile storage (for instance, flash).
- IOAPIC (6) – Memory decoded by OAPICs of the system (must be uncached).
- LAPIC (7) –Memory decoded by local APICs of the system (must be uncached).

REGION LOCATIONS

The following regions are reserved in system memory map usually

- 00000000-0009FFFF – Memory
- 000A0000-000FFFFF – Reserved
- 00100000-???????? – Memory (The???????? Specifies that the top of memory changes depending on
- "reserved" items listed below and any other design-based reserved regions.)
- TSEG – Reserved
- Graphics Stolen Memory – Reserved
- FEC00000-FEC01000* – IOAPIC
- FEE00000-FEE01000* – LAPIC

LOADING THE OPERATING SYSTEM

After memory map is configured, a boot device from the prioritized list of possible bootable partitions is chosen. After that, the OS loader, which loads the OS, is called by using the "Load Image" command or Int 19h.

CHAPTER 2 - COMPUTER MEMORY, APPLICATIONS AND MANAGEMENT

OVERVIEW

In processing, memory alludes to the computer equipment gadgets used to store data for prompt use in a computer; it is synonymous with the expression "essential storage." Computer memory works at a fast, for instance, random-access memory (RAM), as a refinement from storage that gives ease back to access program and information storage, however, offers higher limits. If necessary, the substance of the computer memory can be exchanged to optional storage, through a memory administration system called "virtual memory." An ancient equivalent word for memory is a store.

The expression "memory", signifying "essential storage" or "principle memory", is regularly connected with an addressable semiconductor memory, i.e. incorporated circuits comprising of silicon-based transistors, utilized for instance as essential storage additionally different purposes in computers and other computerized electronic gadgets. There are two primary sorts of semiconductor memory, volatile and non-volatile. Cases of non-volatile memory are flash memory (utilized as optional memory) and ROM, PROM, EPROM and EEPROM memory (utilized for putting away firmware, for example, BIOS). Cases of volatile memory are essential storage, which is regularly powerful random-access memory (DRAM), and quick CPU reserve memory, which is normally static random-access memory (SRAM) that is quick however vitality devouring, offering lower memory areal thickness than DRAM.

Most semiconductor memory is sorted out into memory cells or bistable flip-flounders, each putting away one bit (0 or 1). Flash memory association incorporates both one bit for every memory cell and various bits per cell (called MLC, Multiple Level Cell). The memory cells are gathered into expressions of settled word length, for instance, 1, 2, 4, 8, 16, 32, 64 or 128 bit. Each word can be accessed by a paired address of N-bit, making it conceivable to store 2 brought by N words up in the memory. This infers processor enlists typically are not considered as memory, since they just store single word and do exclude a tending to the component. Ordinary auxiliary storage gadgets are hard circle drives and strong state drives.

It is astonishing what number of various sorts of electronic memory you experience in day by day life. A considerable lot of them have turned into a necessary piece of our vocabulary: RAM, ROM, Cache, Dynamic RAM, Static RAM, Flash memory, Memory Sticks, Virtual Memory, Video memory, BIOS.

COMPUTER MEMORY BASICS

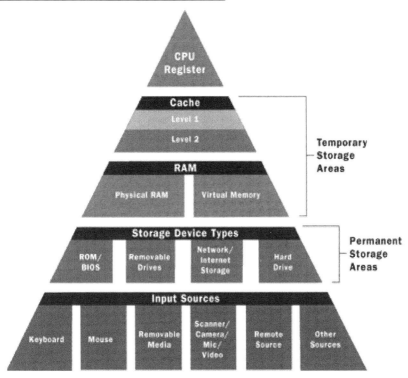

Despite the fact that memory is, in fact, any electronic storage, it is regularly utilized to recognize quick, transitory types of storage. On the off chance that your computer's CPU needed to continually access the hard drive to recover each bit of information it needs, it would work gradually. At the point when the data is kept in memory, the CPU can access it a great deal more rapidly. Most types of memory are proposed to store information incidentally.

As should be obvious in the outline over, the CPU accesses memory as indicated by a particular progression. Regardless of whether it originates from lasting storage (the hard drive) or info (the console), most information goes in random access memory (RAM) first. The CPU then stores bits of information it should access, regularly in reserve, and keeps up certain exceptional directions in the enroll. We'll discuss reserve and registers later.

The greater part of the segments in your computer, for example, the CPU, the hard drive and the working framework, cooperate as a group, and memory is a standout amongst the most fundamental parts of this group. From the minute you turn your computer on until the time you close it down, your CPU is continually utilizing memory. How about we investigate a run of the mill situation:

- You turn the computer on.
- The computer loads information from read-just memory (ROM) and plays out a power-on individual test (POST) to ensure all the significant parts are working legitimately. As a component of this test, the memory controller checks the greater part of the memory addresses with a fast read/compose operation to guarantee that there are no blunders in the memory chips. Perused/compose implies that information is composed of a bit and afterward perused from that bit.
- The computer stacks the fundamental info/yield framework (BIOS) from ROM. The BIOS gives the most fundamental data about storage gadgets, boot arrangement, security, Plug and Play (auto gadget acknowledgment) capacity and a couple of different things.
- The computer stacks the working framework (OS) from the hard crash into the framework's RAM. For the most part, the basic parts of the working framework are kept up in RAM the length of the computer is on. This enables the CPU to have quick access to the working framework, which improves the execution and usefulness of the general framework.
- When you open an application, it is stacked into RAM. To monitor RAM utilization, numerous applications stack just the basic parts of the program at first and after that heap different pieces as required.

- After an application is stacked, any documents that are opened for use in that application are stacked into RAM.
- When you spare a record and close the application, the document is composed to the predetermined storage gadget, and after that, it and the application are cleansed from RAM.

¬In the rundown over, each time something is stacked or opened, it is set into RAM. This just implies it has been placed in the computer's brief storage territory so that the CPU can access that data all the more effortlessly. The CPU asks for the information it needs from RAM, forms it and composes new information back to RAM in a nonstop cycle. In many computers, this rearranging of information between the CPU and RAM happens a large number of times each second. At the point when an application is shut, it and any going with documents are normally cleansed (erased) from RAM to account for new information. On the off chance that the changed records are not spared to a perpetual storage gadget before being cleansed, they are lost.

One basic question about desktop computers that surfaces all the time is, "The reason does a computer require such a variety of memory frameworks?"

TYPES OF COMPUTER MEMORY

A typical computer has:

- *Level 1 and level 2 caches*
- *Normal system RAM*
- *Virtual memory*
- *A hard disk*

Quick, capable CPUs require snappy and simple access to a lot of information with a specific end goal to amplify their execution. If the CPU can't get to the information it needs, it stops and sits tight for it. Current CPUs running at rates of around 1 GigaHertz can devour monstrous measures of information - conceivably billions of bytes for each second. The issue that computer fashioners face is that memory that can stay aware of a 1-gigahertz CPU is to a great degree costly - significantly more costly than anybody can manage the cost of in substantial amounts.

Computer planners have tackled the cost issue by "**tiering**" memory - utilizing costly memory in little amounts and after that sponsorship it up with larger amounts of more affordable memory.

The least expensive read/compose memory in wide utilize today is the hard plate. Hard plates give expansive amounts of reasonable, perpetual storage. You can purchase hard plate space for pennies per megabyte. However, it can take a decent bit of time (moving toward a moment) to peruse a megabyte off a hard circle. Since storage space on a hard circle is so modest and copious, it shapes the last phase of a CPUs memory order, called virtual memory.

The following level of the progressive system is RAM. We talk about RAM in detail in **How RAM Works**, yet a few focuses about RAM are essential here.

The **bit size** of a CPU discloses to you what number of bytes of data it can access from RAM in the meantime. For instance, a 16-bit CPU can prepare 2 bytes at any given moment (1 byte = 8 bits, so 16 bits = 2 bytes), and a 64-bit CPU can handle 8 bytes at any given moment. Megahertz (MHz) is a measure of a CPU's preparing pace, or clock cycle, in millions every second. In this way, a 32-bit 800-MHz Pentium III can conceivably handle 4 bytes at the same time, 800 million times each second (perhaps more in light of pipelining)! The objective of the memory framework is to meet those prerequisites.

A computer's framework RAM alone is not sufficiently quick to coordinate the speed of the CPU. That is the reason you require a store (talked about later). Be that as it may, the speedier RAM is, the better. Most chips today work with a cycle rate of 50 to 70 nanoseconds. The read/compose speed is normally a component of the kind of RAM utilized, for example, DRAM, SDRAM, RAMBUS. We will discuss these different sorts of memory later. To begin with, we should discuss framework RAM.

FRAMEWORK RAM

Framework RAM speed is controlled by transport width and transport speed. Transport width alludes to the quantity of bits that can be sent to the CPU at the same time, and transport speed alludes to the quantity of times a gathering of bits can be sent each second. A transport cycle happens each time information sets out from memory to the CPU. For instance, a 100-MHz 32-bit transport is hypothetically equipped for sending 4 bytes (32 bits isolated by 8 = 4 bytes) of information to the CPU 100 million times each second, while a 66-MHz 16-bit transport can send 2 bytes of information 66 million times each second. On the off chance that you figure it out, you'll see that just changing the transport width from 16 bits to 32 bits and the speed from 66 MHz to 100 MHz in our case considers three-fold the amount of information (400 million bytes versus 132 million bytes) to go through to the CPU consistently.

In all actuality, RAM doesn't more often than not work at ideal speed. Inertness changes the condition profoundly. Inactivity alludes to the quantity of clock cycles expected to peruse a bit of data. For instance, RAM appraised at 100 MHz is equipped for sending a bit in 0.00000001 seconds, yet may take 0.00000005 seconds to begin the read procedure for the principal bit. To make up for dormancy, CPUs utilizes an uncommon procedure called burst mode.

Blasted mode relies on upon the desire that information asked for by the CPU will be put away in consecutive memory cells. The memory controller envisions that whatever the CPU is chipping away freely keep on coming from this same arrangement of memory locations, so it peruses a few back to back bits of information together. This implies just the main bit is liable to the full impact of idleness; perusing progressive bits takes fundamentally less time. The evaluated burst method of memory is ordinarily communicated as four numbers isolated by dashes. The main number discloses to you the quantity of clock cycles expected to start a read operation; the second, third and fourth numbers reveal to you what number of cycles are expected to peruse each back to the back bit in the line, otherwise called the word line. For instance: 5-1-1-1 reveals to you that it takes five cycles to peruse the primary bit and one cycle for each bit after that. The lower these numbers are, the better the execution of the memory.

Blasted mode is frequently utilized as a part of conjunction with pipelining, another method for limiting the impacts of idleness. Pipelining composes information recovery into a kind of sequential construction system handle. The memory controller all the while understands at least one words from memory, sends the present word or words to the CPU and keeps in touch with at least one words to memory cells. Utilized together, burst mode and pipelining can significantly lessen the slack brought on by inertness.

So is there any good reason why you wouldn't purchase the quickest, greatest memory you can get? The speed and width of the memory's transport ought to coordinate the framework's transport. You can utilize memory intended to work at 100 MHz in a 66-MHz framework. However, it will keep running at the 66-MHz speed of the transport, so there is no preferred standpoint, and 32-bit memory won't fit on a 16-bit transport. Indeed, even with a wide and quick transport, despite everything, it takes more time for information to get from the memory card to the CPU than it takes for the CPU to handle the information. That is the place reserves come in.

STORE AND REGISTERS

Stores are intended to mitigate this bottleneck by making the information utilized regularly by the CPU in a split second accessible. This is refined by building a little measure of memory, known as essential or level 1 reserve, directly into the CPU. Level 1 store is little, regularly running between 2 kilobytes (KB) and 64 KB.

The auxiliary or level 2 store normally dwells on a memory card situated close to the CPU. The level 2 reserve has an immediate association with the CPU. A devoted coordinated circuit on the motherboard, the L2 controller, directs the utilization of the level 2 store by the CPU. Contingent upon the CPU, the extent of the level 2 reserve ranges from 256 KB to 2 megabytes (MB). In many frameworks, information required by the CPU is accessed from the store around 95 percent of the time, significantly decreasing the overhead required when the CPU needs to sit tight for information from the primary memory.

Some economical frameworks abstain from the level 2 store inside and out. Numerous superior CPUs now have the level 2 store incorporated with the CPU chip itself. Subsequently, the measure of the level 2 Reserve and whether it is installed (on the CPU) is a noteworthy deciding variable in the execution of a CPU. For more subtle elements on storing, perceive How Caching Works.

A specific kind of RAM, static random access memory (**SRAM**), is utilized essentially for reserve. SRAM utilizes various transistors, ordinarily four to six, for every memory cell. It has an outside door exhibit known as a bistable multivibrator that switches, or flip-flops, between two states. This implies it doesn't need to be consistently revived like DRAM. Every cell will keep up its information the length of it has control. Without the requirement for steady reviving, SRAM can work to a great degree rapidly. Be that as it may, the multifaceted nature of every cell makes it prohibitively costly for use as standard RAM.

The SRAM in reserve can be offbeat or synchronous. Synchronous SRAM is intended to precisely coordinate the speed of the CPU, while offbeat is most certainly not. That smidgen of timing has any effect in execution. Coordinating the CPU's clock speed is something worth being thankful for, so dependably search for synchronized SRAM. (For more data on the different sorts of RAM, perceive How RAM Works.)

The last stride in memory is the registers. These are memory cells incorporated ideal with the CPU that contain the particular information required by the CPU, especially the number juggling and rationale unit (ALU). A vital piece of the CPU itself, they are controlled straightforwardly by the compiler that sends data to the CPU to handle.

VOLATILITY, PRIMARY CLASSIFICATION

Memory can be part into two primary classifications: **volatile** and **nonvolatile**.

Volatile memory loses any information when the framework is killed; it requires steady energy to stay feasible. Most sorts of RAM fall into this classification.

Nonvolatile memory does not lose its information when the framework or gadget is killed. Various sorts of memory fall into this classification. The most well-known is ROM, yet Flash memory storage gadgets, for example, CompactFlash or SmartMedia cards are likewise types of nonvolatile memory.

TYPES OF MEMORY

VOLATILE MEMORY

Volatile memory is computer memory that obliges energy to keep up the putaway data. Most present day semiconductor volatile memory is either static RAM (SRAM) or dynamic RAM (DRAM). SRAM holds its substance the length of the power is associated and is simple for interfacing, yet utilizes six transistors for every bit. Dynamic RAM is more entangled for interfacing and control, requiring standard invigorate cycles to forestall losing its substance, yet utilizes just a single transistor and one capacitor for each bit, enabling it to achieve substantially higher densities and considerably less expensive per-bit costs.

SRAM is not beneficial for desktop framework memory, where DRAM rules, yet is utilized for their reserve recollections. SRAM is typical in little-installed frameworks, which may just need many kilobytes or less. Inevitable volatile memory advances that go for supplanting or contending with SRAM and DRAM incorporate Z-RAM and A-RAM.

NON-VOLATILE MEMORY

Non-volatile memory is computer memory that can hold the put away data notwithstanding when not controlled. Cases of non-volatile memory incorporate read-just memory (see ROM), flash memory, 3D XPoint, most sorts of attractive computer storage gadgets (e.g. hard circle drives, floppy plates and attractive tape), optical plates, and early computer storage strategies, for example, paper tape and punched cards.

Imminent non-volatile memory advances incorporate FeRAM, CBRAM, PRAM, SONOS, RRAM, course memory, NRAM and millipede memory.

MEMORY MANAGEMENT

Legitimate administration of memory is fundamental for a computer framework to work appropriately. Present day working frameworks have complex frameworks to oversee memory appropriately. Inability to do as such can prompt bugs, moderate execution, and best case scenario case, takeover by infections and malevolent programming.

Almost everything a computer software engineer does require him or her to consider how to oversee memory. Notwithstanding putting away a number in memory requires the developer to determine how the memory ought to store it.

MEMORY ADMINISTRATION BUGS

Dishonorable administration of memory is a typical reason for bugs, including the accompanying sorts:

In a math flood, a count brings about a number bigger than the allotted memory grants. For instance, a marked 8-bit whole number permits the numbers −128 to +127. On the off chance that its esteem is 127 and it is told to include one, the computer can't store the number 128 in that space. Such a case will bring about the undesired operation, for example, changing the number's an incentive to −128 rather than +128.

A memory spill happens when a program demands memory from the working framework and stays away forever the memory when it's finished with it. A program with this bug will bite by bit require increasingly memory until the program bombs as it runs out.

A division blames outcomes when a program tries to access memory that it doesn't have consent to access. For the most part, a program doing as such will be ended by the working framework.

A cushion flood implies that a program composes information to the finish of its designated space and after that keeps on composing information to a memory that has been allotted for different purposes. This may bring about whimsical program conduct, including memory access mistakes, off base outcomes, crash, or a break of framework security. They are in this manner the premise of numerous product vulnerabilities and can be malevolently misused.

EARLY COMPUTER FRAMEWORKS

In early computer frameworks, programs regularly determined the area to compose memory and what information to put there. This area was a physical area on the genuine memory equipment. The moderate preparing of such computers did not take into consideration the intricate memory administration frameworks utilized today. Likewise, as most such frameworks were single-assignment, modern frameworks were not required to such an extent.

This approach has its pitfalls. On the off chance that the area indicated is inaccurate, this will make the computer compose the information to some other piece of the program. The consequences of a blunder like this are erratic. Now and again, the erroneous information may overwrite memory utilized by the working framework. Computer wafers can exploit this to make infections and malware.

VIRTUAL MEMORY

Virtual memory is a framework where all physical memory is controlled by the working framework. At the point when a program needs memory, it demands it from the working framework. The working framework then chooses what physical area to put the memory in.

This offers a few favorable circumstances. Computer software engineers never again need to stress over where the memory is physically put away or whether the client's computer will have enough memory. It likewise enables numerous sorts of memory to be utilized. For instance, some memory can be put away in physical RAM chips while another memory is put away on a hard drive. This builds the measure of memory accessible to programs. The working framework will put effectively utilized memory in physical RAM, which is substantially speedier than hard circles. At the point when the measure of RAM is not adequate to run all the present projects, it can bring about a circumstance where the computer invests more energy moving memory from RAM to plate and back than it does finishing errands; this is known as whipping. Virtual memory frameworks, for the most part, incorporate ensured memory, yet this is not the situation.

MEMORY ASSURANCE

Ensured memory is a framework where each program is given a zone of memory to utilize and is not allowed to go outside that range. Utilization of ensured memory incredibly upgrades both the dependability and security of a computer framework.

Without ensured memory, it is conceivable that a bug in one program will change the memory utilized by another program. This will make that other program keep running off of adulterated memory with unusual outcomes. If the working framework's memory is undermined, the whole computer framework may crash and should be rebooted. Now and again programs purposefully modify the memory utilized by different projects. This is finished by infections and malware to assume control computers.

Ensured memory relegates programs their ranges of memory. If the working framework identifies that a program has attempted to change memory that does not have a place with it, the program is ended. Along these lines, just the culpable program crashes, and different projects are not influenced by the blunder.

Secured memory frameworks quite often incorporate virtual memory too.

MEMORY HIERARCHY

The term memory chain of command is utilized as a part of computer engineering while talking about execution issues in computer structural outline, calculation expectations, and the lower level programming develops, for example, including the territory of reference. A "memory chain of command" in computer storage recognizes each level in the "progression" by reaction time. Since reaction time, many-sided quality, and limit are connected, the controlling innovation may likewise recognize the levels.

The many exchanges off in outlining for elite will incorporate the structure of the memory chain of importance, i.e. the size and innovation of every segment. So the different parts can be seen as framing a chain of command of recollections (m1,m2,..., mn) in which every part mi is it might be said subordinate to the following most elevated part mi+1 of the pecking order. To breaking point holding up by more elevated amounts, a lower level will react by filling a cradle and after that motioning to initiate the exchange. There are four noteworthy storage levels.

- Interior – Processor registers and reserve.
- Fundamental – the framework RAM and controller cards.
- On-line mass storage – Secondary storage.
- Disconnected mass storage – Tertiary and Off-line storage.

This is a general memory progressive system organizing. Numerous different structures are helpful. For instance, a paging calculation might be considered as a level for virtual memory when outlining a computer engineering, and one can incorporate a level of nearline storage amongst on the web and disconnected storage.

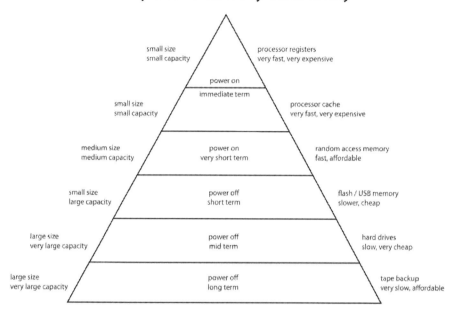

Computer Memory Hierarchy

- Adding multifaceted nature backs off the memory progression.
- CMOS memory innovation extends the Flash space in the memory chain of importance
- One of the primary approaches to building framework execution is limiting how far down the memory chain of importance one needs to go to control information.
- Latency and data transfer capacity are two measurements related with stores and memory. Neither of them is uniform, yet is particular to a specific segment of the memory order.
- Predicting where in the memory chain of command the information lives is troublesome.

- The area in the memory chain of command manages the time required for the prefetch to happen.

The quantity of levels in the memory chain of command and the execution at each level has expanded after some time. For instance, the memory chain of the importance of an Intel Haswell Mobile processor around 2013 is:

Processor registers – the quickest conceivable access (typically 1CPU cycle). Couple of thousand bytes in size

- **Cache -**
- Level 0 (L0) Micro-operations store – 6 KiB in size
- Level 1 (L1) Instruction store – 128 KiB in size
- Level 1 (L1) Data store – 128 KiB in size. Best access speed is around 700 GiB/second
- Level 2 (L2) Instruction and information (shared) – 1 MiB in size. Best access speed is around 200 GiB/second
- Level 3 (L3) Shared reserve – 6 MiB in size. Best access speed is around 100 GB/second
- Level 4 (L4) Shared reserve – 128 MiB in size. Best access speed is around 40 GB/second
- **Main memory (Primary storage)** – Gigabytes in size. Best access speed is around 10 GB/second. On account of a NUMA machine, access times may not be uniform
- **Disk storage (Secondary storage)** – Terabytes in size. Starting at 2013, best access speed is from a strong state drive is around 600 MB/second
- **Nearline storage (Tertiary storage)** – Up to exabytes in size. Starting at 2013, best access speed is around 160 MB/second
- **Offline storage**
  1. The lower levels of the chain of command – from plates downwards – are otherwise called layered storage. The formal qualification between on the web, nearline, and disconnected storage is:
  2. Online storage is promptly accessible for I/O.

45

3. Nearline storage is not promptly accessible, but rather can be made online rapidly without human mediation.
4. Offline storage is not quickly accessible and requires some human intercession to bring on the web.

For instance, dependably on turning circles are on the web, while turning plates that turn down, for example, a huge cluster of sit out of gear plate (MAID), are nearline. Removable media, for example, tape cartridges that can be naturally stacked, as in a tape library, are nearline, while cartridges that must be physically stacked are disconnected.

Most present day CPUs are fast to the point that for most program workloads, the bottleneck is the region of reference of memory accesses and the effectiveness of the reserving and memory exchange between various levels of the chain of importance. Subsequently, the CPU invests a lot of its energy sitting, sitting tight for memory I/O to finish. This is some of the time called the space cost, as a bigger memory question will probably flood a little/quick level and require utilization of a bigger/slower level. The subsequent load on memory utilize is known as weight (separately enlist weight, store weight, and (fundamental) memory weight). Terms for information being absent from a more elevated amount and waiting to be gotten from a lower level are, individually: enlist spilling (because of enlisting weight: Enroll to reserve), store miss (store to principle memory), and (hard) page blame (fundamental memory to the circle).

Present day programming dialects, for the most part, accept two levels of memory, principle memory, and plate storage, however in low-level computing construct and inline constructing agents in dialects, for example, C, registers can be straightforwardly accessed. Taking ideal preferred standpoint of the memory order requires the collaboration of developers, equipment, and compilers (and also basic support from the working framework):

- **Programmers** are in charge of moving information amongst circle and memory through the document I/O.
- **Hardware** is in charge of moving information amongst memory and stores.
- **Optimizing compilers** are in charge of producing code that, when executed, will make the equipment utilize reserves and registers productively.

Numerous software engineers accept one level of memory. This works fine until the application hits an execution divider. At that point, the memory pecking order will be surveyed amid code refactoring.

THE NEW GENERATION OF MEMORY

Normally, memory chips store data in transistors, small three-pronged gadgets that can house electrons. Some memory organization, as Intel and Micron have done away the transistor, putting away data in what is truly only a grid of wires. Each snippet of data sits where two wires cross.

THE THIRD DIMENSION

The "3D" bit demonstrates that those cross-point wire grids can be stacked on top of each other. Fundamentally, these chips store information by changing the electrical resistance at those many cross focuses. This is finished with a small contraption that Fazio calls a "selector." This is like a diode, which can change from low imperviousness to high.

That is unique to memory advances like DRAM and Flash, which utilize transistors. A transistor is a change produced using three essential segments: a source, door, and deplete. At the point when a specific voltage is connected to the door, current streams from the source to the deplete, and the transistor is "on." Apply another voltage, the present stops, and the transistor is "off." 3D XPoint doesn't move current like this. It changes the property of the material. It doesn't attempt to store an electron.

This straightforward design is the thing that enables the chips to store a great deal more information than DRAM (per range). Regardless they aren't as quick as DRAM, yet not at all like DRAM, they're "non-volatile," which means they can hold information notwithstanding when a machine is shut down. Flash is non-volatile as well. However, 3D XPoint is essentially speedier than flash. That additional speed originates from the interesting blend of materials that chip producers use to fabricate the cross section and the selector.

A REAL NEED FOR SPEED

3D XPoint will be incredible for gaming machines. Today, diversion originators are limited in what they can do to the abilities of the framework, and that may well be the situation. Be that as it may, the genuine need is inside the gigantic computer server farms that power the most prevalent web administrations Google, Facebook, Amazon.

In the server farm, these organizations must spread data crosswise over a huge number of machines. With an end goal to speed the storage and recovery of this information, they're supplanting customary hard drives with quicker flash memory, and now and again, they're running databases that keep information in DRAM, evading both hard drives and flash. As depicted 3D XPoint can give still more execution inside these warehoused-sized figuring focuses—something the Facebooks and the Googles are constantly eager for.

In the meantime, the new tech can help more conventional organizations. The commonplace endeavor doesn't store information crosswise over a large number of machines the way Facebook or Google does. In any case, littler outfits are running "in-memory databases"— i.e. in-DRAM databases—on individual machines or little quantities of machines. 3D XPoint can conceivably help here too. It can give more memory per machine.

Figure 3. Reading a bit in a crosspoint array

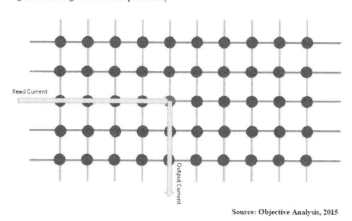

Source: Objective Analysis, 2015

CHAPTER 3: COMPUTER BUSSES, PORTS AND PERIPHERAL DEVICES

OVERVIEW

In computer engineering, a bus (identified with the Latin "omnibus," signifying "for all") is a similar framework that exchanges information between parts inside a computer, or between computers. This expression covers all related equipment parts (wire, optical fiber, and so forth.) and programming, including correspondence conventions.

Early computer busses were parallel electrical wires with numerous associations, yet the term is presently utilized for any physical game plan that gives an indistinguishable coherent usefulness from a parallel electrical bus. Present day computer busses can utilize both parallel and bit-serial associations and can be wired in either a multidrop (electrical parallel) or daisy chain topology, or associated with exchanging center points as if there should arise an occurrence of USB.

FOUNDATION AND TERMINOLOGY

Computer frameworks, for the most part, comprise of three primary parts: the central processing unit (CPU) that processes information, a memory that holds the projects and information to be processed, and I/O (input/output) gadgets as peripherals that speak with the outside world. An early computer may utilize a hand-wired CPU of vacuum tubes, an attractive drum for fundamental memory, and a punch tape and printer for perusing and composing information. In a present day framework, we may discover a multi-center CPU, DDR3 SDRAM for memory, a hard drive for optional stockpiling, an illustrations card and LCD show as a show framework, a mouse and console for the association, and a Wi-Fi association for systems administration. In both illustrations, computer busses of some frame move information between these gadgets.

In most conventional computer structures, the CPU and principle memory have a tendency to be firmly coupled. A microprocessor ordinarily is a solitary chip which has various electrical associations on its sticks that can be utilized to choose an "address" in principle memory and another arrangement of pins to peruse and compose the information put away in that area. By and large, the CPU and memory share flagging qualities and work in synchrony. The bus associating the CPU and memory is one of the characterizing qualities of the framework and regularly alluded to just as the framework bus.

It is conceivable to enable peripherals to speak with memory similarly, connecting connectors as extension cards straightforwardly to the framework bus. This is regularly expert through some institutionalized electrical connector, a few of these shaping the development bus or neighborhood bus. In any case, as the execution contrasts between the CPU and peripherals fluctuates broadly, some arrangement is for the most part expected to guarantee that peripherals don't moderate general framework execution. Numerous CPUs highlight a moment set of pins like those for speaking with memory, however ready to work at altogether different speeds and to utilize diverse conventions. Others utilize savvy controllers to put the information straightforwardly in memory, an idea is known as immediate memory get to. Most current frameworks consolidate both arrangements, where fitting.

As the quantity of potential peripherals developed, utilizing an extension card for each fringe turned out to be progressively untenable. This has prompted the presentation of bus frameworks planned particularly to bolster different peripherals. Basic illustrations are the SATA ports in present day computers, which enable various hard drives to be associated without the requirement for a card. Notwithstanding, these superior frameworks are by and large excessively costly, making it impossible to execute in low-end gadgets, similar to a mouse. This has prompted the parallel advancement of various low-execution bus frameworks for these arrangements, the most widely recognized case being Universal Serial Bus. Every such illustration might be alluded to as fringe busses, in spite of the fact that this wording is not general.

In current frameworks, the execution contrast between the CPU and primary memory has developed so extraordinarily that expanding measures of fast memory is incorporated straightforwardly with the CPU, known as a cache. In such frameworks, CPUs impart utilizing superior busses that work at rates considerably more prominent than memory and speak with memory utilizing conventions like those utilized exclusively for peripherals before. These framework busses are likewise used to speak with most (or every) another fringe, through connectors, which like this converse with different peripherals and controllers. Such frameworks are structurally more like multi computers, imparting over a bus as opposed to a system. In these cases, extension busses are altogether particular and at no time in the future offer any design with their host CPU (and may in truth bolster a wide range of CPUs, just like the case with PCI). What might have once in the past been a framework bus is presently frequently known as a front-side bus.

Given these progressions, the traditional terms "framework," "development" and "fringe" at no time in the future have similar implications. Other normal arrangement frameworks depend on the busses essential part, associating gadgets internally or externally, PCI versus SCSI for example. Nonetheless, numerous normal present day bus frameworks can be utilized for both; SATA and the related eSATA are one case of a framework that would once in the past be depicted as internal, while in certain car applications utilize the external IEEE 1394 in a manner more like a framework bus. Different cases, as InfiniBand and I²C were composed of the begin to be utilized both internally and externally.

INTERNAL BUS

The internal bus, also called internal information bus, a memory bus, framework bus or Front-Side-Bus, interfaces all the internal parts of a computer, for example, CPU and memory, to the motherboard. Internal information busses are additionally alluded to as a nearby bus since they are proposed to interface with neighborhood gadgets. This bus is commonly rather fast and is autonomous of whatever is left of the computer operations.

EXTERNAL BUS

The external bus, or development bus, is comprised of the electronic pathways that interface the diverse external gadgets, for example, printer and so on., to the computer.

USAGE POINTS OF INTEREST

Busses can be parallel busses, which convey information words in parallel on different wires, or serial busses, which convey information in the bit-serial frame. The expansion of additional power and control associations, differential drivers, and information associations toward every path ordinarily implies that most serial busses have a greater number of channels than the base of one utilized as a part of 1-Wire and UNI/O. As information rates increment, the issues of timing skew, control utilization, electromagnetic impedance and crosstalk crosswise over parallel busses turn out to be increasingly hard to evade. One halfway answer for this issue has been to twofold pump the bus. Regularly, a serial bus can be worked at higher general information rates than a parallel bus, in spite of having less electrical associations, because a serial bus intrinsically has no planning skew or crosstalk. USB, FireWire, and Serial ATA are cases of this. Multidrop associations don't function admirably for quick serial busses, so most present day serial busses utilize daisy-chain or center point plans.

Organize associations, for example, Ethernet are not, for the most part, viewed as busses, despite the fact that the distinction is largely theoretical as opposed to down to earth. Credit, for the most part, used to describe a bus is that power is given by the bus to the associated equipment. This underlines the busbar roots of bus design as providing exchanged or circulated control. This bars, like busses, plans, for example, serial RS-232, parallel Centronics, IEEE 1284 interfaces and Ethernet, since these gadgets likewise required separate power supplies. Widespread Serial Bus gadgets may utilize the bus provided control, yet regularly utilize a different power source. This qualification is exemplified by a phone framework with an associated modem, where the RJ11 association and related balanced flagging plan is not viewed as a bus and is undifferentiated from an Ethernet association. A telephone line association plan is not thought to be a bus as for signs, yet the Central Office utilizes busses with cross-bar switches for associations between telephones.

In any case, this qualification—that power is given by the bus—is not the situation in numerous aeronautical frameworks, where information associations, for example, ARINC 429, ARINC 629, MIL-STD-1553B (STANAG 3838), and EFABus (STANAG

3910) are ordinarily alluded to as "information busses" or, at times, "databuses". Such flying information busses are typically described by having a few gear or Line Replaceable Items/Units (LRI/LRUs) associated with a typical, shared media. They may, as with ARINC 429, be simplex, i.e. have a solitary source LRI/LRU or, as with ARINC 629, MIL-STD-1553B, and STANAG 3910, be duplex, permit all the associated LRI/LRUs to act, at various circumstances (half duplex), as transmitters and recipients of information.

HISTORY

After some time, a few gatherings of individuals taken a shot at different computer bus benchmarks, including the IEEE Bus Architecture Standards Committee (BASC), the IEEE "Superbus" contemplate gathering, the open microprocessor activity (OMI), the open microsystems activity (OMI), the "Group of Nine" that created EISA, and so forth.

1ˢᵀGENERATION COMPUTER BUSSES

Early computer busses were packs of wire that connected computer memory and peripherals. Narratively named the "digit trunk," they were named after electrical power busses or busbars. Quite often, there was one bus for memory and at least one separate busses for peripherals. These were gotten to by independent guidelines, with totally extraordinary timings and conventions.

One of the principal difficulties was the utilization of interferes. Early computer programs performed I/O by sitting tight in a circle for the fringe to wind up plainly prepared. This was an exercise in futility for projects that had different undertakings to do. Additionally, if the program endeavored to play out those different errands, it may take too ache for the program to check once more, bringing about the loss of information. Builds in this manner masterminded the peripherals to interfere with the CPU. The hinders must be organized, because the CPU can just execute code for one fringe at any given moment, and a few gadgets are additional time-basic than others.

Top of the line frameworks presented channel controllers, which were little computers committed to taking care of the input and output of a given bus. IBM presented these on the IBM 709 in 1958, and they turned into a typical component of their stages. Other elite merchants like Control Data Corporation executed comparable plans. For the most part, the channel controllers would do their best to run the majority of the bus operations internally, moving information when the CPU was known to be busy somewhere else if conceivable, and just utilizing hinders when important. This significantly diminished CPU stack and gave better general framework execution.

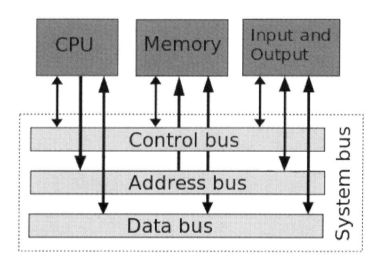

SINGLE FRAMEWORK BUS

To give particularity, memory and I/O busses can be joined into a brought together framework bus. For this situation, a solitary mechanical and electrical framework can be utilized to associate together a large number of the framework parts, or now and again, every one of them.

Later computer programs started to share memory normal to a few CPUs. Access to this memory bus must be organized, also. The basic approach to organizing hinders or bus get to was with a daisy chain. For this situation signs will normally course through the bus in the physical or legitimate request, taking out the requirement for complex planning.

MINIS AND MICROS

Advanced Equipment Corporation (DEC) additionally diminished cost for mass-delivered minicomputers and mapped peripherals into the memory bus, so that the input and output gadgets had all the earmarks of being memory areas. This was actualized in the Unibus of the PDP-11 around 1969.

Early microcomputer bus frameworks were an aloof backplane associated straightforwardly or through cradle speakers to the pins of the CPU. Memory and different gadgets would be added to the bus utilizing a similar address and information sticks as the CPU itself utilized, associated in parallel. Correspondence was controlled by the CPU, which had perused and composed information from the gadgets as though they are squares of memory, utilizing similar directions, all coordinated by a central clock controlling the speed of the CPU. Still, gadgets interfered with the CPU by motioning on isolated CPU pins. For example, a plate drive controller would flag the CPU that new information was prepared to be perused, and soon after that the CPU would move the information by perusing the "memory area" that related to the circle drive. All early microcomputers were worked in this form, beginning with the S-100 bus in the Altair 8800 computer framework.

In a few occasions, most eminently in the IBM PC, albeit comparable physical design can be utilized, directions to get to peripherals (in and out) and memory (mov and others) have not been made uniform by any stretch of the imagination, and still create unmistakable CPU flags, that could be utilized to actualize a different I/O bus.

These straightforward bus frameworks had a genuine downside when utilized for broadly useful computers. All the gear on the bus needed to talk at a similar speed, as it shared a solitary clock.

Expanding the speed of the CPU ends up noticeably harder, in light of the fact that the speed of the considerable number of gadgets must increment also. When it is not reasonable or sparing to have all gadgets as quick as the CPU, the CPU should either enter a holdup state or work at a slower clock recurrence briefly, to converse with different gadgets in the computer. While satisfactory in inserted frameworks, this issue was not endured for long by and large reason, client expandable computers.

Such bus frameworks are likewise hard to design when built from basic off-the-rack hardware. Ordinarily, each additional development card requires numerous jumpers with a specific end goal to set memory addresses, I/O addresses, interfere with needs, and intrude on numbers.

2NDGENERATION COMPUTER BUSSES

"Second Era" bus frameworks like NuBus tended to some of these issues. They normally isolated the computer into two "universes," the CPU and memory on one side, and the different gadgets on the other. A bus controller acknowledged information from the CPU side to be moved to the peripherals side, hence moving the correspondences convention trouble from the CPU itself. This permitted the CPU and memory side to advance independently from the gadget bus, or simply "bus." Gadgets on the bus could converse with each other with no CPU mediation. This prompted much better "true" execution, additionally required the cards to be significantly more mind boggling. These busses additionally regularly tended to speed issues by being "greater" regarding the measure of the information way, moving from 8-bit parallel busses in the original, to 16 or 32-bit in the second, and also including programming setup (now institutionalized as Plug-n-play) to supplant or supplant the jumpers.

However, these more current frameworks imparted one quality to their prior cousins, in that everybody on the bus needed to talk at a similar speed. While the CPU was currently separated and could expand speed, CPUs and memory kept on expanding in speed significantly speedier than the busses they conversed with. The outcome was that the bus rates were presently particularly slower than what a cutting edge framework required, and the machines were left starved for information. An especially basic case of this issue was that video cards rapidly beat even the more current bus frameworks like PCI, and computers started to incorporate AGP just to drive the video card. By 2004 AGP was outgrown again by the top of the line video cards and different peripherals and has been supplanted by the new PCI Express bus.

An expanding number of external gadgets began utilizing their particular bus frameworks too. At the point when circle drives were first presented, they would be added to the machine with a card connected to the bus, which is the reason computers have such a variety of openings on the bus. However, through the 1990s, new frameworks like SCSI and IDE were acquainted with serve this need, leaving most openings in present day frameworks exhaust. Today there are probably going to be around five distinct busses in the run of the mill machine, supporting different gadgets.

3ᴿᴰGENERATION COMPUTER BUSSES

"Third Era" busses have been developing into the market since around 2001, including HyperTransport and InfiniBand. They additionally have a tendency to be extremely adaptable as far as their physical associations, enabling them to be utilized both as internal busses, and also interfacing distinctive machines together. This can prompt complex issues when attempting to benefit distinctive solicitations, such a large amount of the work on these frameworks concerns programming configuration, rather than the equipment itself. By and large, these third era busses tend to look more like a system than the first idea of a bus, with a higher convention overhead required than early frameworks, while additionally enabling different gadgets to utilize the bus without a moment's delay. Busses, for example, Wishbone have been created by the open source equipment development trying to expel further lawful and patent requirements from computer outline.

EXAMPLES OF INTERNAL COMPUTER BUSES:
Parallel

- ASUS Media Bus proprietary, used on some ASUSSocket 7 motherboards
- Computer Automated Measurement and Control (CAMAC) for instrumentation systems
- Extended ISA or EISA
- Industry Standard Architecture or ISA
- Low Pin Count or LPC
- MBus
- MicroChannel or MCA

- Multibus for industrial systems
- NuBus or IEEE 1196
- OPTi local bus used on early Intel 80486 motherboards.
- Conventional PCI
- Parallel ATA (also known as Advanced Technology Attachment, ATA, PATA, IDE, EIDE, ATAPI, etc.) disk/tape peripheral attachment bus
- S-100 bus or IEEE 696, used in the Altair and similar microcomputers
- SBus or IEEE 1496
- SS-50 Bus
- Runway bus, a proprietary front side CPU bus developed by Hewlett-Packard for use by its PA-RISC microprocessor family
- GSC/HSC, a proprietary peripheral bus developed by Hewlett-Packard for use by its PA-RISC microprocessor family
- Precision Bus, a proprietary bus developed by Hewlett-Packard for use by its HP3000 computer family
- STEbus
- STD Bus (for STD-80 [8-bit] and STD32 [16-/32-bit]), FAQ
- Unibus, a proprietary bus developed by Digital Equipment Corporation for their PDP-11 and early VAX computers.
- Q-Bus, a proprietary bus developed by Digital Equipment Corporation for their PDP and later VAX computers.
- VESA Local Bus or VLB or VL-bus
- VMEbus, the VERSAmodule Eurocard bus
- PC/104, PC/104 Plus, PC/104 Express, PCI-104, PCIe-104
- Zorro II and Zorro III, used in Amiga computer systems

Serial

- 1-Wire
- HyperTransport

- I²C
- PCI Express or PCIe
- Serial ATA (SATA)
- Serial Peripheral Interface Bus or SPI bus
- UNI/O
- SMBus

EXAMPLES OF EXTERNAL COMPUTER BUSES:

Parallel

- HIPPI High-Performance Parallel Interface
- IEEE-488 (also known as GPIB, General-Purpose Interface Bus, and HPIB, Hewlett-Packard Instrumentation Bus)
- PC Card, previously known as PCMCIA, much used in laptop computers and other portables, but fading with the introduction of USB and built-in network and modem connections

Serial

- Controller area network ("CAN bus")
- eSATA
- ExpressCard
- Fieldbus
- IEEE 1394 interface (FireWire)
- Lightning
- RS-232
- RS-485
- Thunderbolt (interface)
- USB Universal Serial Bus, used for a variety of external devices
- Examples of internal/external computer buses
- Futurebus
- InfiniBand

- PCI Express External Cabling
- QuickRing
- Scalable Coherent Interface (SCI)
- SCSI Small Computer System Interface, disk/tape peripheral attachment bus
- Serial Attached SCSI (SAS) and other serial SCSI buses
- Thunderbolt
- Yapbus, a proprietary bus developed for the Pixar Image Computer

PERIPHERAL DEVICE DEFINITION

A peripheral is a "gadget that is utilized to place data into or get data out of the computer."

There are two unique sorts of peripherals: input gadgets, which connect with or send information to the computer (mouse, consoles, and so forth.), and output gadgets, which give output to the client from the computer (screens, printers, and so forth.). A few peripherals, for example, touchscreens, may join distinctive gadgets into a solitary equipment part that can be utilized both as an input and output gadget.

A peripheral gadget is, for the most part, characterized as any helper gadget, for example, a computer mouse or console that interfaces with and works with the computer somehow. Different cases of peripherals are picture scanners, tape drives, mouthpieces, amplifiers, webcams, and advanced cameras. Numerous present-day gadgets, for example, advanced watches, cell phones, and tablet computers, have interfaces that enable them to be utilized as a peripheral by desktop computers, in spite of the fact that they do not have subordinate in an indistinguishable path from other peripheral gadgets.

Normal input peripherals incorporate consoles, computer mice, realistic tablets, touchscreens, standardized identification per users, picture scanners, receivers, webcams, diversion controllers, light pens, and computerized cameras. Normal output peripherals incorporate computer shows, printers, projectors, and computer speakers.

A peripheral gadget interfaces with a computer framework to include usefulness. Cases are a mouse, console, screen, printer and scanner. Find out about the distinctive sorts of peripheral gadgets and how they enable you to accomplish more with your computer.

A computer peripheral is a gadget that is associated with a computer, however, is not some portion of the center computer engineering. The center components of a computer are the central processing unit, control supply, motherboard and the computer case that contains those three segments. In fact talking, everything else is viewed as a peripheral gadget. Notwithstanding, this is a fairly limit see, since different components are required for a computer to capacity, for example, a hard drive and arbitrary get to memory (or RAM).

A great many people utilize the term peripheral all the more freely to allude to a gadget external to the computer case. You interface the gadget to the computer to extend the usefulness of the framework. For instance, consider a printer. Once the printer is associated with a computer, you can print out reports. Another approach to take a gander at peripheral gadgets is that they are reliant on the computer framework. For instance, most printers can't do much all alone, and they just wind up plainly utilitarian when associated with a computer framework.

SORTS OF PERIPHERAL DEVICES

There are a wide range of peripheral gadgets, yet they fall into three general classes:

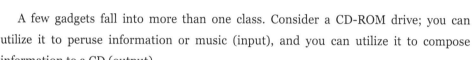

- **Input gadgets**, for example, a mouse and a console
- **Output gadgets**, for example, a screen and a printer
- **Capacity gadgets**, for example, a hard drive or glimmer drive

A few gadgets fall into more than one class. Consider a CD-ROM drive; you can utilize it to peruse information or music (input), and you can utilize it to compose information to a CD (output).

Peripheral gadgets can be external or internal. For instance, a printer is an external gadget that you interface utilizing a link, while an optical plate drive is normally situated inside the computer case. Internal peripheral gadgets are additionally alluded to as incorporated peripherals. At the point when the vast majority allude to peripherals, they normally mean external ones.

The idea of what precisely is "peripheral" is in this manner fairly liquid. For a desktop computer, a console and a screen are considered peripherals - you can undoubtedly associate and separate them and supplant them if necessary. For a portable workstation phone, segments are incorporated into the computer framework and can't be effectively evacuated.

The expression "peripheral" likewise does not mean it is not fundamental for the capacity of the computer. A few gadgets, for example, a printer, can be detached and the computer will continue working fine and dandy. Notwithstanding, expel the screen of a desktop computer, and it turns out to be practically futile.

CASES OF PERIPHERAL DEVICES

Here you can see a run of the mill desktop computer framework with various basic peripheral gadgets.

The central processing unit, motherboard and control supply are the centers computer framework. Extension spaces on the motherboard make it conceivable to associate internal peripherals, for example, a video card or sound card. Other internal peripherals indicated are a hard circle drive and an optical plate drive.

Some examples of **External input peripherals** are display monitor, keyboard scanner and mouse.

Some examples of **External output peripherals** are printers and speakers .

A computer peripheral, or peripheral gadget, is an external protest that gives input and output to the computer. Some basic input gadgets include console, mouse, touchscreen, pen tablet. Joystick, MIDI console, scanner, computerized camera, camcorder, receiver.

Some normal output gadgets include screen, projector, TV screen, printer, plotter, speakers.

There are additionally gadgets that capacity as both input and output gadgets, for example, external hard drives, media card per users, advanced camcorders, computerized blenders, MIDI gear, touchscreens.

While these are a portion of the more typical peripherals, there are numerous different sorts too. Simply recollect that any external gadget that gives input to the computer or gets output from the computer is viewed as a peripheral.

INTRODUCTION

A peripheral is a bit of computer equipment that is added to a computer keeping in mind the end goal to extend its capacities. The term peripheral is utilized to depict those gadgets that are discretionary in nature, rather than equipment that is either requested or constantly required on a fundamental level. There are all various types of peripherals you can include your computer. The primary qualification among peripherals is how they are associated with your computer. They can be associated internally or externally.

BUSSES

A bus is a subsystem that exchanges information between computer parts inside a computer or between computers. Not at all like an indicate point Association, a bus can sensibly interface a few peripherals over a similar arrangement of wires. Each bus characterizes its arrangement of connectors to plug gadgets, cards or links together physically.

There are two sorts of busses: internal and external. Internal busses are associations with different internal segments. External busses are associations with different external parts. There are various types of spaces that internal and external gadgets can associate with.

INTERNAL TYPES OF SLOTS

There are a wide range of sorts of internal busses, yet just a modest bunch of well-known ones. Diverse computers accompanied various types and number of spaces. It is critical to realize what kind and number of spaces you have on your computer before you go out and by a card that matches up to an opening you don't have. PCI

PCI (Peripheral Component Interconnect) is basic in present day PCs. This sort of bus is being prevailing by PCI Express. Average PCI cards utilized as a part of PCs include: organize cards, sound cards, modems, additional ports, for example, USB or serial, TV tuner cards and circle controllers. Video cards have outgrown the abilities of PCI in light of their higher data transmission necessities.

PCI EXPRESS

PCI Express was presented by Intel in 2004. It was intended to supplant the universally useful PCI extension bus and the AGP design card interface. PCI Express is not a bus but rather an indicate point Association of serial connections called paths. PCI Express cards have speedier transmission capacity then PCI cards which make them more perfect for the top of the line video cards.

PCMCIA

PCMCIA (additionally alluded to as PC Card) is the kind of bus utilized for PCs. The name PCMCIA originates from the gathering who built up the standard: Personal Computer Memory Card International Association. PCMCIA was initially intended for computer memory extension, yet the presence of a usable general standard for scratch pad peripherals prompted numerous sorts of gadgets being made accessible in this shape. Average gadgets incorporate system cards, modems, and hard circles.

AGP

AGP (Accelerated Graphics Port) is a rapid indicate point channel for appending a design card to a computer's motherboard, basically to aid the increasing speed of 3D computer illustrations. AGP has been supplanted over the past couple years by PCI Express. AGP cards and motherboards are as yet accessible to purchase, yet they are ending up plainly less normal.

SORTS OF CARDS

VIDEO CARD

A video card (otherwise called representation card) is an extension card whose capacity is to create and output pictures to show. Some video cards offer included capacities, for example, video catch, TV tuner connector, the capacity to interface various screens, and others. Most video cards all offer comparable parts. They incorporate a design processing unit (GPU) which is a committed microprocessor improved for 3D representation rendering. It likewise incorporates video BIOS that contain the essential program that administers the video card's operations and gives the guidelines that enable the computer and programming to interface with the card. On the off chance that the video card is incorporated in the motherboard, it might utilize the computer RAM memory. If it is not, it will have its video memory called Video RAM. This sort of memory can run from 128MB to 2GB.

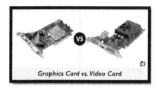
Graphics Card vs. Video Card

A video card additionally has an RAMDAC (Random Access Memory Digital-to-Analog Converter) which assumes liability for turning the computerized signals delivered by the computer processor into a simple flag which can be comprehended by the computer show. Ultimately, they all have outputs, for example, an HD-15 connector (standard screen link), DVI connector, S-Video, composite video or segment video.

SOUND CARD

A sound card is an extension card that encourages the input and output of sound signs to/from a computer under control of computer projects. Average uses for sound cards incorporate giving the sound part to sight and sound applications, for example, music com

EXTERNAL TYPES OF CONNECTIONS

USB

USB (Universal Serial Bus) is a serial bus standard to interface gadgets. USB was intended to enable numerous peripherals to be associated utilizing a solitary institutionalized interface attachment and to enhance the fitting and-play capacities by enabling gadgets to be associated and disengaged without rebooting the computer.

Other helpful components incorporate giving energy to low-utilization gadgets without the requirement for an external power supply and enabling numerous gadgets to be utilized without requiring maker particular, singular gadget drivers to be

introduced. USB is by a wide margin the commanding bus for interfacing external gadgets to your computer.

FIREWIRE

Firewire (in fact known as IEEE 1394 and furthermore known as i.LINK for Sony) is a serial bus interface standard for rapid correspondences and isochronous continuous information exchange, often utilized as a part of a PC. Firewire has supplanted Parallel ports in numerous applications.

It has been received as the High Definition Audio-Video Network Alliance (HANA) standard association interface for A/V (sound/visual) part correspondence and control. All cutting edge advanced camcorders have incorporated this association.

PS/2

The PS/2 connector is utilized for interfacing a few consoles and mice to a PC good computer framework. The console and mouse interfaces are electrically comparative with the fundamental distinction being

that open authority outputs are required on both closures of the console interface to permit bidirectional correspondence. If a PS/2 mouse is associated with a PS/2 console port, the mouse may not be perceived by the computer relying upon the design.

DEVICES

REMOVABLE STORAGE

Similar sorts of CD and DVD drives that could come worked in on your computer can likewise be appended externally. You may just have a CD-ROM drive worked into your computer yet you require a CD author to copy CDs. You can purchase an external CD essayist that associates with your USB port and acts an indistinguishable route from if it was worked into your computer. The same is valid for DVD scholars, Blu-beam drives, and floppy drives. Streak drives have turned out to be exceptionally well-known types of removable stockpiling particularly as the cost of glimmer drives diminishes and the conceivable size for them increments. Streak drives are USB ones either in the frame USB sticks or little, versatile gadgets. USB streak drives are little, quick, removable, rewritable, and enduring. Capacity limits run from 64MB to at least 32gb. A glimmer drive does not have any mechanically determined parts so rather than a hard drive which makes it more sturdy and littler typically.

NON-REMOVABLE STORAGE

Non-removable capacity can be a hard drive that is associated externally. External hard drives have turned out to be exceptionally well known for reinforcements, shared drives among numerous computers, and just growing the measure of hard drive space you have from your internal hard drive. External hard drives come in many shapes, and sizes like glimmer drives do. An external hard drive is associated by USB however you can likewise have an arranged hard drive which will interface with your system which enables all computers on that system to get to that hard drive.

INPUT

Input gadgets are critical to computers. The most widely recognized input gadgets are mice and consoles which scarcely every computer has. Another mainstream directing gadget that may, in the long run, supplant the mouse is a touch screen which you can get on some tablet note pads. Other famous input gadgets incorporate mouthpieces, webcams, and unique mark per users which can likewise be worked into present day portable workstations and desktops. A scanner is another well-known input gadget that may be worked into your printer.

OUTPUT

There are heaps of various types of output gadgets that you can get for your computer. Without a doubt, the most well-known external output gadget is a screen. Other exceptionally well-known output gadgets are printers and speakers. There are heaps of various types of printers and diverse sizes of speakers for your computer.

Screens are associated as a rule through the HD-15 connector on your video card. Printers are associated with a USB port. Speakers have their particular sound out port inherent to the sound card.

CHAPTER 4: HARD DISK DRIVE AND DISK ENCRYPTION

INTRODUCTION

A hard disk drive (HDD), hard drive, hard disk or settled disk is a data storage gadget utilized for storing and recovering digital information utilizing at least one inflexible ("hard") quickly pivoting disks (platters) covered with attractive material. The platters are matched with attractive heads orchestrated on a moving actuator arm, which read and compose data to the platter surfaces. Data is gotten to in an irregular get to way, implying that individual squares of data can be stored and recovered in any request and not just repeatedly. HDDs are a sort of non-volatile memory, holding put away data notwithstanding when fueled off.

First Offered by IBM in 1956, HDDs turned into the predominant optional storage gadget for universally useful computers by the mid 1960s. Consistently enhanced, HDDs have kept up this position into the advanced period of PC's and servers. Nearly more than 200 establishments have created HDD units, however most ebb and flow units are produced via Seagate, Toshiba and Western Digital. Starting at 2015, HDD generation (exabytes every year) and areal thickness are developing, in spite of the factor that unit deliveries are decreasing.

The essential attributes of a HDD are its ability and execution. Limit is indicated in unit prefixes comparing to forces of 1000: a 1-terabyte (TB) drive has a limit of 1,000 gigabytes (GB; where 1 gigabyte = 1 billion bytes). Ordinarily, some of a HDD's ability is inaccessible to the client since it is utilized by the record framework and the computer working framework, and potentially inbuilt repetition for blunder adjustment and recuperation. Execution is showed when it is compulsory to move the heads to a track or barrel (normal get to time) aslo the time it takes for the coveted division to move under the head (normal inactivity, which is an element of the physical rotational speed in cycles every moment), lastly the speed at which the data is transmitted (data rate).

The two most basic shape variables for present day HDDs are 3.5-inch, for desktop computers, and 2.5-inch, principally for portable PCs. HDDs are associated with frameworks by standard interface links, for example, SATA (Serial ATA), PATA (Parallel ATA), USB and SAS (Serial joined SCSI) links.

Starting at 2016, the essential contending innovation for auxiliary storage is streak memory as strong state drives (SSDs), which have higher data exchange rates, better unwavering quality, and fundamentally bring down idleness and get to times, yet HDDs remain the predominant medium for optional storage because of favorable circumstances in cost per bit. In any case, SSDs are supplanting HDDs where speed, control utilization and solidness are more vital contemplations. Crossover drive items have been accessible since 2007. These are a blend of HDD and SSD innovation in a solitary gadget, additionally known by the initialism SSHD.

HISTORY

Improvement of HDD characteristics over time			
Parameter	Started with	Developed to	Improvement
Capacity (formatted)	3.75 megabytes	10 terabytes	2.7-million-to-one
Physical volume	68 cubic feet (1.9 m3)	2.1 cubic inches (34 cc)	56,000-to-one
Weight	2,000 pounds (910 kg)	2.2 ounces (62 g)	15,000-to-one
Average access time	Nearly 600 milliseconds	few milliseconds	Nearly 200-to-one
Price	US$9,200 per megabyte (1961)	$0.032 per gigabyte by 2015	300-million-to-one
Areal density	2,000 bits per square inch	826 gigabits per square inch in 2014	greater than 400-million-to-one

Hard disk drives were presented in 1956 as data storage for an IBM continuous exchange, preparing computer and were produced for use with universally useful centralized server and minicomputers. The primary IBM drive, the 350 RAMAC, was nearly the extent of two coolers and put away 5 million six-piece characters (3.75 megabytes) on a heap of 50 disks.

The IBM 350 **RAMAC disk** storage unit was superseded by the IBM 1301 disk storage unit, which consisted of 50 platters, each one around 1/8-inch thick and 24 crawls in breadth. While the IBM 350 utilized two read/compose heads, pneumatically activated and traveling through two measurements, the 1301 was one of the principal disk storage units to utilize a variety of heads, one for each platter, moving as a solitary unit. Chamber mode read/compose operations were done, while the heads flew around 250 reduced scale creeps over the platter exterior. Head movement cluster relied on a twofold viper arrangement of pressure driven actuators, which guarantees repeatable situating. The 1301 bureau is about the measure of 3 home iceboxes when put next to each other, putting away also be called around 21 million eight-piece bytes. Get to time is around 200 milliseconds.

In mid of 1962, IBM offered the model 1311 disk drive, which was about the size of a clothes washer and put away 2 million characters on a removable disk pack. Clients could buy additional packs and exchange them when required, much like reels of smart tape. Upgraded models of removable pack drives, from IBM and others, turned as the standard in most computer establishments and achieved limits of 300 megabytes by the mid 1980s. Non-removable HDDs were called "settled disk" drives.

Some elite HDDs were produced with just one head for each track (e.g. IBM 2305) so that time would be saved physically moving the heads to a track. Known as settled head or head-per-track disk drives they were exceptionally costly and are no longer underway.

In 1973, IBM presented another kind of HDD codenamed "Winchester". It's essential recognizing highlight was that the disk heads were not pulled back totally from the pile of disk platters when the drive was shut down. Rather, the heads were permitted to "land" on an extraordinary region of the disk surface upon turn down, "taking off" again when the disk was later controlled on. This extraordinarily diminished the cost of the head actuator system, however blocked expelling only the disks from the drive as were finished with the disk packs of the day. Rather, the principal models of "Winchester innovation" drives highlighted a removable disk module, which included both the disk pack and the head get together, leaving the actuator engine in the drive upon evacuation. Later "Winchester" drives abandoned the removable media thought and come back to non-removable platters.

Like the principal removable pack drive, the primary "Winchester" drives utilized platters 14 inches (360 mm) in distance across. After 2 years the fact, architects were investigating the possibility that physically littler platters may offer focal points. Drives with non-removable eight-inch platters showed up, and after that drives that utilized a 5 1/4 in (130 mm) frame consider (a mounting width proportional to that utilized by contemporary floppy disk drives). The last were fundamentally planned for the then-juvenile (PC) showcase.

As the 1980s started, HDDs were an uncommon and extremely costly extra element in PCs, however, by the later part of the 1980s the cost had been reduced to the point where they were standard on everything except the least expensive computers.

Most HDDs in 1980s were often sold to PC end clients as an outside, extra subsystem. The subsystems were not sold under the producer's name of the drive but rather under the subsystem maker's name, for example, Corvus Systems and Tallgrass Technologies, also not under the PC framework producer's name, for example, the ProFile for Apple. The IBM PC/XT in 1983 incorporated an inward 10 MB HDD, and before long interior HDDs multiplied on PCs.

Outside HDDs stayed mainstream for any longer on the Apple Macintosh. Each Macintosh made in the vicinity of 1986 and 1998 had a SCSI port on the back, making outer development straightforward; additionally, more seasoned minimal Macintosh computers did not have effortlessly available hard drive sounds (or on account of the Macintosh 128K, Macintosh 512K, and Macintosh Plus, any hard drive cove whatsoever), so on those models outside SCSI disks were the main sensible choice.

Thailand, in 2011, surges harmed the assembling plants and affected hard disk drive cost antagonistically in the vicinity of 2011 and 2013. Driven by perpetually increasing areal thickness since their formation, HDDs have constantly improved their potentials; a couple highlights are recorded in the table above. In the meantime, showcase application extended from centralized computer, computers of the late 1950s to most mass storage applications including computers and purchaser applications, for example, storage of stimulation substance.

Technology

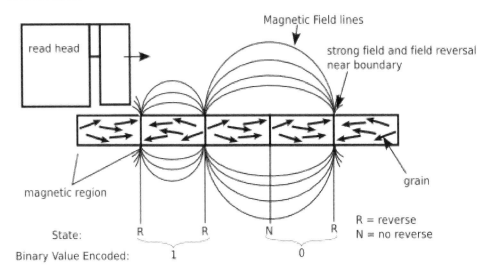

Magnetic cross section and frequency balance encoded binary data

MAGNETIC RECORDING

A HDD records data by charging a thin film of ferromagnetic material on a disk. Successive alters in the course of charge speak to binary data bits. The data is perused from the disk by distinguishing the moves in charge. Client data is encoded utilizing an encoding plan, for example, run-length constrained encoding, which decides how the data is spoken to by the magnetic moves.

A commonplace HDD configuration comprises of a shaft that holds level round disks, likewise called platters, which hold the recorded data. The platters are produced using a non-magnetic material, more often than not aluminum compound, glass, or artistic, and are covered with a shallow layer of magnetic material regularly 10–20 nm inside and out, with an external layer of carbon for assurance. For reference, a standard bit of duplicate paper is 0.07–0.18 millimeters (70,000–180,000 nm).

Outline naming the significant segments of a computer HDD

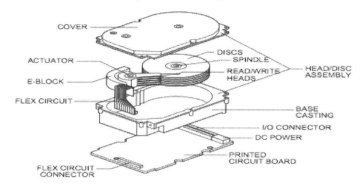

Recording of single magnetization of bits on a 200 MB HDD-platter (recording made noticeable utilizing CMOS-MagView)

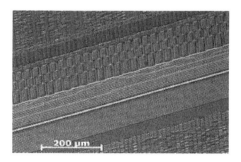

Platters of contemporary HDDs are spun at rates differing from 4,200 RPM in vitality effective, convenient gadgets, to 15,000 RPM for elite servers. The main HDDs spun at 1,200 RPM and, for a long time, 3,600 RPM was the standard. From December 2013, the platters in many customer review HDDs turn at either 5,400 RPM or 7,200 RPM.

Information is composed to, and perused from a platter as it axles past devices called read-and-compose heads that are located to work near the magnetic surface, with their flying tallness regularly in the scope of many nanometers. The read-and-compose head is used to recognize and change the polarization of the material passing instantly under it.

In current drives, there is one set out toward each magnetic platter surface on the axle, straddling on a typical arm. An actuator arm (or get to arm) transfers the heads on a bend (generally radially) over the platters as they turn, enabling each go to get to nearly the whole external of the platter as it turns. The arm is moved consuming a voice curl actuator or in some more seasoned plans a stepper engine. Early hard disk drives composed data at some consistent bits every second, bringing about all tracks having a similar measure of data per track yet current drives (since the 1990s) utilize zone bit recording—expanding the compose speed from inward to external zone and in this manner putting away more data per track in the external zones.

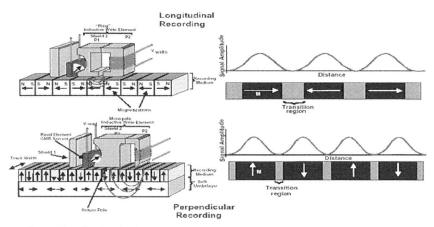

Recording Technologies

Longitudinal recording (standard) and opposite recording graph

In present day drives, the little size of the magnetic locales makes the peril that their magnetic state may be lost in light of warm impacts, thermally incited magnetic insecurity which is regularly called "as far as possible". To pledge this, the platters are protected with two parallel magnetic layers, isolated by a 3-iota layer of the non-magnetic component ruthenium, and the two layers are polarized in inverse introduction, therefore fortifying each other. Another innovation used to beat warm impacts to permit more prominent recording densities is opposite recording, first transported in 2005, and starting at 2007 the innovation was utilized as a part of numerous HDDs.

The 2004, an idea was acquainted with permit additionally increment of the data thickness in magnetic recording, using recording media encompassing of coupled delicate and hard magnetic layers. That purported trade spring media, else called trade coupled composite media, permits excessive writability due to the unite help nature of the subtle layer. In any case, the warm solidness is resolved just by the hardest layer and not affected by the delicate layer.

SEGMENTS

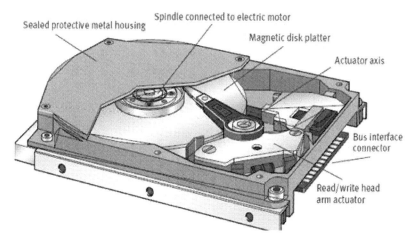

HDD with disks and engine center expelled uncovering copper shaded stator curls encompassing a direction in the focal point of the axle engine. Orange stripe at the brink of the arm is tinny printed-circuit link, axle bearing is in the exclusive and the actuator is in the upper left.

An ordinary HDD has two electric engines; a shaft engine that rotates the disks and an actuator (engine) that places the read/compose head gathering over the turning disks. The disk engine has an outer rotor appended to the disks; the stator windings are settled set up. Inverse the actuator toward the finish of the head bolster arm is the perused compose head; thin printed-circuit links interface the read-compose heads to speaker gadgets mounted at the turn of the actuator. The head bolster arm is light, additionally solid; in current drives, speeding up at the head achieves 550 g.

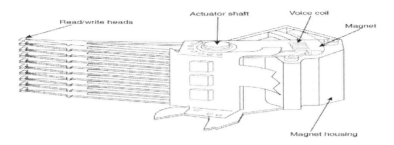

Head stack with an actuator loop on the left and read/compose heads on the privilege

The actuator is a changeless magnet and moving loop engine that swings the heads to the coveted position. A metal plate underpins a squat neodymium-press boron (NIB) high-flux magnet. Underneath this plate is the moving curl, frequently alluded to as the voice loop by similarity to the loop in amplifiers, which is connected to the actuator center point, and underneath that is a moment NIB magnet, mounted on the base plate of the engine (a few drives just have one magnet).

The voice curl itself is molded rather like a pointed stone, and made of doubly covered copper magnet wire. The inward layer is protection, and the external is thermoplastic, which bonds the loop together after it is twisted on a shape, making it self-supporting. The segments of the loop along the two sides of the sharpened stone (which indicate the actuator bearing focus) collaborate with the magnetic field, building up a distracting power that pivots the actuator. Present streaming radially outward along one side of the honed stone and radially inner on alternate delivers the digressive drive. From the off chance that the magnetic field were uniform, each side would create restricting strengths that would counterbalance each other. Thusly, the surface of the magnet is half north shaft and half south post, with the spiral isolating line in the center, making the two sides of the curl see inverse magnetic fields and deliver strengths that include as opposed to crossing out. Streams along the top and base of the loop deliver outspread strengths that don't turn the head.

The HDD's devices control the expansion of the actuator and the turn of the disk, and perform peruses and composes on request from the disk controller. Input of the drive gadgets is refined by methods for exceptional sections of the disk devoted to servo criticism. Either whole concentric circles (on account of devoted servo innovation), or portions scattered with genuine data (on account of implanted servo innovation). The servo criticism upgrades the flag to commotion proportion of the GMR sensors by modifying the voice-curl of the activated arm. The turning of the disk additionally utilizes a servo engine. Present day disk firmware is equipped for booking peruses and composes productively on the platter surfaces and remapping divisions of the media which have fizzled.

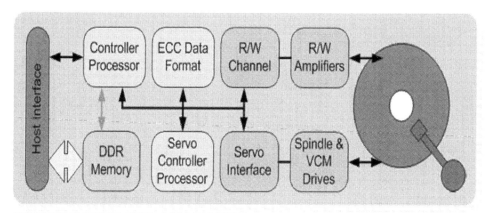

ERROR RATES AND HANDLING

Present day drives make broad utilization of mistake remedy codes (ECCs), especially Reed–Solomon blunder adjustment. These procedures store additional bits, dictated by numerical recipes, for each piece of data; the additional bits enable numerous mistakes to be revised undetectably. The additional bits themselves consume up room on the HDD, yet enable higher recording densities to be utilized without bringing on uncorrectable blunders, bringing about substantially bigger storage capacity. For instance, a run of the mill 1 TB hard disk with 512-byte divisions gives extra capacity of around 93 GB for the ECC data.

In the most up to date drives, starting at 2009, low-thickness equality check codes (LDPC) were supplanting Reed-Solomon; LDPC codes empower execution near the Shannon Limit and therefore give the most astounding storage thickness accessible.

Common hard disk drives endeavor to "remap" the data in a physical part that is neglecting to an extra physical area given by the drive's "extra division pool" (likewise called "save pool"), while depending on the ECC to recuperate put away data while the measure of blunders in an awful segment is still sufficiently low. The S.M.A.R.T (Self-Monitoring, Analysis and Reporting Technology) includes checking the aggregate number of mistakes in the whole HDD settled by ECC (in spite of the fact that not on every single hard drive as the related S.M.A.R.T traits "Hardware ECC Recovered" and "Delicate ECC Correction" are not reliably upheld), and the aggregate number of performed segment remapping, as the event of numerous such blunders may foresee a HDD disappointment.

The "No-ID Format", created by IBM in the mid-1990s, contains information about which parts are terrible and where remapped segments have been found.

Just a minor part of the distinguished mistakes winds up as not correctable. For instance, particular for an undertaking SAS disk (a model from 2013) gauges this division to be one uncorrected blunder in each 1016 bits, and another SAS venture disk from 2013 determines comparable mistake rates. Another cutting edge (starting at 2013) venture SATA disk indicates a blunder rate of under 10 non-recoverable read mistakes in each 1016 bits. An endeavor disk with a Fiber Channel interface, which utilizes 520 byte segments to bolster the Data Integrity Field standard to battle data debasement, indicates comparable blunder rates in 2005.

The most noticeably awful kind of mistakes are those that go unnoticed, and are not by any means identified by the disk firmware or the host working framework. These blunders are known as noiseless data defilement, some of which might be brought about by hard disk drive glitches.

Future improvement

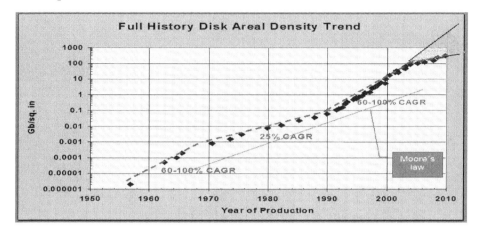

Driving edge hard disk drive areal densities from 1956 through 2009 contrasted with Moore's law.

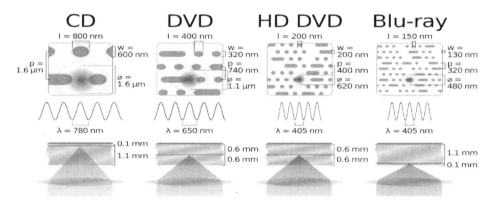

HDD contrasted with CD, DVD and Blu-beam densities

The rate of areal thickness headway was like Moore's law (multiplying at regular intervals) through 2010: 60% every year among 1988–1996, 100% among 1996–2003 and 30% among 2003–2010. Gordon Moore (1997) called the expansion "flooring, while at the same time watching later that development can't proceed until the end of time. Areal thickness progression eased back to 10% every year amid 2011–2014, because of trouble in moving from opposite recording to fresher advancements.

Areal thickness is the reverse of bit cell estimate, so an expansion in areal thickness compares to a lessening in bit cell measure. In 2013, a generation desktop 3 TB HDD (with four platters) would have had an a real thickness of around 500 Gbit/in2 which would have added up to a bit cell involving around 18 magnetic grains (11 by 1.6 grains). Since the mid-2000s areal thickness advance has progressively been tested by a superparamagnetic trilemma including grain estimate, grain magnetic quality and capacity of the make a beeline for compose. Keeping in mind the end goal to keep up worthy flag to commotion littler grains are required; littler grains may self-switch (warm insecurity) unless their magnetic quality is expanded, however known compose head materials can't produce a magnetic field adequate to compose the medium. A few new magnetic storage innovations are being created to overcome or if nothing else lessen this trilemma and subsequently keep up the fierceness of HDDs as for items, for instance, streak memory-based strong state drives (SSDs).

In 2013, Seagate offered one such invention, shingled magnetic recording (SMR). Also, SMR accompanies plan complexities that may bring about diminished compose execution. Other new recording advances that, starting at 2016, still stay being worked on incorporate warmth helped magnetic recording (HAMR), microwave-helped magnetic recording (MAMR), two-dimensional magnetic recording (TDMR), bit-designed recording (BPR), and "current opposite to plane" monster magnetoresistance (CPP/GMR) heads.

The rate of areal thickness development has dipped under the recorded Moore's law amount of 40% every year, and the braking is required to hold on through no less than 2020. Depending on suppositions on plausibility and timing of these innovations, the middle conjecture by industry eyewitnesses and investigators for 2020 and past for areal thickness development is 20% every year with a scope of 10–30%. Possibly for the HAMR innovation in blend with BPR and SMR might be 10 Tbit/in2, which would turn out to be 20 times higher than the 500 Gbit/in2 spoken to by 2013 generation desktop HDDs. Starting at 2015, HAMR HDDs have been deferred quite a long while, and are normal in 2018. They require an alternate engineering, with overhauled media and read/compose heads, new lasers, and new close field optical transducers.

CAPACITY

The storage capacity of a hard disk drive, as detailed by a working framework to the end client, is littler than the sum expressed by a drive or framework maker; this can be brought about by a mix of elements: the working framework utilizing some space, distinctive units utilized while ascertaining capacity, or data excess.

ESTIMATION

Present day hard disk drives appear to their interface as a touching arrangement of intelligent pieces, so the gross drive capacity might be computed by increasing the quantity of squares by the square size. This information is accessible from the maker's item particular, and from the drive itself through utilization of extraordinary working framework utilities that conjure low-level drive summons.

The gross capacity of more seasoned HDDs might be computed as the result of the quantity of chambers per zone, the quantity of bytes per area (most normally 512), and the number of zones of the drive. Some advanced SATA drives additionally report barrel head-area (CHS) values, however these are not genuine physical parameters since the announced numbers are obliged by memorable working framework interfaces. The C/H/S plot has been supplanted by coherent piece tending to (LBA), which is an elementary straight tending to plan that finds hinders by a number file, with the primary square being LBA 0, the second LBA 1, et cetera. Sometimes, to attempt to "constrain fit" the CHS plan to huge capacity drives, the quantity of heads was given as 64, albeit no present day drive has anyplace close to 32 platters: starting at 2013, a common 2 TB hard disk has two 1 TB platters, and 4 TB drives utilize four platters.

In current HDDs, save capacity for imperfection administration is excluded in the distributed capacity; Now, in many early HDDs a specific amount of segments were saved as extras, in this way lessening the capacity accessible to end clients.

For RAID subsystems, data uprightness and adaptation to internal failure necessities likewise decrease the acknowledged capacity. For instance, a RAID1 subsystem will be about a large portion of the aggregate capacity therefore of data reflecting. RAID5 subsystems with x drives, will potentially lose 1/x of capacity to equality. Strike subsystems are various drives that have all the earmarks of being one drive or more drives to the client, however gives a lot of adaptation to non-critical failure. Most RAID merchants utilize some type of checksums to enhance data honesty at the piece level. For some merchants, this includes utilizing HDDs with areas of 520 bytes for each division to contain 512 bytes of client data and eight checksum bytes or utilizing separate 512-byte segments for the checksum data.

In a few frameworks, there might be concealed allotments utilized for framework recuperation that lessen the capacity accessible to the end client.

SYSTEM USE

The introduction of a hard disk drive to its host is dictated by the disk controller. The real introduction may vary considerably from the drive's local interface, especially in centralized computers or servers. Present day HDDs, for example, SAS and SATA drives, show up at their interfaces as a bordering set of legitimate obstructs that are ordinarily 512 bytes in length, however the business is changing to the 4,096-byte coherent pieces design, known as the Advanced Format (AF).

The way toward instating these sensible pieces on the physical disk platters is called low-level designing, which is generally performed at the manufacturing plant and is not regularly changed in the field. As a subsequent stage in setting up a HDD for utilize, abnormal state arranging composes segment and record framework structures into chose intelligent pieces to make the staying coherent squares accessible to the host's working framework and its applications. The document framework uses a share of the disk space to structure the HDD and class out records, storing their document names and the arrangement of disk ranges that speak to the record. Cases of data structures put away on disk to recover documents incorporate the File Allocation Table (FAT) in the DOS record framework and in odes in frequent UNIX record frameworks, and also other working framework data structures (otherwise called metadata). As an outcome, not all the space on a HDD is accessible for client records, however this framework overhead is generally irrelevant.

UNITS

Decimal and binary unit prefixes interpretation				
Capacity advertised by manufacturers		Capacity expected by some consumers		Reported capacity
				Windows, Linux	OS X 10.6+
With prefix	Bytes	Bytes	Diff.		
100GB	100,000,000,000	107,374,182,400	7.37%	93.1 GB, 95,367MB	100 GB
1TB	1,000,000,000,000	1,099,511,627,776	9.95%	931GB, 953,674 MB	1,000GB, 1,000,00MB

FORM FACTORS

The aggregate capacity of HDDs is given by producers in SI-based units, for instance, gigabytes (1GB = 1,000,000,000 bytes) and terabytes (1 TB = 1,000,000,000,000 bytes). The act of utilizing SI-based prefixes (meaning forces of 1,000) in the hard disk drive and computer enterprises goes back to the beginning of computing;] by the 1970s, "million", "mega" and "M" were consistently used as a part of the decimal sense for drive capacity. Be that as it may, limits of memory (RAM, ROM) and CDs are generally cited utilizing a binary elucidation of the prefixes, i.e. utilizing forces of 1024 rather than 1000.

Inside, computers don't speak to either hard disk drive or memory capacity in forces of 1,024, yet revealing it in this way is a tradition. The Microsoft Windows group of working frameworks utilizes the binary tradition when revealing storage capacity, so a HDD offered by its maker as a 1 TB drive is accounted for by these working frameworks as a 931 GB HDD. OS X 10.6 ("Snow Leopard") utilizes decimal tradition when announcing HDD capacity. The default conduct of the df order line utility on Linux is to report the HDD capacity as various 1024-byte units.

The distinction between the decimal and binary prefix elucidation brought on some purchaser perplexity and impelled class activity suits against HDD makers. The affronted revelries contended that the use of decimal prefixes adequately deceived shoppers while the respondents denied any wrongdoing or obligation, stating that their promoting and publicizing gone with all regards with the law and that no class part supported any harms or wounds.

VALUE ADVANCEMENT

HDD cost per byte enhanced at the rate of −40% every year amid 1988–1996, −51% every year amid 1996–2003, and −34% every year amid 2003–2010. The cost change decelerated to −13% every year amid 2011–2014, as areal thickness increment moderated and the 2011 Thailand surges harmed fabricating offices.

Past and present HDD form factors							
Form factor	Status	Length	Width	Height	Largest capacity	Platters (max)	Capacity per platter
3.5-inch	Current	146 mm	101.6 mm	19 or 25.4 mm	10 TB (10/2015)	5 or 7	1149 GB
2.5-inch	Current	100 mm	69.85 mm	5, 7, 9.5 12.5, 15 or 19 mm	4 TB (2015)	5	800 GB
1.8-inch	Obsolete	78.5 mm	54 mm	5 or 8 mm	320 GB (2009)	2	220 GB
8-inch	Obsolete	362 mm	241.3 mm	117.5 mm	?	?	?
5.25-inch FH	Obsolete	203 mm	146 mm	82.6 mm	47 GB (1998)	14	3.36 GB
5.25-inch HH	Obsolete	203 mm	146 mm	41.4 mm	19.3 GB (1998)	4	4.83 GB

1.3-inch	Obsolete	?	43 mm	?	40 GB (2007)	1	40 GB
1-inch (CFII/ZIF/IDE-Flex)	Obsolete	?	42 mm	?	20 GB (2006)	1	20 GB
0.85-inch	Obsolete	32 mm	24 mm	5 mm	8 GB (2004)	1	8 GB

IBM's very first hard drive, the IBM 350, used a heap of fifty 24-inch platters and was of a size practically identical to two vast coolers. In 1962, IBM presented its model 1311 disk, which utilized six 14-inch (ostensible size) platters in a removable pack and was generally the span of a clothes washer. This turned into a standard platter size and drive shape figure for a long time, utilized likewise by different makers. The IBM 2314 utilized platters of an identical size in an eleven-high pack and offered the "drive in a drawer" design, in spite of the fact that the "drawer" was not the entire drive.

Future drives were planned to fit altogether into a skeleton that would mount in a 19-inch rack. Digital's RK05 and RL01 were early cases utilizing single 14-inch platters in removable packs, the complete drive suitable in a 10.5-inch-high rack space (six rack units). In the mid-to-late 1980s the comparably measured Fujitsu Eagle, which utilized (circumstantially) 10.5-inch platters, was a prominent item.

Such vast platters were never utilized with microchip based frameworks. With expanding offers of microcomputers having worked in floppy-disk drives (FDDs), HDDs that would fit to the FDD mountings ended up plainly attractive. Consequently HDD Form components, at first took after those of 8-inch, 5.25-inch, and 3.5-inch floppy disk drives. Since there were no littler floppy disk drives, littler HDD shape elements created from item offerings or industry principles.

8-INCH

9.5 in × 4.624 in × 14.25 in (241.3 mm × 117.5 mm × 362 mm). The 1979, Shugart Associates' SA1000 was the main frame calculates perfect HDD, having similar measurements and a good interface to the 8" FDD.

5.25-INCH

5.75 in × 3.25 in × 8 in (146.1 mm × 82.55 mm × 203 mm). This littler shape consider, first utilized as a part of a HDD via Seagate in 1980, was an indistinguishable size from full-tallness 5 1/4-inch-breadth (130 mm) FDD, 3.25-inches high. This is twice as high as "half tallness"; i.e., 1.63 in (41.4 mm). Maximum desktop models of drives for optical 120 mm disks (DVD, CD) utilize the half tallness 5¼" measurement; however it dropped out of form for HDDs. The organization was institutionalized as EIA-741 and co-distributed as SFF-8501 for disk drives, with other SFF-85xx arrangement models covering related 5.25 inch gadgets (optical drives, and so on.) The Quantum Bigfoot HDD was the last to utilize it in the late 1990s, with "low-profile" (≈25 mm) and "ultra-low-profile" (≈20 mm) high forms.

3.5-INCH

4 in × 1 in × 5.75 in (101.6 mm × 25.4 mm × 146 mm) = 376.77344 cm³. This littler shape variable is like that utilized as a part of a HDD by Rodime in 1983, which was an indistinguishable size from the "half tallness" 3½" FDD, i.e., 1.63 inches high. Today, the 1-inch high ("slimline" or "low-profile") variant of this shape element is the most prominent frame utilized as a part of generally desktops. The organization was institutionalized as far as measurements and places of mounting openings as EIA/ECA-740, co-distributed as SFF-8301.

2.5-INCH

2.75 in × 0.275–0.75 in × 3.945 in (69.85 mm × 7–19 mm × 100 mm) = 48.895–132.715 cm3. This littler shape element was presented by PrairieTek in 1988; there is no comparing FDD. The 2.5-inch drive arrangement is institutionalized in the EIA/ECA-720 co-distributed as SFF-8201; when utilized with particular connectors, more definite determinations are SFF-8212 for the 50-stick (ATA tablet) connector, SAS connector, orSFF-8223 with the SATA and SFF-8222 with the SCA-2 connector.

It came to be broadly utilized for HDDs in cell phones (portable workstations, music players, and so on.) and for strong state drives (SSDs), by 2008 supplanting somewhere in the range of 3.5 inch venture class drives. It is likewise utilized as a part of the PlayStation 3 and Xbox 360 computer game consoles.

Drives 9.5 mm high turned into an informal standard for all aside from the biggest capacity portable PC drives (more often than not having two platters inside); 12.5 mm-high drives, regularly with three platters, are utilized for greatest capacity, however won't fit most smart phones. Endeavor class drives can have a stature up to 15 mm. Seagate discharged a 7 mm drive gone for passage level tablets and top of the line netbooks in December 2009. Western Digital discharged on April 23, 2013 a hard drive 5 mm in tallness particularly gone for UltraBooks.

1.8-INCH

54 mm × 8 mm × 78.5 mm = 33.912 cm³. This frame consider, initially presented by Integral Peripherals in 1993, developed into the ATA-7 LIF with measurements as expressed. For a period it was progressively utilized as a part of digital sound players and subnotebooks, yet its fame diminished to the point where this shape element is progressively uncommon and just a little rate of the general market. There was an endeavor to institutionalize this organization as SFF-8123, however it was crossed out in 2005. SATA correction 2.6 institutionalized the interior Micro SATA connector and gadget measurements.

1-INCH

42.8 mm × 5 mm × 36.4 mm. This frame figure was acquainted 1999 as IBM's Microdrive with fit inside a CF Type II opening. Samsung calls a similar shape calculate "1.3 inch" drive in its item writing.

0.85-INCH

24 mm × 5 mm × 32 mm. Toshiba reported this frame figure January 2004 for use in cell phones and comparative applications, including SD/MMC opening good

HDDs upgraded for video storage on 4G handsets. Toshiba produced a 4 GB (MK4001MTD) and a 8 GB (MK8003MTD) form and holds the Guinness World Record for the littlest HDD.

Starting at 2012, 2.5-inch and 3.5-inch hard disks were the most famous sizes.

By 2009, all makers had stopped the advancement of new items for the 1.3-inch, 1-inch and 0.85-inch frame calculates because of falling costs of blaze memory, which has no moving parts.

While these sizes are usually portrayed by an around right figure in inches, real sizes have for some time been determined in millimeters.

EXECUTION QUALITIES

TIME TO GET TO DATA

The components that utmost an opportunity to get to the data on a HDD are generally identified with the mechanical way of the pivoting disks and moving heads. Look for time is a measure of to what extent it takes the make a beeline for go to the track of the disk that contains data. Rotational idleness is brought about on the grounds that the coveted disk segment may not be specifically under the head when data exchange is asked. These two deferrals are on the request of milliseconds each. The bit rate or data exchange rate (once the head is in the correct position) makes defer which is an element of the quantity of pieces exchanged; regularly moderately little, however can be very long with the exchange of vast touching documents. Postponement may likewise happen if the drive disks are ceased to spare vitality.

A HDD's Normal Access Time is its usual look for time which in fact is an idyllic opportunity to do every single imaginable look for remote by the amount of every imaginable look for, however by and by is verbalized by measurable techniques or just approximated as the season of a look for more than 33% of the quantity of tracks.

DEFRAGMENTATION

Defragmentation is a system used to limit defer in recovering data by moving related things to physically proximate territories on the disk. Some computer working frameworks perform defragmentation consequently. Albeit programmed defragmentation is proposed to decrease get to postponements, execution will be briefly lessened while the technique is in advance.

TIME TO ACCESS

Time to get to data can be enhanced by expanding rotational speed (subsequently diminishing inactivity) or by decreasing the time spent chasing. Expanding areal thickness builds throughput by expanding data rate and by expanding the measure of data under a procedure of heads, in this way conceivably lessening look for movement for a given measure of data. An opportunity to get to data has not stayed aware of throughput expands, which themselves have not remained aware of progress in bit thickness and storage capacity.

LOOK FOR TIME

Normal look for time ranges from under 4 ms for top of the line server drives to 15 ms for versatile drives, with the most widely recognized portable drives at around 12 ms and the most well-known desktop sort ordinarily being around 9 ms. The principal HDD had a normal look for time of around 600 ms; by the center of 1970s HDDs were available with look for times of around 25 ms. Some early PC drives utilized a stepper engine to move the heads, and therefore had look for times as moderate as 80–120 ms, yet this was immediately enhanced by voice curl sort incitation in the 1980s, lessening look for times to around 20 ms. Look for time has kept on enhancing gradually after some time.

Some desktop and tablet phone enable the client to make a tradeoff between look for execution and drive commotion. Speedier look for rates normally require more vitality use to rapidly move the heads over the platter, creating louder commotions from the rotate bearing and more prominent device vibrations as the heads are quickly accelerated amid the begin of the look for movement and slowed toward the finish of the look for movement. Calm operation decreases development speed and quickening rates, however at a cost of lessened look for execution.

LATENCY

Rotational speed [rpm]	Average latency [ms]
15,000	2
10,000	3
7,200	4.16
5,400	5.55
4,800	6.25

Latency or Dormancy is the deferral for the turn of the disk to bring the required disk area under the read-compose system. It depends upon the rotational speed of a disk, measured in cycles every moment (rpm). Normal rotational inertness appears in the table on the privilege, in light of the factual connection that the normal idleness in milliseconds for such a drive is one-a large portion of the rotational period.

DATA EXCHANGE RATE

Starting at 2010, a run of the mill 7,200-rpm desktop HDD has a maintained "disk-to-cushion" data exchange rate up to 1,030 Mbit/sec. This rate relies on upon the track area; the rate is higher for data on the external tracks (where there are more data parts per turn) and lower toward the inward tracks (where there are less data divisions per pivot); and is for the most part to some degree higher for 10,000-rpm drives. A current broadly utilized standard for the "support to-computer" interface is 3.0 Gbit/s SATA, which is capable of sending around 300 megabyte/s (10-bit encoding) from the cushion to the computer, and hence is still serenely in front of today's disk-to-cradle exchange rates. Data exchange rate (read/compose) can be measured by composing an extensive record to disk utilizing extraordinary document generator apparatuses, then perusing back the record. Exchange rate can be impacted by record framework discontinuity and the design of the documents.

HDD data exchange rate relies on the rotational speed of the platters and the data recording thickness. Since warmth and vibration confine rotational speed, propelling thickness turns into the primary technique to enhance successive exchange rates. Higher velocities require an all the more capable axle engine, which makes more warmth. While areal thickness propels by expanding both the quantity of tracks over the disk and the quantity of segments per track, just the last builds the data exchange rate for a given rpm. Since data exchange rate execution just tracks one of the two segments of areal thickness, its execution enhances at a lower rate.

DIFFERENT CONTEMPLATIONS

Other implementation contemplations include quality-balanced value, control use, capable of being heard clamor, and stun resistance.

The Federal Reserve Board has a quality-balanced value record for substantial scale venture storage frameworks including at least three endeavor HDDs and related controllers, racks and links. Costs for these extensive scale storage frameworks enhanced at the rate of –30% every year amid 2004–2009 and –22% every year amid 2009–2014.

INTERFACES AND ACCESS

HDDs are getting into more than one of various transport sorts, including starting at 2011 parallel ATA (PATA, likewise called IDE or EIDE; portrayed before the presentation of SATA as ATA), SCSI, Serial ATA (SATA), Serial Attached SCSI (SAS), and Fiber Channel. Connect hardware is at times used to interface HDDs to transports with which they can't impart locally, for sample, IEEE 1394, USB and SCSI.

Current HDDs display a reliable interface to whatever is left of the computer, regardless of what data encoding plan is utilized inside. Normally a DSP in the devices inside the HDD takes the basicmeek voltages from the read head and uses PRML and Reed–Solomon blunder revision to unravel the area limits and division data, then sends that data out the standard interface. That DSP likewise watches the mistake rate recognized by blunder discovery and rectification, and performs awful segment remapping, data accumulation for Self-Monitoring, Analysis, and Reporting Technology, and other inside assignments.

Current interfaces associate a HDD to a host transport interface connector (today regularly incorporated into the "south extension") with one data/control link. Each drive likewise has an extra power link, generally direct to the power supply unit.

-SCSI, Small Computer System Interface, initially named SASI for Shugart Associates System Interface, was standard on servers, Commodore Amiga, workstations, Atari ST and Apple Macintosh computers through the mid of 1990s, by which time most models had been transitioned to IDE (and later, SATA) family disks. The range restrictions of the data link considers outside SCSI gadgets.

Coordinated Drive Electronics (IDE), later institutionalized under the name AT Attachment (ATA, with the false name P-ATA or PATA (Parallel ATA) retroactively endless supply of SATA) places the HDD controller from the interface card to the disk drive. This institutionalized the host/controller interface, lessen the programming intricacy in the host gadget driver, and diminished framework charge and many-sided quality. The 40-stick IDE/ATA association exchanges 16 bits of data at once on the data link. The data link was initially 40-conductor, yet later higher speed necessities for data exchange to and from the HDD incited an "ultra DMA" mode, called as UDMA. Logically swifter forms of this standard at last included the prerequisite for an 80-conductor variation of a similar link, where half of the conductors gives establishing important to upgraded rapid flag quality by lessening cross talk.

EIDE was an informal refresh (by Western Digital) to the first IDE standard, with the important change being the use of direct memory get to (DMA) to exchange data between the disk and the computer without the inclusion of the CPU, a change later received by the authority ATA guidelines. By straightforwardly exchanging data amongst memory and disk, DMA wipes out the requirement for the CPU to duplicate byte per byte, in this manner enabling it to handle different undertakings while the data exchange happens.

Fiber Channel (FC) is a beneficiary to parallel SCSI interface on big commercial advertise. It is a serial contract. In disk drives for the most part the Fiber Channel Arbitrated Loop (FC-AL) association topology is utilized. FC has substantially more extensive utilization than insignificant disk interfaces, and it is the foundation of storage zone systems (SANs). Since late different contracts for this field, as iSCSI and ATA over Ethernet have been produced too. Surprisingly, drives for the most part use copper bent match links for Fiber Channel, not fiber optics. The last are customarily saved for bigger gadgets, for example, servers or disk exhibit controllers.

Serial Attached SCSI (SAS). The SAS is another time serial correspondence contract for devices intended to take into consideration considerably higher speed data exchanges and is good with SATA. SAS utilizes a mechanically indistinguishable data and power connector to standard 3.5-inch SATA1/SATA2 HDDs, and numerous server-arranged SAS RAID controllers are additionally equipped for tending to SATA HDDs. SAS utilizes serial correspondence rather than the parallel technique found in customary SCSI gadgets yet utilizes SCSI charges.

Serial ATA (SATA). The SATA data link has one data match for differential transmission of data to the device, and one sets for difference getting from the device, much the same as EIA-422. That requires that data be transmitted serially. A comparable differential flagging framework is utilized as a part of RS485, LocalTalk, USB, FireWire, and differential SCSI.

INTEGRITY AND FAILURE

Because of the to a great degree close separating between the heads and the disk surface, HDDs are defenseless against being harmed by a head crash—a disappointment of the disk in which the head scrub over the platter exterior, regularly pounding without end the thin magnetic film and bringing on data misfortune. Head accidents can be brought about by electronic disappointment, a sudden power disappointment, physical stun, defilement of the drive's inner fenced in area, wear and tear, consumption, or ineffectively produced platters and heads.

The HDD's axle framework hinge on the air thins inside the disk fenced in area to bolster the heads at their appropriate flying tallness while the disk pivots. HDDs require a specific scope of air densities keeping in mind the end goal to work appropriately. The association with the outside condition and thickness happens through a little gap in the nook (around 0.5 mm in expansiveness), ordinarily with a channel within (the breather channel). As it was, that the air thickness is too little, then there is insufficient lift for the flying head, so the head gets excessively near the disk, and there is a danger of head accidents and data misfortune. Exceptionally made fixed and pressurized disks are required for dependable, high-height operation, above around 3,000 m (9,800 ft). Current disks incorporate temperature sensors and alter their operation to the working condition. Breather openings can be seen on all disk drives—they more often than not have a sticker alongside them, notice the client not to cover the gaps. The air inside the working drive is always moving as well, being cleared in movement by grinding with the turning platters. This air goes through an inner distribution (or "recirc") channel to eject any additional contaminants from fabricates, any elements or chemicals that may have by one way or another entered the walled in area, and any particles or outgassing produced inside during ordinary operation. High moistness exhibit for expanded timeframes can consume the heads and platters.

For monster magnetoresistive (GMR) heads, precisely, a slight head crash from tainting (that does not oust the magnetic exterior of the disk) still results in the head parenthetically overheating, because of erosion with the disk surface, and can condense the data incomprehensible for a brief period until the head temperature balances out (supposed "warm severity", an issue which can mostly be managed by legitimate electronic sifting of the read flag).

At the point when the rationale leading body of a hard disk comes up short, the drive can regularly be reestablished to working request and the data recouped by supplanting the circuit leading body of one of an indistinguishable hard disk. On account of read-compose head deficiencies, they can be supplanted utilizing particular instruments in a clean free condition. On the off chance that the disk platters are undamaged, they can be moved into an indistinguishable walled in area and the data can be duplicated or cloned onto another drive. In case of disk-platter disappointments, dismantling and imaging of the disk platters might be required. For coherent harm to document frameworks, an assortment of devices, including fsck on UNIX-like frameworks and CHKDSK on Windows, can be utilized for data recuperation. Recuperation from sensible harm can require record cutting.

A typical desire is that hard disk drives outlined and advertised for server utilize will bomb less often than shopper review drives normally utilized as a part of desktop computer. In any case, two free reviews via Carnegie Mellon University and Google found that the "review" of a drive does not identify with the drive's dissatisfaction rate.

A 2011 depressed of research into SSD and magnetic disk disappointment designs by Tom's Hardware condensed examine discoveries as takes after:

- Mean time between disappointments (MTBF) does not demonstrate dependability; the annualized disappointment rate is higher and typically more applicable.
- Magnetic disks don't have a particular inclination to come up short amid early utilize, and temperature just has a minor impact; rather, disappointment rates consistently increment with age.
- S.M.A.R.T. cautions of mechanical issues however not different issues influencing dependability, and is in this way not a solid marker of condition.
- Disappointment rates of drives sold as "big business" and "purchaser" are "particularly comparative", in spite of the fact that these drive sorts are tweaked for their diverse working situations.
- In drive exhibits, one drive's disappointment essentially expands the transient possibility of a moment drive fizzling.

SHOWCASE FRAGMENTS

DESKTOP HDDS

They regularly store between 60 GB and 4 TB and turn at 5,400 to 10,000 rpm, and have a media exchange rate of 0.5 Gbit/s or higher (1 GB = 109 bytes; 1 Gbit/s = 109 piece/s). As of August 2014, the most noteworthy capacity desktop HDDs store 8 TB.

PORTABLE (TABLET) HDDS

Smaller than their desktop and enterprise partners, they have a bent to be slower and have bring down capacity. Versatile HDDs turn at 4,200 rpm, 5,200 rpm, 5,400 rpm, or 7,200 rpm, with 5,400 rpm being commonplace. 7,200 rpm drives have a trend to be more overpriced and have littler restrictions, while 4,200 rpm models more often than not have high storage limits. In view of littler platter(s), portable HDDs by and large have bring down capacity than their more prominent desktop counterparts. There are likewise 2.5-inch drives turning at 10,000 rpm, which have a place with the endeavor section with no aim to be utilized as a part of tablets.

ENDEAVOR HDDS

Regularly utilized with numerous client computers running endeavor programming. Cases are: exchange handling databases, web foundation (email, webserver, online business), logical figuring programming, and near line storage administration programming. Endeavor drives normally work persistently ("day in and day out") in requesting conditions while conveying the most astounding conceivable execution without relinquishing unwavering quality. Greatest capacity is not the essential objective, and thus the drives are regularly offered in limits that are generally low in connection to their cost.

The speediest venture HDDs turn at 10,000 or 15,000 rpm, and can accomplish consecutive media exchange speeds over 1.6 Gbit/s and a maintained exchange rate up to 1 Gbit/s. Drives working at 10,000 or 15,000 rpm use smaller platters to alleviate expanded power prerequisites (as they have less air drag) and in this way for the most part have brought down capacity than the most elevated capacity desktop drives. Venture HDDs are ordinarily associated through Serial Attached SCSI (SAS) or Fiber

Channel (FC). Some reinforced different ports, so they can be linked with a repetitive host transport connector.

Venture HDDs can have division sizes bigger than 512 bytes (regularly 520, 524, 528 or 536 bytes). The extra per-area space can be utilized by hardware RAID controllers or applications for putting away Data Integrity Field (DIF) or Data Integrity Extensions (DIX) data, bringing about higher unwavering quality and avoidance of noiseless data defilement.

CUSTOMER GADGETS HDDS

They incorporate drives implanted into digital video recorders and car vehicles. The previous are designed to give an ensured gushing capacity, even notwithstanding read and compose mistakes, while the last are worked to face bigger measures of stun.

MANUFACTURERS AND SALES

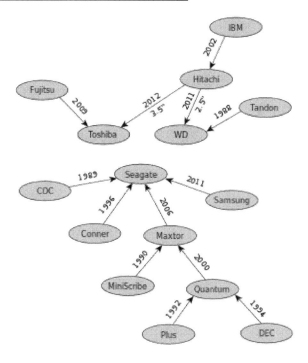

More than 200 organizations have produced HDDs after some time. Be that as it may, solidifications have moved generation into only three producers today: Western Digital, Seagate, and Toshiba.

Overall incomes for disk storage were $32 billion in 2013, down around 3% from 2012. Annualized shipments worldwide were 470 million units amid the initial seventy five percent of 2015, down 16% and 30% from the relating quarters of 2014 and 2011. Another source reports 552 million units sent in 2013, contrasted with 578 million in 2012, and 622 million in 2011. The evaluated 2015 pieces of the pie are around 40–45% each for Seagate and Western Digital and 13–16% for Toshiba. The two biggest producers report that the normal deals cost is $60 per HDD unit in 2015.

OUTER HARD DISK DRIVES

Outer hard disk drives ordinarily associate by means of USB; variations utilizing USB 2.0 interface by and large have slower data exchange rates when contrasted with inside mounted hard drives associated through SATA. Fitting and play drive usefulness offers framework similarity and elements huge storage alternatives and versatile plan. As of March 2015, accessible capacities with respect to outer hard disk drives run from 500 GB to 8 TB.

Outer hard disk drives are normally accessible as pre-collected incorporated items, yet might be additionally gathered by consolidating an outside walled in area (with USB or other interface) with an independently obtained drive. They are accessible in 2.5-inch and 3.5-inch sizes; 2.5-inch variations are ordinarily called compact outer drives, while 3.5-inch variations are alluded to as desktop outside drives. "Compact" drives are bundled in littler and lighter walled in areas than the "desktop" drives; moreover, "versatile" drives utilize control given by the USB association, while "desktop" drives require outside power blocks.

Components, for example, biometric security or various interfaces (for instance, Firewire) are accessible at a higher cost. There are pre-collected outside hard disk drives that, when taken out from their nooks, can't be utilized inside in a portable workstation or desktop computer because of installed USB interface on their written circuit sheets, and lack of SATA (or Parallel ATA) interfaces.

VISUAL PORTRAYAL

Hard disk drives are customarily symbolized as an adapted pile of platters or as a barrel, and are thusly found in different charts; here and there, they are portrayed with little lights to demonstrate data get to. In most present day graphical client conditions (GUIs), hard disk drives are spoken to by a representation or photo of the drive nook.

In GUIs, hard disk drives are regularly symbolized with a drive symbol

Two chambers in a RAID graph, symbolizing a variety of disks

DISK ENCRYPTION

Disk encryption is an innovation which secures information by changing over it into indistinguishable code that can't be deciphered effortlessly by unapproved individuals. Disk encryption utilizes disk encryption programming or hardware to encode all of data that goes on a disk or disk volume. Disk encryption averts unapproved access to data storage.

Expressions full disk encryption (FDE) or entire disk encryption frequently mean that everything on disk is encoded – including the projects that can scramble bootable working framework allotments – when some portion of the disk is essentially not scrambled. On frameworks that utilization an ace boot record (MBR), that piece of the disk remains non encoded. Some hardware-based full disk encryption frameworks can really scramble a whole boot disk, including the MBR.

STRAIGHTFORWARD ENCRYPTION

Straightforward encryption, otherwise called ongoing encryption and on-the-fly encryption (OTFE), is a technique utilized by some disk encryption programming. "Straightforward" alludes to the way that data is naturally scrambled or unscrambled as it is stacked or spared.

With straightforward encryption, the records are open promptly after the key is given, and the whole volume is commonly mounted as though it were a physical drive, making the documents similarly as available as any decoded ones. No data put away on a scrambled volume can be perused (unscrambled) without utilizing the right secret key/keyfile(s) or rectify encryption keys. The whole record framework inside the volume is encoded (counting document names, organizer names, document substance, and other meta-data).

To be straightforward to the end client, straightforward encryption as a rule requires the utilization of gadget drivers to empower the encryption procedure. In spite, of the fact that executive get to rights are regularly required to introduce such drivers, encoded volumes can commonly be utilized by typical clients without these rights.

When all is said in done, each strategy in which data is straightforwardly encoded on compose and unscrambled on read can be called straightforward encryption.

DISK ENCRYPTION VERSUS FILESYSTEM-LEVEL ENCRYPTION

Disk encryption does not supplant record encryption in all circumstances. Disk encryption is in some cases utilized as a part of conjunction with filesystem-level encryption with the aim of giving a more secure execution. Since disk encryption by and large uses a similar key for scrambling the entire volume, all data is decryptable when the framework runs. Be that as it may, some disk encryption arrangements utilize numerous keys for scrambling distinctive parcels. In the event that an assailant accesses the computer at run-time, the aggressor approaches all records. Traditional record and organizer encryption rather permits diverse keys for various segments of the disk. In this way an assailant can't separate information from still-encoded records and organizers.

Not at all like disk encryption, filesystem-level encryption does not commonly encode filesystem metadata, for example, the index structure, record names, change timestamps or sizes.

DISK ENCRYPTION AND TRUSTED PLATFORM MODULE

Put stock in Platform Module (TPM) is a safe cryptoprocessor implanted in the motherboard that can be utilized to confirm a hardware gadget. Since each TPM chip is novel to a specific gadget, it is fit for performing stage confirmation. It can be utilized to check that the framework looking for the get to is the normal framework.

A set number of disk encryption arrangements have bolster for TPM. These usage can wrap the unscrambling key utilizing the TPM, in this manner tying the hard disk drive (HDD) to a specific gadget. In the event that the HDD is expelled from that specific gadget and put in another, the unscrambling procedure will fall flat. Recuperation is conceivable with the unscrambling secret key or token.

In spite of the fact that this has the favorable position that the disk can't be expelled from the gadget, it may make a solitary purpose of disappointment in the encryption. For instance, if something happens to the TPM or the motherboard, a client would not have the capacity to get to the data by interfacing the hard drive to another computer, unless that client has a different recuperation key.

USAGE

There are numerous devices accessible in the market that take into consideration disk encryption. Be that as it may, they change extraordinarily in elements and security. They are isolated into three principle classifications: programming based, hardware-based inside the storage gadget, and hardware-based somewhere else, (for example, CPU or host transport connector). Hardware-based full disk encryption inside the storage gadget are called self-scrambling drives and have no effect on execution at all. Moreover, the media-encryption key never leaves the gadget itself and is hence not accessible to any infection in the working framework.

The Trusted Computing Group Opal drive gives industry acknowledged institutionalization to self-encoding drives. Outer hardware is extensively quicker than the product based arrangements in spite of the fact that CPU variants may even now have an execution affect, and the media encryption keys are not too ensured.

All answers for the boot drive require a Pre-Boot Authentication part which is accessible for a wide range of arrangements from various sellers. It is imperative in all cases that the confirmation qualifications are typically a noteworthy potential shortcoming since the symmetric cryptography is normally solid.

PASSWORD/DATA RECOVERY MECHANISM

Secure and safe recuperation systems are fundamental to the vast scale arrangement of any disk encryption arrangements in an endeavor. The arrangement must give a simple yet secure approach to recoup passwords (in particular data) on the off chance that the client leaves the organization without notice or overlooks the secret word.

CHALLENGE/REACTION SECRET WORD RECUPERATION INSTRUMENT

Challenge/Response secret word recuperation instrument enables the watchword to be recouped in a safe way. It is offered by a predetermined number of disk encryption arrangements.

A few advantages of test/reaction watchword recuperation:

- No requirement for the client to convey a disk with recuperation encryption key.
- No mystery data is traded amid the recuperation procedure.
- No information can be sniffed.
- Does not require a system association, i.e. it works for clients that are at a remote area.

ERI DOCUMENT WATCHWORD RECUPERATION COMPONENT

An Emergency Recovery Information (ERI) document gives another option to recuperation if a test reaction component is unfeasible because of the cost of helpdesk agents for little organizations or usage challenges.

A few advantages of ERI record recuperation:

- Little organizations can utilize it without usage troubles
- No mystery data is traded amid the recuperation procedure.
- No information can be sniffed.
- Does not require a system association, i.e. it works for clients that are at a remote area.

SECURITY CONCERNS

Most full disk encryption plans are defenseless against a cool boot assault, whereby encryption keys can be stolen by frosty booting a machine officially running a working framework, then dumping the substance of memory before the data vanishes. The assault depends on the data remanence property of computer memory, whereby data bits can take up to a few minutes to corrupt after power has been expelled. Indeed, even a Trusted Platform Module (TPM) is not powerful against the assault, as the working framework needs to hold the unscrambling keys in memory with a specific end goal to get to the disk.

Full disk encryption is likewise defenseless when a computer is stolen when suspended. As wake-up does not include a BIOS boot grouping, it commonly does not request the FDE secret word. Hibernation, interestingly goes through a BIOS boot succession, and is sheltered.

All product based encryption frameworks are helpless against different side channel assaults, for example, acoustic cryptanalysis and hardware keyloggers. Conversely, self-encoding drives are not helpless against these assaults since the hardware encryption key never leaves the disk controller.

FULL DISK ENCRYPTION

BENEFITS

Full disk encryption has a few advantages contrasted with normal document or organizer encryption, or encoded vaults. The accompanying are a few advantages of disk encryption:

1. Almost everything including the swap space and the brief documents is scrambled. Encoding these documents is imperative, as they can uncover vital classified data. With a product execution, the bootstrapping code can't be scrambled nonetheless. (For instance, BitLocker Drive Encryption leaves a decoded volume to boot from, while the volume containing the working framework is completely encoded.)
2. With full disk encryption, the choice of which individual documents to scramble is not surrendered over to clients' watchfulness. This is vital for circumstances in which clients won't not need or may neglect to encode delicate documents.
3. Prompt data pulverization, for example, basically decimating the cryptographic keys, renders the contained data pointless. In any case, if security towards future assaults is a worry, cleansing or physical annihilation is prompted.

THE BOOT KEY ISSUE

One issue to address in full disk encryption is that the squares where the working framework is put away should be decoded before the OS can boot, implying that the key must be accessible before there is a UI to request a secret word. Most Full Disk Encryption arrangements use Pre-Boot Authentication by stacking a little, exceptionally secure working framework which is entirely secured and hashed versus framework factors to check for the respectability of the Pre-Boot part. A few usage, for example, BitLocker Drive Encryption can make utilization of hardware, for example, a Trusted Platform Module to guarantee the respectability of the boot condition, and in this manner disappoint assaults that objective the boot loader by supplanting it with an altered variant. This guarantees verification can occur in a controlled domain without the likelihood of a bootkit being utilized to subvert the pre-boot unscrambling.

With a Pre-Boot Authentication condition, the key used to scramble the data is not decoded until an outside key is contribution to the framework.

Answers for putting away the outside key include:

- Username/secret word
- Utilizing a smartcard in mix with a PIN
- Utilizing a biometric validation strategy, for example, a unique mark
- Utilizing a dongle to store the key, expecting that the client won't enable the

Dongle to be stolen with the tablet or that the dongle is encoded also.

- Utilizing a boot-time driver that can request a watchword from the client
- Utilizing a system trade to recuperate the key, for example as a component of a PXE boot
- Utilizing a TPM to store the decoding key, avoiding unapproved access of the unscrambling key or subversion of the boot loader.
- Utilize a mix of the above

Every one of these conceivable outcomes have fluctuating degrees of security; be that as it may, most are superior to a decoded disk.

CHAPTER 5: SCSI DRIVES AND RAID ARRAYS FUNCTIONALITY

INTRODUCTION

A computer is brimming with busses - highways that take data and power from one place to another. For instance, when you plug an MP3 player or advanced camera into your computer, you're presumably utilizing a universal serial bus (USB) port. Your USB port is great at conveying the information and power required for little electronic gadgets that do things like make and store pictures and music documents. In any case, that bus isn't sufficiently enormous to bolster an entire computer, a server or bunches of gadgets at the same time.

For that, you would require something more like SCSI. SCSI initially remained for Small Computer System Interface, yet it's truly outgrown the "little" assignment. It's a quick bus that can associate loads of gadgets to a computer in the meantime, including hard drives, scanners, CD-ROM/RW drives, printers and tape drives. Different advances, similar to serial-ATA (SATA), have to a great extent supplanted it in new frameworks, yet SCSI is still being used. This article will survey SCSI basics and give you heaps of data on SCSI sorts and details.

SCSI BASICS

SCSI CONNECTOR

SCSI depends on a more seasoned, restrictive bus interface called Shugart Associates System Interface (SASI). SASI was initially created in 1981 by Shugart Associates in conjunction with NCR Corporation. In 1986, the American National Standards Institute (ANSI) endorsed SCSI (articulated "scuzzy"), an adjusted form of SASI. SCSI utilizes a controller to send and get information and energy to SCSI-empowered gadgets, like hard drives and printers.

SCSI has a few advantages. It's genuinely quick, up to 320 megabytes for each second (MBps). It's been around for over 20 years, and it's been altogether tried, so it has a notoriety for being dependable. Like Serial ATA and FireWire, it gives you a chance to put various things on one bus. SCSI additionally works with most computer frameworks.

In any case, SCSI additionally has some potential issues. It has constrained framework BIOS support, and it must be arranged for every computer. There's likewise, no normal SCSI programming interface. At last, all the distinctive SCSI sorts have diverse paces, bus widths, and connectors, which can confound. When you know the significance behind "Quick," "Ultra" and "Wide," however, it's straightforward. We'll take a gander at these SCSI sorts next.

Single-Ended Parallel SCSI icon

SCSI TYPES

Name	Specification	# of Devices	Bus Width	Bus Speed	MBps
Asynchronous SCSI	SCSI-1	8	8 bits	5 MHz	4 MBps
Synchronous SCSI	SCSI-1	8	8 bits	5 MHz	5 MBps
Wide	SCSI-2	16	16 bits	5 MHz	10 MBps
Fast	SCSI-2	8	8 bits	10 MHz	10 MBps
Fast/Wide	SCSI-2	16	16 bits	10 MHz	20 MBps
Ultra	SCSI-3 SPI	8	8 bits	20 MHz	20 MBps
Ultra/Wide	SCSI-3 SPI	8	16 bits	20 MHz	40 MBps
Ultra2	SCSI-3 SPI-2	8	8 bits	40 MHz	40 MBps
Ultra2/Wide	SCSI-3 SPI-2	16	16 bits	40 MHz	80 MBps
Ultra3	SCSI-3 SPI-3	16	16 bits	40 MHz	160 MBps
Ultra320	SCSI-3 SPI-4	16	16 bits	80 MHz	320 MBps

Distinctive mixes of multiplied bus speed multiplied clock speed and SCSI-3 determinations have prompted heaps of SCSI varieties.

SCSI has three essential particulars:

SCSI-1

The first detail created in 1986, SCSI-1 is currently old. It highlighted a bus width of 8 bits and clock speed of 5MHz.

SCSI-2:

Adopted in 1994, this particular incorporated the Common Command Set (CCS) - 18 charges considered a flat out need for support of any SCSI gadget. It likewise had the choice to twofold the clock speed to 10 MHz (Fast), twofold the bus width from to 16 bits and incremented the quantity of gadgets to 15 (Wide), or do both (Fast/Wide). SCSI-2 likewise included order lining, enabling gadgets to store and organize summons from the host computer.

SCSI-3:

This determination appeared in 1995 and incorporated a progression of littler principles inside its general extension. An arrangement of norms including the SCSI Parallel Interface (SPI), which is the way that SCSI gadgets speak with each other, has kept on advancing inside SCSI-3. Most SCSI-3 particulars start with the term Ultra, for example, Ultra for SPI varieties, Ultra2 for SPI-2 varieties and Ultra3 for SPI-3 varieties. The Fast and Wide assignments work simply like their SCSI-2 partners. SCSI-3 is the standard right now being used.

Distinctive mixes of multiplied bus speed multiplied clock speed and SCSI-3 particulars have prompted bunches of SCSI varieties. The outline on this page analyzes a few of them. Huge numbers of the slower ones are at no time in the future being used - we've included them for correlation.

SCSI CONTROLLER

Notwithstanding the expanded bus speed, Ultra320 SCSI utilizes packeted information exchange, expanding its proficiency. Ultra2 was additionally the last sort of having a "limited," or 8-bit, bus width.

These SCSI sorts are parallel - bits of information travel through the bus at the same time as opposed to each one in turn. The most current sort of SCSI, called Serial Attached SCSI (SAS), utilizes SCSI orders yet transmits information serially. SAS utilizes an indicate serial guide association toward move information at 3.0 gigabits for each second, and every SAS port can bolster up to 128 gadgets or expanders.

All the distinctive SCSI assortments utilize controllers and links to interface with gadgets. We'll take a gander at this procedure next.

CONTROLLERS, DEVICES, AND CABLES

A SCSI controller organizes between the greater part of alternate gadgets on the SCSI bus and the computer. Additionally called a host connector, the controller can be a card that you connect to an accessible opening, or it can be incorporated with the motherboard. The SCSI BIOS is likewise on the controller. This is a little ROM or Flash memory chip that contains the product expected to get to and control the gadgets on the bus.

Every SCSI gadget must have a one of a kind identifier (ID) with the goal for it to work legitimately. For instance, if the bus can bolster sixteen gadgets, their IDs, indicated through a hardware or programming setting, run from zero to 15. The SCSI controller itself must utilize one of the IDs, normally the most elevated one, leaving space for 15 different gadgets on the bus.

Internal gadgets associate with a SCSI controller with a strip link. External SCSI gadgets join to the controller in a daisy chain utilizing a thick, round link. (Serial Attached SCSI gadgets utilize SATA links.) In a daisy chain, every gadget associates with the following one in line. Thus, external SCSI gadgets regularly have two SCSI connectors - one to associate with the past gadget in the chain, and the other to interface with the following gadget. The link itself ordinarily comprises of three layers:

INWARD LAYER:

The most ensured layer, this contains the real information being sent.

MEDIA LAYER:

Contains the wires that send control summons to the gadget.

EXTERNAL LAYER:

Includes wires that convey equality data, which guarantees that the information is right.

Distinctive SCSI varieties utilize diverse connectors, which are frequently inconsistent with each other. These connectors more often than not utilize 50, 68 or 80 pins. SAS utilizes littler, SATA-good connectors.

When the majority of the gadgets on the bus are introduced and have their particular IDs, each end of the bus must be shut. We'll take a gander at how to do this next.

SCSI TERMINATION

Some SCSI eliminators are incorporated with the SCSI gadget, while others may require an external eliminator like this one.

On the off chance that the SCSI bus were left open, electrical signs sent down the bus could reflect back and meddle with correspondence amongst gadgets and the SCSI controller. The arrangement is to end the bus, shutting each end with a resistor circuit. If the bus underpins both internal and external gadgets, then the keep going gadget on every arrangement must be ended.

Sorts of SCSI end can be assembled into two principle classifications: detached and dynamic. The inactive end is commonly utilized for SCSI frameworks that keep running at the standard clock speed and have a separation of under 3 feet (1 m) from the gadgets to the controller. The dynamic end is utilized for Fast SCSI frameworks or frameworks with gadgets that are more than 3 feet (1 m) from the SCSI controller.

SIGNALING

SCSI additionally utilizes three sorts of bus flagging, which likewise influence ends. Flagging is the way that the electrical motivations are sent over the wires.

SINGLE-ENDED (SE)

The controller creates the flag and pushes it out to all gadgets on the bus over a single information line. Every gadget goes about as a ground. Therefore, the flag rapidly starts to debase, which limits SE SCSI to a greatest of around 10 ft (3 m). SE flagging is normal in PCs.

HIGH-VOLTAGE DIFFERENTIAL (HVD)

Often utilized for servers, HVD utilizes a couple of way to deal with motioning, with a high information line and an information low line. Every gadget on the SCSI bus has a flag handset. At the point when the controller speaks with the gadget, gadgets along the bus get the flag and retransmit it until it achieves the objective gadget. This takes into account substantially more prominent separations between the controller and the gadget, up to 80 ft (25 m).

LOW-VOLTAGE DIFFERENTIAL (LVD)

LVD is a minor departure from HVD and works similarly. The enormous contrast is that the handsets are littler and incorporated with the SCSI connector of every gadget. This makes LVD SCSI gadgets more reasonable and enables LVD to utilize less power to impart. The drawback is that the greatest separation is half of HVD - 40 ft (12 m).

AN ACTIVE TERMINATOR

Both HVD and LVD ordinarily utilize uninvolved terminators, despite the fact that the separation amongst gadgets and the controller can be considerably more prominent than 3ft (1m). This is on account of the handsets guarantee that the flag is solid from one end of the bus to the next.

SCSI COMMAND PROTOCOL

Notwithstanding a wide range of hardware executions, the SCSI models additionally incorporate a broad arrangement of command definitions. The SCSI command engineering was initially characterized for parallel SCSI busses, however, has been conveyed forward with insignificant change for use with iSCSI and Serial SCSI. Different advances which utilize the SCSI command set incorporate the ATA Packet Interface, USB Mass Storage class, and FireWire SBP-2.

In SCSI wording, correspondence happens between an initiator and an objective. The initiator sends a command to the objective, which then reacts. SCSI commands are sent in a Command Descriptor Block (CDB). The CDB comprises a one-byte operation code taken after by at least five bytes containing command-particular parameters.

Toward the finish of the command arrangement, the objective returns a status code byte, for example, 00h for achievement, 02h for a blunder (called a Check Condition), or 08h for busy. At the point when the objective returns a Check Condition in light of a command, the initiator normally then issues a SCSI Request Sense command keeping in mind the end goal to get a key code qualifier (KCQ) from the objective. The Check Condition and Request Sense grouping include an exceptional SCSI protocol called a Contingent Allegiance Condition.

There are 4 classes of SCSI commands: N (non-data), W (composing data from initiator to target), R (perusing data), and B (bidirectional). There are around 60 diverse SCSI commands altogether, with the most generally utilized being:

1. **Test unit prepared:** Queries gadget to check whether it is prepared for data exchanges (plate spun up, media stacked, and so forth.).
2. **Request:** Returns essential gadget data.
3. **Ask for sense:** Returns any blunder codes from the past command that restored a mistake status.
4. **Send indicative and Receive analytic outcomes:** runs a straightforward individual test, or a specific test characterized in a demonstrative page.
5. **Begin/Stop unit:** Spins circles all over, or loads/empties media (CD, tape, and so forth.).

6. **Perused limit:** Returns stockpiling limit.
7. **Design Unit:** Prepares a capacity medium for utilize. In a plate, a low-level arrangement will happen. Some tape drives will delete the tape because of this command.
8. **Perused (four variations):** Reads data from a gadget.
9. **Compose (four variations):** Writes data to a gadget.
10. **Log sense:** Returns current data from log pages.
11. **Mode sense:** Returns current gadget parameters from mode pages.
12. **Mode Select:** Sets gadget parameters in a mode page.

Every gadget on the SCSI bus is allocated a remarkable SCSI distinguishing proof number or ID. Gadgets may envelop numerous consistent units, which are tended to by legitimate unit number (LUN). Basic gadgets have only one LUN; more mind-boggling gadgets may have different LUNs.

An "immediate get to" (i.e. circle sort) stockpiling gadget comprises of various intelligent pieces, tended to by Logical Block Address (LBA). A common LBA compared to 512 bytes of capacity. The utilization of LBAs has developed over some time. Thus four diverse command variations are accommodated perusing and composing data. The Read(6) and Write(6) commands contain a 21-bit LBA address. The Read(10), Read(12), Read Long, Write(10), Write(12), and Write Long commands all contain a 32-bit LBA address in addition to different other parameter alternatives.

The limit of a "successive get to" (i.e. tape-sort) gadget is not determined in light of the fact that it depends, in addition to other things, on the length of the tape, which is not recognized in a machine-clear manner. Perused and compose operations on a consecutive get to gadget start at the present tape position, not at a particular LBA. The piece measure on successive get to gadgets can either be settled or variable, contingent upon the particular gadget. Tape gadgets, for example, half-inch 9-track tape, DDS (4mm tapes physically like DAT), Exabyte, and so on., bolster variable square sizes.

RAID

SCSI is regularly used to control an excess cluster of free circles (RAID). Different innovations, similar to serial-ATA (SATA), can likewise be utilized for this reason. More up to date SATA drives have a tendency to be speedier and less expensive than SCSI drives.

A will be a progression of hard drives regarded as one major drive. These drives can read and compose data in the meantime, known as striping. The controller figures out which drive gets which lump of data. While that drive composes the data, the controller sends data to or understands it from another drive.

Additionally, enhances adaptation to non-critical failure through reflecting and equality. Reflecting makes a correct copy of one drive's data on a moment hard drive. Equality utilizes at least three hard drives, and data is composed successively to each drive, aside from the last one. The last drive stores a number that speaks to the entirety of the data on alternate drives.

WHAT IS RAID?

In 1987, Patterson, Gibson, and Katz at the University of California, Berkeley, distributed a paper entitled "A Case for Redundant Arrays of Inexpensive Disks (RAID)". This paper portrayed different sorts of plate clusters, alluded to by the acronym RAID. The fundamental thought of RAID was to join different little, modest plate drives into a variety of circle drives which yields execution surpassing that of a Single Large Expensive Drive (SLED). Furthermore, this variety of drives appears to the computer as a single intelligent stockpiling unit or drive.

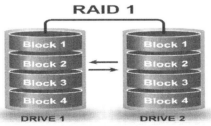

115

The Mean Time Between Failure (MTBF) of the cluster will be equivalent to the MTBF of an individual drive, separated by the quantity of drives in the exhibit. Along these lines, the MTBF of a variety of drives would be too low for some application prerequisites. Nonetheless, circle clusters can be made blame tolerant by needlessly putting away data in different ways.

Five sorts of exhibit models, RAID-1 through RAID-5, were characterized by the Berkeley paper, each giving circle adaptation to internal failure and each offering diverse exchange offs in components and execution. Notwithstanding these five excess cluster models, it has turned out to be prevalent to allude to a non-repetitive exhibit of plate drives as an RAID-0 cluster.

DATA STRIPING

Basic to RAID is "striping," a strategy for linking different drives into one consistent stockpiling unit. Striping includes apportioning each drive's storage room into stripes which might be as little as one area (512 bytes) or as vast as a few megabytes. These stripes are then interleaved round-robin, so that the consolidated space is made on the other hand out of stripes from each drive. As a result, the storage room of the drives is rearranged like a deck of cards. The kind of use condition, I/O or data serious, decides if extensive or little stripes ought to be utilized.

Most multi-client working frameworks today, similar to NT, Unix, and Netware, bolster covered plate I/O operations over different drives. In any case, with a specific end goal to amplify throughput for the circle subsystem, the I/O stack must be adjusted over every one of the drives so that each drive can be kept busy however much as could be expected. In a different drive framework without striping, the circle I/O load is never splendidly adjusted. A few drives will contain data records which are every now and again got to, and a few drives will just once in a while be gotten to. In I/O concentrated conditions, execution is streamlined by striping the drives in the cluster with stripes sufficiently substantial so that each record conceivably falls altogether inside one stripe. This guarantees the data and I/O will be equitably appropriated over the cluster, enabling each drive to take a shot at an alternate I/O operation, and subsequently amplify the quantity of concurrent I/O operations which can be performed by the exhibit.

In data escalated situations and single-client frameworks which get to extensive records, little stripes (regularly one 512-byte division long) can be utilized so that each record will traverse over every one of the drives in the cluster, each drive putting away a piece of the data from the record. This causes long record gets to be performed quicker since the data move happens in parallel on different drives. Sadly, little stripes discount various covered I/O operations, since every I/O will ordinarily include all drives. In any case, working frameworks like DOS which don't permit covered plate I/O, won't be adversely affected. Applications, for example, on-request video/sound, therapeutic imaging, and data securing, which use long record gets to, will accomplish ideal execution with little stripe clusters.

A potential downside to utilizing little stripes is that synchronized shaft drives are required with a specific end goal to shield execution from being debased when short records are gotten to. Without synchronized shafts, each drive in the exhibit will be at various arbitrary rotational positions. Since an I/O can't be finished until each drive has gotten to its piece of the record, the drive which takes the longest will decide when the I/O finishes. The more drives in the exhibit, the more the normal get to time for the cluster approaches the most pessimistic scenario single-drive get to time. Synchronized shafts guarantee that each drive in the cluster achieves its data in the meantime. The get to the time of the exhibit will, therefore, be equivalent to the normal get to the time of a single drive instead of moving toward the most pessimistic scenario get to time.

THE DIFFERENT RAID LEVELS

RAID-0

RAID Level 0 is not repetitive, henceforth does not fit the "RAID" acronym. In level 0, data is part crosswise overdrives, bringing about higher data throughput. Since no repetitive data is put away, execution is great. However, the disappointment of any circle in the cluster brings about data misfortune. This level is ordinarily alluded to as striping.

RAID-1

RAID Level 1 gives repetition by composing all data to at least two drives. The execution of a level 1 exhibit has a tendency to be quicker on peruses and slower on composes contrasted with a single drive, yet if either drive bombs, no data is lost. This is a decent passage level excess framework, since just two drives are required; be that as it may, since one drive is utilized to store a copy of the data, the cost per megabyte is high. This level is ordinarily alluded to as reflecting.

RAID-2

RAID Level 2, which utilizes Hamming mistake revision codes, is intended for use with drives which don't have worked in blunder identification. All SCSI drives bolster worked in mistake recognition, so this level is of little utilize when utilizing SCSI drives.

RAID-3

RAID Level 3 stripes data at a byte level over a few drives, with equality, put away on one drive. It is generally like level 4. Byte-level striping requires hardware bolster for effective utilize.

RAID-4

RAID Level 4 stripes data at a piece level over a few drives, with equality, put away on one drive. The equality data permits recuperation from the disappointment of any single drive. The execution of a level 4 cluster is useful for peruses (the same as level 0). Composes, in any case, require that equality data be refreshed each time. This moderates little arbitrary composes, specifically, however huge composes or consecutive composes are genuinely quick. Since just a single drive in the exhibit stores excess data, the cost per megabyte of a level 4 cluster can be genuinely low.

RAID-5

RAID Level 5 is like level 4, yet conveys equality among the drives. This can speed little sends in multiprocessing frameworks since the equality circle does not turn into a bottleneck. Since equality data must be skipped on each drive amid peruses, nonetheless, the execution for peruses has a tendency to be extensively lower than a level 4 cluster. The cost per megabyte is the same on level 4.

SYNOPSIS

- RAID-0 is the speediest and most productive cluster sort, however, offers no adaptation to internal failure.
- RAID-1 is the variety of decision for execution basic, blame tolerant conditions. Moreover, RAID-1 is the main decision for adaptation to non-critical failure if close to two drives are wanted.
- RAID-2 is occasionally utilized today since ECC is installed in all present day circle drives.
- RAID-3 can be utilized as a part of data escalated or single-client conditions which get to long successive records to accelerate data exchange. Be that as it may, RAID-3 does not permit various I/O operations to be covered and requires synchronized-axle drives to maintain a strategic distance from execution corruption with short records.
- RAID-4 offers no preferences over RAID-5 and does not bolster different synchronous compose operations.
- RAID-5 is the best decision in multi-client situations which are not compose execution touchy. Be that as it may, no less than three, and all the more ordinarily five drives are required for RAID-5 clusters.

HOW TO DEAL WITH RAID

HARDWARE RAID

The hardware based framework deals with the RAID subsystem freely from the host and exhibits to the host just a single circle for every RAID cluster. Along these lines, the host doesn't need to know about the RAID subsystems(s).

1. THE CONTROLLER BASED HARDWARE ARRANGEMENT

DPT's SCSI controllers are a decent case for a controller based RAID arrangement.

The astute controller deals with the RAID subsystem freely from the host. The favorable position over an external SCSI - SCSI RAID subsystem is that the controller can traverse the RAID subsystem over different SCSI channels and by this evacuate the constraining variable external RAID arrangements have: The exchange rate over the SCSI bus.

2. THE EXTERNAL HARDWARE ARRANGEMENT (SCSI - SCSI RAID)

An external RAID box moves all RAID taking care of "knowledge" into a controller that is sitting in the external circle subsystem. The entire subsystem is associated with the host using an ordinary SCSI controller and appears to the host as a single or numerous circles.

This arrangement has downsides contrasted with the controller based arrangement: The single SCSI divert utilized as a part of this arrangement makes a bottleneck.

More current advances like Fiber Channel can facilitate this issue, particularly if they permit to trunk various channels into a Storage Area Network.

4 SCSI drives can as of now totally surge a parallel SCSI bus, since the normal exchange size is around 4KB and the command exchange overhead - which is even in Ultra SCSI still done nonconcurrently - takes a large portion of the bus time.

PROGRAMMING RAID

- The MD driver in the Linux portion is a case of a RAID arrangement that is totally hardware free.

The Linux MD driver underpins at present RAID levels 0/1/4/5 + direct mode.

- Under Solaris, you have the Solstice DiskSuite and Veritas Volume Manager which offer RAID-0/1 and 5.
- Adaptecs AAA-RAID controllers are another illustration, they have no RAID usefulness at all on the controller, they rely on upon external drivers to give all external RAID usefulness.

They are fundamentally just different single AHA2940 controllers which have been coordinated on one card. Linux recognizes them as AHA2940 and treats them in like manner.

Each OS needs its extraordinary driver for this sort of RAID arrangement; this is mistake inclined and not exceptionally good.

HARDWARE VERSUS PROGRAMMING RAID

Much the same as whatever other application, programming based exhibits possess have framework memory, devour CPU cycles and are working framework subordinate. By battling with different applications that are running simultaneously for host CPU cycles and memory, programming based exhibits debase general server execution. Additionally, dissimilar to hardware-based exhibits, the execution of a product construct cluster is straightforwardly needy in light of server CPU execution and load.

Aside from the exhibit usefulness, hardware-based RAID plans have almost no just the same as programming based executions. Since the host CPU can execute client applications while the cluster connector's processor all the while executes the exhibit capacities, the outcome is genuine hardware multi-entrusting. Hardware clusters additionally don't possess any host framework memory, nor are they working framework subordinate.

Hardware exhibits are additionally very blamed tolerant. Since the exhibit rationale is situated in hardware, programming is NOT required to boot. Some product clusters, in any case, will neglect to boot if the boot drive in the exhibit comes up short. For instance, a cluster actualized in programming must be practical when the exhibit programming has been perused from the circles and is memory-occupant. What happens if the server can't stack the cluster programming because the circle that contains the blame tolerant programming has fizzled? Programming based executions regularly require a different boot drive, which is excluded in the exhibit.

A plate exhibit controller is a gadget which deals with the physical circle drives and displays them on the computer as coherent units. It quite often executes hardware RAID, in this manner, it is here and there alluded to as RAID controller. It likewise regularly gives extra circle store.

A circle cluster controller name is frequently despicable abbreviated to a plate controller. The two ought not to be confounded as they give altogether different usefulness.

FRONT-END AND BACK-END SIDE

A circle cluster controller gives front-end interfaces and back-end interfaces.

Back-end interface speaks with controlled circles. Henceforth protocol is normally ATA (a.k.a. PATA; inaccurately called IDE), SATA, SCSI, FC or SAS.

Front-end interface speaks with a computer's host connector (HBA, Host Bus Adapter) and employments:

- one of ATA, SATA, SCSI, FC; these are mainstream protocols utilized by plates, so by utilizing one of them, a controller may straightforwardly copy a circle for a computer
- somewhat less mainstream protocol devoted for a particular arrangement: FICON/ESCON, iSCSI, HyperSCSI, ATA over Ethernet or InfiniBand
- A single controller may utilize diverse protocols for back-end and front-end correspondence. Numerous venture controllers utilize FC on front-end and SATA on the back-end.

VENTURE CONTROLLERS

In a cutting edge undertaking design plate exhibit controllers (some of the time likewise called capacity processors, or SPs) are parts of physically autonomous walled in areas, for example, circle clusters put in a capacity territory arrange (SAN) or system appended capacity (NAS) servers.

Those external plate clusters are typically acquired as a coordinated subsystem of RAID controllers, circle drives, control supplies, and administration programming. It is up to controllers to give propelled usefulness (different merchants name these in an unexpected way):

- Programmed failover to another controller (straightforward to computers transmitting data)
- Long-running operations performed without downtime
- Shaping another RAID set
- Reproducing corrupted RAID set (after a plate disappointment)
- Adding a circle to online RAID set
- Expelling a circle from a RAID set (uncommon usefulness)
- Apportioning a RAID set to separate volumes/LUNs

BASIC CONTROLLERS

A basic plate exhibit controller may fit inside a computer, either as a PCI development card or simply manufactured onto a motherboard. Such a controller typically gives have bus connector (HBA) usefulness itself to spare physical space. Thus it is once in a while called a RAID connector.

As of February 2007, Intel began incorporating their particular Matrix RAID controller in their more upmarket motherboards, giving control more than 4 gadgets and an extra 2 SATA connectors, and totaling 6 SATA associations (3Gbit/s each). For in reverse similarity one IDE connector ready to interface 2 ATA gadgets (100 Mbit/s) is likewise present.

<u>CONCLUSION</u>

While hardware RAID controllers were accessible for quite a while, they required costly SCSI hard drives and gone for the server and top of the line figuring market. SCSI innovation points of interest incorporate permitting up to 15 devices on one bus, autonomous data exchanges, hot-swapping, considerably higher MTBF.

Around 1997, with the presentation of ATAPI-4 (and in this way the Ultra-DMA-Mode 0, which empowered quick data-exchanges with less CPU use) the main ATA RAID controllers were presented as PCI extension cards. Those RAID frameworks advanced toward the purchaser showcase, where the clients needed the adaptation to the non-critical failure of RAID without putting resources into costly SCSI drives.

ATA drives make it conceivable to fabricate RAID frameworks at lower taken a toll than with SCSI, yet most ATA RAID controllers do not have a devoted cushion or elite XOR hardware for equality count. Subsequently, ATA RAID performs moderately inadequately contrasted with most SCSI RAID controllers. Moreover, data security endures if there is no battery reinforcement to complete composes hindered by a power blackout.

CHAPTER 6: INSIDE OF AN OPEN-SOURCE SATA CORE

For a few applications, it might be alluring to store the gained data for later examination. In any case, the measure of data would immediately surpass the RAM stockpiling capacity, so it is important to store the data on a devoted stockpiling device, for example, a hard drive. To do as such, one of the business standard hard drive interfaces must be utilized. Accordingly, SATA is by all accounts a reasonable decision, since it includes high throughput for capacity, as appeared in Table 1.

SATA Version	Maximum Speed
SATA Generation 1 (SATA I)	1.5Gb/s, 150MB/s
SATA Generation 2 (SATA II)	3.0Gb/s, 300MB/s
SATA Generation 3 (SATA III)	6.0Gb/s, 600MB/s

Table 1: SATA Generations and Speeds

The SATA protocol utilizes a layered approach, wherein each layer utilizes administrations of the layer beneath it and presents administrations to the layer above it. At the most elevated amount, a genuinely Basic Read/Write interface is displayed to applications wishing to store data, while the lower layers do numerous mind-boggling changes, synchronization, and hand-shaking. The engineering of SATA will be talked about in more detail in the blink of an eye.

SATA OVERVIEW

Serial ATA is a fringe interface made in 2003 to supplant Parallel ATA, otherwise called IDE. Hard drive velocities were getting quicker, and would soon outpace the abilities of the more established standard—the speediest PATA speed accomplished was 133MB/s, while SATA started at 150MB/s and was composed on account of future execution. Likewise, more up to date silicon innovations utilized lower voltages than PATA's 5V least. The strip links utilized for PATA were additionally an issue; they were wide and blocked wind current, had a short maximum length limitation, and required many sticks and flag lines.

SATA has various elements that make it better than Parallel ATA. The flagging voltages are low, and the links and connectors are little. SATA has outpaced hard drive execution, so the interface is not a bottleneck in a framework. It likewise has various new elements, including hot-plug bolster.

SATA is an indicate point design, where each SATA interface contains just two devices: an SATA host (commonly a computer) and the capacity device. If a framework requires different capacity devices, each SATA connection is looked after independently. This disentangles the protocol and enables every capacity device to use the full abilities of the bus all the while, not at all like in the PATA engineering where the bus is shared.

To facilitate the move to the new standard, SATA keeps up in reverse similarity with PATA. To do this, the Host Bus Adapter (HBA) keeps up an arrangement of shadow registers that copy the registers utilized by PATA. The disk likewise keeps up an arrangement of these registers. At the point when an enroll esteem is changed, the enlist set is sent over the serial line to keep both arrangements of registers synchronized. This considers the product drivers to be freethinker about the interface being utilized.

SATA utilizes a layered design, portrayed in Figure 3. The most elevated layer is the Application Layer, which speaks to the product utilizing the SATA device. Underneath that is the Command Layer, which triggers arrangement of Transport Layer activities to execute a PATA command. Next is the Transport Layer, which handles making and organizing Frame Information Structures (FISes), and the legitimate successions of FISes. Underneath that is the Link Layer, which encodes the FISes, handles control flags, and checks for FIS honesty. The least layer is the Physical Layer, which handles the transmission and gathering of the genuine electrical flag and looks after arrangement. It additionally deals with building up the connection, utilizing what is known as Out-of-band (OOB) flagging.

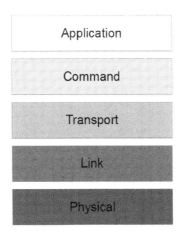

Figure 3: SATA Layer Architecture

Each layer gives administrations to the layer above it. This takes into consideration each layer to "unique away" the points of interest of the layers beneath it and rearranges the outlined procedure. The layers will be talked about in more profundity in the blink of an eye.

NOTES ON TERMINOLOGY

While examining SATA, various words can allude to a similar thing, and words could have distinctive implications in different settings. To keep away from uncertainty, in this report, we will attempt to be reliable in the utilization and significance of the accompanying terms.

DWORD:

Although this term is regularly utilized as a part of the setting of a specific processor or processor family, here it alludes to 32 bits of data, or 4 bytes. This is predictable with other SATA writing. Nonetheless, take note of that a Dword is encoded as 40 bits while hanging in the balance. In spite of the size change, this is still alluded to as a "Dword" because the encoded data is never controlled straightforwardly, and once decoded, will again be 32 bits.

CORE, HOST BUS ADAPTER (HBA):

This alludes to the SATA configuration being displayed in this work. That is, the hardware that interfaces with a disk and handles the SATA protocol.

HOST:

This alludes to the framework that is interfacing with the disk, and incorporates the HBA. A case of a host would be a PC or the SSD board. Since the SATA protocol is topsy-turvy, "Host" can likewise allude to the host's side of the protocol.

DISK, DEVICE:

This alludes to the hard drive with which we are imparting. In spite of the fact that disk is unambiguous, the device could allude to any number of things. In this work, "device" alludes to the hard disk, unless setting demonstrates something else.

OUTLINE INFORMATION STRUCTURE (FIS):

A Frame Information Structure, or FIS, is a single data payload that is sent over the SATA connect. These are similar to "bundles" in system wording. There are numerous sorts of FISes, and every one of them are wrapped by Start of Frame (SOF) and End of Frame (EOF) primitives. The protocol characterizes legitimate successions of FISes for data exchange. At least one of these FISes will be Data FISes, that contain the data to be perused or composed. The maximum size of a single FIS is 8KB.

SATA DETAILS

PHYSICAL LAYER

The physical layer is the most reduced layer of the SATA protocol stack. It handles the electrical flag being sent over the link. The physical layer additionally handles some other vital perspectives, for example, resets and speed arrangement.

SATA utilizes low-voltage differential flagging (LVDS). Rather than sending 1's and 0's in respect to a shared belief, the data being sent depends on the distinction in voltage between two conductors sending data. As it were, there is a TX+ and a TX-flag. A rationale 1 compares to a high TX+ and a low TX-; and the other way around for a rationale 0. SATA utilizes a ±125mV voltage swing.

This plan was decided for different reasons. For one, it enhances imperviousness to the commotion. A source of obstruction will probably influence both conductors similarly since they are parallel to each other. Be that as it may, an adjustment in voltage on both conductors does not change the contrast between them, so the flag will at present be effortlessly recuperated. Low-voltage differential flagging likewise lessens electromagnetic impedance (EMI), and the lower flagging voltages imply that less power is utilized.

OUT-OF-BAND SIGNALING

As expressed before, the physical layer is additionally in charge of link statement and resets. Be that as it may, in what capacity can a host and a device convey to introduce the link if they don't have a link with which to impart? The plan that SATA uses is gotten out-of-band (or OOB) flagging.

Under this plan, it is accepted that the host and the device can recognize the nearness or nonattendance of a flag, regardless of the possibility that they can't yet translate that flag. OOB signs are that—regardless of whether an in-band flag is there. By driving TX+ and TX-to a similar basic voltage (so not a rationale 1 or a rationale 0), one gathering can transmit an OOB "absence of the flag."

Link instatement is performed by sending a sequence of OOB primitives, which are characterized examples of flag/no-flag. There are three characterized primitives: COMRESET, COMINIT, and COMWAKE. Every primitive comprises of six "blasts" of a present flag, with sit without moving time in the middle. The seasons of each burst are characterized as far as "Generation 1 Unit Intervals" (U), which is an ideal opportunity to send 1 bit at the SATA I rate of 1.5Gb/s.

Table 2 demonstrates the meanings of the primitives. There are additionally genuinely free resistances characterized for each flag. Note likewise that COMRESET and COMINIT have a similar definition—the main distinction is that COMRESET is sent by the host, and COMINIT is sent by the device.

OOB Signal	Burst Length Inter-burst Idle Time
COMRESET	106ns (160U)320ns (480U)
COMINIT	106ns 320ns
COMWAKE	106ns 106ns

Table 2: OOB Primitive Definitions

The COMRESET flag, sent by the host, is utilized to reset the link. Taking after a COMRESET, the OOB introduction sequence is performed once more. COMRESET can likewise be sent over and over to hold the link in a reset state.

THE OOB SEQUENCE

The instatement state machine for the host takes after this sequence to set up correspondences with the disk. This sequence is delineated in Figure 4.

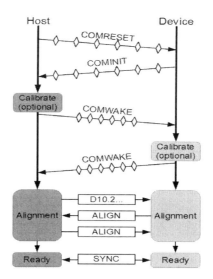

Figure 4: OOB Initialization Sequence

Initial, a COMRESET is sent. The host then sits tight for a COMINIT from the device.

On the off chance that no COMINIT is gotten, the host can send more COMRESETs until it gets one, and accept that no device is associated until it does. In the wake of accepting COMINIT, the host is offered time to adjust its beneficiary and transmitter alternatively. For instance, it might be important to modify flag parameters or end impedances. The host then sends a COMWAKE to the device and expects the same consequently. After this, the host holds up to get an ALIGN primitive (an in-band flag which will be clarified presently).

In the interim, it sends a "dial-tone" to the device: a rotating example of 1's and 0's. This was intended as a cost-sparing element so that disks with shabby oscillators could rather utilize the dial-tone as a source of the perspective clock for locking.

It is additionally at this phase speed transaction is performed. The device will send ALIGN primitives at the quickest speed it backings and sit tight for the host to recognize them. If it doesn't get an affirmation, then it tries the following most minimal speed, et cetera until an assention is found. On the other hand, if the host bolsters speedier rates than the device, then ALIGN primitives it gets will seem "extended"; the host can then back off to suit. At the point when the host gets legitimate ALIGN primitives, it sends ALIGNs back to recognize. Both sides then send SYNC or other non-ALIGN primitives, and the link is prepared.

8B/10B ENCODING

The Physical Layer additionally handles encoding the data before sending it. The plan utilized as a part of SATA is 8b/10b encoding, which is likewise utilized as a part of PCI Express, USB 3.0, and numerous other rapid protocols. 8b/10b Encoding has various properties that make it helpful for this reason.

One essential capacity of 8b/10b encoding is clock recuperation. Under this plan, there are never more than five ones or zeros in succession. At the end of the day, there are many pieces moves in the data stream. This enables the recipient to recoup the clock utilizing a PLL or by oversampling the data. This is imperative for serial data, as generally a flood of 12 ones in succession, for instance, could be deciphered as 11 or 13 ones.

The encoding of data maps every byte to a 10-bit character, rather than an 8-bit one. Just 10-bit characters that have enough moves are utilized. Additionally, the plan tries to keep up DC Balance and uses the 10-bit designs with an equivalent number of zeros. Be that as it may, there are insufficient of these to oblige the 256 conceivable estimations of a byte, so likewise those examples with 6 zeros and 4 ones (or the other way around) are utilized.

The encoder monitors the running divergence to keep up DC Balance. The running divergence changes each time an uneven example is sent. For instance, if a 10-bit character with 6 zeros and 4 ones was recently sent, the running dissimilarity is currently negative.

The following character along these lines must have a positive difference (4 zeros and 6 ones) or nonpartisan dissimilarity (5 and 5). Along these lines, huge numbers of the bytes have two encodings—one positive and the other negative. The present running divergence figures out which encoded an incentive to utilize. Running difference additionally goes about as a way to recognize transmission blunders.

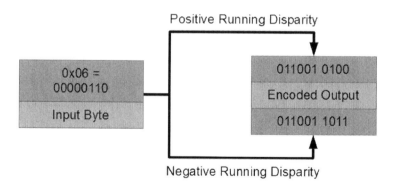

Figure 5: 8b/10b Encoding Example

Note: In this encoding case, take note of that the quantity of zeros in the yield is distinctive relying upon the present divergence. Both of the encodings compare to similar data byte (0x06, or D6.0 in the encoding table).

THE COMMA AND THE ALIGN PRIMITIVE

Notwithstanding the 256 substantial data encodings for every byte (alluded to as Dx.x images), there are additionally unique control images that can be sent. These don't relate to a data byte and are alluded to as Kx.x images, or K characters. SATA utilizes two K characters: K28.3 and K28.5. The first is utilized to recognize link layer primitives, and the other is the comma character.

The comma is an exceptional character that is utilized to decide byte alignment in the data stream. We've as of now talked about how 8b/10b encoding gives enough moves in the stream to recuperate a clock (basically giving piece alignment), yet it would not be conceivable to disentangle the genuine characters being sent on the off chance that it is not known where they start and end.

The comma is a unique character since it is the main place in the data stream where there are five zeros or five ones consecutively (contingent upon uniqueness), trailed by two bits of the inverse. Hence, the beneficiary can recognize this one of a kind example and realize that it is a comma, and accordingly, discover the 10-bit limits between the images.

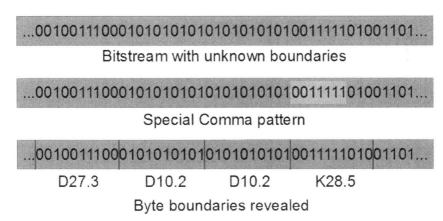

Figure 6: Comma Alignment Example

In SATA, the comma is utilized as a component of the ALIGN primitive. Link Layer primitives, which will be talked about presently, are 4 bytes in length and dependably start with a K character. The ALIGN is the just a single to contain the comma, K28.5. That is the reason it is utilized as a major aspect of the link instatement method, so that byte limits can be resolved before endeavoring to send data.

The SATA protocol additionally determines that no less than two ALIGNs must be sent each 256 Dwords, and they should be sent in sets. This happens notwithstanding when data is being sent. This guarantees the byte limit is not lost, and both the host and the disk must send these ALIGNs. It likewise goes about as an approach to oversee little recurrence contrasts between the sender and beneficiary. For instance, if the sender's clock is running somewhat quicker than the receiver's, the recipient's support may in the long run flood. Since ALIGNs are occasionally sent, and they are not data-imperative, they can be dropped to keep this from happening.

SPREAD-SPECTRUM CLOCKING

To additionally diminish EMI, the SATA determination requires that a collector has the capacity to bolt to a bitstream that utilizations spread-spectrum clocking (SSC). SSC is a plan wherein the line rate does not remain consistent but rather fluctuates somewhat after some time. This spreads the discharges over a more extensive recurrence extend. The handsets on the Virtex-4 can get SSC signals, yet does not utilize it when transmitting.

LINK LAYER

The link layer is the following layer and is specifically over the physical layer. This layer is in charge of exemplifying data payloads and deals with the protocol for sending and getting them. A data payload that is sent is known as a Frame Information Structure (FIS). The link layer likewise gives some different administrations to guaranteeing data uprightness, dealing with flow control, and diminishing EMI.

The host and the disk each have their own particular transmit match in an SATA link, and hypothetically data could be sent in both headings all the while. Nonetheless, this does not happen. Rather, the beneficiary sends "backchannel" data to the sender that demonstrates the status of the move in advance. For example, if a mistake were to be identified mid-transmission, for example, a uniqueness blunder, the recipient could inform the sender of this.

The link layer utilizes an arrangement of characterized Link Layer Primitives to play out these capacities. Primitives are every 4 Dwords in length and begin with the control character K28.3 (aside from ALIGN, as talked about above). The accompanying table records the vast majority of the characterized primitives and their incentive in hexadecimal before encoding. The use of these will be talked about in more detail.

Table 3: Link Layer Primitives

Primitive	Hex-Representation
ALIGN	0x7B4A4ABC
SYNC	0xB5B5957C
X_RDY	0x5757B57C
R_RDY	0x4A4A957C
SOF	0x3737B57C
R_IP	0x5555B57C
HOLD	0xD5D5AA7C
HOLD_ACK	0x9595AA7C
EOF	0xD5D5B57C
WTRM	0x5858B57C
R_OK	0x3535B57C
R_ERR	0x5656B57C
CONT	0x9999AA7C

Table 3: Link Layer Primitives

ALIGN

This primitive, as examined in the past area, enables the beneficiary to decide the byte limits in the data stream. A couple of them is sent no less than each 256 Dwords paying little heed to what express the link layer is in.

SYNC:

SYNC is utilized to show that the line is sit out of gear. At the point when edges are not being sent, both the host and the disk will send this primitive. This primitive additionally has an uncommon capacity called the "Match up Escape." If the host sends an SYNC, the line is compelled to go sit without moving, ending every present exchange. The disk must react SYNC. Along these lines, if the host needs to issue a delicate reset, it can do as such.

X_RDY

This primitive shows that there is data that is prepared to be sent. It will be sent over and again by the disk or host until it is recognized. If both sides are at the same time sending X_RDY, it is normal that the host will down. R_RDY: Indicates that the gathering is prepared to get a FIS. This primitive is utilized to recognize X_RDY, or can be sent preemptively if an exchange is normal.

SOF

A primitive that flags the begin of an FIS (Start of Frame). The following Dwords sent after this are data.

R_IP

Receive In Progress. This is a backchannel primitive that is utilized by a beneficiary to show that it is presently accepting the FIS.

HOLD

The HOLD primitive is utilized for flow control administration, which will be talked about in more detail in a matter of seconds.

HOLD_ACK

Acknowledges a HOLD.

EOF

A primitive that flags the finish of a FIS. No more data will be sent until another FIS exchange is begun. It likewise demonstrates that the past Dword was the CRC.

WTRM

Waiting for Termination. This is sent more than once after EOF by the sender of a FIS. It demonstrates that the sender is sitting tight for affirmation of the edge.

R_OK

This primitive is sent by the recipient to demonstrate that the FIS was gotten effectively, and that the CRC was right.

R_ERR

This primitive demonstrates that there was a blunder with the gathering of the FIS. No doubt, the CRC was erroneous. Be that as it may, it could likewise show an equality blunder.

CONT

The CONT primitive is utilized to diminish EMI made by primitives. There are ordinarily where a similar primitive is sent more than once, and this would make certain frequencies have more EMI clamor. The CONT primitive dispenses with that issue by utilizing pseudo-arbitrarily produced refuse data. In the event that a sender would send many rehashed primitives, rather it can send CONT. The recipient ought to then treat the CONT, and all the accompanying irregular data, as though the first primitive was all the while being sent. This proceeds until another substantial primitive is gotten (none of the garbage data are K characters). For instance, a sender may send SYNC, SYNC, CONT, XXXX, XXXX, ..., X_RDY. The CONT shows that the recipient ought to "imagine" that

SYNCs are as yet being sent, up until the following legitimate primitive (X_RDY). By utilizing junk data rather than rehashed primitives, the EMI is disseminated over a more extensive spectrum.

Figure 7: Link Layer Primitives in real life

In this screen catch from the Chipscope troubleshooting device, we see that the host is sending WTRM while the disk sends R_IP. It then sends CONT taken after by some refuse data, which ought to be dealt with as a proceeded with R_IP.

PMREQ_P/PMREQ_S/PMACK/PMNAK

These primitives encourage control administration. Be that as it may, they are not executed in this work nor are they vital for right SATA operation. In this way, they won't be talked about further. For more data with respect to these primitives.

A commonplace FIS exchange occurs as takes after. The sender shows that they have data to send utilizing X_RDY. The sender then sits tight for R_RDY from the beneficiary. The sender then sends a (single) SOF, trailed by the data to be sent. At the point when the beneficiary sees the SOF, it will change from sending R_RDY to R_IP. When the majority of the data in the FIS has been sent, the CRC is sent, trailed by EOF. The sender then begins sending WTRM until it gets R_OK, R_ERR, or SYNC. The last two demonstrate a blunder, with SYNC meaning a protocol or obscure mistake. The recipient, after getting EOF, checks the CRC, which it knows is the past Dword. It then answers either R_OK or R_ERR. The sender recognizes the R_OK or R_ERR by sending SYNC. The recipient then likewise sends SYNC, the line has come back to sit out of gear, and the exchange is finished. This procedure is outlined in Figure 8.

FLOW CONTROL

As expressed some time recently, HOLD and HOLD_ACK are the primitives utilized for flow control. They are utilized as a part of two circumstances to impermanent respite the transmission of data amidst a FIS. The primary circumstance is if the beneficiary's cushion is getting full and can't acknowledge any more data. For instance, this could happen if a hard drive can't compose data as quick as the protocol permits. The beneficiary would then change from sending R_IP to HOLD. The sender would then delay the sending of data and react with HOLD_ACK. At the point when there is at the end of the day enough room in the cradle, the collector sends R_IP once more, and the sender can continue sending the data.

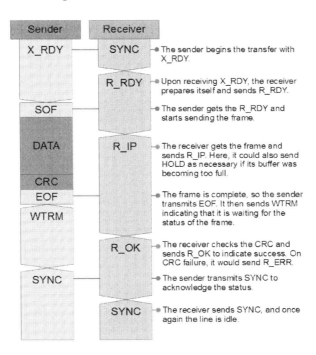

The second circumstance happens when the transmitter is sitting tight for more data to send. For this situation, the sender sends HOLD until it is prepared to keep on sending data. At the end of the day, HOLD_ACK is sent in answer.

Obviously, these primitives don't go down the link quickly. There is a deferral between the time that a HOLD is sent and the time that the HOLD is gotten. Be that as it may, this could prompt data misfortune if the sending gathering was not yet mindful of the asked for HOLD and kept on sending data. Hence, the protocol determines a maximum postponement, alluded to as the maximum flag dormancy or the HOLD inertness. This inertness incorporates the time on the wire, as well as an opportunity to translate, decipher, and respond to the HOLD.

The HOLD inactivity is determined as an opportunity to send 20 Dwords. Along these lines, a recipient can send a HOLD when there are 20 Dwords of space left in its cushion and no data will be lost. Before 20 more Dwords of data arrive, the sender will have changed to HOLD_ACK.

CRC

SATA utilizes a Cyclic Redundancy Check (CRC) on every last FIS to guarantee data trustworthiness. The CRC utilized is CRC-32, a similar that is utilized for Ethernet and some different protocols. This CRC can dependably recognize up to no-account blunders on data hinders as expansive as 2064 Dwords. In this way, the CRC places a cutoff on the maximum size of a FIS. The point of confinement is characterized to be 2049 Dwords for SATA.

SCRAMBLING

As expressed in area 3.2, one of the capacities that the link layer performs is EMI diminishment. The CONT primitive does this for primitives, however it is likewise accomplished for FISes. The substance of an edge, including the CRC, are mixed before being sent. To do this, the data is XORed (a bitwise select OR operation) with a pseudo-irregular number generator. In particular, the PRNG utilized is a Galois Linear Feedback Shift Register (LFSR).

Toward the begin of each casing, the scrambler is reset. The collector, utilizing a similar Galois LFSR, can then descramble the data by again XORing the data with the yield of the scrambler. Primitives are never mixed, even those sent amidst a casing, (for example, HOLD and ALIGN).

TRANSPORT LAYER

The transport layer is in charge of building, conveying, and accepting Frame Information Structures. It characterizes the configuration of each FIS and the legitimate sequence of FISes that can traded.

The primary byte of each FIS characterizes the sort. The second byte contains sort subordinate control fields. The accompanying table records a portion of the sorts of FISes that are characterized, and the estimation of their sort field.

Table 4: FIS Types

FIS Type	Type Value
Enroll – Host to Device	0x27
Enroll – Device to Host	0x34
Data	0x46
DMA Activate	0x39

Various different FIS sorts are characterized; however they are not actualized in this work. For more points of interest on different FIS sorts.

The Register FIS sorts are utilized to exchange the substance of the shadow registers to the device, and the device enlists back to the host. These registers reflect those utilized for PATA, and are the methods by which commands are activated. A portion of the pertinent fields are the Command field, which holds the PATA command to be executed; the tending to fields; and the part number fields. A part is 512 bytes.

The Data FIS is an exceptionally straightforward FIS. After the sort field, the rest of the principal Dword is held. Taking after that is the genuine data to be conveyed. The maximum length of the data for a single FIS is 8KB. This is to guarantee that the CRC is equipped for checking the data.

The DMA Activate FIS is sent by the device to demonstrate that it is prepared to get data. After a compose ask for has been made, the disk may need to set itself up before it can get data. For instance, it might need to flush its cradle or move the make a beeline for the right area. It is a short FIS, comprising just of a single Dword. It contains the FIS sort and whatever remains of the bits are saved.

For read and compose operations, the sequence of legitimate FISes is genuinely straightforward. To play out a read, the host sends a Register – Host to Device (H2D

141

Register) FIS to the disk with the PATA read command in the Command field. It then holds up to get at least one Data FISes (contingent upon the length of the operation) from the disk. From that point forward, the device will send a D2H Register FIS to show its status.

Compose operations are genuinely comparable. The host again sends a H2D Register FIS to the disk, however now with the PATA compose command. It then anticipates a DMA Activate FIS, demonstrating that the disk is prepared. It then sends a Data FIS. On the off chance that the operation is bigger than 8KB, the host must sit tight for another DMA Activate before sending every Data FIS. After the operation is finished, the device will again send a D2H Register FIS with status data.

SATA CONCLUSION

In general, SATA is an exceptionally appropriate protocol for the mass stockpiling outline. It takes into consideration rapid stockpiling good with any hard drive or SSD accessible available. Additionally, it is an exceptionally robust protocol, making it appropriate for utilize essentially all over the place. Every last casing has a CRC to ensure against bit blunders. Low-voltage differential flagging includes commotion invulnerability and reductions control expended. There are likewise various techniques utilized to decrease EMI.

CHAPTER 7: CUDA AND GPU ACCELERATION OF IMAGE PROCESSING

OVERVIEW

CUDA remains for the "Compute Unified Device Architecture", which is a free software stage given by NVidia. It empowers clients to control GPUs by composing programs much the same as C++. All CUDA software can be downloaded from CUDA Zone. CUDA is fundamentally the same as in nature to cores on a CPU. You may have a double or quad-center CPU, and that is the nearest simple to CUDA cores that the vast majority will have any involvement with.

Nonetheless, CUDA cores have a tendency to be more particular for the stream, preparing rather than summed up like a CPU, so there's less rationale to copy making it simpler to fit more CUDA cores onto a GPU.

All things considered, CUDA's essential utilize is by all accounts for permitting the GPU to be utilized for more universally useful assignments, such as encoding recordings, or even equipment increasing the speed of video deciphering. For gaming, I would go more for things like memory transport transmission capacity, and memory and GPU clock speeds. On the off chance that you can discover a card that additionally has more CUDA cores contrasted with a fundamentally the same as a card, then surprisingly better, yet I'd put CUDA cores far down on the rundown for gaming.

Indeed, even simply considering GPUs, while NVidia is the most prevalent, it's not by any means the only amusement around the local area; there are additionally AMD's (ATI's). They utilize OpenCL, which the Kronos bunch marks. It is an alternate API for GPU-like (stream, SIMD) preparing. OpenCL is a standard, and you can run OpenCL-composed code on NVidia equip. However it won't keep running as quick as CUDA code.

Utilizing CUDA enables the developer to exploit the monstrous parallel registering energy of a NVidia graphics card keeping in mind the end goal to do the broadly useful calculation. Before proceeding with, it merits discussing this for a smidgen longer.

MULTICORE CPU AND GPU

CPUs like Intel Core 2 Duo and AMD Opteron are great at doing maybe a couple of assignments at once and doing those undertakings rapidly. Graphics cards, then again, are great at doing a monstrous number assignments in the meantime and doing those undertakings rapidly. To place this into viewpoint, assume you have a 20-inch screen with a standard determination of 1,920 x 1200. An NVidia graphics card has the computational capacity to ascertain the shade of 2,304,000 unique pixels, all the time. Keeping in mind the end goal to achieve this accomplishment, graphics cards utilize handfuls, even many ALUs. Luckily, NVidia's ALUs are completely programmable, which empowers us to bridle an exceptional measure of computational power into the programs that we compose.

As expressed beforehand, CUDA gives the developer a chance to exploit the many ALUs inside a graphics processor, which is substantially more intense than the modest bunch of ALUs accessible in any CPU. In any case, this puts the farthest point on the sorts of uses that are appropriate to CUDA.

CUDA IS JUST APPROPRIATE FOR PROFOUNDLY PARALLEL CALCULATIONS

Keeping in mind the end goal to run productively on a GPU, you need a large number of strings. For the most part, threads should you have, as much as possible. On the off chance that you have a calculation that is for the most part serial, then it doesn't bode well to utilize CUDA. Numerous serial calculations do have parallel counterparts, yet many don't. If you can't separate your issue into no less than a thousand strings, then CUDA likely is not the best answer for you.

CUDA IS TO A GREAT DEGREE APPROPRIATE FOR CALCULATING

On the off chance that there is one thing that CUDA exceeds expectations at, it is calculating. The GPU is completely equipped for doing 32-bit number and skimming point operations. Truth be told, it GPUs are more suited for skimming point calculations, which makes CUDA a superb for calculating. A portion of the higher end graphics cards do have twofold skimming point units. However, there is just a single 64-bit coasting point unit for each 16 32-bit gliding point units. So utilizing twofold skimming point numbers with CUDA ought to be kept away from on the off chance that they aren't completely essential for your application.

CUDA IS APPROPRIATE FOR HUGE DATASETS

Most present day CPUs have two or three megabytes of L2 reserve because most programs have high information coherency. Nonetheless, when working rapidly over a huge dataset, say 500 megabytes, the L2 store may not be as useful. The memory interface for GPUs is altogether different from the memory interface of CPUs. GPUs utilize enormous parallel interfaces keeping in mind the end goal to associate with its memory. For instance, the GTX 280 utilizations a 512-piece interface to its superior GDDR-3 memory. This kind of interface is roughly 10 times speedier than a run of the mill CPU to the memory interface, which is awesome. It is significant that most NVidia graphics cards don't have more than 1 gigabyte of memory. NVidia offers uncommon CUDA compute cards which have up to four gigabytes of slam locally available, yet these cards are more costly than cards initially expected for gaming.

COMPOSING A KERNEL IN CUDA

As expressed beforehand, CUDA can be taken the full preferred standpoint of when writing in C. This is uplifting news since most developers are exceptionally acquainted with C. Likewise expressed already, the principle thought of CUDA is to have a huge number of strings executing in parallel. What wasn't expressed is that these strings will be executing the exceptionally same capacity, known as a kernel. Understanding what the kernel is and how it functions is basic to your prosperity when composing an application that utilizations CUDA. The thought is that despite the fact that the greater part of the strings of your program are executing a similar capacity, the greater part of the strings will work with an alternate dataset. Each string will know its particular ID and based on its ID, it will figure out which bits of information to chip away at. Try not to stress, stream control like 'if, for, while, do, and so on.' are altogether upheld.

COMPOSING PROGRAMS WITH CUDA

One imperative thing to recollect is that your whole program DOES NOT should be composed in CUDA. In case you're composing an extensive application, finish with a UI, and numerous different capacities, then the vast majority of your code will be composed in C++ or whatever your dialect of decision is. At that point, when something to a great degree computationally extreme is required, your program can call the CUDA kernel work you composed. So the primary thought is that CUDA ought to just be utilized for the most computationally extreme segments of your program.

CUDA WITHOUT A GRAPHICS CARD

While CUDA is particularly intended to keep running on NVidia's graphics cards, it can likewise keep running on any CPU. Though the program will never have the capacity to run about as quick on a CPU, it will be in any case work.

DEVICE ARCHITECTURE: STREAMING MULTIPROCESSOR (SM)

1 SM contains 8 scalar cores

- Up to 8 cores can run at the same time
- Each center executes indistinguishable guideline set or dozes
- SM plans directions crosswise over cores with 0 overhead
- Up to 32 strings might be planned at once, called a twist, however, max 24 twists dynamic in 1 SM
- Thread-levelmemory-sharing bolstered by means of Shared Memory
- Register memory is neighborhood to string, and isolated among all pieces on SM
- ATI Stream software environment.
- Memory progression in OpenCL programming model.

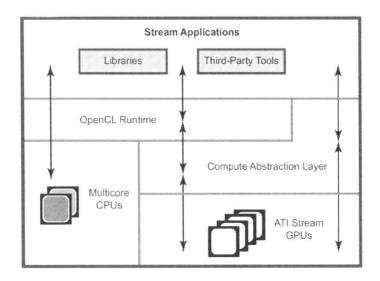

ATI Stream software environment

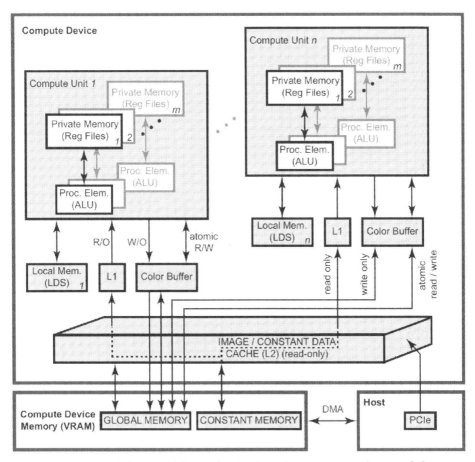

Memory hierarchy in OpenCL programming model.

TRANSPARENT SCALABILITY

- Hardware is allowed to appoint squares to any processor whenever
- A kernel scales over any number of parallel processors

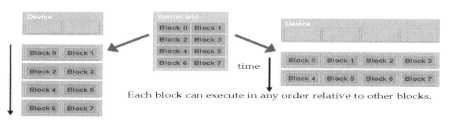

Each block can execute in any order relative to other blocks.

SM WARP SCHEDULING

- SM equipment executes zero- overhead Warp booking
- Warps whose next direction has its operands prepared for utilization are eligible for execution
- Eligible Warps are chosen for execution on an organized booking arrangement
- All strings in a Warp execute a similar guideline when chosen
- 4 clock cycles expected to dispatch a similar guideline for all strings in a Warp in G80
- If one worldwide memory gets to be required for each 4 directions
- An insignificant of 13 Warps are expected to endure 200-cycle memory inactivity entirely.

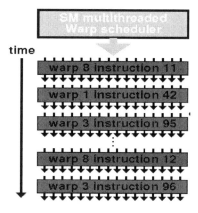

COMPUTATIONAL CAPACITIES

Current GPUs utilize the greater part of their transistors to do figurings identified with 3D computer graphics. They were first used to quicken the memory-serious work of surface mapping and rendering polygons, later adding units to quicken geometric estimations, for example, the turn and interpretation of vertices into various arrange frameworks. Later advancements in GPUs incorporate support for programmable shaders which can control vertices and surfaces with a large number of similar operations bolstered by CPUs, oversampling and insertion methods to diminish associating, and high-exactness shading spaces. Since a large portion of these calculations includes a framework and vector operations, specialists and researchers have progressively concentrated the utilization of GPUs for non-graphical figurings.

Notwithstanding the 3D equipment, today's GPUs incorporate essential 2D increasing speed and framebuffer capacities (typically with a VGA similarity mode). More current cards like AMD/ATI HD5000-HD7000 even need 2D quickening; it must be copied by 3D equipment.

GPU QUICKENED VIDEO TRANSLATING

Most GPUs made since 1995 support the YUV shading space and equipment overlays, vital for advanced video playback, and numerous GPUs made since 2000 additionally bolster MPEG primitives, for example, movement remuneration and iDCT. This procedure of equipment quickened video translating, where parts of the video unraveling procedure and video present handling are offloaded on the GPU equipment, is regularly alluded to as "GPU quickened video disentangling", "GPU helped video interpreting", "GPU equipment quickened video deciphering" or "GPU equipment helped video unraveling".

Later graphics cards even translate superior quality video on the card, offloading the focal handling unit. The most widely recognized APIs for GPU quickened video deciphering are DxVA for Microsoft Windows working framework and VDPAU, VAAPI, XvMC, and XvBA for Linux-based and UNIX-like working frameworks. All aside from XvMC are equipped for deciphering recordings encoded with MPEG-1, MPEG-2, MPEG-4

ASP (MPEG-4 Part 2), MPEG-4 AVC (H.264/DivX 6), VC-1, WMV3/WMV9, Xvid/OpenDivX (DivX 4), and DivX 5 codecs, while XvMC is just fit for unraveling MPEG-1 and MPEG-2.

VIDEO DECODING PROCESSES THAT CAN BE ACCELERATED

The video decoding processes that can be accelerated by today's modern GPU hardware are:

- Motion compensation (mocomp)
- Inverse discrete cosine transform (iDCT)
- Inverse telecine 3:2 and 2:2 pull-down correction
- Inverse modified discrete cosine transform (iMDCT)
- In-loop deblocking filter
- Intra-frame prediction
- Inverse quantization (IQ)
- Variable-length decoding (VLD), more commonly known as slice-level

ACCELERATION

- Spatial-worldly deinterlacing and programmed entwine/dynamic source identification
- Bitstream preparing (Context-versatile variable-length coding/Context-versatile twofold number-crunching coding) and flawless pixel situating.

GPU FRAMES

GRAPHICS CARDS

Devoted graphics cards The GPUs of the most effective class ordinarily interface with the motherboard by methods for an extension opening, for example, PCI Express (PCIe) or Accelerated Graphics Port (AGP) and can more often than not be supplanted or updated without breaking a sweat, expecting the motherboard is equipped for supporting the redesign. A couple of graphics cards still utilize Peripheral Component Interconnect

(PCI) openings, however, their transmission capacity is limited to the point that they are by and large utilized just when a PCIe or AGP space is not accessible.

A devoted GPU is not removable, nor does it fundamentally interface with the motherboard in a standard form. The expression "devoted" alludes to the way that committed graphics cards have RAM that is committed to the card's utilization, not to the way that most devoted GPUs are removable. Devoted GPUs for convenient computers are most generally interfaced through a non-standard and frequently exclusive opening because of size and weight imperatives. Such ports may at present be viewed as PCIe or AGP as far as their consistent host interface, regardless of the possibility that they are not physically tradable with their partners.

Advancements, for example, SLI by NVidia and CrossFire by AMD permit different GPUs to draw pictures at the same time for a solitary screen, expanding the preparing power accessible for graphics.

INTEGRATED GRAPHICS SOLUTIONS

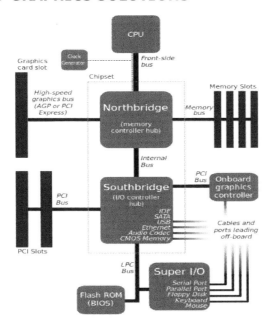

The position of an integrated GPU in a northbridge/southbridge system layout

151

The position of an integrated GPU in a northbridge/southbridge framework design.

Integrated graphics solutions, shared graphics solutions, or integrated graphics processors (IGP) use a bit of a computer's framework RAM as opposed to devoted graphics memory. IGPs can be integrated onto the motherboard as a feature of the chipset, or inside an indistinguishable kick the bucket from CPU (like AMD APU or Intel HD Graphics). On certain motherboards

AMD's IGPs can utilize devoted side port memory. This is a different settled square of elite memory that is devoted for use by the GPU. In mid-2007, computers with integrated graphics represent around 90% of all PC shipments. These solutions are less exorbitant to execute than devoted graphics solutions, however, have a tendency to be less fit. Truly, integrated solutions were frequently viewed as unfit to play 3D recreations or run graphically concentrated programs, however, could run less serious programs, for example, Adobe Flash. Cases of such IGPs would be offerings from SiS and VIA around 2004. In any case, present day integrated graphics processors, for example, AMD Accelerated Processing Unit, and Intel HD Graphics are more than equipped for taking care of 2D graphics or low anxiety 3D graphics.

As a GPU is to a great degree memory concentrated, an integrated arrangement may wind up going after the as of now moderately moderate framework RAM with the CPU, as it has negligible or no committed video memory. IGPs can have up to 29.856 GB/s of memory transmission capacity from framework RAM; however graphics cards can appreciate up to 264 GB/s of data transfer capacity between its RAM and GPU center. This data transmission is what is alluded to as the memory transport and can be execution restricting. More seasoned integrated graphics chipsets needed equipment change and lighting, however, more current ones incorporate it.

HYBRID SOLUTIONS

This more up to date class of GPUs contends with integrated graphics in the low-end desktop and journal markets. The most well-known usage of this are ATI's HyperMemory and NVidia's TurboCache.

Hybrid graphics cards are to some degree more costly than integrated graphics, however a great deal more affordable than devoted graphics cards. These offer memory with the framework and have a little-devoted memory store, to compensate for the high idleness of the framework RAM. Advances inside PCI Express can make this conceivable. While these solutions are some of the time publicized as having as much as 768MB of RAM, this alludes to what amount can be imparted to the framework memory.

STREAM PROCESSING AND GENERAL PURPOSE GPUS (GPGPU)

It is winding up plainly progressively regular to utilize a universally useful graphics handling unit (GPGPU) as an adjusted type of stream processor. This idea turns the enormous computational energy of a current graphics quickening agent's shader pipeline into universally useful processing power, instead of being hard-wired exclusively to do graphical operations. In specific applications requiring gigantic vector operations, this can yield a few requests of extent higher execution than an ordinary CPU. The two biggest discrete (see "Committed graphics cards" above) GPU architects, ATI and NVidia, are starting to seek after this approach with a variety of uses. Both NVidia and ATI have cooperated with Stanford University to make a GPU-based customer for the Folding@home disseminated processing venture, for protein collapsing estimations. In specific conditions, the GPU computes forty times speedier than the regular CPUs customarily utilized by such applications.

GPGPU can be utilized for some sorts of embarrassingly parallel undertakings including beam following. They are for the most part suited to high-throughput sort calculations that display information parallelism to abuse the wide vector width SIMD architecture of the GPU.

Besides, GPU-based elite computers are beginning to assume a noteworthy part in vast scale modeling. Three of the 10 most capable supercomputers on the planet exploit GPU acceleration.

NVidia cards bolster API expansions to the C programming dialect, for example, CUDA and OpenCL. CUDA is particularly for NVidia GPUs while OpenCL is intended to work over a huge number of architectures including GPU, CPU, and DSP (utilizing particular seller SDKs). These advancements permit determined capacities (kernels) from an ordinary C program to keep running on the GPU's stream processors. This makes C programs fit for exploiting a GPU's capacity to work on substantial frameworks in parallel, while as yet making utilization of the CPU when proper. CUDA is likewise the main API to enable CPU-based applications to straightforwardly get to the assets of a GPU for more universally useful registering without the impediments of utilizing a graphics API.

Since 2005 there has been enthusiasm for utilizing the execution offered by GPUs for transformative calculation by and large, and for quickening the wellness assessment in hereditary programming specifically. Most methodologies assemble straight or tree programs on the host PC and exchange the executable to the GPU to be run. Ordinarily, the execution favorable position is just gotten by running the single dynamic program all the while on numerous case issues in parallel, utilizing the GPU's SIMD architecture. In any case, generous acceleration can likewise be acquired by not arranging the programs, and rather exchanging them to the GPU, to be translated there. Acceleration can then be acquired by either translating various programs at the same time, at the same time running different case issues, or blends of both. A current GPU (e.g. 8800 GTX or later) can promptly at the same time decipher countless little programs.

EXTERNAL GPU (EGPU)

An external GPU is a graphics processor situated outside of the lodging of the computer. External graphics processors are frequently utilized with smartphones. Tablets may have a generous measure of RAM and an adequately capable focal handling unit (CPU), however, regularly do not have an effective graphics processor (and rather have a less capable yet more vitality proficient on-board graphics chip). On-board graphics chips are regularly not sufficiently capable of playing the most recent diversions, or for different undertakings (video altering, ...).

Like this, it is alluring to have the capacity to join a GPU to some external transport of a journal. PCI Express is the main transport regularly utilized for this reason. The port might be, for instance, an ExpressCard or mPCIe port (PCIe ×1, up to 5 or 2.5 Gbit/s separately) or a Thunderbolt 1, 2, or 3 port (PCIe ×4, up to 10, 20, or 40 Gbit/s individually). Those ports are just accessible on certain journal frameworks.

External GPUs have had minimal authority merchant bolster. This has not prevented devotees from making their own particular DIY eGPU solutions.

APPLICATIONS

- GPU bunch
- Mathematica incorporates worked in support for CUDA and OpenCL GPU execution
- MATLAB acceleration utilizing the Parallel Computing Toolbox and MATLAB Distributed Computing Server, and also outsider bundles like Jacket.
- Molecular modeling on GPU
- Deeplearning4j, open-source, conveyed profound learning for Java. Machine vision and literary subject modeling toolbox.

GPU ORGANIZATIONS

Many organizations have created GPUs under various brand names. In 2009, Intel, NVidia, and AMD/ATI were the piece of the overall industry pioneers, with 49.4%, 27.8% and 20.6% piece of the pie individually. In any case, those numbers incorporate Intel's integrated graphics solutions as GPUs. Not including those numbers, NVidia and ATI control almost 100% of the market starting at 2008. Furthermore, S3 Graphics (possessed by VIA Technologies) and Matrox create GPUs.

Deals In 2013, 438.3 million GPUs were delivered universally, and the figure for 2014 was 414.2million

CHAPTER 8: ARCHITECTURE AND OPERATION OF A WATCHDOG TIMER

OVERVIEW

A watchdog timer is an electronic timer that is utilized to recognize and recuperate from PC breakdowns. Amid typical operation, the PC consistently restarts the watchdog timer to keep it from slipping by, or "timing out." On the off chance that, because of an equipment fault or program blunder, the PC neglects to restart the watchdog, the timer will pass and produce a timeout flag. The timeout flag is utilized to start corrective activity or actions. The corrective actions ordinarily incorporate putting the PC framework in a protected state and reestablishing typical framework operation.

Watchdog timers are found in installed frameworks and other PC controlled gear where people can't without much of a stretch get to the hardware or would be not able to respond to faults in a timely way. In such frameworks, the PC can't rely on upon a human to reboot it on the off chance that it hangs; it must act naturally dependent. For instance, remotely installed frameworks, for example, space tests are not physically available to human administrators; these could turn out to be for all time handicapped on the off chance that they were not able independently to recoup from faults. A watchdog timer is utilized in cases like these. Watchdog timers may likewise be utilized when running untrusted code in a sandbox, to confine the CPU time accessible to the code and in this way keep a few sorts of dissent of-administration assaults.

ARCHITECTURE AND OPERATION

WATCHDOG RESTART

The demonstration of restarting a watchdog timer is alluded to as "kicking the canine" or other comparative terms; this is commonly done by keeping in touch with a watchdog control port. Then again, in microcontrollers that have a coordinated watchdog timer, the watchdog is sometimes kicked by executing a unique machine dialect guideline. A case of this is the CLRWDT (clear watchdog timer) guideline found in the direction set of some PIC microcontrollers.

In PCs that are running working frameworks, watchdog resets are typically conjured through a gadget driver. For instance, in the Linux working framework, a client space program will kick the watchdog by associating with the watchdog gadget driver, normally by composing a zero character to/dev/watchdog. The gadget driver, which serves to extract the watchdog equipment from client space projects, is additionally used to design the time-out period and begin and stop the timer.

SINGLE-STAGE WATCHDOG

Watchdog timers come in numerous designs, and many enable their arrangements to be changed. Microcontrollers frequently incorporate a coordinated, on-chip watchdog. In different PCs, the watchdog may live in a close-by chip that interfaces straightforwardly to the CPU, or it might be situated on an outer extension card in the PC's undercarriage. The watchdog and CPU may share a typical clock motion, as appeared in the piece chart beneath, or they may have autonomous clock signals.

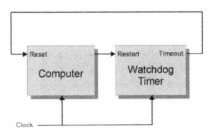

MULTISTAGE WATCHDOG

At least two timers are sometimes fell to frame a multistage watchdog timer, where every timer is alluded to as a timer stage, or essentially a stage. For instance, the square outline underneath demonstrates a three-stage watchdog. In a multistage watchdog, just the main stage is kicked by the processor. Upon first stage timeout, a corrective activity is started, and the following stage in the course is begun. As each resulting stage times out, it triggers a corrective activity and begins the following stage. Upon definite stage timeout, a corrective activity is started. However, no other stage is begun in light of the fact that the finish of the course has been come to. Normally, single-stage watchdog timers are utilized just to restart the PC, while multistage watchdog timers will consecutively trigger a progression of corrective actions, with the last stage setting off a PC restart.

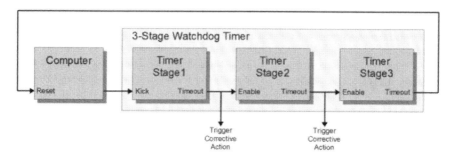

TIME INTERVALS

Watchdog timers may have either settled or programmable time intervals. Some watchdog timers enable the time interim to be customized by choosing from among a couple of selectable, discrete esteems. In others, the interim can be modified to subjective esteems. Normally, watchdog time intervals extend from ten milliseconds to a moment or more. In a multistage watchdog, every timer may have its own, extraordinary time interim.

CORRECTIVE ACTIONS

A watchdog timer may start any of a few sorts of corrective activity, including processor reset, non-maskable intrude, maskable interfere with, power cycling, safeguard state initiation, or mixes of these. Contingent upon its architecture, the kind of corrective activity or actions that a watchdog can trigger might be settled or programmable. A few PCs require a beat flag to conjure a processor reset. In such cases, the watchdog commonly triggers a processor reset by initiating an interior or outer heartbeat generator, which like this makes the required reset beats.

In inserted frameworks and control frameworks, watchdog timers are frequently used to enact safeguard hardware. Whenever actuated, the safeguard hardware compels all control yields to safe states (e.g., kills engines, warmers, and high-voltages) to avert wounds and gear harm while the fault holds on. In a two-stage watchdog, the beginner is regularly used to initiate safeguard yields and begin the second timer stage; the second stage will reset the PC if the fault can't be redressed before the timer slips by.

Watchdog timers are sometimes used to trigger the recording of framework state data—which might be valuable amid fault recuperation—or investigate data (which might be helpful for deciding the reason for the fault) onto an industrious medium. In such cases, a moment timer—which is begun when the novice slips by—is regularly used to reset the PC later, after permitting adequate time for information recording to finish. This enables time for the data to be spared, yet guarantees that the PC will be reset regardless of the possibility that the recording procedure falls flat.

For instance, the above outline demonstrates a conceivable arrangement for a two-stage watchdog timer. Amid ordinary operation, the PC consistently kicks Stage1 to keep a timeout. On the off chance that the PC neglects to kick Stage1 (e.g., because of an equipment fault or programming blunder), Stage1 will in the long run timeout. This occasion will begin the Stage2 timer and, at the same time, advise the PC (by methods for a non-maskable intrude on) that a reset is fast approaching. Until Stage2 times out, the PC may endeavor to record state data, investigate data, or both. The PC will be reset upon Stage2 timeout.

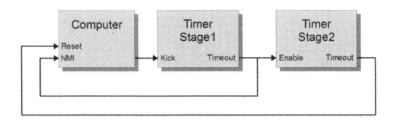

FAULT DETECTION

A PC framework is regularly composed so that its watchdog timer will be kicked just if the PC regards the framework useful. The PC decides if the framework is useful by directing at least one fault detection tests and it will kick the watchdog just if all tests have passed. In PCs that are running a working framework and different procedures, a single, basic test might be lacking to ensure ordinary operation, as it could neglect to recognize an inconspicuous fault condition and like this enable the watchdog to be kicked despite the fact that a fault condition exists.

For instance, on account of the Linux working framework, a client space watchdog daemon may kick the watchdog intermittently without playing out any tests. For whatever length of time that the daemon runs regularly, the framework will be ensured against genuine framework crashes, for example, a bit freeze. To identify less serious faults, the daemon can be arranged to perform tests that cover asset accessibility (e.g., adequate memory and record handles, sensible CPU time), proof of expected process movement (e.g., framework daemons running, particular documents being available or refreshed), overheating, and system action, and framework particular test scripts or projects may likewise be run.

An endless supply of a fizzled test, the Linux watchdog daemon may endeavor to play out a product started restart, which can be desirable over an equipment reset as the record frameworks will be securely unmounted, and fault data will be logged. In any case, it is basic to have the protection of the equipment timer as a product restart can flop under various fault conditions. As a result, this is a double stage watchdog with the product restart involving the primary stage and the equipment reset the second stage.

To shield a watchdog timer from resetting your framework, you must kick it routinely. In any case, that is not everything to watchdog science. We will look at the utilization and testing of a watchdog, and additionally the combination of a watchdog into a multitasking domain.

Making appropriate utilization of a watchdog timer is not as straightforward as restarting a counter. On the off chance that you have a watchdog timer in your framework, you should pick the timeout period, painstakingly, guarantee that the watchdog timer is tried consistently, and, on the off chance that you are multitasking, screen the majority of the assignments. Furthermore, the recuperation actions you execute can bigly affect general framework unwavering quality.

A watchdog timer is a bit of equipment, regularly incorporated with a microcontroller that can bring about a processor reset when it judges that the framework has hung, or is at no time in the future executing the right arrangement of code. This article will examine precisely the kind of disappointments a watchdog can recognize, and the choices that must be made in the plan of your watchdog framework. The main portion of the article will accept that there is no RTOS exhibit. The second half covers a plan for making utilization of a watchdog in a multi-entrusting framework.

The equipment part of a watchdog is a counter that is set to a specific esteem and afterward tallies down towards zero. It is the obligation of the product to set the tally to its unique esteem regularly enough to guarantee that it never achieves zero. On the off chance that it reaches zero, it is expected that the product has flopped in some way and the CPU is reset.

In different writings, you will see different terms for restarting the timer: strobing, stroking or refreshing the watchdog. Be that as it may, in this article we will utilize the more visual representation of a man kicking the pooch occasionally—with expressions of remorse to creature mates. On the off chance that the man quits kicking the canine, the puppy will exploit the hesitation

It is additionally conceivable to plan the equipment so that kick that happens too early will bring about a nibble, yet with a specific end goal to utilize such a framework, exceptionally exact learning of the planning qualities of the principle circle of your program is required.

ERRORS WE CAUGHT

An appropriately composed watchdog component ought to, in any event, get occasions that hang the framework. In electrically boisterous situations, a power glitch may degenerate the program counter, stack pointer, or information in RAM. The product would crash very quickly, regardless of the possibility that the code is totally bug-free. This is precisely the kind of transient disappointment that watchdogs will get.

Bugs in programming can likewise make the framework hang, on the off chance that they prompt an endless circle, an incidental hop out of the code range of memory, or a gridlock condition (in multitasking circumstances). It is desirable over fix the underlying driver, as opposed to getting the watchdog to get the pieces. In a complex implanted framework, it may not be conceivable to ensure that there are no bugs, yet by utilizing a watchdog, you can ensure that none of those bugs will hang the framework uncertainly.

FIRST AID

Once your watchdog has chomped, you need to choose what move to make. The equipment will more often than not attest the processor's reset line, yet different actions are likewise conceivable. For instance, when the watchdog nibbles it might specifically impair an engine, draw in an interlock, or sound a caution until the product recuperates. Such actions are particularly imperative to leave the framework in a protected state if, for reasons unknown, the framework's product can't keep running by any means (maybe because of chip demise) after the disappointment.

A microcontroller with an inside watchdog will quite often contain a status bit that gets set when a nibble happens. By analyzing this bit in the wake of rising up out of a watchdog-instigated reset, we can choose whether to keep running, change to a safeguard state, and additionally show a blunder message. In any event, you ought to tally such occasions, so that a constantly errant application won't be restarted uncertainly. A sensible approach may be to close the framework down if three watchdog chomps happen in one day.

On the off chance that we need the framework to recuperate rapidly, the instatement after a watchdog reset ought to be significantly shorter than power-on introduction. A conceivable alternate route is to avoid a portion of the gadget's individual tests. Then again, in a few frameworks it is ideal to do a full arrangement of individual tests since the main driver of the watchdog timeout may be recognized by such a test.

As far as the outside world, the recuperation might be immediate, and the client may not know a reset happened. The recuperation time will be the length of the watchdog timeout in addition to the time it takes the framework to reset and play out its introduction. How well the gadget recoups relies on upon how much relentless information the gadget requires, and whether that information is put away frequently and perused after the framework resets.

SANITY CHECKS

Kicking the puppy on a standard interim demonstrates that the product is running. It is regularly a smart thought to kick the puppy just if the framework passes some sanity check, as appeared in Figure 1:

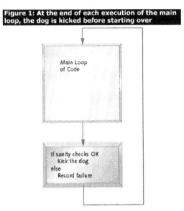

Figure 1: At the end of each execution of the main loop, the dog is kicked before starting over

Main Loop of Code

If sanity checks OK
  Kick the dog
else
  Record failure

Stack profundity, number of supports apportioned, or the status of some mechanical part might be checked before choosing to kick the canine. Great outline of such checks will build the group of errors that the watchdog will distinguish.

One approach is to clear various banners before each circle is begun, as appeared in Figure 2:

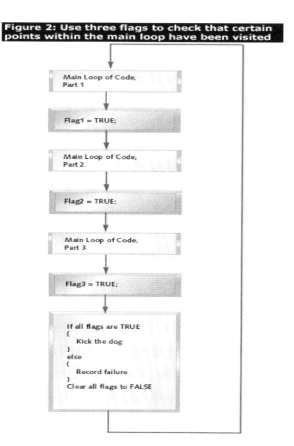

Figure 2: Use three flags to check that certain points within the main loop have been visited

Main Loop of Code, Part 1

Flag1 = TRUE;

Main Loop of Code, Part 2

Flag2 = TRUE;

Main Loop of Code, Part 3

Flag3 = TRUE;

```
If all flags are TRUE
{
    Kick the dog
}
else
{
    Record failure
}
Clear all flags to FALSE
```

Each banner is set at one point insider savvy. At the base of the circle the pooch is kicked, however first the banners are verified that the greater part of the vital focuses insider savvy have been gone to. The multitasking approach talked about later depends on a comparative arrangement of sanity banners.

For a particular disappointment, it is regularly a smart thought to attempt to record the cause (potentially in NVRAM), since it might be hard to build up the cause after the reset. On the off chance that the watchdog nibble is because of a bug (would that be a bug chomp?) then whatever other data you can record about the condition of the framework, or the as of now dynamic assignment will be significant when attempting to analyze the issue.

PICKING THE TIMEOUT INTERIM

Any security chain is just in the same class as its weakest connection, and if the product strategy used to choose when to kick the pooch is bad, then utilizing watchdog equipment can make your framework less dependable. On the off chance that you don't completely comprehend the planning qualities of your program, you may pick a timeout interim that is too short. This could prompt periodic resets of the framework, which might be hard to analyze. The contributions to the framework, and the recurrence of intrudes, can influence the length of a single circle.

One approach is to pick an interim which is a few seconds in length. Utilize this approach when you are just attempting to reset a framework that has certainly hung, however you would prefer not to do an itemized investigation of the planning of the framework. This is a vigorous approach. A few frameworks require quick recuperation, however for others, the main necessity is that the framework is not left in a hung state inconclusively. For these more languid frameworks, there is no compelling reason to do exact estimations of the most pessimistic scenario time of the program's fundamental circle to the closest millisecond.

When picking the timeout you may likewise need to consider the best measure of harm the gadget can do between the first disappointment and the watchdog gnawing. With a gradually reacting framework, for example, a substantial warm mass, it might be worthy to hold up 10 seconds before resetting. Such quite a while can ensure that there will be no false watchdog resets. On a restorative ventilator, 10 seconds would have been awfully long to leave the patient unassisted, yet in the event that the gadget can recuperate inside a moment then the disappointment will have negligible effect, so a decision of a 500ms timeout may be proper. When making such counts, make certain to incorporate the time taken for the gadget to fire up and also the timeout time of the watchdog itself.

One genuine illustration is the Space Shuttle's fundamental motor controller. 1 The watchdog timeout is set at 18ms, which is shorter than one noteworthy control cycle. The reaction to the watchdog gnawing is to change over to the reinforcement PC. This instrument enables control to go from a fizzled PC to the reinforcement before the motor has sufficient energy to play out any irreversible actions.

While regarding the matter of timeouts, it merits calling attention to that some watchdog circuits permit the first timeout to be extensively longer than the timeout utilized for whatever remains of the intermittent checks. This permits the processor time to instate, without worrying about the watchdog gnawing.

While the watchdog can regularly react sufficiently quick to stop mechanical frameworks, it offers little assurance for harm that should be possible by programming alone. Consider a territory of non-unpredictable RAM which might be overwritten with refuse information if some circle leaves control. It is likely that such an overwrite would happen far speedier than a watchdog could identify the fault. For those circumstances you require some other insurance, for example, a checksum. The watchdog is truly only one layer of assurance, and ought to frame some portion of an exhaustive wellbeing net.

DUPLICATING THE INTERIM

On the off chance that you are not building the watchdog equipment yourself, then you may have little say in deciding the longest interim accessible. On some microcontrollers the inherent watchdog has a most extreme timeout on the request of a couple of hundred milliseconds. It you conclude that you need additional time, you have to increase that in programming.

Say the equipment gives a 100ms timeout, yet your strategy says that you just need to check the framework for sanity each 300ms. You should kick the pooch at an interim shorter than 100ms, however just do the sanity check each third time the kick capacity is called. This approach may not be reasonable for a single circle plan if the principle circle could take longer than 100ms to execute.

One probability is to move the sanity look at to an interfere. The hinder would be called each 100ms, and would then kick the canine. On each third interfere with the intrude on capacity would check a banner that demonstrates that the primary circle is as yet turning. This banner is set toward the finish of the principle circle, and cleared by the hinder when it has perused it.

On the off chance that you adopt the strategy of kicking the watchdog from an interfere with, it is key to have a beware of the principle circle, for example, the one portrayed in the past passage. Else it is conceivable to get into a circumstance where the fundamental circle has hung, yet the interfere with keeps on kicking the canine, and the watchdog never gets an opportunity to reset the framework.

SELF-TEST

Expect that the watchdog equipment bombs such that it never chomps. How might you ever know? At the point when the framework works, such a fault is not evident. The fault would just be found when some disappointment that ordinarily prompts a reset, rather prompts a hung framework. In the event that such a disappointment was adequate, you could never have disturbed with the watchdog in the first place.

On the off chance that you think watchdog disappointment is an uncommon thing, reconsider. Numerous frameworks contain a way to impair the watchdog, similar to a jumper that interfaces the watchdog yield to the reset line. This is fundamental for some test modes, and for troubleshooting with any instrument that can stop the program. On the off chance that the jumper drops out, or an administration architect who expelled the jumper for a test neglects to supplant it, the watchdog will be rendered toothless.

The least difficult path for a gadget to do a start-up self-test is to enable the watchdog to timeout, bringing on a processor reset. To abstain from circling limitlessly along these lines, it is important to recognize the power-on case from the watchdog reset case. In the event that the reset was because of a power-on, then play out this test, yet in the event that the reset was because of a watchdog nibble, then we may as of now be running the test. Generally you will need to compose an incentive in RAM that will be protected through a reset, so you can check if the reset was because of a watchdog test or to a genuine disappointment. A counter ought to be augmented while waiting for the reset. After the reset, check the counter to perceive to what extent you needed to sit tight for the timeout, so you are certain that the watchdog bit after the right interim.

In the event that you are checking the quantity of watchdog resets keeping in mind the end goal to choose if the framework ought to surrender attempting, then make sure that you don't unintentionally tally the watchdog test reset as one of those.

MULTITASKING

A watchdog technique has four targets in a multitasking framework:

- To distinguish a legitimately working framework
- To distinguish an interminable circle in any of the undertakings
- To identify gridlock including at least two undertakings
- To identify if some lower need errands are not getting the opportunity to run in light of the fact that higher need assignments are hoarding the CPU

Commonly, insufficient planning data is accessible on the conceivable ways of any offered assignment to check for a base execution time or to set as far as possible on an errand to be precisely the time taken for the longest way. Thusly, while every single limitless circle are identified, a blunder that makes a circle execute various additional cycles may go undetected by the watchdog component. Various different contemplations must be considered to make any plan attainable:

The additional code added to the ordinary errands (as particular from an assignment made for observing undertakings) must be little, to decrease the probability of getting to be noticeably inclined to errors itself. The measure of framework assets utilized, particularly CPU cycles, must be sensible.

The arrangement I will portray was utilized on a medicinal ventilator running on the RTXC continuous working framework. The thought was inexactly impacted by Agustus P. Lowell's article "The Care and Feeding of Watchdogs," which portrays an approach to incorporate the watchdog plot with the RTOS itself. Not at all like Lowell's plan, nonetheless, this plan can keep running on top of any RTOS, without obliging changes to the RTOS code. This plan utilizes an assignment committed to the watchdog. This errand awakens at a customary interim and checks the sanity of every single other assignment in the framework. On the off chance that all assignments finish the test, the watchdog is kicked. The watchdog screen errand keeps running at a higher need than the assignments it is checking.

THE WAY OF THE UNDERTAKINGS

Most undertakings have some base period amid which they are required to run. An errand may keep running in response to a timer that happens at a customary interim. These assignments have a begin point through which they go in every execution circle. These errands are alluded to as normal assignments. Different assignments react to outside occasions, the recurrence of which can't be anticipated. These errands are alluded to as waiting assignments.

First we will talk about how the plan will function if all assignments are general and after that we will clarify what additional work must be accomplished for waiting undertakings.

The watchdog timeout can be the most extreme time amid which every single general undertaking have had an opportunity to keep running from their begin point through one full circle back to their begin point once more. Each undertaking has a banner which can have two esteems, ALIVE and UNKNOWN. The banner is later perused and composed by the screen. The screen's employment is to wake up before the watchdog timeout terminates and check the status of each banner. On the off chance that all banners contain the esteem ALIVE, each errand got its swing to execute and the watchdog might be kicked. A few undertakings may have executed a few circles and set their banner to ALIVE a few times, which is worthy. Subsequent to kicking the watchdog, the screen sets the greater part of the banners to UNKNOWN. When the screen undertaking executes once more, the greater part of the UNKNOWN banners ought to have been overwritten with ALIVE. Figure 3 demonstrates a case with three assignments:

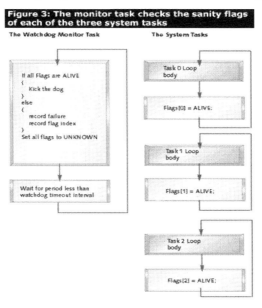

Figure 3: The monitor task checks the sanity flags of each of the three system tasks

WAITING ASSIGNMENTS

Waiting assignments can't be ensured to go through their begin point inside any limited measure of time. These errands typically have at least one focuses at which they are waiting on an outer occasion, for example, a client key activity or correspondence from another processor. At those focuses, the banners are set to the esteem ASLEEP. After the hold up, the banner is set to ALIVE, and the procedure proceeds as portrayed previously. The screen changes its plan as takes after: if the screen checks the banners and sees the esteem ASLEEP, it views that state as substantial. In this way, if all banners are either ASLEEP or ALIVE then the watchdog is kicked.

The inconvenience is that if an undertaking sets a banner to ASLEEP and never shows signs of change it back, it generally finishes the test and any stop or unending circles in that errand go undetected. In this way, one of our guidelines is that the line of code taking after the line where the banner is set to ASLEEP should play out the hold up, typically utilizing one of the blocking capacity calls from the working framework. The guideline which takes after the hold up must set the banner to ALIVE. For instance:

- myFlag = ASLEEP;
- KS_wait(KEY_PRESS_HAPPENED);
- myFlag = ALIVE;

Since there are no conditions or branches in this grouping, no arrangement of conditions enable the assignment to proceed with the banner in the ASLEEP state.

Once the banner has been set to ALIVE, the undertaking must raced to some point where the banner is again set to ALIVE or ASLEEP, before the screen errand has room schedule-wise to clear the banner to UNKNOWN and hold up one timeout period. Many assignments have just a single place where they tend to an outside occasion and set the banner to ASLEEP. Those errands must finish one full circle and be back at the three lines appeared above in less time than the screen's timeout.

Take note of that this component is not utilized on all blocking calls to the working framework; it is utilized for the holds up that are subject to occasions for which a limited return time can't be ensured. There are still a few worries with this plan. On the off chance that a stop happens that includes holds up in various waiting errands while each of the waiting undertakings has its banner set to ASLEEP, the screen can't recognize the fault. Keeping in mind the end goal to maintain a strategic distance from this trap, a chart can be physically made to demonstrate each errand with a bolt to the undertakings it attends to (drawing bolts just for holds up that set the assignment banner to ASLEEP). On the off chance that there is a total circle (for instance, Task1 attends to Task2; Task2 tends to Task3; and Task3 tends to Task1), then these sits tight are not really waiting for outer occasions and you ought to consider whether the assignment banner ought to be set to ASLEEP at all of these focuses. On the off chance that such a circle can't be kept away from, an additional timeout could be determined to one of the holds up (expecting that your RTOS underpins timed holds up), and this timeout would give insurance against a halt. This timeout could be far longer than the watchdog timeout period. On account of this additional timer timing out, the framework would be judged to be in gridlock.

At times, you may relegate two banners to one undertaking. The banners could then be set to ALIVE at various focuses inside the errand's primary circle. This would get an issue where an undertaking was stuck in a circle that reset one of the banners however skirted some fundamental piece of its work. The screen would just view the undertaking as solid if both banners are set to ALIVE inside every period.

For waiting errands, the majority of the undertakings' banners are set to ASLEEP at the waiting point and every one of them set to ALIVE promptly a short time later.

For instance, if an errand was distributed two banners called myFlag1 and myFlag2 then the succession of calls when this assignment is waiting is as per the following:

- myFlag1 = ASLEEP;
- myFlag2 = ASLEEP;
- KS_wait (KEY_PRESS_HAPPENED);
- myFlag1 = ALIVE;
- myFlag2 = ALIVE;

CONCURRENT ACCESS

Since composes of a single byte are nuclear, it is protected to utilize a single byte as a banner for a single assignment. Regardless of when the undertaking switch happens, it is difficult to get an illicit esteem kept in touch with the byte.

On account of the monitor, the byte is perused and after that composed. Hypothetically, an undertaking switch between the read and the compose could change the condition of the byte, and after that that change would be overwritten by the monitor. This can never happen if the monitor is a higher need assignment than the errands being monitored. The errands being monitored never perused the banner. They just keep in touch with it.

MONITOR INTERVAL

As expressed, the timeout interval must be sufficient for the greater part of the errands being monitored to finish no less than one circle. In the event that there is a major contrast between the shortest undertaking circle and the longest then the assignments with shorter execution times may just be getting checked after a couple of hundred circles. The rundown of banners can be separated into high recurrence banners and low recurrence banners. Each time the monitor is stirred, the high recurrence assignments' banners are checked, however the low recurrence errands' banners are just kept an eye on each nth cycle, where n is the proportion between the high and low recurrence.

DEBUGGING

When testing and debugging the framework, it is a smart thought to run the framework with the watchdog timeout set more tightly than it ordinarily will be in the field. This will help recognize any of the ways in the code that are fringe.

It is likewise a smart thought to introduce the monitor undertaking right on time in the advancement cycle, since that will demonstrate how the framework responds to the genuine bugs in the monitored assignments amid improvement. Amid debugging, dependably put a breakpoint in the monitor undertaking at the point where it identifies a fizzled hail. At that point a fizzled assignment is recognized promptly, as well as utilize the debugger to take a gander at its state and make sense of why it missed its due date.

NEED OF MONITORING UNDERTAKING

This watchdog plan is composed on the presumption that the monitoring undertaking is running at a higher need than any of the assignments that it is monitoring. This has one disadvantage. It implies that it might take up CPU cycles when another undertaking might attempt to meet some hard continuous target. In the event that you're monitoring assignment performs checks other than the banners depicted here, and if those checks expend a great deal of CPU cycles, you might need to consider modifying this plan to one where the monitoring errand keeps running at a lower need. In the event that you do this, you should guarantee that the watchdog assignment is booked to run all the more regularly with the goal that it won't be conceded for so long by a high need errand that it doesn't strobe the equipment watchdog in time. For instance, you may plan it to kick the pooch each 25ms, despite the fact that the equipment watchdog just requires a kick each 50ms. It will then survive a 25ms postponement created when a higher need assignment is running.

Utilizing a lower need assignment will enhance the capacity of high need errands to meet their hard constant targets. The detriment of such an approach is, to the point that you lose the chance to record the personality of the errand that neglects to set its banner to ALIVE, which is helpful debugging data. I additionally trust that it is harder to guarantee that there are no conditions where an appropriately working framework will bolt out the monitoring errand for enough time to get an undesirable kick.

At the point when the lower need errand is the monitoring assignment, you will likewise need to address the likelihood that another undertaking may interfere with the monitoring assignment while the banners are being refreshed. The suppositions made in the "Concurrent access" segment at no time in the future hold, and the other errand may refresh the banner that the monitoring undertaking has as of now read, however before the monitoring assignment has an opportunity to keep in touch with it. One alternative is to utilize an asset bolt on the arrangement of banners. Another choice is to guarantee that looking at and refreshing the banner in the monitoring assignment is executed as a nuclear perused and-change operation, which might be accessible as a single CPU opcode, or your RTOS may give an office.

DEBILITATING THE WATCHDOG TIMER

It is conceivable to for all time incapacitate the WDT from resetting a framework on the off chance that it won't be utilized. Programming may set the HALT piece to keep the timer from achieving zero. This keeps the WDT from creating a SMI. Programming may set the NO_REBOOT bit. This keeps the WDT from rebooting the stage on the off chance that it achieves zero. To be protected, the SMI handler ought to set the NO_REBOOT bit. This keeps errant programming from clearing the bit and hence bringing about a reset. The equipment strap might be utilized to forestall reboots totally.

<u>CONCLUSION</u>

A decent watchdog system requires cautious thought of both programming and equipment. It additionally requires watchful thought of what move to make when the disappointment is distinguished. When you outline with watchdog equipment, ensure you choose at an opportune time precisely how you plan to make best utilization of it, and you will receive the rewards of a more vigorous framework.

CHAPTER 9: THE KERNEL BOOT PROCESS

INTRODUCTION

The chapter is about booting at the subtle elements of the Kernel to perceive how a working system begins life after computers boot up straight up to the point where the boot loader, in the wake of stuffing the Kernel picture into memory, is going to bounce into the Kernel passage point.

In registering, the Kernel is a PC program that oversees input/output demands of programming, and makes an interpretation of them into data processing guidelines for the central processing unit and other electronic segments of a PC. The Kernel is a major some portion of an advanced PC's working system.

A Kernel connects the application software to the hardware of a computer.

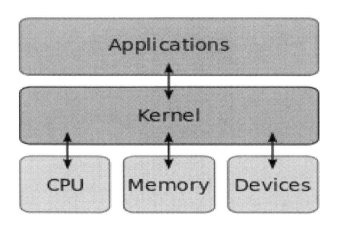

The basic code of the Kernel is typically stacked into an ensured territory of memory, which keeps it from being overwritten by other, less habitually utilized parts of the working system or by applications. The Kernel plays out its undertakings, for example, executing procedures and taking care of intrudes, in Kernel space, while everything a client typically does, for example, composing content in a word processor or running projects in a GUI (graphical UI), is done in client space. This partition counteracts client data and Kernel data from meddling with each other and thereby reducing execution or making the system end up noticeably insecure (and perhaps slamming).

At the point when a procedure makes solicitations of the Kernel, the demand is known as a system call. Different Kernel outlines vary by the way they oversee system calls and assets. For instance, a solid Kernel executes all the working system guidelines in a similar deliver space so as to enhance the execution of the system. A microKernel runs the majority of the working system's experience forms in the client space, to make the working system more secluded and, therefore, less demanding to keep up.

ELEMENTS OF THE KERNEL

The Kernel's essential capacity is to intercede access to the PC's assets, including CPU, RAM, I/O assets.

THE CENTRAL PROCESSING UNIT (CPU)

This central segment of a PC system is in charge of running or executing programs. The Kernel assumes liability for choosing whenever which of the many running projects ought to be assigned to the processor or processors (each of which can as a rule run just a single program at any given moment).

ARBITRARY ACCESS MEMORY (RAM)

Arbitrary access memory is utilized to store both program guidelines and data. Normally, both should be available in memory all together for a program to execute. Regularly various projects will need access to memory, much of the time requesting more memory than the PC has accessible. The Kernel is in charge of choosing which memory each procedure can utilize, and figuring out what to do when insufficient memory is accessible.

INPUT/OUTPUT (I/O) DEVICES

I/O devices incorporate such peripherals as consoles, mice, circle drives, printers, arrange connectors, and show devices. The Kernel allots demands from applications to perform I/O to a suitable device and gives advantageous strategies to utilizing the device (normally dreamy to the point where the application does not have to know execution subtle elements of the device).

Enter viewpoints vital in asset management are the meaning of an execution area (address space) and the assurance component used to intervene the accesses to the assets inside a space.

Bits likewise more often than not give techniques to synchronization and correspondence between procedures called between process correspondence (IPC).

A Kernel may execute these elements itself, or depend on a portion of the procedures it hurries to give the offices to other procedures, in spite of the fact that for this situation it must give a few methods for IPC to enable procedures to access the offices given by each other.

At last, a Kernel must furnish running projects with a technique to make solicitations to access these offices.

DEVICE MANAGEMENT

To perform valuable capacities, forms require access to the peripherals associated with the PC, which are controlled by the piece through device drivers. A device driver is a PC program that empowers the working system to interface with an equipment device. It furnishes the working system with data of how to control and speak with a specific bit of equipment. The driver is a critical and indispensable piece to a program application. The outline objective of a driver is deliberation; the capacity of the driver is to interpret the OS-ordered capacity calls (programming calls) into device-particular calls.

In theory, the device ought to work accurately with the appropriate driver. Device drivers are utilized for such things as video cards, sound cards, printers, scanners, modems, and LAN cards. The normal levels of deliberation of device drivers are:

On the equipment side:

- Interfacing straightforwardly.
- Using an abnormal state interface (Video BIOS).

- Using a lower-level device driver (record drivers utilizing plate drivers).
- Simulating work with equipment, while accomplishing something totally extraordinary.

On the product side:

- Allowing the working system guide access to equipment assets.
- Implementing just primitives.
- Implementing an interface for non-driver programming (Example: TWAIN).
- Implementing a dialect, at times abnormal state (Example PostScript).

For instance, to demonstrate the client something on the screen, an application would make a demand to the portion, which would forward the demand to its show driver, which is then in charge of really plotting the character/pixel.

A part should keep up a rundown of accessible devices. This rundown might be known ahead of time (e.g. on an implanted system where the portion will be revamped if the accessible equipment changes), arranged by the client (run of the mill on more seasoned PCs and on systems that are not intended for individual utilize) or recognized by the working system at run time (regularly called attachment and play). In an attachment and play system, a device supervisor initially plays out a sweep on various equipment transports, for example, Peripheral Component Interconnect (PCI) or Universal Serial Bus (USB), to recognize introduced devices, then scans for the fitting drivers.

As device management is an extremely OS-particular point, these drivers are dealt with diversely by every sort of piece outline, yet for each situation, the bit needs to give the I/O to enable drivers to physically access their devices through some port or memory area. Important choices must be made when planning the device management system, as in a few outlines accesses may include setting switches, making the operation extremely CPU-concentrated and effortlessly bringing on a noteworthy execution overhead.

Since I have an observational bowed I'll interface vigorously to the hotspots for Linux Kernel 2.6.25.6 at the Linux Cross Reference. The sources are exceptionally clear in the event that you know about C-like sentence structure; regardless of the possibility that you miss a few subtle elements you can get the significance of what's occurring. The fundamental impediment is the absence of setting around a portion of the code, for example, when or why it runs or the basic elements of the machine. I plan to give a touch of that specific situation. Because of a ton of fun stuff - like hinders and memory - gets just a gesture for the time being. The article closes with the highlights for the Windows boot.

Now in the Intel x86 boot story the processor is running in genuine mode, can address 1MB of memory, and RAM resembles this for a cutting edge Linux system:

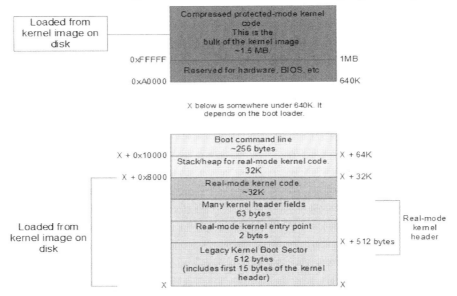

RAM contents after boot loader is done

The Kernel picture has been stacked to memory by the boot loader utilizing the BIOS plate I/O administrations. This picture is a precise of the document in your hard drive that contains the Kernel, e.g. /boot/vmlinuz-2.6.22-14-server. The picture is part into two pieces: a little part containing the real-mode Kernel code is stacked underneath the

179

640K obstruction; the greater part of the Kernel, which keeps running in ensured mode, is stacked after the principal megabyte of memory.

The activity begins in the real-mode Kernel header presented previously. This district of memory is utilized to actualize the Linux boot convention between the boot loader and the Kernel. A portion of the qualities there are perused by the boot loader while doing its work. These incorporate courtesies, for example, an intelligible string containing the Kernel variant, additionally pivotal data like the measure of the real-mode Kernel piece. The boot loader additionally composes qualities to this district, for example, the memory address for the order line parameters given by the client in the boot menu. Once the boot loader is done it has filled in the greater part of the parameters required by the Kernel header. It's then time to bounce into the Kernel section point. The chart beneath demonstrates the code grouping for the Kernel introduction, alongside source indexes, records, and line numbers:

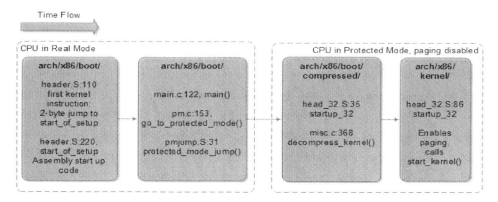

Architecture-specific Linux Kernel Initialization

The early Kernel start-up for the Intel design is in document curve/x86/boot/header.S. It's in low level computing construct, which is uncommon for the Kernel everywhere except basic for boot code. The begin of this record really contains boot part code, a left over from the days when Linux could work without a boot loader. These days this boot segment, if executed, just prints a "bugger_off_msg" to the client and reboots. Modern boot loaders overlook this inheritance code. After the boot area code we have the initial 15 bytes of the real-mode Kernel header; these two sorts out indicate 512 bytes, the span of a run of the mill plate division on Intel hardware.

After these 512 bytes, at offset 0x200, we locate the primary direction that keeps running as a component of the Linux Kernel: the real-mode section point. It's in header.S:110 and it is a 2-byte hop composed specifically in machine code as 0x3aeb. You can confirm this by running hexdump on your Kernel picture and seeing the bytes at that offset – only a once-over to verify everything is ok to ensure it's not each of a fantasy. The boot loader hops into this area when it is done, which thusly hops to header.S:229 where we have a customary get together standard called start_of_setup. This short routine sets up a stack, zeroes the bss portion (the range that contains static factors, so they begin with zero esteems) for the real-mode Kernel and afterward hops to great old C code at curve/x86/boot/main.c:122.

fundamental() does some housekeeping like identifying memory format, setting a video mode, and so on. It then calls go_to_protected_mode (). Prior to the CPU can be set to ensured mode, in any case, a couple assignments must be finished. There are two fundamental issues: hinders and memory. In real-mode the interfere with vector table for the processor is dependably at memory address 0, while in ensured mode the area of the intrude on vector table is put away in a CPU enroll called IDTR. In the interim, the interpretation of intelligent memory addresses (the ones projects control) to direct memory addresses (a crude number from 0 to the highest point of the memory) is diverse between real-mode and secured mode. Secured mode requires an enlist called GDTR to be stacked with the address of a Global Descriptor Table for memory. So go_to_protected_mode() calls setup_idt() and setup_gdt() to introduce a transitory intrude on descriptor table and worldwide descriptor table.

We're presently prepared for the dive into ensured mode, which is finished by protected_mode_jump, another gathering schedule. This routine empowers secured mode by setting the PE bit in the CR0 CPU enroll. Now we're running with paging handicapped; paging is a discretionary element of the processor, even in secured mode, and there's no requirement for it yet. What's vital is that we're at no time in the future limited to the 640K boundary and can now deliver up to 4GB of RAM. The normal then calls the 32-bit Kernel section point, which is startup_32 for packed Kernels. This routine does some fundamental enroll introductions and calls decompress_Kernel(), a C capacity to do the genuine decompression.

The decompress_Kernel() prints the natural "Decompressing Linux... " message. Decompression occurs set up and once it's done the uncompressed Kernel picture has overwritten the packed one imagined in the primary graph. Henceforth the uncompressed substance additionally begin at 1MB. decompress_Kernel() then prints "done." and the ameliorating "Booting the Kernel." By "Booting" it implies a hop to the last section point in this entire story, given to Linus by God himself on Mountain Halti, which is the secured mode Kernel passage point toward the begin of the second megabyte of RAM (0x100000). That sacrosanct area contains a routine called, uh, startup_32. Be that as it may, this one is in an alternate registry, you see.

The second incarnation of startup_32 is likewise a get together standard, however it contains 32-bit mode instatements. It clears the bss fragment for the secured mode Kernel (which is the genuine Kernel that will now keep running until the machine reboots or close down), sets up the last worldwide descriptor table for memory, manufactures page tables so paging can be turned on, empowers paging, introduces a stack, makes the last interfere with descriptor table, lastly hops to the engineering free Kernel start-up, start_Kernel(). The chart beneath demonstrates the code stream for the last leg of the boot:

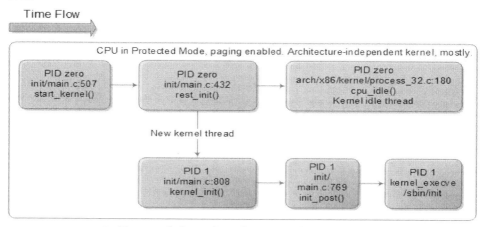

Architecture-independent Linux Kernel Initialization

182

start_Kernel() looks more like commonplace Kernel code, which is about all C and machine free. The capacity is an extensive rundown of calls to instatements of the different Kernel subsystems and data structures. These incorporate the scheduler, memory zones, time keeping, et cetera. start_Kernel() then calls rest_init(), and soon thereafter things are all working. rest_init() makes a Kernel string passing another capacity, Kernel_init(), as the passage point. rest_init() then calls calendar() to kickstart errand planning and goes to rest by calling cpu_idle(), which is the sit without moving string for the Linux Kernel. cpu_idle() runs always thus processes zero, which has it. At whatever point there is work to do – a runnable procedure – handle zero gets booted out of the CPU, just to return when no runnable procedures are accessible.

Be that as it may, here's the kicker for us. This sit without moving circle is the finish of the long string we took after since boot, it's the last descendent of the main bounce executed by the processor after catalyst. The majority of this wreckage, from reset vector to BIOS to MBR to boot loader to real-mode Kernel to secured mode Kernel, every last bit of it leads appropriate here, bounce by hop by hop it closes in the sit without moving circle for the boot processor, cpu_idle(). Which is really sort of cool. Be that as it may, this can't be the entire story otherwise the PC would do no work.

Now, the Kernel string began beforehand is prepared to kick in, dislodging process 0 and its sit still string. Thus it does, and soon thereafter Kernel_init() begins running since it was given as the string section point. Kernel_init() is in charge of instating the rest of the CPUs in the system, which have been stopped since boot. The majority of the code we've seen so far has been executed in a solitary CPU, called the boot processor. As the other CPUs, called application processors, are begun they come up in real-mode and must gone through a few instatements too. Huge numbers of the code ways are normal, as should be obvious in the code for startup_32, however there are slight forks taken by the late-coming application processors. At last, Kernel_init() calls init_article(), which tries to execute a client mode prepare in the accompanying request:/sbin/init,/and so on/init,/container/init, and/canister/sh. On the off chance that all fall flat, the Kernel will freeze. Fortunately init is more often than not there, and begins running as PID 1. It checks its setup record to make sense of which procedures to dispatch, which may incorporate X11 Windows, programs for signing in on the comfort, organize daemons, et cetera. Consequently closes the boot procedure so far another Linux box begins running some place. May your uptime be long and untroubled.

The procedure for Windows is comparable from multiple points of view, given the basic design. A significant number of similar issues are confronted and comparative instatements must be finished. With regards to boot one of the greatest contrasts is that Windows packs the majority of the real-mode Kernel code, and a portion of the underlying ensured mode code, into the boot loader itself (C:\NTLDR). So as opposed to having two areas in a similar Kernel picture, Windows utilizes diverse paired pictures. Additionally Linux totally isolates boot loader and Kernel; in a way this consequently drops out of the open source handle. The graph underneath demonstrates the primary bits for the Windows Kernel:

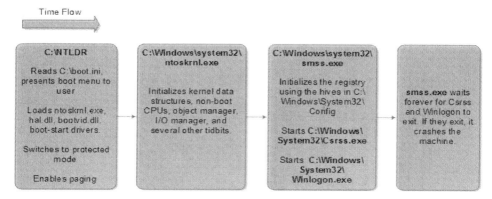

Windows Kernel Initialization

The Windows client mode start-up is actually altogether different. There's no/sbin/init, yet rather Csrss.exe and Winlogon.exe. Winlogon brings forth Services.exe, which begins the majority of the Windows Services, and Lsass.exe, the neighborhood security authentication subsystem. The great Windows login discourse keeps running with regards to Winlogon.

CHAPTER 10: ARM ARCHITECTURE AND RISC APPLICATIONS

OVERVIEW

ARM, initially Acorn RISC Machine, later Advanced RISC Machine, is a group of Reduced Instruction Set Computing (RISC) structures for computer processors, designed for different conditions. English organization ARM Holdings builds up the engineering and licenses it to different organizations, who outline their own particular items that execute one of those designs—including frameworks on-chips (SoC) that consolidate memory, interfaces, radios, and so forth. It additionally plans centers that actualize this instruction set and licenses these outlines to various organizations that consolidate those center outlines into their own particular items.

On the off chance that you've given careful consideration to cell phones and tablets you've likely known about the expression "ARM" used to allude to the equipment inside. It's tossed around left and right, frequently as a state of separation from tablets and desktops, which utilize Intel x86. The Key To ARM Is RISC.

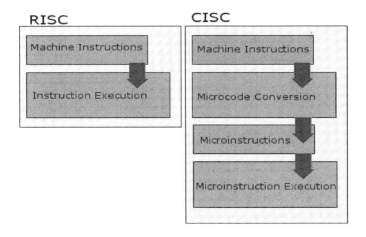

RISC is, in its broadest shape, a plan reasoning for processors. It originates from a conviction that a processor with a moderately basic instruction set will be more proficient than one which is more perplexing. The term initially returned into utilization in the 1980s with an examination extend called Berkeley RISC that researched the conceivable outcomes of this way to deal with plan and afterward made processors in light of it.

All ARM processors are viewed as RISC plans, however this doesn't mean much since RISC itself is essentially a way to deal with outline as opposed to a mechanical standard or processor design. Still, an essential comprehension of RISC appropriately outlines ARM.

ARM'S BASICS

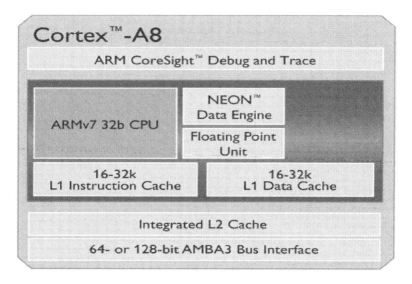

ARM alludes to itself as an architecture, which can bring about a misconception when contrasted with Intel. Intel gives each new chip plan its own one of a kind code and discusses each as another architecture – notwithstanding when there's regularly numerous likenesses and they all utilization a similar instruction set (x86). ARM, then again, regards its outlines as an unbroken family. Updates are as yet a piece of the ARM architecture. They're quite recently given another variant number.

The attribute that is most pertinent to shoppers is not the small scale architecture (the physical outline of the chip) however rather the instruction set. The instruction set is the fundamental set of abilities and elements a processor makes accessible to programming. It figures out what number-crunching can be utilized, how reserve ought to be distributed and the request in which instructions ought to be executed. Programming intended for one instruction set can't be utilized on another unless it's changed.

Smaller scale architectures and instruction sets can't be isolated on the grounds that the architecture is a physical articulation of the instruction set. This is the reason ARM-based processors have a tendency to be little, productive and generally moderate. The basic instruction set requires a little, basic outline with less transistors. Transistors expend power and increment kick the bucket measure (which expands creation cost), so having as few as conceivable is perfect while choosing a processor for a cell phone or tablet.

ARM'S BUSINESS IS DIFFERENT

Discussing ARM processors in general can be troublesome on the grounds that there are such a large number of accessible and their execution shifts. It's illogical. By what method can Apple have ARM processors that are speedier than the opposition when it's utilizing a similar architecture?

This happens in light of how ARM Holdings, the organization that is in charge of ARM, works together. ARM Holdings is just a plan organization. They deal with the instruction set and outline new forms of the center architecture and after that permit it to different organizations. Those organizations can then enhance it and match it with whatever equipment appears to be suitable.

It comprehends that ARM's center architecture is just a processor. It doesn't deal with remote availability. It doesn't deal with illustrations. It doesn't deal with USB or different types of wired network. The greater part of that is the duty of other equipment licensees match the architecture.

This is the main reason that there are such varieties of variations of ARM on the market and why they perform in an unexpected way. Apple has a whole in-house building staff that deals with its ARM processors. Different organizations, as Qualcomm and Texas Instruments, go about as center men. They take the ARM architecture, match it with an assortment of equipment, and afterward re-offer it as a "framework on-a-chip" for cell phones and tablets.

WHAT DOES ARM MEAN FOR CONSUMERS

To a shopper, ARM can be thought of as a biological community. Programming intended for ARM will just work on ARM. Windows RT applications, for instance, don't chip away at a PC with Windows 8. Alterations must be made to a program to bounce from ARM to x86.

Working frameworks that work on one ARM gadget ought to take a shot at others. That is the reason there are so many of Android adjustments and why Android can conceivably be stacked onto tablets from HP and BlackBerry. Apple messes with the biological community a bit, in any case, in light of the fact that the source code of iOS is not accessible. Endeavoring to port iOS to other ARM gadgets is practically inconceivable without it.

ARM likewise implies bring down power draw and lower execution in respect to x86. This is not set in stone, be that as it may, in light of the fact that both architectures are changing after some time. Intel is striving to make forms of its processors with to a great degree low power draw. Also, ARM Holdings is endeavoring to enhance the execution of its plans.

WILL ARM BE IN YOUR PC

There have been a couple endeavors to offer customary gadgets with ARM processors that work like conventional PCs. Motorola sold a console dock for the Atrix cell phone and promoted it as a portable PC substitution. ASUS offers a line of Android tablets with console docks. What's more, Samsung now offers a Chromebook that keeps running on ARM.

Such endeavors hint a tempest of potential encompassing ARM, yet foreseeing the tempest's way and power is unthinkable. Current ARM architectures are essentially behind the execution Intel's slowest processors (don't worry about it its standard line of Core processors). Nvidia says that it is dealing with a processor utilizing ARM's architecture that will rival Intel, yet it's not clear how this is being proficient or when a completed item may be discharged.

For the time being the potential risk of ARM remains a dim cloud not too far off of the potential PC space. It looks undermining, yet a solid risk presently can't seem to show. Is ARM a fearsome tempest or basically a couple shadowed mists that will in the end scatter? That remaining parts to be seen.

OAK SEED RISC MACHINE: ARM2

The official Acorn RISC Machine extend begun in October 1983. They picked VLSI Technology as the silicon accomplice, as they were a wellspring of ROMs and custom chips for Acorn. Wilson and Furber drove the plan. They executed it with a comparable effectiveness ethos as the 6502. A key plan objective was accomplishing low-dormancy input/yield (interfere with) taking care of like the 6502. The 6502's memory get to architecture had given engineers a chance to deliver quick machines without exorbitant direct memory get to equipment.

The primary examples of ARM silicon worked appropriately when initially got and tried on 26 April 1985.

The primary ARM application was as a moment processor for the BBC Micro, where it helped in creating reenactment programming to complete advancement of the bolster chips (VIDC, IOC, MEMC), and accelerated the CAD programming utilized as a part of ARM2 improvement. Wilson hence reworked BBC BASIC in ARM low level computing construct. The top to bottom learning picked up from planning the instruction set empowered the code to be exceptionally thick, making ARM BBC BASIC as to a great degree great test for any ARM emulator. The first point of a primarily ARM-based computer was accomplished in 1987 with the arrival of the Acorn Archimedes. In 1992, Acorn yet again won the Queen's Award for Technology for the ARM.

The ARM2 highlighted a 32-bit information transport, 26-bit address space and 27 32-bit registers. Eight bits from the program counter enlist were accessible for different purposes; the main six bits (accessible in light of the 26-bit address space)

189

filled in as status banners, and the last two bits (accessible on the grounds that the program counter was dependably word-adjusted) were utilized for setting modes. The deliver transport was stretched out to 32 bits in the ARM6, yet program code still needed to exist in the initial 64 MB of memory in 26-bit similarity mode, because of the held bits for the status banners. The ARM2 had a transistor tally of only 30,000, contrasted with Motorola's six-year-more established 68000 model with around 40,000. A lot of this straightforwardness originated from the absence of microcode (which speaks to around one-quarter to 33% of the 68000) and from (like most CPUs of the day) excluding any reserve. This straightforwardness empowered low power utilization, yet preferable execution over the Intel 80286. A successor, ARM3, was delivered with a 4 KB store, which additionally enhanced execution.

The new Apple-ARM work would inevitably develop into the ARM6, first discharged in mid 1992. Apple utilized the ARM6-based ARM610 as the reason for their Apple Newton PDA. In 1994, Acorn utilized the ARM610 as the primary focal handling unit (CPU) in their RiscPC computers. DEC authorized the ARM6 architecture and created the StrongARM. At 233 MHz, this CPU drew just a single watt (most up to date forms draw comparably less). The work later on was passed to Intel as a piece of a claim settlement, and Intel accepted the open door to supplement their i960 line with the StrongARM. Intel later built up its own superior usage named XScale, which it has since sold to Marvell. The Transistors tally of the ARM center remained basically a similar size all through these progressions; ARM2 had 30,000 transistors, while ARM6 became just to 35,000.

MARKET SHARE

In 2005, around 98% of every single cell phone sold, utilized no less than one ARM processor. In 2010, makers of chips in light of ARM architectures detailed shipments of 6.1 billion ARM-based processors, speaking to 95% of cell phones, 35% of computerized TVs and set-beat boxes and 10% of laptops. By 2011, ARM architecture of the 32-bit, was the most generally utilized architecture in cell phones and the most mainstream 32-bit one in implanted frameworks. In 2013, 10 billion were delivered and "ARM-based chips are found in about 60 percent of the world's cell phones".

CORE LICENSE

ARM Holdings' essential business is offering IP cores, which licensees use to make microcontrollers (MCUs), CPUs, and frameworks on-chips in light of those cores. The first outline producer joins the ARM core with different parts to create an entire gadget, commonly one that can be worked in existing semiconductor fabs effortlessly and still convey generous execution. The best execution has been the ARM7TDMI with many millions sold. Atmel has been an antecedent outline focus in the ARM7TDMI-based implanted framework.

The ARM architectures utilized as a part of cell phones, PDAs and other cell phones territory from ARMv5 to ARMv6, utilized as a part of low-end gadgets, to ARMv7-An utilized as a part of current top of the line gadgets. ARMv7 incorporates an equipment drifting point unit (FPU), with enhanced speed contrasted with programming based coasting point.

In 2009, a few producers presented netbooks in light of ARM architecture CPUs, in direct rivalry with netbooks in view of Intel Atom. As indicated by examiner firm IHS iSuppli, by 2015, ARM ICs might be in 23% of all tablets.

ARM Holdings offers an assortment of permitting terms, fluctuating in cost and expectations. ARM Holdings gives to all licensees an integratable equipment depiction of the ARM core and additionally total programming advancement toolset (compiler, debugger, programming improvement unit) and the privilege to offer made silicon containing the ARM CPU.

SoC bundles incorporating ARM's core plans incorporate Nvidia Tegra's initial three eras, CSR plc's Quatro family, ST-Ericsson's Nova and NovaThor, Silicon Labs' Precision32 MCU, Texas Instruments' OMAP items, Samsung's Hummingbird and Exynos items, Apple's A4, A5, and A5X, and Freescale's i.MX.

Fabless licensees, who wish to incorporate an ARM core into their own chip configuration, are typically just keen on getting a prepared to-make confirmed IP core. For these clients, ARM Holdings conveys an entryway netlist portrayal of the picked ARM core, alongside a disconnected reenactment model and test projects to help plan reconciliation and check. More goal-oriented clients, including incorporated gadget producers (IDM) and foundry administrators, gain the processor IP in synthesizable RTL (Verilog) frame. With the synthesizable RTL, the client can perform design level improvements and expansions. This enables the fashioner to accomplish intriguing outline objectives not generally conceivable with an unmodified netlist (high clock speed, low power utilization, instruction set augmentations, and so forth.). While ARM Holdings does not concede the licensee the privilege to exchange the ARM architecture itself, licensees may uninhibitedly offer fabricated item, for example, chip gadgets, assessment sheets and finish frameworks. Dealer foundries can be a unique case; not exclusively are they permitted to offer completed silicon containing ARM cores, they for the most part hold the privilege to re-fabricate ARM cores for different clients.

ARM Holdings costs its IP in view of saw esteem. Bring down performing ARM cores ordinarily have bring down permit costs than higher performing cores. In execution terms, a synthesizable core costs more than a hard full scale (blackbox) core. Confusing value matters, a trader foundry that holds an ARM permit, for example, Samsung or Fujitsu, can offer fab clients reduced permitting costs. In return for procuring the ARM core through the foundry's in-house configuration benefits, the client can diminish or dispose of installment of ARM's forthright permit expense.

Contrasted with committed semiconductor foundries, (for example, TSMC and UMC) without in-house configuration administrations, Fujitsu/Samsung charge a few times more for every fabricated wafer. For low to mid volume applications, a plan benefit foundry offers bring down general evaluating (through sponsorship of the permit charge). For high volume mass-created parts, the long haul cost decrease achievable through lower wafer evaluating diminishes the effect of ARM's NRE (Non-Recurring Engineering) costs, improving the devoted foundry a decision.

Organizations that have planned chips with ARM cores incorporate Amazon.com's Annapurna Labs auxiliary, Analog Devices, Apple, AppliedMicro, Atmel,Nvidia, NXP, Qualcomm, Renesas, Samsung Electronics, Broadcom, Cypress Semiconductor, Freescale Semiconductor (now NXP Semiconductors), ST Microelectronics and Texas Instruments.

STRUCTURAL PERMIT

Organizations can likewise get an ARM structural permit for outlining their own CPU cores utilizing the ARM instruction sets. These cores must consent completely with the ARM architecture. Organizations that have composed cores that execute an ARM architecture incorporate Apple, AppliedMicro, Broadcom, Nvidia, Qualcomm, and Samsung Electronics.

CORES

CORTEX-A	Cortex-A5, Cortex-A7, Cortex-A9, Cortex-A15, Cortex-A17, Cortex-A32, Cortex-A35, Cortex-A53, Cortex-A57, Cortex-A72
CORTEX-R	Cortex-R4, Cortex-R5, Cortex-R7, Cortex-R8
CORTEX-M	Cortex-M0, Cortex-M0+, Cortex-M1, Cortex-M3, Cortex-M4, Cortex-M7
SECURCORE	SC300, SC100, SC000

ARM CORTEX APPLICATION PROCESSORS

CORTEX-A SERIES - HIGH PERFORMANCE PROCESSORS FOR FEATURE RICH OPERATING SYSTEMS

The greater part of our Cortex-A processors convey uncommon 32-bit performance for the best computing, and with the new Cortex-A72 processor and both the Cortex-A57 and Cortex-A53 processors conveying consolidated 32-bit and 64-bit performance, empowering cutting edge versatile, systems administration and server items. The new Cortex-A35 is the ARM's most effective 32/64-bit ARMv8-A processor, focusing on the following billion section level cell phone clients. The processors are accessible in single-core and multi-core assortments, conveying up to four handling units with the capacity to coordinate NEON™ mixed media preparing squares and propelled Floating Point execution units.

APPLICATIONS INCLUDE:

- Cell phones
- Netbooks
- Tablets
- Advanced TV
- Home Gateways
- Servers and Networking
- ARM Cortex Real-time Embedded Processors

CORTEX-R SERIES - EXCEPTIONAL PERFORMANCE FOR ONGOING APPLICATIONS

Cortex Real-time Embedded processors have been created for profoundly implanted continuous applications where the requirement for low power and quick and deterministic intrude on control are adjusted with uncommon performance and solid similarity with existing stages.

APPLICATIONS INCLUDE:

- Car slowing mechanisms
- Powertrain arrangements
- Mass stockpiling controller
- Organizing and Printing
- Modems and correspondences
- ARM Cortex Embedded Processors

CORTEX-M SERIES - COST-TOUCHY ANSWERS FOR DETERMINISTIC MICROCONTROLLER APPLICATIONS

Cortex-M arrangement processors have been created fundamentally for the microcontroller area where the requirement for quick, exceptionally deterministic, intrude on administration is combined with the longing for to a great degree low entryway number and most minimal conceivable power utilization.

APPLICATIONS INCLUDE:

- Microcontrollers
- Blended flag gadgets
- Savvy sensors
- Car body hardware and airbags
- ARM Specialist Processors

SECURCORE™

- Processors for high security applications

FPGA CORES

- Processors for FPGA

ARM Specialist Processors are intended to meet the requesting needs of particular markets. SecurCore processors are used inside the security markets for versatile SIMs and distinguishing proof applications and incorporate various innovations to recognize and stay away from security assaults while conveying remarkable performance.

ARM likewise creates processors for FPGA textures, empowering clients to quickly achieve market while keeping up similarity with conventional ARM gadgets. Furthermore the texture autonomous nature of these processors empowers designers to pick the objective gadget which is ideal for their application as opposed to be bolted to a particular seller.

Albeit most datapaths and CPU registers in the early ARM processors were 32-bit, addressable memory was restricted to 26 bits.

ARMv3 incorporated a similarity mode to bolster the 26-bit locations of prior forms of the architecture. This similarity mode discretionary in ARMv4, and expelled in ARMv5.

A rundown of sellers who actualize ARM cores in their outline (application particular standard items (ASSP), microchip and microcontrollers) is given by ARM Holdings.

RUNDOWN OF APPLICATIONS OF ARM CORES

ARM cores are utilized as a part of various items, especially PDAs and cell phones. Some computing illustrations are Microsoft's original Surface and Surface 2, Apple's iPads, and Asus' Eee Pad Transformer tablet computers. Others incorporate Apple's iPhone cell phone and iPod compact media player, Canon PowerShot computerized cameras, Nintendo DS handheld amusement consoles and TomTom turn-by-turn route frameworks.

In 2005, ARM Holdings participated in the improvement of Manchester University's computer, SpiNNaker, which utilized ARM cores to recreate the human cerebrum.

ARM chips are additionally utilized as a part of Raspberry Pi, BeagleBoard, BeagleBone, PandaBoard and other single-board computers, since they are little, modest and devour next to no power.

32-BIT ARCHITECTURE

The 32-bit ARM architecture, for example, ARMv7-An, is the most generally utilized architecture in cell phones.

Since 1995, theReference Manual for the ARM Architecture has been the essential wellspring of documentation on the ARM processor architecture and instruction set, recognizing interfaces that all ARM processors are required to support, (for example, instruction semantics) from usage points of interest that may change. The architecture has developed after some time, and form seven of the architecture, ARMv7, characterizes three architecture "profiles":

- A-profile, the "Application" profile, actualized by 32-bit cores in the Cortex-An arrangement and by some non-ARM cores;

- R-profile, the "Ongoing" profile, actualized by cores in the Cortex-R arrangement
- M-profile, the "Microcontroller" profile, actualized by most cores in the Cortex-M arrangement.

In spite of the fact that the architecture profiles were first characterized for ARMv7, ARM in this way characterized the ARMv6-M architecture (utilized by the Cortex M0/M0+/M1) as a subset of the ARMv7-M profile with less instructions.

CPU MODES

But in the M-profile, the 32-bit ARM architecture indicates a few CPU modes, contingent upon the executed architecture highlights. At any minute in time, the CPU can be in just a single mode, yet it can change modes because of outside occasions (intrudes) or automatically.

CLIENT MODE:

The main non-favored mode.

FIQ MODE:

A favored mode that is entered at whatever point the processor acknowledges a FIQ intrude.

IRQ MODE:

A favored mode that is entered at whatever point the processor acknowledges an IRQ intrude.

MANAGER (SVC) MODE:

A favored mode entered at whatever point the CPU is reset or when a SVC instruction is executed.

PREMATURELY END MODE:

A special mode that is entered at whatever point a prefetch prematurely end or information prematurely end exemption happens.

INDISTINCT MODE:

A special mode that is entered at whatever point a vague instruction exemption happens.

FRAMEWORK MODE (ARMV4 OR MORE):

The main special mode that is not entered by an exemption. It must be entered by executing an instruction that unequivocally keeps in touch with the mode bits of the CPSR.

SCREEN MODE (ARMV6 AND ARMV7 SECURITY EXTENSIONS, ARMV8 EL3):

A screen mode is acquainted with bolster TrustZone augmentation in ARM cores.

HYP MODE (ARMV7 VIRTUALIZATION EXTENSIONS, ARMV8 EL2):

A mode of hypervisor that backings Popek and Goldberg virtualization necessities for the non-secure operation of the CPU.

INSTRUCTION SET

The first (and ensuing) ARM execution was hardwired without microcode, similar to the significantly easier 8-bit 6502 processor utilized as a part of earlier Acorn microcomputers.

The 32-bit ARM architecture (and the 64-bit architecture generally) incorporates the accompanying RISC highlights:

STACK/STORE ARCHITECTURE

3. No support for unaligned memory gets to in the first form of the architecture. ARMv6 and later, aside from some microcontroller forms, bolster unaligned gets to for half-word and single-word load/store instructions with a few constraints, for example, no ensured atomicity.

4. Uniform 16× 32-bit enlist document (counting the program counter, stack pointer and the connection enroll).

5. Settled instruction width of 32 bits to simplicity deciphering and pipelining, at the cost of diminished code thickness. Afterward, the Thumb instruction set included 16-bit instructions and expanded code thickness.
6. For the most part single clock-cycle execution.

ADDITIONAL DESIGN FEATURES

To make up for the less complex outline, contrasted and processors like the Intel 80286 and Motorola 68020, some extra plan elements were utilized:

1. Contingent execution of most instructions lessens branch overhead and makes up for the absence of a branch indicator.
2. Number juggling instructions modify condition codes just when wanted.
3. 32-bit barrel shifter can be utilized without performance punishment with most number juggling instructions and address computations.
4. Has effective listed tending to modes.
5. A connection enlist underpins quick leaf work calls.
6. A basic, however quick, 2-need level interfere with subsystem has exchanged enlist banks.

NUMBER-CRUNCHING INSTRUCTIONS

ARM incorporates whole number math operations for include, subtract, and increase; a few variants of the architecture likewise bolster separate operations.

ARM bolsters 32-bit x 32-bit increases with either a 32-bit result or 64-bit result, however Cortex-M0/M0+/M1 cores don't bolster 64-bit comes about. Some ARM cores likewise bolster 16-bit x 16-bit and 32-bit x 16-bit duplicates.

The partition instructions are just incorporated into the accompanying ARM architectures:

- -ARMv7-M and ARMv7E-M architectures dependably incorporate partition instructions.

- -ARMv7-R architecture dependably incorporates separate instructions in the Thumb instruction set, however alternatively in its 32-bit instruction set.
- -ARMv7-An architecture alternatively incorporates the partition instructions. The instructions won't not be actualized, or executed just in the Thumb instruction set, or executed in both the Thumb and ARM instruction sets, or actualized if the Virtualization Extensions are incorporated.

REGISTERS

Registers R0 through R7 are the same over all CPU modes; they are never managed an account. Registers R8 through R12 are the same over all CPU modes with the exception of FIQ mode. FIQ mode has its own particular unmistakable R8 through R12 registers.

R13 and R14 are saved money over all favored CPU modes aside from framework mode. That is, every mode that can be entered on account of an exemption has its own R13 and R14. These registers for most of the part contain the stack pointer and the arrival address from capacity calls, individually.

ALIASES:

- R13 is also referred to as SP, the Stack Pointer.
- R14 is also referred to as LR, the Link Register.
- R15 is also referred to as PC, the Program Counter.

The Current Program Status Register (CPSR) has the following 32 bits.

- M (bits 0–4) is the processor mode bits.
- T (bit 5) is the Thumb state bit.
- F (bit 6) is the FIQ disable bit.
- I (bit 7) is the IRQ disable bit.
- A (bit 8) is the imprecise data abort disable bit.
- E (bit 9) is the data endianness bit.

- IT (bits 10–15 and 25–26) is the if-then state bits.
- GE (bits 16–19) is the greater-than-or-equal-to bits.
- DNM (bits 20–23) is the do not modify bits.
- J (bit 24) is the Java state bit.
- Q (bit 27) is the sticky overflow bit.
- V (bit 28) is the overflow bit.
- C (bit 29) is the carry/borrow/extend bit.
- Z (bit 30) is the zero bit.
- N (bit 31) is the negative/less than bit.

CONDITIONAL EXECUTION

Practically every ARM instruction has a restrictive execution highlight called predication, which is actualized with a 4-bit condition code selector (the predicate). To take into account unequivocal execution, one of the four-piece codes makes the instruction be constantly executed. Most other CPU architectures just have condition codes on branch instructions.

In spite of the fact that the predicate takes up four of the 32 bits in an instruction code, and along these lines chops down fundamentally on the encoding bits accessible for removals in memory get to instructions, it stays away from branch instructions when producing code for little if articulations. Aside from disposing of the branch instructions themselves, this jam the bring/decipher/execute pipeline at the cost of just a single cycle for every skipped instruction.

The standard example of conditional execution is the subtraction-based Euclidean algorithm:

In the C programming language, the loop is:

while (i != j) // We enter the loop when i<j or i>j, not when i==j

{

if (i > j) // When i>j we do that

201

```
            i -= j;

    else      // When i<j we do that (since i!=j is checked in while condition)

        j -= i;

    }
```

In ARM assembly, the loop is transformed into:

```
    do

    {

        if    (i > j) // When i>j we do that

            i -= j;

        else if (i < j) // When i<j we do that

            j -= i;

        else

            ;        // When i==j we do nothing

    }

    while (i != j);   // We do nothing into the loop and leave the loop when i==j
```

and coded as:

```
loop:  CMP   Ri, Rj    ; set condition "NE" if (i != j),

              ;           "GT" if (i > j),

              ;         or "LT" if (i < j)

    SUBGT  Ri, Ri, Rj  ; if "GT" (Greater Than), i = i-j;

    SUBLT  Rj, Rj, Ri  ; if "LT" (Less Than), j = j-i;
```

BNE loop   ; if "NE" (Not Equal), then loop

which stays away from the branches around the then and else conditions. On the off chance that Ri and Rj are equivalent then neither of the SUB instructions will be executed, killing the requirement for a restrictive branch to actualize the while check at the highest point of the circle, for instance had SUBLE (not exactly or equivalent) been utilized.

One of the ways that Thumb code gives a more thick encoding is to expel the four piece selector from non-branch instructions.

DIFFERENT ELEMENTS

Another element of the instruction set is the capacity to overlap moves and pivots into the "data preparing" (number juggling, coherent, and enroll enlist move) instructions, so that, for instance, the C explanation

a += (j << 2);

could be rendered as a solitary word, single-cycle instruction:

Include Ra, Ra, Rj, LSL #2

This outcomes in the common ARM program being denser than anticipated with less memory gets to; in this manner the pipeline is utilized all the more productively.

The ARM processor additionally has includes once in a while observed in other RISC architectures, for example, PC-relative tending to (without a doubt, on the 32-bit ARM the PC is one of its 16 registers) and pre-and post-increase tending to modes.

The ARM instruction set has expanded after some time. Some early ARM processors (before ARM7TDMI), for instance, have no instruction to store a two-byte amount.

PIPELINES AND OTHER USAGE ISSUES

The ARM7 and prior usage have a three-organize pipeline; the stages being get, unravel and execute. Higher-performance plans, for example, the ARM9, have further pipelines: Cortex-A8 has thirteen phases. Extra usage changes for higher performance incorporate a speedier snake and more broad branch expectation rationale. The contrast between the ARM7DI and ARM7DMI cores, for instance, was an enhanced multiplier; consequently the additional "M".

COPROCESSORS

The ARM architecture (pre-ARMv8) gives a non-meddlesome method for amplifying the instruction set utilizing "coprocessors" that can be tended to utilizing MCR, MRC, MRRC, MCRR, and comparable instructions. The coprocessor space is isolated intelligently into 16 coprocessors with numbers from 0 to 15, coprocessor 15 (cp15) being saved for some run of the mill control capacities like dealing with the stores and MMU operation on processors that have one.

In ARM-based machines, fringe gadgets are basically connected to the processor by mapping their physical registers into the memory space of ARM, into the coprocessor space, or by interfacing with another gadget (a transport) that thus connects to the processor. Coprocessor gets to have bring down idleness, so a few peripherals—for instance a XScale intrude on controller—are available in both routes: through memory and through coprocessors.

In different cases, chip architects just incorporate equipment utilizing the coprocessor instrument. For instance, a picture preparing motor may be a little ARM7TDMI core joined with a coprocessor that has particular operations to bolster a particular set of HDTV transcoding primitives.

DEBUGGING

All cutting edge ARM processors incorporate equipment debugging offices, enabling programming debuggers to perform operations, for example, stopping, venturing, and break pointing of code beginning from reset. These offices are manufactured utilizing JTAG bolster, however some more up to date cores alternatively bolster ARM's own particular two-wire "SWD" convention. In ARM7TDMI cores, the "D" spoke to JTAG debug bolster, and the "I" spoke to nearness of an "EmbeddedICE" debug module. For ARM7 and ARM9 core eras, EmbeddedICE over JTAG was an accepted debug standard, however not compositionally ensured.

The ARMv7 architecture characterizes essential debug offices at a design level. These incorporate breakpoints, watch points and instruction execution in a "Debug Mode"; comparable offices were additionally accessible with EmbeddedICE. Both "stop mode" and "screen" mode debugging are bolstered. The genuine transport component used to get to the debug offices is not compositionally determined, but rather executions by and large incorporate JTAG bolster.

There is a different ARM "CoreSight" debug architecture, which is not structurally required by ARMv7 processors.

DSP ENHANCEMENT INSTRUCTIONS

To enhance the ARM architecture for advanced flag handling and mixed media applications, DSP instructions were added to the set. These are implied by an "E" for the sake of the ARMv5TE and ARMv5TEJ architectures. E-variations additionally suggest T, D, M and I.

The new instructions are basic in computerized flag processor architectures. They incorporate minor departure from marked multiply–accumulate, soaked include and subtract, and check driving zeros.

SIMD AUGMENTATIONS FOR SIGHT AND SOUND

Presented in ARMv6 architecture, this was a forerunner to the progressed SIMD innovation otherwise called NEON.

Jazelle DBX (Direct Bytecode eXecution) is a method that permits Java Bytecode to be executed specifically in the ARM architecture as a third execution state (and instruction set) close by the current ARM and Thumb-mode. Bolster for this state is implied by the "J" in the ARMv5TEJ architecture, and in ARM9EJ-S and ARM7EJ-S core names. Bolster for this state is required beginning in ARMv6 (aside from the

ARMv7-M profile), however more up to date cores just incorporate a unimportant usage that gives no equipment quickening.

THUMB

To enhance assembled code-thickness, processors since the ARM7TDMI (discharged in 1994) have included the Thumb instruction set, which have their own particular state. (The "T" in "TDMI" demonstrates the Thumb include.) When in this express, the processor executes the Thumb instruction set, a conservative 16-bit encoding for a subset of the ARM instruction set. A large portion of the Thumb instructions are specifically mapped to typical ARM instructions. The space-sparing originates from making a portion of the instruction operands understood and restricting the quantity of conceivable outcomes contrasted with the ARM instructions executed in the ARM instruction set state.

In Thumb, the 16-bit opcodes have less usefulness. For instance, no one but branches can be contingent, and numerous opcodes are confined to getting to just 50% of the majority of the CPU's universally useful registers. The shorter opcodes give enhanced code thickness by and large, despite the fact that a few operations require additional instructions. In circumstances where the memory port or transport width is obliged to under 32 bits, the shorter Thumb opcodes permit expanded performance contrasted and 32-bit ARM code, as less program code may should be stacked into the processor over the compelled memory data transfer capacity.

Implanted equipment, for example, the Game Boy Advance, regularly have a little measure of RAM open with an entire 32-bit datapath; the larger part is gotten to by means of a 16-bit or smaller optional datapath. In this circumstance, it as a rule bodes well to order Thumb code and hand-streamline a couple of the most CPU-escalated segments utilizing full 32-bit ARM instructions, setting these more extensive instructions into the 32-bit transport available memory.

The main processor with a Thumb instruction decoder was the ARM7TDMI. All ARM9 and later families, including XScale, have incorporated a Thumb instruction decoder.

THUMB-2

Thumb-2 innovation was presented in the ARM1156 core, reported in 2003. Thumb-2 broadens the restricted 16-bit instruction set of Thumb with extra 32-bit instructions to give the instruction set more broadness, in this way delivering a variable-length instruction set. An expressed go for Thumb-2 was to accomplish code thickness like Thumb with performance like the ARM instruction set on 32-bit memory.

Thumb-2 broadens the Thumb instruction set with bit-field control, table branches and restrictive execution. In the meantime, the ARM instruction set was reached out to keep up equal usefulness in both instruction sets. Another "Bound together Assembly Language" (UAL) bolsters era of either Thumb or ARM instructions from a similar source code; renditions of Thumb seen on ARMv7 processors are basically as competent as ARM code (counting the capacity to compose interfere with handlers). This requires a touch of care, and utilization of another "IT" (assuming then) instruction, which allows up to four progressive instructions to execute in light of a tried condition, or on its backwards. When accumulating into ARM code, this is overlooked, however when arranging into Thumb it creates a real instruction. For instance:

```
; if (r0 == r1)
CMP r0, r1
ITE EQ      ; ARM: no code ... Thumb: IT instruction
; then r0 = r2;
MOVEQ r0, r2  ; ARM: conditional; Thumb: condition via ITE 'T' (then)
; else r0 = r3;
MOVNE r0, r3  ; ARM: conditional; Thumb: condition via ITE 'E' (else)
; recall that the Thumb MOV instruction has no bits to encode "EQ" or "NE"
```

All ARMv7 chips bolster the Thumb instruction set. All chips in the Cortex-An arrangement, Cortex-R arrangement, and ARM11 arrangement strengthen both "ARM instruction set "and "Thumb instruction set", while chips in the Cortex-M arrangement bolster just the Thumb instruction set.

THUMB EXECUTION ENVIRONMENT (THUMBEE)

ThumbEE (incorrectly called Thumb-2EE in some ARM documentation), marketed as Jazelle RCT (Runtime Compilation Target), was reported in 2005, first showing up in the Cortex-A8 processor. ThumbEE is a fourth Instruction set state, rolling out little improvements to the Thumb-2 developed Thumb instruction set. These progressions make the instruction set especially suited to code produced at runtime (e.g. by JIT compilation) in oversaw Execution Environments. ThumbEE is a target for languages, for example, Java, C#, Perl, and Python, and enables JIT compilers to yield littler assembled code without affecting performance.

New elements given by ThumbEE incorporate programmed invalid pointer minds each heap and store instruction, an instruction to play out a cluster limits check, and uncommon instructions that call a handler. What's more, since it uses Thumb-2 innovation, ThumbEE gives access to registers r8-r15 (where the Jazelle/DBX Java VM state is held). Handlers are little areas of every now and again called code, normally used to actualize abnormal state languages, for example, designating memory for another question. These progressions originated from repurposing a modest bunch of opcodes, and knowing the core is in the new ThumbEE Instruction set state.

On 23 November 2011, ARM Holdings deployed any utilization of the ThumbEE instruction set, and ARMv8 expels bolster for ThumbEE.

FLOATING-POINT (VFP)

VFP (Vector Floating Point) innovation is a FPU (Floating-Point Unit) coprocessor augmentation to the ARM architecture (executed distinctively in ARMv8 - coprocessors not characterized there). It gives ease single-accuracy and twofold exactness floating-point calculation completely consistent with the ANSI/IEEE Std 754-1985 Standard for Binary Floating-Point Arithmetic. VFP gives floating-point calculation appropriate to a wide range of applications, for example, PDAs, cell phones, voice pressure and decompression, three-dimensional representation and advanced sound, printers, set-best boxes, and car applications. The VFP architecture was proposed to bolster execution of short "vector mode" instructions yet these worked on every vector component consecutively and in this manner did not offer the performance of genuine single instruction, various data (SIMD) vector parallelism. This vector mode was subsequently evacuated soon after its presentation, to be supplanted with a great deal more intense NEON Advanced SIMD unit.

A few gadgets, for example, the ARM Cortex-A8 have a chopped down VFPLite module rather than a full VFP module, and require about ten times more clock cycles per glide operation. Pre-ARMv8 architecture actualized floating-point/SIMD with the coprocessor interface. Other floating-point as well as SIMD units found in ARM-based processors utilizing the coprocessor interface incorporate FPA, FPE, iwMMXt, some of which were executed in programming by catching however could have been actualized in equipment. They give a portion of an indistinguishable usefulness from VFP yet are not opcode-perfect with it.

VFPV1 OR VFPV2

A discretionary augmentation to the ARM instruction set in the ARMv5TE, ARMv5TEJ and ARMv6 architectures. VFPv2 has 16 64-bit FPU registers.

VFPV3 OR VFPV3-D32

Executed on most Cortex-A8 and A9 ARMv7 processors. It is in reverse good with VFPv2, aside from that it can't trap floating-point special cases. VFPv3 has 32 64-bit FPU registers as standard, adds VCVT instructions to change over between scalar, buoy and twofold, adds prompt mode to VMOV with the end goal that constants can be stacked into FPU registers.

VFPV3-D16

As above, yet with just 16 64-bit FPU registers. Executed on Cortex-R4 and R5 processors and the Tegra 2 (Cortex-A9).

VFPV3-F16

Exceptional; it bolsters IEEE754-2008 half-accuracy (16-bit) floating point.

VFPV4 OR VFPV4-D32

Actualized on the Cortex-A12 and A15 ARMv7 processors, Cortex-A7 alternatively has VFPv4-D32 on account of a FPU with NEON. VFPv4 has 32 64-bit FPU registers as standard, includes both half-accuracy augmentations and melded increase gather instructions to the components of VFPv3.

VFPV4-D16

As above, however it has just 16 64-bit FPU registers. Actualized on Cortex-A5 and A7 processors (if there should be an occurrence of a FPU without NEON).

VFPV5-D16-M

Executed on Cortex-M7 when single and twofold exactness floating-point core alternative exists.

In Debian Linux and subordinates armhf (ARM hard buoy) alludes to the ARMv7 architecture including the extra VFP3-D16 floating-point equipment augmentation (and Thumb-2) above.

Programming bundles and cross-compiler apparatuses utilize the armhf versus arm/armel postfixes to separate.

PROGRESSED SIMD (NEON)

The Advanced SIMD expansion (otherwise known as NEON or "MPE" Media Processing Engine) is a consolidated 64-and 128-piece SIMD instruction set that gives institutionalized increasing speed to media and flag preparing applications. NEON is incorporated into all Cortex-A8 gadgets however is discretionary in Cortex-A9 gadgets. NEON can execute MP3 sound translating on CPUs running at 10 MHz and can run the GSM versatile multi-rate (AMR) discourse codec at close to 13 MHz. It highlights an exhaustive instruction set, isolate enlist documents and free execution equipment. NEON bolsters 8-, 16-, 32-and 64-bit whole number and single-exactness (32-bit) floating-point data and SIMD operations for taking care of sound and video preparing and representation and gaming handling. In NEON, the SIMD bolsters up to 16 operations in the meantime. The NEON equipment shares a similar floating-point registers as utilized as a part of VFP. Gadgets, for example, the ARM Cortex-A8 and Cortex-A9 bolster 128-piece vectors yet will execute with 64 bits at any given moment, while more up to date Cortex-A15 gadgets can execute 128 bits at any given moment.

ProjectNe10 is ARM's initially open source extend (from its origin). The Ne10 library is a set of normal, helpful capacities written in both NEON and C (for similarity). The library was made to enable engineers to utilize NEON advancements without learning NEON however it additionally fills in as a set of profoundly enhanced NEON inherent and get together code cases for normal DSP, number juggling and picture handling schedules. The code is accessible on GitHub.

SECURITY EXPANSIONS (TRUSTZONE)

The Security Extensions, marketed as TrustZone Technology, is in ARMv6KZ and later application profile architectures. It gives a minimal effort contrasting option to adding another committed security core to a SoC, by giving two virtual processors upheld by equipment based get to control. This gives the application a chance to core switch between two states, alluded to as universes (to lessen perplexity with different names for capacity spaces), so as to keep data from spilling from the more put stock in world to the less confided in world. This world switch is for the most part orthogonal to all different abilities of the processor, along these lines every world can work autonomously of the other while utilizing a similar core. Memory and peripherals are then made mindful of the working universe of the core and may utilize this to give get to control to privileged insights and code on the gadget.

Regular applications of TrustZone Technology are to run a rich working framework in the less confided in world, and littler security-specific code in the more put stock in world (named TrustZone Software, a TrustZone streamlined rendition of the Trusted Foundations Software created by Trusted Logic Mobility), permitting significantly more tightly advanced rights administration for controlling the utilization of media on ARM-based gadgets, and keeping any unapproved utilization of the gadget. Trusted Foundations Software was obtained by Gemalto. Giesecke and Devrient built up an opponent execution named Mobicore. In April 2012 ARM Gemalto and Giesecke and Devrient consolidated their TrustZone portfolios into a joint wander Trustonic. Open Virtualization and T6 are open source usage of the put stock in world architecture for TrustZone.

Practically speaking, since the particular usage points of interest of TrustZone are restrictive and have not been openly revealed for audit, it is hazy what level of affirmation is accommodated a given danger demonstrate.

NO-EXECUTE PAGE INSURANCE

As of ARMv6, the ARM architecture bolsters no-execute page insurance, which is alluded to as XN, for eXecute Never.

EXPANSIVE PHYSICAL ADDRESS EXTENSION

The Large Physical Address Extension, which develops the physical address estimate from 32 bits to 40 bits, was added to the ARMv7-An architecture in 2011.

ARMV8-R

The ARMv8-R sub-architecture, declared after the ARMv8-A, shares a few elements aside from that it is not 64-bit.

64/32-BIT ARCHITECTURE

ARMV8-A

Detailed in October 2011, ARMv8-A (consistently called ARMv8 regardless of the way that not all varieties are 64-bit, for instance, ARMv8-R) addresses a noteworthy change to the ARM architecture. It incorporates a 64-bit architecture, named "AArch64", and another "A64" instruction set. AArch64 outfits customer space comparability with ARMv7-An ISA, the 32-bit architecture, in that insinuated as "AArch32" and the old 32-bit instruction set, now named "A32". The Thumb instruction sets are implied as "T32" and have no 64-bit accomplice. ARMv8-A grants 32-bit applications to be executed in a 64-bit OS, and a 32-bit OS to be under the control of a 64-bit hypervisor. ARM detailed their Cortex-A53 and Cortex-A57 cores on 30 October 2012. Apple was the first to release an ARMv8-An impeccable core (Apple A7) in a buyer thing (iPhone 5S). AppliedMicro, using a FPGA, was the first to demo ARMv8-A.The first ARMv8-A SoC from Samsung is the Exynos 5433 in the Galaxy Note 4, which highlights two bundles of four Cortex-A57 and Cortex-A53 cores in a big.LITTLE setup; be that as it may it will run just in AArch32 mode.

Both AArch32& AArch64, ARMv8-A makes VFPv3/v4 and advanced SIMD (NEON) standard. It in like manner incorporates cryptography instructions supporting AES and SHA-1/SHA-256.

ARMV8.1-A

In December 2014, ARMv8.1-An, a refresh with "incremental advantages over v8.0", was declared. The enhancements fall into two classes:

1. Changes to the instruction set
2. Changes to the special case model and memory interpretation \Expected "item presentations mid-2015" with server CPU producers liable to embrace and Apple "will probably bounce to the new architecture". "The incremental updates in ARMv8.1-A spin around memory tending to, security, virtualization and throughput. ARMv8-A code will keep running on v8.1 cores."

AARCH64 HIGHLIGHTS

1. New instruction set, A64
2. Has 31 universally useful 64-bit registers.
3. Has devoted SP or zero enlist.
4. The program counter (PC) is no longer open as an enlist.
5. Instructions are still 32 bits in length and generally the same as A32 (with LDM/STM instructions and most restrictive execution dropped).
6. Has combined burdens/stores (set up of LDM/STM).
7. No predication for most instructions (with the exception of branches).
8. Most instructions can take 32-bit or 64-bit contentions.
9. Addresses thought to be 64-bit.
10. Progressed SIMD (NEON) improved
11. Has 32× 128-piece registers (up from 16), likewise available by means of VFPv4.
12. Bolsters twofold accuracy floating point.
13. Completely IEEE 754 consistent.
14. AES encode/decode and SHA-1/SHA-2 hashing instructions additionally utilize these registers.
15. Another special case framework

16. Less managed an account registers and modes.
17. Memory interpretation from 48-bit virtual locations in view of the current Large Physical Address Extension (LPAE), which was intended to be effectively reached out to 64-bit Working framework bolster and 32-bit working frameworks

RECORDED WORKING FRAMEWORKS

The initial 32-bit ARM-based PC, the Acorn Archimedes, ran a between time working framework called Arthur, which advanced into RISC OS, utilized on later ARM-based frameworks from Acorn and different sellers. Some Acorn machines likewise had a Unix port called RISC iX.

INSTALLED WORKING FRAMEWORKS

The 32-bit ARM architecture is bolstered by countless and constant working frameworks, including Android, Linux, FreeRTOS, VxWorks, Windows Embedded Compact, Windows 10 IoT Core, ChibiOS/RT, DRYOS, eCos, Integrity,QNX, RIOT, RTEMS, RTXC Quadros, Nucleus PLUS, NuttX, MicroC/OS-II, PikeOS, ThreadX, MQX, T-Kernel, OSE, OS-9.

CONSTANT WORKING FRAMEWORKS

SCIOPTA has a first evidence of-idea usage running.

CELL PHONE WORKING FRAMEWORKS

The 32-bit ARM architecture is the essential equipment environment for most cell phone working frameworks, for example, Android, iOS, Windows Phone,BlackBerry OS/BlackBerry, Windows RT, Chrome OS, Bada10,Firefox OS, Sailfish, MeeGo, Tizen, Ubuntu Touch, , Symbian, and webOS.

DESKTOP/SERVER WORKING FRAMEWORKS

The 32-bit ARM architecture is upheld by RISC OS and different Unix-like working frameworks including BSD (NetBSD, FreeBSD, OpenBSD), OpenSolaris and different Linux disseminations, for example, Debian, Gentoo, and Ubuntu.

64-BIT WORKING FRAMEWORKS

Cell phone working frameworks

iOS bolsters ARMv8-An in iOS 7 and later on 64-bit Apple SoCs.

Android underpins ARMv8-An in Android Lollipop (5.0) and later.

DESKTOP/SERVER WORKING FRAMEWORKS

Bolster for ARMv8-A was converged into the Linux portion rendition 3.7 in late 2012.

ARMv8-An is upheld by various Linux circulations, for example, Debian, Fedora, open SUSE. Bolster for ARMv8-A was converged into FreeBSD in late 2014.

PORTING TO 32-OR 64-BIT ARM WORKING FRAMEWORKS

Windows applications recompiled for ARM and connected with Winelib – from the Wine venture can keep running on 32-bit or 64-bit ARM in Linux (or FreeBSD or other sufficiently good working frameworks).

Intel's x86 parallels, e.g. at the point when not extraordinarily incorporated for ARM, work with Wine (on Linux, OS X and that's only the tip of the iceberg); and have been exhibited on ARM, with QEMU, however don't work at full speed or same capacity as with Winelib.

CHAPTER 11ARDUINO AND OPEN SOURCE HARDWARE AND SOFTWARE

PHILOSOPHY

Arduino is an open-source prototyping stage in light of simple to-utilize hardware and software. Arduino boards can read inputs - light on a sensor, a finger on a catch, or a Twitter message - and transform it into an output - actuating an engine, turning on a LED, distributing something on the web. You can guide your board by sending an arrangement of directions to the microcontroller on the board. To do as such you utilize the Arduino programming dialect (in light of Wiring), and the Arduino Software (IDE), in view of Processing.

Throughout the years, Arduino has been the cerebrum of thousands of ventures, from regular items to complex logical instruments. An overall group of producers - understudies, specialists, craftsmen, software engineers, and experts - has assembled around this open-source stage, their commitments have signified an extraordinary measure of available information that can be of incredible help to tenderfoots and specialists alike.

Arduino was conceived at the Ivrea Interaction Design Institute as a simple apparatus for quick prototyping, gone for understudies without a foundation in gadgets and programming. When it achieved a more extensive group, the Arduino board began changing to adjust to new needs and difficulties, separating its offer from straightforward 8-bit boards to items for IoT applications, wearable, 3D printing, and installed situations. All Arduino boards are totally open-source, enabling clients to manufacture them freely and inevitably adjust them to their specific needs. The software, as well, is open-source, and it is becoming through the commitments of clients around the world.

WHY ARDUINO

On account of its basic and open client encounter, Arduino has been utilized as a part of thousands of various ventures and applications. The Arduino software is anything but difficult to-use for tenderfoots, yet sufficiently adaptable for cutting edge clients. It keeps running on Mac, Windows, and Linux. Instructors and understudies utilize it to manufacture minimal effort logical instruments, to demonstrate science and material science standards, or to begin with programming and mechanical autonomy. Planners and designers construct intuitive models, performers and specialists utilize it for establishments and to explore different avenues regarding new melodic instruments. Creators, obviously, utilize it to fabricate a number of the tasks displayed at the Maker Faire, for instance. Arduino is a key apparatus to learn new things. Anybody - kids, specialists, craftsmen, software engineers - can begin tinkering simply taking after the well ordered directions of a pack, or sharing thoughts online with different individuals from the Arduino people group.

There are numerous different microcontrollers and microcontroller stages accessible for physical processing. Parallax Basic Stamp, Netmedia's BX-24, Phidgets, MIT's Handyboard, and numerous others offer comparative usefulness. These apparatuses take the untidy subtle elements of microcontroller programming and wrap it up in a simple to-utilize bundle. Arduino additionally rearranges the way toward working with microcontrollers, however it offers some preferred standpoint for instructors, understudies, and intrigued novices over different frameworks:

- **Inexpensive** - Arduino boards are generally modest contrasted with other microcontroller stages. The slightest costly adaptation of the Arduino module can be amassed by hand, and even the pre-collected Arduino modules cost under $50

- **Cross-stage** - The Arduino Software (IDE) keeps running on Windows, Macintosh OSX, and Linux working frameworks. Most microcontroller frameworks are restricted to Windows.

- **Simple, clear programming condition** - The Arduino Software (IDE) is anything but difficult to-use for apprentices, yet sufficiently adaptable for cutting edge clients to exploit also. For educators, it's helpfully in view of the Processing programming condition, so understudies figuring out how to program in that condition will be acquainted with how the Arduino IDE functions.

- **Open source and extensible software** - The Arduino software is distributed as open source apparatuses, accessible for expansion by experienced developers.

The dialect can be extended through C++ libraries, and individuals needing to comprehend the specialized points of interest can make the jump from Arduino to the AVR C programming dialect on which it's based. So also, you can include AVR-C code straightforwardly into your Arduino programs in the event that you need to.

- **Open source and extensible hardware** - The arrangements of the Arduino boards are distributed under a Creative Commons permit, so experienced circuit originators can make their own particular variant of the module, broadening it and enhancing it. Indeed, even generally unpracticed clients can fabricate the breadboard variant of the module to see how it functions and spare cash.

The venture depends on microcontroller board plans, produced by a few merchants, utilizing different microcontrollers. These frameworks give sets of computerized and simple I/O sticks that can be interfaced to different extension boards ("shields") and different circuits. The boards highlight serial correspondences interfaces, including USB on a few models, for stacking programs from PCs. For programming the microcontrollers, the Arduino extend gives an incorporated advancement condition (IDE) in view of the Processing venture, which incorporates bolster for the C and C++ programming dialects.

The principal Arduino was presented in 2005, expecting to give an economical and simple route for beginners and experts to make gadgets that collaborate with their condition utilizing sensors and actuators. Normal cases of such gadgets proposed for apprentice specialists incorporate straightforward robots, indoor regulators, and movement identifiers.

Arduino boards are accessible economically in preassembled frame, or as do-it-without anyone's help packs. The hardware plan particulars are openly accessible, permitting the Arduino boards to be fabricated by anybody. Adafruit Industries evaluated in mid-2011 that more than 300,000 authority Arduinos had been economically delivered, and in 2013 that 700,000 authority boards were in clients' grasp.

HISTORY

Colombian understudy Hernando Barragán made the Wiring improvement stage as his Master's postulation extend in 2004 at the Interaction Design Institute Ivrea in Ivrea,

Italy. Massimo Banzi and Casey Reas (known for his work on Processing) were bosses for his postulation. The thought was to make economical and basic apparatuses for non-architects to make advanced tasks. The Wiring stage comprised of a hardware PCB with an ATmega128 microcontroller, a coordinated advancement condition (IDE) in light of Processing and library capacities for simple programming of the microcontroller.

In 2005, Massimo Banzi, alongside David Mellis (an IDII understudy at the time) and David Cuartielles, included support for the less expensive ATmega8 microcontroller to Wiring. Be that as it may, rather than proceeding with the work on Wiring they forked (or replicated) the Wiring source code and began running it as a different venture, called Arduino.

The Arduino's underlying center group comprised of Massimo Banzi, David Cuartielles, Tom Igoe, Gianluca Martino, and David Mellis.

The name "Arduino" originates from a bar in Ivrea, where a portion of the organizers of the venture used to meet. The bar, thus, has been named after Arduin of Ivrea, who was the margrave of Ivrea and King of Italy from 1002 to 1014.

Taking after the consummation of the Wiring stage, its lighter, more affordable forms were made and made accessible to the open-source group; related analysts, including David Cuartielles, advanced the thought. The Arduino's underlying center group comprised of Massimo Banzi, David Cuartielles, Tom Igoe, Gianluca Martino and David Mellis.

HARDWARE

An early Arduino board with a RS-232 serial interface (upper left) and an Atmel ATmega8 microcontroller chip (dark, bring down right); the 14 computerized I/O pins are situated at the top and the six simple information pins at the lower right.

An Arduino board truly comprises of an Atmel 8-, 16-or 32-bit AVR microcontroller (despite the fact that since 2015 other producers' microcontrollers have been utilized) with corresponding parts that encourage programming and fuse into different circuits. An essential part of the Arduino is its standard connectors, which gives clients a chance to associate the CPU board to an assortment of compatible extra modules known as shields. A few shields speak with the Arduino board straightforwardly over different pins, however many shields are separately addressable by means of an I²C serial transport—such a variety of shields can be stacked and utilized as a part of parallel. Before 2015 Official Arduinos had utilized the Atmel megaAVR arrangement of chips, particularly the ATmega8, ATmega168, ATmega328, ATmega1280, and ATmega2560 and in 2015 units by different makers were included. A modest bunch of different processors have additionally been utilized by Arduino perfect gadgets.

Most boards incorporate a 5 V straight controller and a 16 MHz precious stone oscillator (or clay resonator in a few variations), albeit a few plans, for example, the LilyPad keep running at 8 MHz and get rid of the installed voltage controller because of particular frame calculate limitations. An Arduino's microcontroller is additionally pre-modified with a boot loader that streamlines transferring of projects to the on-chip streak memory, contrasted and different gadgets that normally require an outer developer. This makes utilizing an Arduino more clear by permitting the utilization of a normal computer as the software engineer. As of now, optiboot bootloader is the default bootloader introduced on Arduino UNO.

At a theoretical level, when utilizing the Arduino incorporated improvement condition, all boards are customized over a serial association. Its execution changes with the hardware adaptation. Some serial Arduino boards contain a level shifter circuit to change over between RS-232 rationale levels and TTL-level signs. Current Arduino boards are customized by means of Universal Serial Bus (USB), actualized utilizing USB-to-serial connector chips, for example, the FTDI FT232.

A few boards, for example, later-display Uno boards, substitute the FTDI chip with a different AVR chip containing USB-to-serial firmware, which is reprogrammable by means of its own ICSP header. Different variations, for example, the Arduino Mini and the informal Boarduino, utilize a separable USB-to-serial connector board or link, Bluetooth or different techniques, when utilized with conventional microcontroller apparatuses rather than the Arduino IDE, standard AVR ISP writing computer programs is utilized.

The Arduino board uncovered the vast majority of the microcontroller's I/O pins for use by different circuits. The Diecimila, Duemilanove, and current Uno give 14 computerized I/O pins, six of which can create beat width adjusted signs, and six simple inputs, which can likewise be utilized as six advanced I/O pins. These pins are on the highest point of the board, by means of female 0.10-inch (2.5 mm) headers. A few module application shields are likewise monetarily accessible. The Arduino Nano, and Arduino-good Bare Bones Board and Boarduino boards may give male header sticks on the underside of the board that can connect to solderless breadboards.

There are numerous Arduino-good and Arduino-inferred boards. Some are practically equal to an Arduino and can be utilized reciprocally. Many upgrade the fundamental Arduino by including output drivers, regularly for use in school-level training to streamline the development of carriages and little robots. Others are electrically comparable yet change the frame calculate, now and again holding similarity with shields, once in a while not. A few variations utilize totally unique processors, with shifting levels of similarity.

OFFICIAL BOARDS

The first Arduino hardware was made by the Italian organization Smart Projects. Some Arduino-marked boards have been planned by the American organizations SparkFun Electronics and Adafruit Industries. Seventeen renditions of the Arduino hardware have been economically created to date.

Example Arduino boards

- Arduino Diecimila in Stoicheia
- Arduino Duemilanove (rev 2009b)
- Arduino UNO
- Arduino Leonardo
- Arduino Mega
- Arduino MEGA 2560 R3 (front side)

- Arduino MEGA 2560 R3 (rear)

- Arduino Nano

- Arduino Due

- (ARM Cortex-M3 center)

- LilyPad Arduino (rev 2007)

- Arduino Yun

SHIELDS

Arduino and Arduino-perfect boards utilize printed circuit extension boards called "shields", which connect to the regularly provided Arduino stick headers. Shields can give engine controls, GPS, Ethernet, LCD, or breadboarding (prototyping). Various shields can likewise be made DIY.

Example Arduino shields

- Numerous shields can be stacked. In this case the top shield contains a solderless breadboard.

- Sink terminal breakout shield a wing-sort organize

- Adafruit Motor Shield with screw terminals for association with engines

- AdafruitDatalogging Shield with a Secure Digital (SD) card space and continuous clock (RTC) chip

- HackARobot Fabric Shield – intended for Arduino Nano to attach engines and sensors, for example, spinner or GPS, and other breakout boards, for example, WiFi, Bluetooth, RF, and so forth.

SOFTWARE

Arduino programs might be composed in any programming language with a compiler that produces parallel machine code. Atmel gives an advancement situation to their microcontrollers, AVR Studio and the fresher Atmel Studio.

The Arduino extend gives the Arduino incorporated improvement condition (IDE), which is a cross-stage application written in Java. It started from the IDE for the Processing programming language extend and the Wiring venture. It is intended to acquaint programming with specialists and different newcomers new to software advancement. It incorporates a code proofreader with elements, for example, linguistic structure highlighting, support coordinating, and programmed space, and gives basic a single tick system to assembling and stacking programs to an Arduino board. A program composed with the IDE for Arduino is known as a "portray".

The Arduino IDE bolsters the C and C++ programming languages utilizing extraordinary principles of code association. The Arduino IDE supplies a software library called "Wiring" from the Wiring venture, which gives numerous regular information and output methods. An average Arduino C/C++ portray comprise of two capacities that are aggregated and connected with a program stub fundamental() into an executable cyclic official program:

- **setup():**a capacity that runs once toward the begin of a program and that can instate settings.

- **loop():**a capacity called over and over until the board controls off.

After gathering and connecting with the GNU toolchain, additionally included with the IDE conveyance, the Arduino IDE utilizes the program avrdude to change over the executable code into a content document in hexadecimal coding that is stacked into the Arduino board by a loader program in the board's firmware.

TEST PROGRAM

An average program for a starting Arduino developer flickers a light-radiating diode (LED) on and off. This program is generally stacked in the Arduino board by the producer. In the Arduino condition, a client may compose such a program as appeared:

```
#define LED_PIN 13
voidsetup(){
```

```
pinMode(LED_PIN,OUTPUT);// Enable pin 13 for digital output

}

voidloop(){

digitalWrite(LED_PIN,HIGH);// Turn on the LED

delay(1000);// Wait one second (1000 milliseconds)

digitalWrite(LED_PIN,LOW);// Turn off the LED

delay(1000);// Wait one second

}
```

Most Arduino boards contain a LED and a heap resistor associated between stick 13 and ground which is an advantageous component for some tests.

DEVELOPMENT

Arduino is an open-source hardware: the Arduino hardware reference outlines are disseminated under a Creative Commons Attribution Share-Alike 2.5 permit and are accessible on the Arduino Web webpage. Design and creation documents for a few adaptations of the Arduino hardware are likewise accessible. The source code for the IDE is accessible and discharged under the GNU General Public License, variant 2.

In spite of the fact that the hardware and software outlines are unreservedly accessible under copyleft licenses, the engineers have asked for that the name "Arduino" be restrictive to the official item and not be utilized for subordinate works without consent. The official arrangement archive on the utilization of the Arduino name underlines that the venture is open to fusing work by others into the official item. A few Arduino-good items economically discharged have maintained a strategic distance from the "Arduino" name by utilizing "- duino" name variations.

APPLICATIONS

- Xoscillo, an open-source oscilloscope
- Scientific gear, for example, the Chemduino

- Arduinome, a MIDI controller gadget that emulates the Monome
- OBDuino, an excursion computer that uses the on-board diagnostics interface found in most present day autos
- Ardupilot, ramble software/hardware
- ArduinoPhone, a do-it-without anyone's help cellphone
- GertDuino, an Arduino mate for the Raspberry Pi
- Water quality testing platform]
- Homemade CNC utilizing Arduino and DC engines with close circle control by Homofaciens

ACKNOWLEDGMENTS

The Arduino extend got a privileged specify in the Digital Communities class at the 2006 Prix ArsElectronica.

LEGAL QUESTION

In mid 2008, the five prime supporters of the Arduino extend made an organization, Arduino LLC, to hold the trademarks related with Arduino. The fabricate and offer of the boards was to be finished by outside organizations, and Arduino LLC would get a sovereignty from them. The establishing local laws of Arduino LLC indicated that each of the five organizers exchange responsibility for Arduino brand to the recently framed organization.

Toward the finish of 2008, Gianluca Martino's organization, Smart Projects, enrolled the Arduino trademark in Italy and kept this a mystery from the other fellow benefactors for around two years. This was uncovered when the Arduino organization attempted to enroll the trademark in different ranges of the world (they initially enlisted just in the US), and found that it was at that point enrolled in Italy. Arrangements with Gianluca and his organization to bring the trademark under control of the first Arduino organization were not effective, and in 2014 Smart Projects started declining to pay eminences. Keen Projects delegated another CEO, Mr. Musto, who renamed the organization to Arduino SRL and made a site named arduino.org, duplicating the designs and format of the first Arduino.cc. This brought about a crack in the Arduino development group, and albeit all Arduino boards are as yet accessible to buyers, and the plans are open source, the ramifications of this are dubious.

In May 2015, "Genuino" was made far and wide as another trademark, held by Arduino LLC, and is right now being utilized as Arduino LLC's image name outside of the US.

CHAPTER 12: CHANNEL MULTIPLEXING, BANDWIDTH, DATA RATE AND CAPACITY

INTRODUCTION

This chapter gives a short diagram of channel multiplexing procedures like FDM, TDM and so on and with respect to how they are utilized as a part of computer correspondence.

Channel multiplexing is the way toward part or sharing the capacity of a fast channel/media transmission connect to shape numerous low capacity/low speed sub-channels. Each such sub-channel can then be utilized by numerous end hubs as devoted connections. Multiplexing should ordinarily be possible in various areas like time, recurrence and space (and even blends of these).

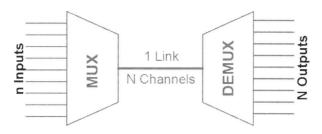

CHANNEL MULTIPLEXING

For computer correspondence, however multiplexing strategies like TDM, FDM were at first utilized for the most part in spine joins associating different data trades, later they have permeated broadly into the get to/last mile interfaces as well, including inside home systems.

TIME DIVISION MULTIPLEXING (TDM)

In TDM, a fast data channel/connection is made to convey data of numerous associations/end hubs in various time openings, in a round robin form. TDM is comparable in idea to multitasking computers, where the fundamental processor does different assignments at the same time. In multitasking processors, however the processor executes just a single assignment at any moment of time and continues carrying between numerous errands in some request, in light of the rapid in which it executes, each undertaking thinks as if the processor is devoted just to it.

Likewise, in TDM, data of every association are divided into smaller units, with the goal that they fit inside scaled down time openings. The connection transmits these little units of data from numerous associations in a round robin design, occasionally distributing a smaller than expected time opening for every client, in the time space.

In TDM, the essential rehashing unit is a casing. A TDM outline comprises of a settled number of time openings. Each time space inside an edge conveys data having a place with a particular end hub/association. In this manner, different consistent sub-channels/connections are made inside a solitary channel. It is likewise conceivable to give numerous spaces inside a casing to a similar client, consequently having the arrangement of having a distinctive capacity sub-channels inside a similar connection.

Expecting that there are "n" end clients, each requiring a connection with a capacity of X Kbps, at that point to effectively multiplex these each end client on a channel, the channel's capacity should be at any rate equivalent to n times X Kbps.

The Figure given beneath illustrates a specimen TDM conspire with 4 clients being served in a round robin form in the time space.

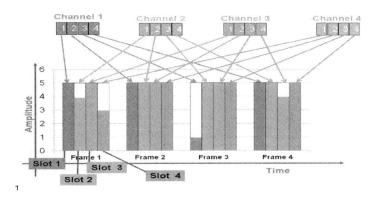

An example TDM frame with 4 time slots serving 4 different users

228

In the illustration given in the figure, the TDM principle channel servers a sum of four clients and subsequently make four sub-channels. Every client's data is conveyed in a particular space inside each edge. For e.g. Channel-1's (User 1) data are constantly conveyed in the primary space of each casing.

The essential guideline of any TDM based convention continues as before as portrayed above, however, there are numerous variations, in light of

- the transmission speed

- number of edges generated every second

- the number of times openings inside each casing

- the outline structure and so on.

TDM is normally utilized as a part of WAN digital transmission joins, in both trunk and get to networks. ISDN (Integrated Services Digital Network) is a case of a convention utilizing TDM at the get to network, to interface home clients to their closest ISP, utilizing the neighborhood circle (phone connect). In ISDN, there are an aggregate of 3 sub-channels, with two of them known as B-Channels (Bearer Channels), each with a capacity of 64Kbps being utilized to convey data and the third known as D-Channel with a capacity of 16Kbps being utilized to convey flagging data.

Standard T1/E1 serial connections are traditional cases of TDM based conventions and are utilized as trunk connections between data trades. While T1 underpins a total rate of 1.54 Mbps with support for 24 sub-channels, each with a capacity of 64Kbps, E1 bolsters a total rate of 2.08 Mbps with support for 32 sub-channels, each with a capacity of 64Kbps. TDM joins with higher capacity incorporate T2, T3 and SONET Optical connections.

Time Division Duplex (TDD) is a type of TDM, where inside the same TDM outline, a few spaces are utilized for uplink bearing (end hubs to network) and a few openings are utilized in the downlink course (network to end hubs), along these lines empowering full duplex correspondence utilizing the same TDM interface.

FREQUENCY DIVISION MULTIPLEXING (FDM)

In FDM, the range (frequency range) of a high capacity connection is partitioned into various non-covering interims/bearers. Data of various end hubs are then balanced utilizing these diverse transporters, so that the resultant flag of each end hub possesses an alternate area in the frequency space. Between each adjoining bearers, a little watch band is left unused, so as not to bring about impedance between firmly separated transporters.

In FDM, at any moment of time, we would have electromagnetic signs relating to every hub/sub-channel, not at all like in TDM, where at any moment of time, the channel would just have electromagnetic flag having a place with one end hub/sub-channel. This appears in the chart given underneath.

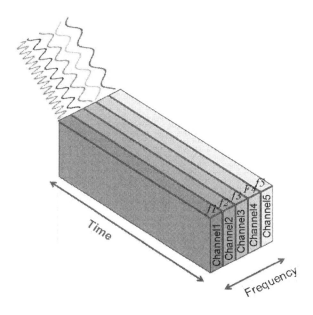

1

An example FDM with 6 different frequency carriers coexisting simultaneously in the time domain

Customary FM Radio and Broadcast TV are traditional cases of utilizations utilizing FDM, where data having a place with each radio station/TV channel is adjusted over an alternate transporter, as appeared in the chart given beneath.

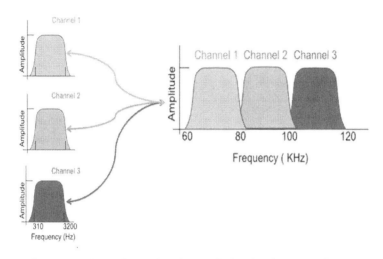

Three baseband channels regulated onto distinctive frequency bearers to separate them in the frequency space

In computer correspondence, the idea of essential FDM and variations of FDM are broadly utilized both in LAN and WAN conditions. DSL and link modem connections are common cases of physical layer conventions utilizing FDM for accomplishing high data rates. In DSL, which additionally utilizes the standard phone last mile neighborhood circle line, various sub-transporters, each with a data transmission of 4KHz. are utilized to convey clients data. The baseband district from 0 to 4KHZ is left for fundamental POTS voice calls. Over this, some number of sub-bearers are apportioned for upstream activity and a higher number of sub-transporters are designated for downstream movement. So also, link modem has a separate frequency band for upstream movement and a scope of sub-transporters for downstream activity.

An illustration chart demonstrating the sub-transporter range assignment for POTS, DSL upstream and downstream bearings are given in the graph underneath:

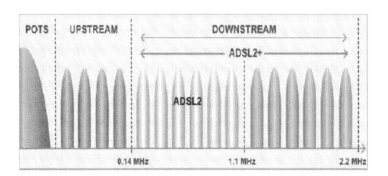

FDM being utilized as a part of ADSL, with various frequency sub-transporters for POTS, ADSL upstream and ADSL downstream

In DSL, to accomplish high data rates, a line coding system like QAM is utilized on top of each sub-bearer. Along these lines both FDM and line coding methods are joined at the physical layer to accomplish high broadband data rates.

FDM is additionally utilized as a part of a few variations of Fast Ethernet (100 Mbps) and Gigabit Ethernet (1000 Mbps) LAN conventions, where various transporters are utilized to accomplish the general data rate bolstered by the hidden physical layer.

VARIATIONS OF FDM

Wavelength Division Multiplexing (WDM) and DWDM (Dense-WDM) utilized as a part of optical Networks, depend on standards like FDM, aside from that their transporters depend on various wavelengths rather than various frequencies

Frequency Division Duplexing (FDD) is a type of FDM, where some arrangement of frequencies/bearers are utilized for conveying uplink direction activity and some other arrangement of frequencies are utilized for conveying downlink movement, along these lines empowering full duplex correspondence utilizing FDM.

Spread Spectrum strategies are variations of FDM, where the data is conveyed or spread over an extensive variety of frequency spectrum. In ordinary FDM, a solitary bearer is utilized to convey data relating to an end hub. Be that as it may, in Spread spectrum strategies, different transporters are utilized to convey data comparing to an end hub, with every bearer conveying a little bit of data. FHSS (Frequency Hopping Spread Spectrum), DSS (Direct Sequence Spread Spectrum) and OFDM (Orthogonal Frequency Division Multiplexing) are distinctive sorts of spread spectrum strategies.

In **FHSS**, the frequency of the transporter fluctuates from moment to moment, though in DSS, data is part into littler units and all the while conveyed by different bearers, as appeared in the chart given underneath

In frequency hopping, the carrier frequency follows a pattern which is known only to the sender and receiver

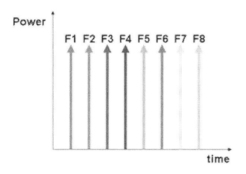

A FHSS where 8 unique bearers are utilized, with data hopping on top of various transporters in a pre-decided request

CDMA (Code Division Multiple Access) is a type of DSS, where a codeword is consolidated with data to spread the flag over an extensive variety of spectrum.

OFDM is a type of DSS that is broadly utilized as a part of Wireless LAN conventions (802.11 a/g), wherein an arrangement of transporters that are orthogonal (don't meddle with each other) are utilized to convey the data motion, as appeared in the graph underneath.

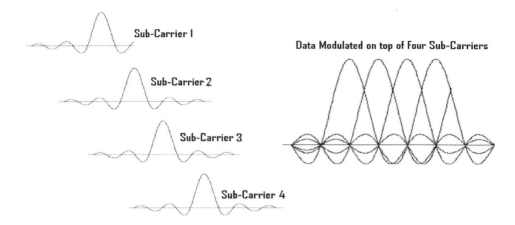

An OFDM conspire where 4 orthogonal frequency sub-transporters are utilized to spread the data over a more extensive spectrum. Orthogonal Frequency Division Multiplexing (OFDM) is utilized for both wired and remote networks

SPACE DIVISION MULTIPLEXING (SDM)

In SDM, a similar arrangement of frequencies or same arrangement of TDM signs are utilized as a part of two better places that are geologically wide separated in space, so one doesn't meddle with the other. Cell correspondence, where a similar arrangement of bearer frequencies are reused (frequency reuse) in cells that are not near each other is a great case of SDM. Another case of SDM is the FM radio communicate, where a similar arrangement of bearer frequencies are utilized as a part of various urban areas that are geologically separated. These are cases of systems where SDM and FDM are consolidated.

MIX OF FDM, TDM AND SDM

GSM (Global System for Mobile Communication) convention consolidates both TDM and FDM, to accomplish full duplex remote correspondence between the mobile handsets and the base stations. While one arrangement of frequencies are utilized as base bearers from mobile handsets to base station, another arrangement of non-covering frequencies are utilized as base transporters from base stations to mobile handsets, accordingly making utilization of FDM standards. Inside every transporter,

GSM utilizes TDM, to convey voice and data having a place with various mobile clients all the while, each in various time spaces. Moreover a similar arrangement of transporter frequencies and TDM plans are reused past a specific least separation, along these lines making utilization of SDM. In this manner GSM is a case convention that utilizations FDM, TDM and SDM.

CONNECTION BETWEEN BANDWIDTH, DATA RATE AND CHANNEL CAPACITY

Some time recently, broadly expounding, knowing the meanings of the accompanying terms would offer assistance:

FLAG BANDWIDTH – the transmission capacity of the transmitted flag or the scope of frequencies present in the flag, as compelled by the transmitter.

CHANNEL BANDWIDTH – the scope of flag data transfer capacities permitted by a correspondence channel without huge loss of vitality (weakening).

CHANNEL CAPACITY OR MAXIMUM DATA RATE – the most extreme rate (in bps) at which data can be transmitted over a given correspondence connection, or channel.

When all is said in done, data is passed on by change in estimations of the flag in time. Since frequency of a flag is a direct measure of the rate of progress in estimations of the flag, the more the frequency of a flag, more is the achievable data rate or data exchange rate. This can be illustrated by taking the case of both a simple and a digital flag.

On the off chance that we take simple transmission line coding methods like Binary ASK, Binary FSK or Binary PSK, data is exchanged by adjusting the property of a high frequency transporter wave. On the off chance that we increment the frequency of this transporter wave to a higher esteem, at that point this lessens the bit interim T (= 1/f) term, subsequently empowering us to exchange more bits every second.

Essentially, in the event that we take digital transmission strategies like NRZ, Manchester encoding and so on., these signs can be displayed as occasional signs and thus is made out of a limitless number of sinusoids, comprising of a principal frequency (f) and its sounds. Here as well, the bit interim (T) is equivalent to the equal of the principal frequency (T = 1/f). Subsequently, if the principal frequency is expanded, at that point this would speak to a digital flag with shorter piece interim and consequently this would build the data rate.

In this way, regardless of whether it is simple or digital transmission, an expansion in the transfer speed of the flag, suggests a comparing increment in the data rate. For e.g. on the off chance that we twofold the flag transmission capacity, at that point the data rate would likewise twofold.

By and by anyway, we can't continue expanding the flag transmission capacity unendingly. The media transmission connect or the correspondence channel goes about as a police and has confinements on the greatest data transfer capacity that it would permit. Aside from this, there are institutionalization transmission limitations that entirely restrict the flag data transmission to be utilized. So the achievable data rate is impacted more by the channel's transfer speed and clamor attributes than the flag transmission capacity.

Nyquist and Shannon have given strategies for figuring the channel capacity (C) of transfer speed restricted correspondence channels.

NYQUIST CRITERIA FOR MOST EXTREME DATA RATE FOR SILENT CHANNELS

Given a silent channel with data transfer capacity B Hz, Nyquist expressed that it can be utilized to convey right around 2B flag changes (images) every second.

The opposite is additionally valid, to be specific for accomplishing a flag transmission rate of 2B images for every second over a channel, it is sufficient if the channel permits signals with frequencies up to B Hz.

Another ramifications of the above outcome is the examining hypothesis, which expresses that for a flag whose most extreme transmission capacity is f Hz, it is sufficient to test the signs at 2f tests for every second with the end goal of quantization (A/D transformation) and furthermore for reproduction of the flag at the collector (D/A change). This is on account of, regardless of the possibility that the signs are tested at a higher rate than 2f (and in this way including the higher consonant segments), the channel would in any case sift through those higher frequency segments.

Likewise, images could have more than two distinct esteems, similar to the case in line coding plans like QAM, QPSK and so on. In such cases, every image esteem could speak to more than 1 digital piece.

Nyquist's formulae for multi-level motioning for a quiet channel is

C = 2 * B * log M,

where C is the channel capacity in bits every second, B is the most extreme data transmission permitted by the channel, M is the quantity of various flagging esteems or images and log is to the base 2.

For instance, expect a quiet 3-kHz channel.

1. If paired signs are utilized, at that point M= 2 and thus greatest channel capacity or achievable data rate is C = 2 * 3000 * log 2 = 6000 bps.

2. Similarly, if QPSK is utilized rather than parallel flagging, at that point M = 4. All things considered, the greatest channel capacity is C = 2 * 3000 * log 4 = 2 * 3000 * 2 = 12000bps.

In this manner, hypothetically, by expanding the quantity of flagging esteems or images, we could continue expanding the channel capacity C uncertainly. In any case, be that as it may, by and by, no channel is silent thus we can't just continue expanding the quantity of images uncertainly, as the recipient would not have the capacity to recognize diverse images within the sight of channel commotion.

It is here that Shannon's hypothesis proves to be useful, as he indicates a most extreme hypothetical utmost for the channel capacity C of a boisterous channel.

SHANNON'S CHANNEL CAPACITY CRITERIA FOR LOUD CHANNELS

Given a corresponding channel with data transfer capacity of B Hz. what's more, a flag to-clamor proportion of S/N, where S is the flag power and N is the commotion power, Shannon's formulae for the most extreme channel capacity C of such a channel is

C = B log (1 + S/N)

For instance, for a channel with data transmission of 3 KHz and with a S/N estimation of 30 DB, similar to that of a run of the mill phone line, the greatest channel capacity is

C = 3000 * log (1 + 30) = 30000 bps (approx.)

Utilizing the past cases of Nyquist criteria, we saw that for a channel with transfer speed 3 KHz, we could twofold the data rate from 6000 bps to 12000 bps., by utilizing QPSK rather than paired motioning as the line encoding system. Utilizing Shannon's criteria for a similar channel, we can reason that independent of the line encoding method utilized, we can't build the channel capacity of this channel past 30000bps.

By and by, be that as it may, because of beneficiary requirements and because of outer clamor sources, Shannon's hypothetical utmost is never accomplished practically speaking.

Accordingly, to compress the connection between transfer speed, data rate and channel capacity,

When all is said in done, the more noteworthy the flag data transmission, the higher the data conveying capacity

In any case, transmission system and collector's capacity restrain the transfer speed that can be transmitted. Consequently the data rate relies on upon:

- Available data transfer capacity for transmission

- Channel capacity and Signal-to-Noise Ratio

- Receiver Capability

Progressively the frequency distributed, increasingly the channel transmission capacity, increasingly the handling ability of the beneficiary, more prominent the data exchange rate that can be accomplished.

CHAPTER 13: CPU VS. SOC – THE BATTLE FOR THE FUTURE OF COMPUTING

CENTRAL PROCESSING UNIT

A central processing unit (CPU) is the electronic circuitry inside a computer that does the directions of a computer program by playing out the essential arithmetic, logical, control and input/output (I/O) operations determined by the guidelines. The term has been utilized as a part of the computer business at any rate since the mid 1960s. Customarily, the expression "CPU" alludes to a processor, all the more particularly to its processing unit and control unit (CU), recognizing these core components of a computer from outside segments, for example, fundamental memory and I/O circuitry.

The shape, plan and usage of CPUs have changed through the span of their history, however their key operation remains practically unaltered. Chief segments of a CPU incorporate the arithmetic logic unit (ALU) that performs arithmetic and logic operations, processor enlists that supply operands to the ALU and store the consequences of ALU operations, and a control unit that brings guidelines from memory and "executes" them by coordinating the planned operations of the ALU, registers and different parts.

Most present day CPUs are microprocessors, which means they are contained on a solitary integrated circuit (IC) chip. An IC that contains a CPU may likewise contain memory, fringe interfaces, and different segments of a computer; such integrated gadgets are differently called microcontrollers or systems on a chip (SoC). A few computers utilize a multi-core processor, which is a solitary chip containing at least two CPUs called "cores"; in that unique situation, single chips are in some cases alluded to as "Sockets". Cluster processors or vector processors have numerous processors that work in parallel, with no unit considered central.

Transistor CPUs

The outline many-sided quality of CPUs expanded as different advancements encouraged building littler and more solid electronic gadgets. The primary such change accompanied the approach of the transistor. Transistorized CPUs amid the 1960s at no time in the future must be worked out of cumbersome, untrustworthy, and delicate exchanging components like vacuum tubes and transfers. With this change more perplexing and solid CPUs were constructed onto one or a few printed circuit sheets containing discrete (individual) parts.

In 1964, IBM presented its System/360 computer engineering that was utilized as a part of a progression of computers equipped for running similar projects with various speed and execution. This was huge when most electronic computers were incongruent with each other, even those made by a similar producer. To encourage this change, IBM used the idea of a microprogram (regularly called "microcode"), which still observes across the board use in present day CPUs. The System/360 engineering was popular to the point that it commanded the centralized server computer showcase for quite a long time and left a heritage that is as yet proceeded by comparable present day computers like the IBM zSeries. In 1965, Digital Equipment Corporation (DEC) presented another powerful computer gone for the logical and research advertises, the PDP-8.

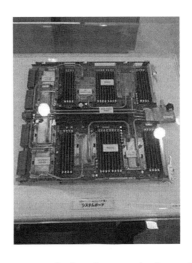

Transistor-based computers had a few particular points of interest over their antecedents. Beside encouraging expanded unwavering quality and lower control utilization, transistors likewise enabled CPUs to work at considerably higher rates in light of the short exchanging time of a transistor in contrast with a tube or hand-off. On account of both the expanded unwavering quality and additionally the drastically expanded speed of the exchanging components (which were only transistors at this point), CPU check rates in the many megahertz were acquired amid this period. Moreover while discrete transistor and IC CPUs were in overwhelming utilization, new elite outlines like SIMD (Single Instruction Multiple Data) vector processors started to show up. These early test plans later offered ascend to the period of specific supercomputers like those made by Cray Inc. what's more, Fujitsu Ltd.

LITTLE SCALE JOINING CPUS

Amid this period, a technique for assembling many interconnected transistors in a smaller space was created. The integrated circuit (IC) enabled countless to be made on a solitary semiconductor-based pass on, or "chip". At first just extremely fundamental non-particular computerized circuits, for example, NOR doors were scaled down into ICs.

CPUs in view of these "building piece" ICs are by and large alluded to as "little scale coordination" (SSI) gadgets. SSI ICs, for example, the ones utilized as a part of the Apollo direction computer, normally contained up to a couple score transistors. To construct a whole CPU out of SSI ICs required a great many individual chips, yet at the same time devoured substantially less space and power than prior discrete transistor plans.

IBM's System/370 take after on to the System/360 utilized SSI ICs as opposed to Solid Logic Technology discrete-transistor modules. DEC's PDP-8/I and KI10 PDP-10 additionally changed from the individual transistors utilized by the PDP-8 and PDP-10 to SSI ICs, and there to a great degree well known PDP-11 line was initially worked with SSI ICs however was in the long run actualized with LSI segments once these ended up plainly down to earth.

VAST SCALE MIX CPUS

Lee Boysel distributed persuasive articles, including a 1967 "pronouncement", which depicted how to fabricate what might as well be called a 32-bit centralized server computer from a generally modest number of substantial scale mix circuits (LSI). At the time, the best way to fabricate LSI chips, which are chips with a hundred or more entryways, was to manufacture them utilizing a MOS procedure (i.e., PMOS logic, NMOS logic, or CMOS logic). Nonetheless, a few organizations kept on building processors out of bipolar chips on the grounds that bipolar intersection transistors were such a great amount of speedier than MOS chips; for instance, Datapoint constructed processors out of TTL chips until the mid 1980s.

243

Individuals assembling rapid computers needed them to be quick, so in the 1970s they constructed the CPUs from little scale mix (SSI) and medium-scale mix (MSI) 7400 arrangement TTL doors. At the time, MOS ICs were slow to the point that they were viewed as helpful just in a couple specialty applications that required low power.

As the microelectronic innovation propelled, an expanding number of transistors were put on ICs, diminishing the amount of individual ICs required for an entire CPU. MSI and LSI ICs expanded transistor checks to hundreds, and after that thousands. By 1968, the quantity of ICs required to manufacture an entire CPU had been diminished to 24 ICs of eight distinct sorts, with every IC containing around 1000 MOSFETs. A distinct difference with its SSI and MSI ancestors, the main LSI execution of the PDP-11 contained a CPU made out of just four LSI integrated circuits.

MICROPROCESSORS

Intel-80486DX2 microprocessor die (Dimension: 12×6.75 mm), in its packaging

In the 1970s, the essential developments by Federico Faggin (Silicon Gate MOS ICs with self-adjusted entryways alongside his new arbitrary logic plan system) changed the outline and execution of CPUs until the end of time. Since the presentation of the main financially accessible microprocessor (the Intel 4004) in 1970, and the principal generally utilized microprocessor (the Intel 8080) in 1974, this class of CPUs has totally surpassed all other central processing unit usage techniques. Centralized server and minicomputer makers of the time, propelled restrictive IC improvement projects to overhaul their more seasoned computer models, and inevitably created direction set perfect microprocessors that were in reverse good with their more established equipment and programming. Consolidated with the approach and inevitable achievement of the universal PC, the term CPU is currently connected solely to microprocessors. A few CPUs (signified cores) can be joined in a solitary processing chip.

On a Vaio E series laptop motherboard built-in Intel Core-i5 CPU (on the right side, under the heat pipe)

Past eras of CPUs were executed as discrete segments and various little integrated circuits (ICs) on at least one circuit sheets. Microprocessors, then again, are CPUs fabricated on few ICs; typically only one. The general littler CPU estimate, thus of being executed on a solitary kick the bucket, implies quicker exchanging time as a result of physical elements like diminished entryway parasitic capacitance. This has enabled synchronous microprocessors to have clock rates running from many megahertz to a few gigahertz. Moreover, as the capacity to build exceedingly little transistors on an IC has expanded, the many-sided quality and number of transistors in a solitary CPU has expanded many crease. This broadly watched pattern is portrayed by Moore's law, which has turned out to be a genuinely exact indicator of the development of CPU (and other IC) intricacy.

While the unpredictability, size, development, and general type of CPUs have changed immensely since 1950, it is prominent that the fundamental outline and capacity has not changed much by any stretch of the imagination. All regular CPUs

245

today can be precisely portrayed as von Neumann put away program machines. As the previously mentioned Moore's law keeps on remaining constant, concerns have emerged about the cutoff points of integrated circuit transistor innovation. Extraordinary scaling down of electronic doors is causing the impacts of marvels like electro relocation and subthreshold spillage to end up plainly a great deal more noteworthy. These more up to date concerns are among the many components making specialists explore new techniques for figuring, for example, the quantum computer, and additionally to grow the utilization of parallelism and different strategies that broaden the value of the established von Neumann demonstrate.

OPERATION

The basic operation of most CPUs, paying little heed to the physical frame they take, is to execute a grouping of put away instructions that is known as a program. The instructions to be executed are kept in some sort of computer memory. Almost all CPUs take after the fetch, decode and execute ventures in their operation, which are all in all known as the instruction cycle.

After the execution of an instruction, the whole procedure rehashes, with the following instruction cycle regularly fetching the following in-grouping instruction on account of the augmented an incentive in the program counter. In the event that a bounce instruction was executed, the program counter will be adjusted to contain the address of the instruction that was hopped to and program execution proceeds regularly. In more mind boggling CPUs, numerous instructions can be fetched, decoded, and executed all the while. This area depicts what is for the most part alluded to as the "exemplary RISC pipeline", which is very basic among the straightforward CPUs utilized as a part of numerous electronic gadgets (regularly called microcontroller). It to a great extent overlooks the vital part of CPU store, and accordingly the get to phase of the pipeline.

A few instructions control the program counter as opposed to creating result information straightforwardly; such instructions are for the most part called "bounced" and encourage program conduct like circles, restrictive program execution (using a contingent hop), and presence of capacities. In a few processors, some different instructions change the condition of bits in a "banners" enlist. These banners can be utilized to impact how a program acts, since they regularly show the result of different operations. For instance, in such processors a "look at" instruction assesses two esteems and sets or clears bits in the banners enroll to demonstrate which one is more prominent or whether they are equivalent; one of these banners could then be utilized by a later bounce instruction to decide program stream.

FETCH

The initial step, fetch, includes recovering an instruction (which is spoken to by a number or succession of numbers) from program memory. The instruction's location (address) in program memory is controlled by a program counter (PC), which stores a number that distinguishes the address of the following instruction to be fetched. After an instruction is fetched, the PC is increased by the length of the instruction with the goal that it will contain the address of the following instruction in the grouping. Regularly, the instruction to be fetched must be recovered from moderately moderate memory, making the CPU slow down while sitting tight for the instruction to be returned. This issue is to a great extent addressed in present day processors by reserves and pipeline architectures.

DECODE

The instruction that the CPU fetches from memory figures out what the CPU will do. In the decode step, performed by the circuitry known as the instruction decoder, the instruction is changed over into signs that control different parts of the CPU.

The route in which the instruction is translated is characterized by the CPU's instruction set architecture (ISA). Frequently, one gathering of bits (that is, a "field") inside the instruction, called the opcode, demonstrates which operation is to be performed, while the rest of the fields as a rule give supplemental data required for the operation, for example, the operands. Those operands might be indicated as a consistent esteem (called a prompt esteem), or as the location of an esteem that might be a processor enlists or a memory address, as controlled by some addressing mode.

In some CPU plans the instruction decoder is executed as a hardwired, unchangeable circuit. In others, a microprogram is utilized to make an interpretation of instructions into sets of CPU design flags that are connected consecutively over numerous clock beats. Now and again the memory that stores the microprogram is rewritable, rolling out it conceivable to improvement the route in which the CPU decodes instructions.

EXECUTE

After the fetch and decode steps, the execute step is performed. Contingent upon the CPU architecture, this may comprise of a solitary activity or a succession of activities. Amid each activity, different parts of the CPU are electrically associated so they can play out all or part of the coveted operation and after that the activity is finished, ordinarily in light of a clock beat. All the time the outcomes are composed to an inside CPU enroll for fast access by consequent instructions. In different cases results might be composed to slower, yet more affordable and higher limit fundamental memory.

For instance, if an expansion instruction is to be executed, the arithmetic logic unit (ALU) inputs are associated with a couple of operand sources (numbers to be summed), the ALU is arranged to play out an expansion operation so that the whole of its operand inputs will show up at its output, and the ALU output is associated with capacity (e.g., an enroll or memory) that will get the entirety. At the point when the clock beat happens, the total will be exchanged to capacity and, if the subsequent entirety is too substantial (i.e., it is bigger than the ALU's output word measure), an arithmetic flood banner will be set.

STRUCTURE AND EXECUTION

Hardwired into a CPU's circuitry is an arrangement of essential operations, it can perform, called an instruction set. Such operations may include, for instance, including or subtracting two numbers, contrasting two numbers, or bouncing to an alternate piece of a program. Every fundamental operation is spoken to by a specific blend of bits, known as the machine dialect opcode; while executing instructions in a machine dialect program, the CPU chooses which operation to perform by "deciphering" the opcode. An entire machine dialect instruction comprises of an opcode and, by and large, extra bits that indicate contentions for the operation (for instance, the numbers to be summed on account of an expansion operation). Going up the multifaceted nature scale, a machine dialect program is a gathering of machine dialect instructions that the CPU executes.

The real numerical operation for every instruction is performed by a combinational logic circuit inside the CPU's processor known as the arithmetic logic unit or ALU. When all is said in done, a CPU executes an instruction by fetching it from memory, utilizing its ALU to play out an operation, and afterward putting away the outcome to memory. Next to the instructions for whole number science and logic operations, different other machine instructions exist, for example, those for stacking information from memory and putting away it back, expanding operations, and scientific operations on floating-point numbers performed by the CPU's floating-point unit (FPU).

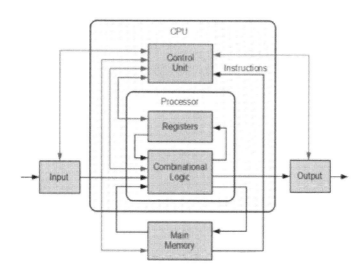

Diagram of a basic uni-processor-CPU computer. Data flow indicates in Black lines, Red lines show control flow; arrows present the flow of directions.

CONTROL UNIT

The control unit of the CPU contains circuitry that utilizations electrical signs to guide the whole computer system to do put away program instructions. The control unit does not execute program instructions; rather, it guides different parts of the system to do as such. The control unit speaks with both the ALU and memory.

ARITHMETIC LOGIC UNIT

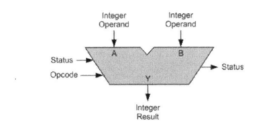

Figurative image of an ALU (Input and output Signals)

The arithmetic logic unit (ALU) is a computerized circuit inside the processor that performs whole number arithmetic and bitwise logic operations. The inputs to the ALU are the information words to be worked on (called operands), status data from past operations, and a code from the control unit demonstrating which operation to perform. Contingent upon the instruction being executed, the operands may originate from inner CPU registers or outer memory, or they might be constants created by the ALU itself.

At the point when all input signals have settled and engendered through the ALU circuitry, the consequence of the performed operation shows up at the ALU's outputs. The outcome comprises of both an information word, which might be put away in an enlist or memory, and status data that is commonly put away in a unique, interior CPU enroll held for this reason.

MEMORY MANAGEMENT UNIT

Most top of the line microprocessors (in desktop, tablet, server computers) have a memory management unit, making an interpretation of logical addresses into physical

RAM addresses, giving memory assurance and paging capacities, valuable for virtual memory. Easier processors, particularly microcontrollers as a rule do exclude a MMU.

INTEGER RANGE

Each CPU speaks to numerical esteems particularly. For instance, some early advanced computers spoke to numbers as recognizable decimal (base 10) numeral system esteems, and others have utilized more abnormal portrayals, for example, ternary (basc three). Almost all current CPUs speak to numbers in double shape, with every digit being spoken to by some two-esteemed physical amount, for example, a "high" or "low" voltage.

$$\overset{\text{32s}}{1}\ \overset{\text{16s}}{0}\ \overset{\text{8s}}{1}\ \overset{\text{4s}}{0}\ \overset{\text{2s}}{0}\ \overset{\text{1s}}{0}$$

A six-piece word containing the double encoded portrayal of decimal esteem 40. Most present day CPUs utilize word sizes that are an energy of two, for instance 8, 16, 32 or 64 bits.

Identified with numeric portrayal is the size and exactness of integer numbers that a CPU can speak to. On account of a double CPU, this is measured by the quantity of bits (critical digits of a twofold encoded integer) that the CPU can prepare in one operation, which is regularly called "word estimate", "bit width", "information way width", "integer exactness", or "integer measure". A CPU's integer estimate decides the range of integer esteems it can straightforwardly operate on. For instance, a 8-bit CPU can specifically control integers spoken to by eight bits, which have a range of 256 (28) discrete integer esteems.

Integer range can likewise influence the quantity of memory locations the CPU can straightforwardly address (an address is an integer esteem speaking to a particular memory location). For instance, if a double CPU utilizes 32 bits to speak to a memory address then it can specifically address 232 memory locations. To bypass this impediment and for different reasons, a few CPUs utilize components, (for example, bank exchanging) that enable extra memory to be addressed.

CPUs with bigger word sizes require more circuitry and thusly are physically bigger, taken a toll more, and expend more power (and subsequently generate more warmth). Thus, littler 4-or 8-bit microcontrollers are generally utilized as a part of current applications despite the fact that CPUs with substantially bigger word sizes, (for example, 16, 32, 64, even 128-piece) are accessible. At the point when higher execution is required, in any case, the advantages of a bigger word measure (bigger information ranges and address spaces) may exceed the detriments. A CPU can have inside information ways shorter than the word size to diminish size and cost. For instance, despite the fact that the IBM System/360 instruction set was a 32-bit instruction set, the System/360 Model 30 and Model 40 had 8-bit information ways in the arithmetic logical unit, so that a 32-bit include required four cycles, one for every 8 bits of the operands, and, despite the fact that the Motorola 68k instruction set was a 32-bit instruction set, the Motorola 68000 and Motorola 68010 had 16-bit information ways in the arithmetic logical unit, so that a 32-bit include required two cycles.

To increase a portion of the favorable circumstances managed by both lower and higher piece lengths, numerous instruction sets have diverse piece widths for integer and floating-point information, permitting CPUs actualizing that instruction set to have distinctive piece widths for various parts of the gadget. For instance, the IBM System/360 instruction set was essentially 32 bit, however upheld 64-bit floating-point esteems to encourage more noteworthy exactness and range in floating point numbers. The System/360 Model 65 had a 8-bit viper for decimal and settled point parallel arithmetic and a 60-bit snake for floating-point arithmetic. Numerous later CPU outlines utilize comparative blended piece width, particularly when the processor is implied for broadly useful utilization where a sensible adjust of integer and floating-point capacity is required.

CLOCK RATE

Most CPUs are synchronous circuits, which implies they utilize a clock flag to pace their successive operations. The clock flag is created by an outer oscillator circuit that generates a reliable number of heartbeats each second as an intermittent square wave. The recurrence of the clock beats decides the rate at which a CPU executes instructions and, therefore, the quicker the clock, the more instructions the CPU will execute each second.

To guarantee legitimate operation of the CPU, the clock time frame is longer than the most extreme time required for all signs to engender (move) through the CPU. In setting the clock time frame to an esteem well over the most pessimistic scenario spread deferral, it is conceivable to plan the whole CPU and the way it moves information around the "edges" of the rising and falling clock flag. This has the upside of disentangling the CPU fundamentally, both from an outline viewpoint and a segment tally point of view. Notwithstanding, it likewise conveys the detriment that the whole CPU must wait on its slowest components, despite the fact that a few parts of it are substantially speedier. This confinement has to a great extent been made up for by different strategies for expanding CPU parallelism (see beneath).

Be that as it may, engineering enhancements alone don't explain the majority of the downsides of all inclusive synchronous CPUs. For instance, a clock flag is liable to the postponements of some other electrical flag. Higher clock rates in progressively complex CPUs make it more hard to keep the clock motion in stage (synchronized) all through the whole unit. This has driven numerous present day CPUs to require different indistinguishable clock signs to be given to abstain from postponing a solitary flag fundamentally enough to make the CPU glitch. Another real issue, as clock rates increment drastically, is the measure of warmth that is dispersed by the CPU. The continually changing clock makes numerous segments switch paying little respect to whether they are being utilized around then. By and large, a segment that is exchanging utilizes more vitality than a component in a static state. In this way, as clock rate builds, so does vitality utilization, making the CPU require more warmth scattering as CPU cooling arrangements.

One technique for managing the exchanging of unneeded segments is called clock gating, which includes killing the clock flag to unneeded parts (viably handicapping them). Be that as it may, this is frequently viewed as hard to execute and along these lines does not see regular use outside of low-power outlines. One remarkable late CPU outline that utilizations broad clock gating is the IBM PowerPC-based Xenon utilized as a part of the Xbox 360; that way, control necessities of the Xbox 360 are incredibly decreased. Another technique for addressing a portion of the issues with a worldwide clock flag is the expulsion of the clock flag out and out. While evacuating the worldwide clock flag makes the outline procedure extensively more perplexing from numerous points of view, nonconcurrent (or clockless) plans convey checked preferences in power utilization and warmth dispersal in correlation with comparable synchronous outlines. While fairly unprecedented, whole nonconcurrent CPUs have been worked without using a worldwide clock flag. Two eminent cases of this are the ARM consistent AMULET and the MIPS R3000 good MiniMIPS.

Instead of thoroughly evacuating the clock flag, some CPU plans enable certain parts of the gadget to be nonconcurrent, for example, utilizing offbeat ALUs in conjunction with superscalar pipelining to accomplish some arithmetic execution picks up. While it is not through and through clear whether absolutely offbeat plans can perform at an equivalent or preferred level over their synchronous counterparts, it is apparent that they do in any event exceed expectations in less complex math operations. This, joined with their fantastic power utilization and warmth scattering properties, makes them extremely appropriate for implanted computers.

PARALLELISM

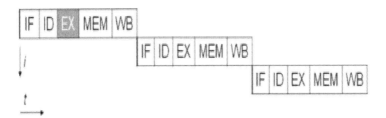

Subscalar CPU's Figure, in which it takes 15 clock cycles to complete 3 commands.

The portrayal of the essential operation of a CPU offered in the past area depicts the least complex frame that a CPU can take. This kind of CPU, more often than not alluded to as subscalar, operates on and executes one instruction on maybe a couple bits of information at once that is short of what one instruction for each clock cycle (IPC < 1).

This procedure offers ascend to an innate wastefulness in subscalar CPUs. Since just a single instruction is executed at once, the whole CPU must sit tight for that instruction to finish before continuing to the following instruction. Subsequently, the subscalar CPU gets "hung up" on instructions which take more than one clock cycle to finish execution. Notwithstanding including a moment execution unit (see beneath) does not enhance execution much; as opposed to one pathway being hung up, now two pathways are hung up and the quantity of unused transistors is expanded. This outline, wherein the CPU's execution assets can operate on just a single instruction at any given moment, can just achieve scalar execution (one instruction for each clock cycle, IPC = 1). In any case, the execution is about dependably subscalar (short of what one instruction for each clock cycle, IPC < 1).

Endeavors to accomplish scalar and better execution have brought about an assortment of outline procedures that make the CPU act not so much directly but rather more in parallel. When alluding to parallelism in CPUs, two terms are for the most part used to group these plan methods:

INSTRUCTION-LEVEL PARALLELISM (ILP)

ILP which tries to build the rate at which instructions are executed inside a CPU (that is, to expand the usage of on-bite the dust execution assets);

TASK-LEVEL PARALLELISM (TLP)

TLP which proposes to build the quantity of strings or procedures that a CPU can execute all the while.

Every approach contrasts both in the courses in which they are executed, and in addition the relative viability they bear the cost of in expanding the CPU's execution for an application.

INSTRUCTION-LEVEL PARALLELISM

Instruction pipelining and Superscalar processor

IF	ID	EX	MEM	WB				
	IF	ID	EX	MEM	WB			
		IF	ID	EX	MEM	WB		
			IF	ID	EX	MEM	WB	
				IF	ID	EX	MEM	WB

Essential five-organize pipeline. In the most ideal situation, this pipeline can support a fruition rate of one instruction for every clock cycle.

One of the most straightforward techniques used to fulfill expanded parallelism is to start the initial steps of instruction fetching and disentangling before the earlier instruction completes the process of executing. This is the least complex type of a system known as instruction pipelining, and is used in all advanced broadly useful CPUs. Pipelining enables more than one instruction to be executed at any given time by separating the execution pathway into discrete stages. This partition can be contrasted with a sequential construction system, in which an instruction is made more total at each phase until it leaves the execution pipeline and is resigned.

Pipelining does, be that as it may, present the likelihood for a circumstance where the aftereffect of the past operation is expected to finish the following operation; a condition frequently named information reliance strife. To adapt to this, extra care must be taken to check for these sorts of conditions and postpone a segment of the instruction pipeline if this happens. Actually, fulfilling this requires extra circuitry, so pipelined processors are more unpredictable than subscalar ones (however not very altogether so). A pipelined processor can turn out to be very almost scalar, repressed just by pipeline slows down (an instruction spending more than one clock cycle in a phase).

IF	ID	EX	MEM	WB				
IF	ID	EX	MEM	WB				
	IF	ID	EX	MEM	WB			
	IF	ID	EX	MEM	WB			
		IF	ID	EX	MEM	WB		
		IF	ID	EX	MEM	WB		
			IF	ID	EX	MEM	WB	
			IF	ID	EX	MEM	WB	
				IF	ID	EX	MEM	WB
				IF	ID	EX	MEM	WB

A straightforward superscalar pipeline. By fetching and dispatching two instructions at any given moment, a most extreme of two instructions for every clock cycle can be finished.

256

Facilitate change upon the possibility of instruction pipelining prompted the improvement of a strategy that declines the sit without moving time of CPU segments significantly further. Outlines that are said to be superscalar incorporate a long instruction pipeline and multiple indistinguishable execution units. In a superscalar pipeline, multiple instructions are perused and gone to a dispatcher, which chooses whether or not the instructions can be executed in parallel (all the while). On the off chance that so they are dispatched to accessible execution units, bringing about the capacity for a few instructions to be executed at the same time. All in all, the more instructions a superscalar CPU can dispatch at the same time to holding up execution units, the more instructions will be finished in a given cycle.

The vast majority of the trouble in the plan of a superscalar CPU architecture lies in making a compelling dispatcher. The dispatcher should have the capacity to rapidly and accurately decide if instructions can be executed in parallel, and in addition dispatch them so as to keep however many execution units occupied as could be expected under the circumstances. This requires the instruction pipeline is filled as frequently as could be expected under the circumstances and offers ascend to the need in superscalar architectures for noteworthy measures of CPU reserve. It likewise makes peril keeping away from methods like branch forecast, theoretical execution, and out-of-request execution urgent to keeping up abnormal amounts of execution. By endeavoring to anticipate which branch (or way) a contingent instruction will take, the CPU can limit the quantity of times that the whole pipeline must hold up until a restrictive instruction is finished. Theoretical execution regularly gives unassuming execution increments by executing bits of code that may not be required after a restrictive operation finishes. Out-of-request execution to some degree rearranges the request in which instructions are executed to decrease delays because of information conditions. Likewise in the event of single instruction stream, multiple information stream—a situation when a ton of information from a similar sort must be handled—, present day processors can incapacitate parts of the pipeline so that when a solitary instruction is executed ordinarily, the CPU skirts the fetch and decode stages and in this manner enormously expands execution on specific events, particularly in very dull program motors, for example, video creation programming and photograph processing.

For the situation where a segment of the CPU is superscalar and part is not, the part which is not endures an execution punishment because of planning slows down. The Intel P5 Pentium had two superscalar ALUs which could acknowledge one instruction for every clock cycle each, however its FPU couldn't acknowledge one instruction for each clock cycle. Along these lines the P5 was integer superscalar yet not floating point superscalar. Intel's successor to the P5 architecture, P6, added superscalar capacities to its floating point highlights, and in this manner managed a critical increment in floating point instruction execution.

Both basic pipelining and superscalar configuration increment a CPU's ILP by enabling a solitary processor to finish execution of instructions at rates outperforming one instruction for every clock cycle. Most present day CPU plans are at any rate fairly superscalar, and almost all universally useful CPUs outlined in the most recent decade are superscalar. In later years a portion of the accentuation in outlining high-ILP computers has been moved out of the CPU's equipment and into its product interface, or ISA. The strategy of the very long instruction word (VLIW) causes some ILP to wind up inferred specifically by the product, lessening the measure of work the CPU must perform to help ILP and in this way decreasing the outline's many-sided quality.

TASK-LEVEL PARALLELISM

Another strategy of accomplishing execution is to execute multiple strings or procedures in parallel. This region of research is known as parallel figuring. In Flynn's scientific classification, this strategy is known as multiple instruction stream, multiple information stream (MIMD).

One innovation utilized for this reason for existing was multiprocessing (MP). The underlying kind of this innovation is known as symmetric multiprocessing (SMP), where few CPUs share a cognizant perspective of their memory system. In this plan, every CPU has extra equipment to keep up a continually a la mode perspective of memory. By staying away from stale perspectives of memory, the CPUs can cooperate on a similar program and programs can migrate starting with one CPU then onto the next. To expand the quantity of participating CPUs past a modest bunch, plans, for example, non-uniform memory access (NUMA) and catalog based intelligibility conventions were presented in the 1990s. SMP systems are constrained to few CPUs while NUMA systems have been worked with a large number of processors. At first, multiprocessing was assembled utilizing multiple discrete CPUs and sheets to execute the interconnect between the processors. At the point when the processors and their interconnect are altogether executed on a solitary chip, the innovation is known as chip-level multiprocessing (CMP) and the single chip as a multi-core processor.

It was later perceived that better grain parallelism existed with a solitary program. A solitary program may have a few strings (or capacities) that could be executed separately or in parallel. A portion of the most punctual cases of this innovation actualized input/output processing, for example, coordinate memory access as a separate string from the calculation string. A more broad way to deal with this innovation was presented in the 1970s when systems were intended to run multiple calculation strings in parallel. This innovation is known as multi-threading (MT). This approach is viewed as more practical than multiprocessing, as just few parts inside a CPU is imitated to bolster MT instead of the whole CPU on account of MP.

In MT, the execution units and the memory system including the reserves are shared among multiple strings. The drawback of MT is that the equipment bolster for multithreading is more obvious to programming than that of MP and consequently chief programming like working systems need to experience bigger changes to bolster MT. One kind of MT that was actualized is known as worldly multithreading, where one string is executed until it is slowed down sitting tight for information to come back from outside memory. In this plan, the CPU would then rapidly setting switch to another string which is prepared to run, the switch frequently done in one CPU clock cycle, for example, the UltraSPARC Technology. Another kind of MT is known as synchronous multithreading, where instructions of multiple strings are executed in parallel inside one CPU clock cycle.

For a very long while from the 1970s to mid 2000s, the concentration in planning elite universally useful CPUs was to a great extent on accomplishing high ILP through innovations, for example, pipelining, stores, superscalar execution, out-of-request execution, and so on. This pattern finished in expansive, control hungry CPUs, for example, the Intel Pentium 4. By the mid 2000s, CPU planners were upset from accomplishing higher execution from ILP systems because of the developing uniqueness between CPU working frequencies and primary memory working frequencies and raising CPU control dispersal attributable to more recondite ILP procedures.

CPU originators at that point acquired thoughts from business registering markets, for example, exchange processing, where the total execution of multiple programs, otherwise called throughput figuring, was more critical than the execution of a solitary string or process.

This inversion of accentuation is prove by the multiplication of double and more core processor outlines and remarkably, Intel's more up to date plans taking after its less superscalar P6 architecture. Late outlines in a few processor families show CMP, including the x86-64 Opteron and Athlon 64 X2, the SPARC UltraSPARC T

DATA PARALLELISM

A less normal, however progressively essential worldview of processors (and without a doubt, figuring all in all) bargains with information parallelism. The processors talked about before are altogether alluded to as some kind of scalar gadget. As the name infers, vector processors manage multiple bits of information with regards to one instruction. This stands out from scalar processors, which manage one bit of information for every instruction. Utilizing Flynn's scientific classification, these two plans of managing information are for the most part alluded to as a solitary instruction stream, multiple information stream (SIMD) and single instruction stream, single information stream (SISD), separately. The immense utility in making processors that arrangement with vectors of information lies in improving tasks that have a tendency to require a similar operation (for instance, a total or a spot item) to be performed on a vast arrangement of information. Some great cases of these sorts of tasks are mixed media applications (pictures, video, and sound), and also many sorts of logical and designing tasks. Though a scalar processor must finish the whole procedure of fetching, unraveling, and executing every instruction and incentive in an arrangement of information, a vector processor can play out a solitary operation on a relatively extensive arrangement of information with one instruction. Obviously, this is just conceivable when the application has a tendency to require many strides which apply one operation to an expansive arrangement of information.

Most early vector processors, for example, the Cray-1, were asSoCiated solely with logical research and cryptography applications. Be that as it may, as interactive media has to a great extent moved to advanced media, the requirement for some type of SIMD when all is said in done reason processors has turned out to be critical. Not long after incorporation of floating-point units begun to wind up plainly typical all in all reason processors, details for and usage of SIMD execution units likewise started to show up for universally useful processors. Some of these early SIMD details like HP's Multimedia Acceleration eXtensions (MAX) and Intel's MMX were integer-as it were. This ended up being a noteworthy obstacle for some product engineers, since a considerable lot of the applications that advantage from SIMD basically manage floating-point numbers. Continuously, these early plans were refined and revamped into a portion of the normal, present day SIMD particulars, which are typically asSoCiated with one ISA. Some outstanding present day illustrations are Intel's SSE and the PowerPC-related AltiVec (otherwise called VMX).

PERFORMANCE

The performance or speed of a processor relies on upon, among numerous different components, the clock rate (by and large given in multiples of hertz) and the instructions per clock (IPC), which together are the elements for the instructions every second (IPS) that the CPU can perform. Many announced IPS esteems have spoken to "pinnacle" execution rates on fake instruction groupings with few branches, while reasonable workloads comprise of a blend of instructions and applications, some of which take more time to execute than others. The performance of the memory chain of command likewise enormously influences processor performance, an issue scarcely considered in MIPS counts. Due to these issues, different state sanctioned tests, regularly called "benchmarks" for this reason, for example, SPECint—have been produced to endeavor to quantify the genuine viable performance in usually utilized applications.

Processing performance of computers is expanded by utilizing multi-core processors, which basically is stopping at least two individual processors (called cores in this sense) into one integrated circuit. In a perfect world, a double core processor would be about twice as capable as a solitary core processor. By and by, the performance pick up is far littler, just around half, because of flawed programming calculations and usage. Expanding the quantity of cores in a processor (i.e. double core, quad-core, and so on.) builds the workload that can be dealt with. This implies the processor can now deal with various nonconcurrent occasions, intrudes, and so on which can incur significant damage on the CPU when overpowered. These cores can be thought of as various floors in a processing plant, with each floor taking care of an alternate task. Here and there, these cores will deal with an indistinguishable tasks from cores adjoining them if a solitary core is insufficient to deal with the data.

Because of particular capacities of present day CPUs, for example, hyper-threading and uncore, which include sharing of genuine CPU assets while going for expanded usage, checking performance levels and equipment use continuously turned into a more unpredictable task. As a reaction, a few CPUs execute extra equipment logic that screens real use of different parts of a CPU and gives different counters accessible to programming; a case is Intel's Performance Counter Monitor innovation.

SYSTEM ON A CHIP

The AMD Geode is a x86 perfect system on a chip

A system on a chip or system on chip (SoC or SOC) is an integrated circuit (IC) that integrates all segments of a computer or other electronic system into a solitary chip. It might contain computerized, simple, blended flag, and frequently radio-recurrence works—all on a solitary chip substrate. SoCs are very normal in the versatile hardware showcase in view of their low power utilization. A run of the mill application is in the zone of installed systems.

The diverge from a microcontroller is one of degree. Microcontrollers ordinarily have under 100 kB of RAM (frequently only a couple of kilobytes) and regularly truly are single-chip-systems, while the term SoC is commonly utilized for all the more capable processors, fit for running programming, for example, the desktop forms of Windows and Linux, which require outer memory chips (streak, RAM) to be valuable, and which are utilized with different outside peripherals. To put it plainly, for bigger systems, the term system on a chip is metaphor, showing specialized bearing more than reality: a high level of chip combination, driving toward lessened assembling costs, and the creation of littler systems. Numerous systems are excessively perplexing, making it impossible to fit on only one chip worked with a processor streamlined for only one of the system's tasks.

When it is not practical to develop a SoC for a specific application, an option is a system in bundle (SiP) including various chips in a solitary bundle. In extensive volumes, SoC is accepted to be more savvy than SiP since it builds the yield of the creation and on the grounds that its bundling is less complex.

Another alternative, as observed for instance in higher end PDAs is bundle on bundle stacking amid board get together. The SoC incorporates processors and various computerized peripherals, and arrives in a ball matrix bundle with lower and upper associations. The lower balls interface with the board and different peripherals, with the upper balls in a ring holding the memory transports used to access NAND streak and DDR2 RAM. Memory bundles could originate from multiple sellers.

AMD Am286ZX/LX, SoC in view of 80286

STRUCTURE

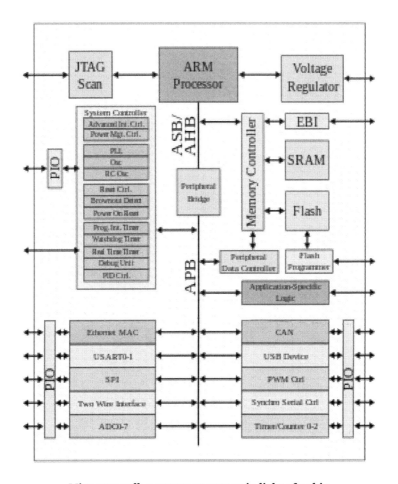

Microcontroller-construct system in light of a chip

A common SoC comprises of:

➢ A microcontroller, microprocessor or computerized flag processor (DSP) core – multiprocessor SoCs (MPSoC) having more than one processor core.

➢ Memory pieces including a determination of ROM, RAM, EEPROM and streak memory

- Timing sources including oscillators and stage bolted circles
- Peripherals including counter-clocks, continuous clocks and power-on reset generators
- Outside interfaces, including industry benchmarks, for example, USB, FireWire, Ethernet, USART, SPI
- Simple interfaces including ADCs and DACs
- Voltage controllers and power management circuits
- **A Bus/transport** – either exclusive or industry-standard, for example, the AMBA transport from ARM Holdings – associates these pieces. DMA controllers course information straightforwardly between outside interfaces and memory, bypassing the processor core and along these lines expanding the information throughput of the SoC.

CONFIGURATION STREAM

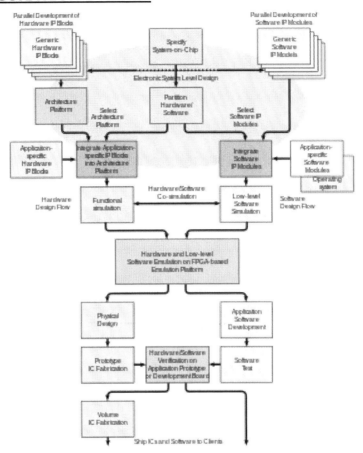

System-on-a-chip configuration stream

A SoC comprises of both the equipment, portrayed above, and the product controlling the microcontroller, microprocessor or DSP cores, peripherals and interfaces. The plan stream for a SoC intends to build up this equipment and programming in parallel.

Most SoCs are created from pre-qualified equipment hinders for the equipment components portrayed above, together with the product drivers that control their operation. Of specific significance are the convention stacks that drive industry-

266

standard interfaces like USB. The equipment pieces are assembled utilizing CAD apparatuses; the product modules are integrated utilizing a product advancement condition.

Chips are checked for logical rightness before being sent to foundry. This procedure is called useful confirmation and it represents a huge segment of the time and vitality exhausted in the chip plan life cycle (despite the fact that the regularly cited figure of 70% is likely an embellishment). With the developing intricacy of chips, equipment check dialects like SystemVerilog, SystemC, e, and OpenVera are being utilized. Bugs found in the confirmation stage are accounted for to the creator.

Generally, engineers have utilized recreation quickening, copying as well as a FPGA model to check and troubleshoot both equipment and programming for SoC plans before tapeout. With high limit and quick aggregation time, increasing speed and copying are intense advances that give wide perceivability into systems. Both advances, notwithstanding, operate gradually, on the request of MHz, which might be essentially slower – up to 100 times slower – than the SoC's working recurrence. Speeding up and copying boxes are likewise very substantial and costly at over US$1,000,000. FPGA models, conversely, utilize FPGAs specifically to empower architects to approve and test at, or near, a system's full working recurrence with genuine boosts. Apparatuses, for example, Certus are utilized to embed tests in the FPGA RTL that mention signals accessible for objective fact. This is utilized to troubleshoot equipment, firmware and programming cooperations over multiple FPGAs with abilities like a logic analyzer.

Once the equipment of the SoC is repaired, the place-and-course period of the outline of an integrated circuit or application-particular integrated circuit (ASIC) happens before it is manufactured.

FABRICATION

SoCs can be manufactured by a few advances, including:

> Full custom
> Standard cell
> Field-programmable gate array (FPGA)

SoC outlines as a rule expend less power and have a lower cost and higher unwavering quality than the multi-chip systems that they supplant. What's more, with less bundles in the system, get together expenses are decreased also.

In any case, as most VLSI plans, the aggregate cost is higher for one vast chip than for a similar usefulness dispersed more than a few littler chips, due to lower yields and higher non-repeating designing expenses.

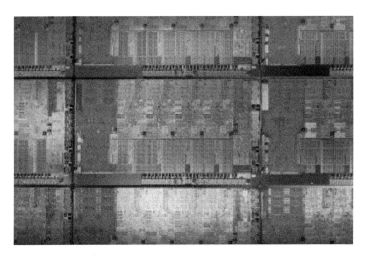

After over 50 years at the highest point of the load, the CPU at long last has some opposition from an upstart called the SoC. For a considerable length of time, you could stroll into a shop and unhesitatingly choose another computer in view of its CPU — and now, everywhere you look, from cell phones to tablets and even a few portable workstations, there are SoCs.

Try not to stress, however, CPUs and SoCs are entirely comparable, and practically everything you think about CPUs can likewise be connected to SoCs.

Notwithstanding the immense accentuation put on CPU innovation and performance, it is at last a very quick adding machine. It fetches information from memory, and afterward plays out some sort of arithmetic (include, duplicate) or logical (and, or, not) operation on that information. The more costly/complex the CPU, the more information it can handle, the speedier your computer.

A CPU itself is not a PC, however — an entire system of other silicon chips is required for that. There must be memory to hold the information, a sound chip to decode and open up your music, a designs processor to draw pictures on your screen, and many littler segments that all have a very essential task.

A SoC, or system-on-a-chip to give its full name, integrates these parts into a solitary silicon chip. Along with a CPU, a SoC as a rule contains a GPU (an illustrations processor), memory, USB controller, control management circuits, and remote radios (Wi-Fi, 3G, 4G LTE, et cetera). While a CPU can't work without many different chips, it's conceivable to construct finish computers with only a solitary SoC.

THE DISTINCTION BETWEEN A SOC AND CPU

The main preferred standpoint of a SoC is its size: A SoC is just a tiny bit bigger than a CPU, but then it contains significantly greater usefulness. On the off chance that you utilize a CPU, it's very difficult to make a computer that is littler than 10cm (4 inches) squared, simply in light of the quantity of individual chips that you have to crush in. Utilizing SoCs, we can put finish computers in cell phones and tablets, and still have a lot of space for batteries.

Because of its very abnormal state of reconciliation and substantially shorter wiring, a SoC likewise utilizes significantly less power — once more, this is a major reward with regards to portable registering. Eliminating the quantity of physical chips implies that it's significantly less expensive to fabricate a computer utilizing a SoC, as well.

Regular PC motherboard (left) versus the fundamental iPad 3 circuit board (right). This picture is generally proportional.

The main genuine detriment of a SoC is an entire absence of adaptability. With your PC, you can put in another CPU, GPU, or RAM whenever — you can't do likewise for your cell phone. Later on you may have the capacity to purchase SoCs that you can space in, but since everything is integrated this will be inefficient and costly in the event that you just need to include more RAM.

ARE CPUS IN TRANSIT OUT

Eventually, SoCs are the subsequent stage after CPUs. In the long run, SoCs will totally devour CPUs. We are as of now observing this with AMD's Llano and Intel's Ivy Bridge CPUs, which integrate a memory controller, PCI Express, and a designs processor onto a similar chip. There will dependably be a business opportunity for broadly useful CPUs, particularly where power and impression are less of an issue, (for example, supercomputers). Versatile and wearable gadgets are the eventual fate of computers, however, as are SoCs.

This fight just applies to the portable market however, and perhaps things like integrated sheets for media focuses and such, yet positively not for desktops, not to mention servers.

CPUs are, and will dependably be the intense blocks of torque that are at the establishment of capable system, SoCs are fit for portable figuring and integrated registering, however they can't stay aware of the capable x86 based CPUs.

Without a doubt, an ever increasing number of parts are integrated into CPUs, however that is totally unique in relation to SoCs, with a CPU you're making inquiries like 'regardless of whether to integrate a memory controller and perhaps basic GPU', with SoCs you're making inquiries like 'regardless of whether to integrate an auxiliary or tertiary interchanges subsystem for Wi-Fi, 3/4G, Bluetooth, or the total memory'.

Yes, for portable stages I think SoCs will make increasingly territory, seeing they're a great deal more power proficient and little, yet when there's any unclear requirement for torque, CPUs and GPUs are placed in separately. Since the improvement of Smartphones and Tablet PC we will soon observe Tablet PC in bigger sizes, why not in 20"? Samsung have as of late declared that they will begin making Amoled shows on adaptable polyamide substrate that will have mark Samsung Youm.

SoC IC will be made in 3D tech expected years where recollections, both DRAM and non-unstable recollections like NAND Flash or surprisingly better with Memristor or different sorts of ReRAM can be made in this 3D IC like IBM and 3M 3D was reported in September 2011, that they will begin to market in end of 2013 (for server processor creators) in end of 2014 to the semiconductor business.

The main current performance increment for PC's that is as yet taking after Moore's Law is performance per watt. Indeed, even the cost per transistor is not dropping as quick as it was on the grounds that the Fab expenses are quickening. Servers will be dropping all the heritage PC parts that consume half of the vitality fundamental for running them. The name of the diversion will be vitality productivity. Removing a large portion of the physical board expected to run a computer cuts the cost of the computer itself also. The iPad 2 costs presumably $35 while the little PC board it was contrasted with is most likely $135 with RAM included. The SoC's have been multiplying in performance every year. The PC has not multiplied over the most recent 3 years. Surely, Intel is seeing the iPad as an immense danger to its reality. Why else would they be spending so much cash advertising thin shape consider tablets? Apple utilizes Intel chips in its own note pads, why Intel doesn't consider this to be a win for their market? Apple is not the only one in doing this either. AMD just acquired the startup that is running SoC servers. What will happen if ARM chips can coordinate Intel in performance? My figure is that will occur in when in 3 years.

Not that I'm a specialist in the venture world, however I know for top of the line shoppers, secluded, adaptable systems is an ABSOLUTE must, particularly on restricted spending plans. Besides, for non-24 hour operation, yielding performance to meet warm and power envelopes is likewise a negative. These two alone will mean the SoC will never totally supplant the CPU. Indeed, even to include further, certain applications have diverse necessities. Gaming, for instance, has an accentuation on Graphics performance, and the designs necessities climb significantly speedier than the prerequisites of CPU's. This by itself implies redesigning SoCs will be very costly. With the secluded system, I can overhaul a maturing GPU and still keep the CPU because of generally unobtrusive CPU prerequisites of gaming. I can at present have a very respectable gaming system with a Core 2 Duo combined with the correct designs processor (say a Radeon 6950). This implies I can inhale new life into a maturing machine at a small amount of the cost. I am just for SoC's, yet they will battle in the market with various requests in view of their rigidity.

I might want to point out that the primary single chip CPU (as it applies to how you're utilizing the term) was the Intel 4004, worked in 1970 - About 45 years prior. Next, I need to point out that it was an awesome propel when computers went from having multiple chips utilized for each kind of task, to utilizing a solitary chip with every one of the systems required for general processing. I don't worry about us utilizing the SoC expression casually to allude to a chip with a specific arrangement of integrated peripherals, however at one time, that was the same than the idea of a CPU.

We simply have new peripherals. Diverse things will in the end be added to the chip bite the dust as they move toward becoming benchmarks, and taken off in the event that they are at no time in the future required. Likewise, as chips turn out to be more best in class, they will have the capacity to cover more capacities also. HD video used to require very much an excessive amount of energy to integrate onto a chip with different capacities, and now, it comes standard. SoC is only an old idea with another name.

So the freshest integrated illustrations will fulfill 80-90 percent of the market. From that point, the integrated versus discrete illustrations will go here and there for some time with discrete designs gradually losing piece of the overall industry until it is only a specialty thing for specific experts, and a couple gamers with very outrageous setups. That point will most likely involve an integrated realistic arrangement coming to the heart of the matter where it show 4K determination at 16 times the polygon fill rate of a PS3 or Xbox360. I would evaluate in the 10-15 year range, however by at that point, desktops themselves will be a decently specialty thing.

Toward the end, this is "Shrewd Devices versus Substantial Computers" or something else "Integrated Motherboards versus Multi-Applicable Mother Boards". On the off chance that a CPU is coercively fastened into a motherboard as yet requiring an indistinguishable parts from some time recently, it will be more invaluable. Macintosh and numerous different organizations have been doing this to their computers for so long it barely bodes well. That is the reason "Macintosh versus PCs" are as yet a fight, on the off chance that you need an organization that does everything for you? Or, on the other hand need an organization that offers it all and you can pick what you need from it and another organization. This article has nothing to do with the vanishing of old computer parts it's truly exactly how we sort out them.

CHAPTER 14: DIGITAL SIGNAL PROCESSING USING ADC AND DAC

OVERVIEW

The majority of the signals straightforwardly experienced in science and designing are persistent: light power that progression with separation; voltage that fluctuates after some time; a substance response rate that relies on upon temperature, and so forth. Analog-to-Digital Conversion (ADC) and Digital-to-Analog Conversion (DAC) are the procedures that enable digital computers to communicate with these ordinary signals.

Digital data is unique in relation to its constant partner in two critical regards: it is inspected, and it is quantized. Both of these confine how much data a digital signal can contain. This article is about data administration: understanding what data you have to hold, and what data you can bear to lose. Thusly, this manages the choice of the examining recurrence, number of bits, and sort of analog sifting required for changing over between the analog and digital domains.

QUANTIZATION

Initial, a touch of trivia. As you most likely are aware, it is a digital computer, not a digit computer. The data prepared is called digital data, not digit data. Why at that point, is analog-to-digital transformation largely called: digitize and digitization, as opposed to digitalize and digitalization? The appropriate response is nothing you would anticipate. At the point when gadgets got around to developing digital methods, the restorative group had as of now grabbed the favored names up almost a century prior. Digitalize and digitalization intends to manage the heart stimulant digitalis.

Figure 3-1 demonstrates the electronic waveforms of a run of the mill analog-to-digital transformation. Figure (an) is the analog signal to be digitized. As appeared by the names on the chart, this signal is a voltage that fluctuates after some time. To make the numbers simpler, we will expect that the voltage can change from 0 to 4.095 volts, comparing to the digital numbers in the vicinity of 0 and 4095 that will be delivered by a 12 bit digitizer. See that the piece outline is broken into two areas, the specimen and-hold (S/H), and the analog-to-digital converter (ADC). As you presumably learned in gadgets classes, the example and-hold is required to keep the voltage entering the ADC steady while the change is occurring. In any case, this is not the reason it is appeared here; breaking the digitization into these two phases is an imperative hypothetical model for understanding digitization. The way that it happens to look like normal hardware is only a blessed reward.

As appeared by the contrast amongst (an) and (b), the yield of the specimen and-hold is permitted to change just at occasional interims, at which time it is made indistinguishable to the momentary estimation of the info signal. Changes in the info signal that happen between these examining times are totally overlooked. That is, testing changes over the free factor (time in this case) from consistent to discrete.

As appeared by the distinction amongst (b) and (c), the ADC produces a whole number an incentive in the vicinity of 0 and 4095 for each of the level districts in (b). This presents a blunder, since every level can be any voltage in the vicinity of 0 and 4.095 volts. For instance, both 2.56000 volts and 2.56001 volts will be changed over into digital number 2560. As it were, quantization changes over the reliant variable (voltage in this case) from consistent to discrete.

See that we painstakingly abstain from looking at (an) and (c), as this would bump the inspecting and quantization together. It is critical that we dissect them independently in light of the fact that they debase the signal in various routes, and in addition being controlled by various parameters in the hardware. There are likewise situations where one is utilized without the other. For example, examining without quantization is utilized as a part of exchanged capacitor channels.

To start with we will take a gander at the impacts of quantization. Any one specimen in the digitized signal can have a most extreme blunder of ±½ LSB (Least Significant Bit, language for the separation between neighboring quantization levels). Figure (d) demonstrates the quantization mistake for this specific illustration, found by subtracting (b) from (c), with the fitting changes. At the end of the day, the digital yield (c), is comparable to the ceaseless information (b), in addition to a quantization mistake (d). A critical component of this examination is that the quantization blunder seems particularly like arbitrary clamor.

This sets the phase for an essential model of quantization mistake. By and large, quantization brings about simply the expansion of a particular measure of irregular clamor to the signal. The added substance commotion is consistently appropriated between $\pm \frac{1}{2}$ LSB, has a mean of zero, and a standard deviation of 1/LSB (0.29 LSB). For instance, passing an analog signal through a 8 bit digitizer includes a rms clamor of: 0.29/256 , or around 1/900 of the full scale esteem. A 12bit change includes a clamor of: 0.29/4096 "" 1/14,000, while a 16 bit transformation includes: 0.29/65536 "" 1/227,000 . Since quantization mistake is an irregular commotion, the quantity of bits decides the exactness of the data. For instance, you may put forth the expression: "We expanded the accuracy of the estimation from 8 to 12 bits." This model is greatly effective, in light of the fact that the irregular clamor produced by quantization will just add to whatever commotion is as of now present in the analog signal.

For instance, envision an analog signal with a greatest adequacy of 1.0 volt, and an irregular commotion of 1.0 millivolt rms. Digitizing this signal to 8 bits brings about 1.0 volt getting to be noticeably digital number 255, and 1.0 millivolt getting to be plainly 0.255 LSB. Irregular clamor signals are consolidated by including their differences. That is, the signals are included quadrature: sqrt A 2 + sqrt B 2 = C . The aggregate clamor on the digitized signal is = 0.386 LSB. This is an expansion of around half over the clamor as of now in the analog signal. Digitizing this same signal to 12 bits would deliver practically no expansion in the commotion, and nothing would be lost because of quantization. At the point when confronted with the choice of what number of bits are required in a framework, ask two inquiries: (1) How much commotion is now present in the analog signal? (2) How much commotion can be endured in the digital signal?

At the point when isn't this model of quantization legitimate? Just when the quantization mistake can't be dealt with as irregular. The main normal event of this is the point at which the analog signal stays at about a similar incentive for some sequential specimens, as is shown in Fig.3-2a. The yield stays stuck on the same digital number for some specimens in succession, despite the fact that the analog signal might be switching up to ±½ LSB. Rather than being an added substance irregular clamor, the quantization mistake now resembles a thresholding impact or abnormal twisting.

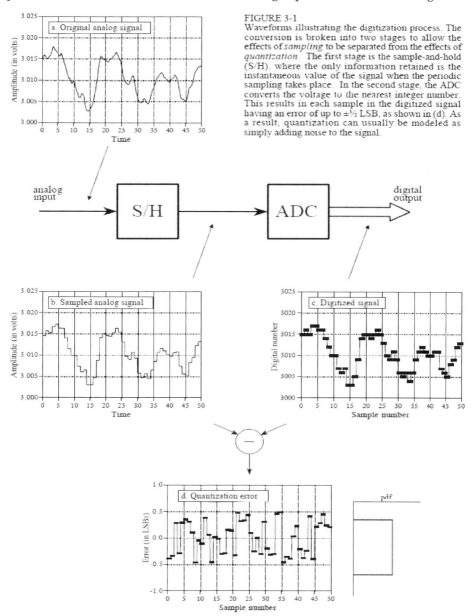

FIGURE 3-1
Waveforms illustrating the digitization process. The conversion is broken into two stages to allow the effects of *sampling* to be separated from the effects of *quantization*. The first stage is the sample-and-hold (S/H), where the only information retained is the instantaneous value of the signal when the periodic sampling takes place. In the second stage, the ADC converts the voltage to the nearest integer number. This results in each sample in the digitized signal having an error of up to ±½ LSB, as shown in (d). As a result, quantization can usually be modeled as simply adding noise to the signal.

DITHERING

Dithering is a typical strategy for enhancing the digitization of these gradually fluctuating signals. a little measure of irregular clamor is added to the analog signal. In this case, the additional clamor is typically disseminated with a standard deviation of 2/3 LSB, bringing about a crest to-top sufficiency of around 3 LSB. Figure (c) indicates how the expansion of this dithering clamor has influenced the digitized signal. Notwithstanding when the first analog signal is changing by not as much as ±½ LSB, the additional clamor makes the digital yield haphazardly flip between neighboring levels.

To see how this enhances the circumstance, envision that the info signal is a consistent analog voltage of 3.0001 volts, making it one-tenth of the path between the digital levels 3000 and 3001. Without dithering, taking 10,000 specimens of this signal would deliver 10,000 indistinguishable numbers, all having the estimation of 3000. Next, rehash the idea try different things with a little measure of dithering clamor included. The 10,000 esteems will now waver between (at least two) levels, with around 90% having an estimation of 3000, and 10% having an estimation of 3001. Taking the normal of every one of the 10,000 esteems brings about something near 3000.1. Despite the fact that a solitary estimation has the inalienable ±½ LSB confinement, the insights of countless specimens can improve. This is a significant unusual circumstance including commotion gives more data.

Circuits for dithering can be very refined, for example, utilizing a computer to create arbitrary numbers, and afterward going them through a DAC to deliver the additional clamor. After digitization, the computer can subtract the arbitrary numbers from the digital signal utilizing drifting point math.

This exquisite method is called subtractive dither, however is just utilized as a part of the most expound frameworks. The most straightforward technique, despite the fact that not generally conceivable, is to utilize the clamor effectively show in the analog signal for dithering.

THE SAMPLING THEOREM

The meaning of appropriate sampling is very straightforward. Assume you test a consistent signal in some way. On the off chance that you can precisely recreate the analog signal from the examples, you more likely than not done the sampling legitimately. Regardless of the possibility that the inspected data seems confounding or fragmented, the key data has been caught on the off chance that you can turn around the procedure.

Figure 3-3 demonstrates a few sinusoids previously, then after the fact digitization. The ceaseless line speaks to the analog signal entering the ADC, while the square markers are the digital signal leaving the ADC. In (a), the analog signal is a consistent DC esteem, a cosine wave of zero recurrence. Since the analog signal is a progression of straight lines between each of the specimens, the greater part of the data expected to remake the analog signal is contained in the digital data. As indicated by our definition, this is legitimate sampling.

The sine wave appeared in (b) has a recurrence of 0.09 of the sampling rate. This may speak to, for instance, a 90 cycle/second sine wave being tested at 1000 specimens/second. Communicated in another route, there are 11.1 examples assumed control over each total cycle of the sinusoid. This circumstance is more entangled than the past case, in light of the fact that the analog signal can't be recreated by just drawing straight lines between the data focuses. Do these specimens legitimately speak to the analog signal? The appropriate response is yes, in light of the fact that no other sinusoid, or mix of sinusoids, will create this example of tests (inside the sensible requirements recorded beneath). These examples compare to just a single analog signal, and thusly the analog signal can be precisely remade. Once more, an occurrence of legitimate sampling.

In (c), the circumstance is made more troublesome by expanding the sine wave's recurrence to 0.31 of the sampling rate. This outcomes in just 3.2 examples for each sine wave cycle. Here the examples are sparse to the point that they don't seem to take after the general pattern of the analog signal. Do these specimens legitimately speak to the analog waveform? Once more, the appropriate response is yes, and for the very same reason. The examples are an interesting portrayal of the analog signal. The greater part of the data expected to remake the constant waveform is contained in the digital data. How you approach doing this will be talked about later in this article. Clearly, it must be more complex than simply drawing straight lines between the data focuses. As interesting as it appears, this is legitimate sampling as indicated by our definition.

In (d), the analog recurrence is pushed significantly higher to 0.95 of the sampling rate, with a unimportant 1.05 examples for each sine wave cycle. Do these examples legitimately speak to the data? No, they don't! The examples speak to an alternate sine wave from the one contained in the analog signal. Specifically, the first sine wave of 0.95 recurrence distorts itself as a sine wave of 0.05 recurrence in the digital signal. This wonder of sinusoids changing recurrence amid sampling is called associating. Similarly as a criminal may go up against an expected name or character (a nom de plume), the sinusoid accept another recurrence that is not its own. Since the digital data is at no time in the future exceptionally identified with a specific analog signal, an unambiguous remaking is unimaginable. There is nothing in the examined data to recommend that the first analog signal had a recurrence of 0.95 instead of 0.05. The sine wave has shrouded its actual character totally; the ideal wrongdoing has been submitted! As indicated by our definition, this is a case of uncalled for sampling.

This line of thinking prompts a turning point in DSP, the sampling theorem. Every now and again this is known as the Shannon sampling theorem, or the Nyquist sampling theorem, after the creators of 1940s papers on the theme. The sampling theorem shows that a consistent signal can be appropriately tested, just on the off chance that it doesn't contain recurrence parts over one-portion of the sampling rate. For example, a sampling rate of 2,000 specimens/second requires the analog signal to be made out of frequencies underneath 1000 cycles/second. On the off chance that frequencies over this utmost are available in the signal, they will be associated to frequencies in the vicinity of 0 and 1000 cycles/second, consolidating with whatever data that was genuinely there.

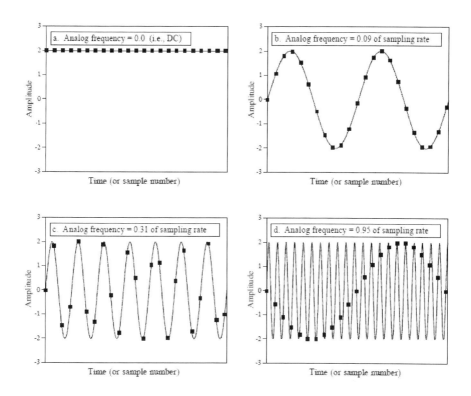

FIGURE 3-3

Illustration of proper and improper sampling. A continuous signal is sampled *properly* if the samples contain all the information needed to recreated the original waveform. Figures (a), (b), and (c) illustrate *proper sampling* of three sinusoidal waves. This is certainly not obvious, since the samples in (c) do not even appear to capture the shape of the waveform. Nevertheless, each of these continuous signals forms a unique one-to-one pair with its pattern of samples. This guarantees that reconstruction can take place. In (d), the frequency of the analog sine wave is greater than the Nyquist frequency (one-half of the sampling rate). This results in *aliasing*, where the frequency of the sampled data is different from the frequency of the continuous signal. Since aliasing has corrupted the information, the original signal cannot be reconstructed from the samples.

Two terms are generally utilized while talking about the sampling theorem: the Nyquist frequency and the Nyquist rate. Sadly, their importance is not institutionalized.

To comprehend this, consider an analog signal made out of frequencies amongst DC and 3 kHz. To legitimately digitize this signal it must be examined at 6,000 examples/sec (6 kHz) or higher. Assume we test at 8,000 specimens/sec (8 kHz), permitting frequencies amongst DC and 4 kHz to be appropriately spoken to. In this circumstance there are four vital frequencies: (1) the most astounding frequency in the signal, 3 kHz; (2) twice this frequency, 6 kHz; (3) the sampling rate, 8 kHz; and (4) one-a large portion of the sampling rate, 4 kHz. Which of these four is the Nyquist frequency and which is the Nyquist rate? It depends who you inquire! The greater parts of the conceivable blends are utilized. Luckily, most creators are mindful to characterize how they are utilizing the terms.

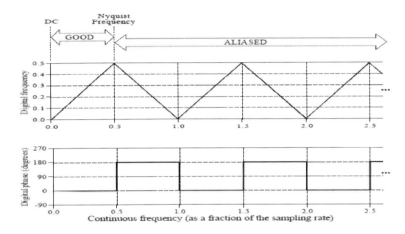

FIGURE 3-4
Conversion of analog frequency into digital frequency during sampling. Continuous signals with a frequency less than one-half of the sampling rate are directly converted into the corresponding digital frequency. Above one-half of the sampling rate, aliasing takes place, resulting in the frequency being misrepresented in the digital data. Aliasing always changes a higher frequency into a lower frequency between 0 and 0.5. In addition, aliasing may also change the phase of the signal by 180 degrees.

Figure 3-4 indicates how frequencies are changed amid associating. The key indicate recollect is that a digital signal can't contain frequencies over one-a large portion of the sampling rate (i.e., the Nyquist frequency/rate). At the point when the frequency of the consistent wave is beneath the Nyquist rate, the frequency of the examined data is a match. In any case, when the ceaseless signal's frequency is over the Nyquist rate, associating changes the frequency into something that can be spoken to in the inspected data. As appeared by the crisscrossing line in Fig. 3-4, each consistent frequency over the Nyquist rate has a relating digital frequency in the vicinity of zero and one-a large portion of the sampling rate. In the event that there happens to be a sinusoid as of now at this lower frequency, the associated signal will add to it, bringing about lost data. Associating is a twofold revile; data can be lost about the higher and the lower frequency. Assume you are given a digital signal containing a frequency of 0.2 of the sampling rate.

On the off chance that this signal were gotten by legitimate sampling, the first analog signal more likely than not had a frequency of 0.2. In the event that associating occurred amid sampling, the digital frequency of 0.2 could have originated from any of a vast number of frequencies in the analog signal: 0.2, 0.8, 1.2, 1.8, 2.2.

Similarly as associating can change the frequency amid sampling, it can likewise change the stage. For instance, glance back at the associated signal in Fig. 3-3d. The associated digital signal is modified from the first analog signal; one is a sine wave while the other is a negative sine wave. As it were, associating has changed the frequency and presented a 180° stage move. Just two stage movements are conceivable: 0° (no stage move) and 180° (reversal). The zero stage move happens for analog frequencies of 0 to 0.5, 1.0 to 1.5, 2.0 to 2.5, and so forth. A modified stage happens for analog frequencies of 0.5 to 1.0, 1.5 to 2.0, 2.5 to 3.0, et cetera.

Presently we will plunge into a more point by point investigation of sampling and how associating happens. Our general objective is to comprehend what happens to the data when a signal is changed over from a ceaseless to a discrete frame. The issue is, these are altogether different things; one is a consistent waveform while the other is a variety of numbers. This "one type to a totally different type" correlation makes the examination extremely troublesome. The arrangement is to present a hypothetical idea called the motivation prepare.

Figure 3-5a demonstrates an illustration analog signal. Figure (c) demonstrates the signal examined by utilizing a drive prepare. The drive prepare is a nonstop signal comprising of a progression of restricted spikes (motivations) that match the first signal at the sampling moments. Every motivation is imperceptibly thin. Between these sampling times the estimation of the waveform is zero. Remember that the motivation prepare is a hypothetical idea, not a waveform that can exist in an electronic circuit.

Since both the first analog signal and the motivation prepare are constant waveforms, we can make an "apples-apples" correlation between the two.

Presently we have to look at the connection between the motivation prepare and the discrete signal (a variety of numbers). This one is simple; regarding data content, they are indistinguishable. On the off chance that one is known, it is trifling to ascertain the other. Think about these as various finishes of an extension going between the analog and digital universes. This implies we have accomplished our general objective once we comprehend the results of changing the waveform in Fig. 3-5a into the waveform in Fig. 3.5c.

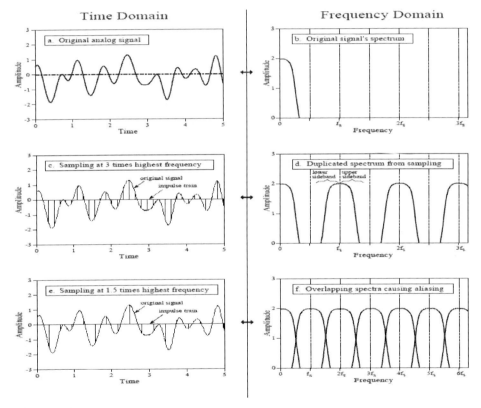

FIGURE 3-5
The sampling theorem in the time and frequency domains. Figures (a) and (b) show an analog signal composed of frequency components between zero and 0.33 of the sampling frequency, f_s. In (c), the analog signal is sampled by converting it to an impulse train. In the frequency domain, (d), this results in the spectrum being duplicated into an infinite number of upper and lower sidebands. Since the original frequencies in (b) exist undistorted in (d), proper sampling has taken place. In comparison, the analog signal in (e) is sampled at 0.66 of the sampling frequency, a value exceeding the Nyquist rate. This results in aliasing, indicated by the sidebands in (f) overlapping.

Three consistent waveforms are appeared in the left-hand section in Fig. 3-5. The relating frequency spectra of these signals are shown in the right-hand segment. This ought to be a commonplace idea from your insight into gadgets; each waveform can be seen as being made out of sinusoids of shifting plentifulness and frequency. Later we will talk about the frequency space in detail.

Figure (a) demonstrates an analog signal we wish to test. As demonstrated by its frequency range in (b), it is made just out of frequency segments in the vicinity of 0 and around 0.33 fs, where fs is the sampling frequency we plan to utilize. For instance, this may be a discourse signal that has been sifted to evacuate all frequencies over 3.3 kHz. Correspondingly, fs would be 10 kHz (10,000 examples/second), our proposed sampling rate.

Sampling the signal in (a) by utilizing a motivation prepare produces the signal appeared in (c), and its frequency range appeared in (d). This range is a duplication of the range of the first signal. Each various of the sampling frequency, fs, 2fs, 3fs, 4fs, and so on., has gotten a duplicate and a left-for-right flipped duplicate of the first frequency range. The duplicate is known as the upper sideband, while the flipped duplicate is known as the lower sideband.

Sampling has generated new frequencies. Is this legitimate sampling? The appropriate response is yes, in light of the fact that the signal in (c) can be changed once more into the signal in (a) by dispensing with all frequencies above ½fs. That is, an analog low-pass channel will change over the drive prepare, (b), again into the first analog signal, (a).

In the event that you are as of now comfortable with the essentials of DSP, here is a more specialized clarification of why this unearthly duplication happens. (Overlook this passage in the event that you are new to DSP). In the time area, sampling is accomplished by increasing the first signal by a motivation prepare of solidarity adequacy spikes. The frequency range of this solidarity abundancy motivation prepare is additionally a solidarity adequacy drive prepare, with the spikes happening at products of the sampling frequency, fs, 2fs, 3fs, 4fs, and so on. At the point when two time space signals are increased, their frequency spectra are convolved. This outcomes in the first range being copied to the area of each spike in the motivation prepare's range. Seeing the first signal as made out of both positive and negative frequencies represents the upper and lower sidebands, individually. This is the same as abundancy regulation.

Figure (e) demonstrates a case of ill-advised sampling, coming about because of too low of sampling rate. The analog signal still contains frequencies up to 3.3 kHz, however the sampling rate has been brought down to 5 kHz. See that fS , 2fS , 3fS · along the even hub are separated nearer in (f) than in (d).

The frequency range, (f), demonstrates the issue: the copied segments of the range have attacked the band in the vicinity of zero and one-portion of the sampling frequency. In spite of the fact that (f) demonstrates these covering frequencies as holding their separate personality, in real practice they include framing a solitary confounded wreckage. Since there is no real way to separate the covering frequencies, data is lost, and the first signal can't be recreated. This cover happens when the analog signal contains frequencies more noteworthy than one-a large portion of the sampling rate, that is, we have demonstrated the sampling theorem.

DIGITAL-TO-ANALOG CONVERSION

In principle, the most straightforward technique for digital-to-analog conversion is to pull the examples from memory and change over them into a drive prepare. This is illustrated in Fig. 3-6a, with the comparing frequency range in (b). As simply portrayed, the first analog signal can be impeccably recreated by passing this drive prepare through a low-pass channel, with the cutoff frequency equivalent to one-portion of the sampling rate. At the end of the day, the first signal and the drive prepare have indistinguishable frequency spectra underneath the Nyquist frequency (one-a large portion of the sampling rate). At higher frequencies, the drive prepare contains a duplication of this data, while the first analog signal contains nothing (accepting associating did not happen).

While this technique is numerically immaculate, it is hard to generate the required restricted heartbeats in hardware. To get around this, about all DACs operate by holding the last an incentive until another example is gotten. This is known as a zeroth-arrange hold, what might as well be called the specimen and-hold utilized amid ADC. (A first-arrange hold is straight lines between the focuses, a moment arrange hold utilizes parabolas,..). The zeroth-arrange hold delivers the staircase appearance appeared in (c).

In the frequency area, the zeroth-arrange hold brings about the range of the motivation, prepare being duplicated by the dull bend appeared in (d), given by the condition:

High frequency sufficiency decreases because of the zeroth-arrange hold. This bend is plotted in Fig. 3-6d. The sampling frequency is spoken to by fS . For f = 0, H(f) = 1.

$$H(f) = \left| \frac{\sin(\pi f / f_s)}{\pi f / f_s} \right|$$

This is of the general form: sin (rcx) /(rcx), called the sinc function or sinc(x)

On the off chance that you as of now have extensive experience with this material, the zeroth-arrange hold can be comprehended as the convolution of the motivation prepare with a rectangular heartbeat, having a width equivalent to the sampling time frame. This outcomes in the frequency area being duplicated by the Fourier change of the rectangular heartbeat, i.e., the sinc work. In Fig. (d), the light line demonstrates the frequency range of the drive prepare (the "right" range), while the dull line demonstrates the sinc. The frequency range of the zeroth request hold signal is equivalent to the result of these two bends.

The analog channel used to change over the zeroth-arrange hold signal, (c), into the remade signal, (f), needs to do two things: (1) expel all frequencies over one-portion of the sampling rate, and (2) help the frequencies by the proportional of the zeroth-request hold's impact, i.e., 1/sinc(x). This adds up to an intensification of around 36% at one-portion of the sampling frequency. Figure (e) demonstrates the perfect frequency reaction of this analog channel.

This 1/sinc(x) frequency lift can be taken care of in four ways: (1) disregard it and acknowledge the outcomes, (2) outline an analog channel to incorporate the 1/sinc(x) reaction, (3) utilize a favor multirate procedure depicted later in this article, or (4) make the adjustment in programming before the DAC.

Before leaving this segment on sampling, we have to disperse a typical myth about analog versus digital signals. As this article has appeared, the measure of data conveyed in a digital signal is restricted in two ways: First, the quantity of bits per test confines the determination of the reliant variable. That is, little changes in the signal's sufficiency might be lost in the quantization commotion. Second, the sampling rate constrains the determination of the autonomous variable, i.e., firmly separated occasions in the analog signal might be lost between the examples. This is another method for saying that frequencies over one-a large portion of the sampling rate are lost.

Here is the myth: "Since analog signals utilize persistent parameters, they have unendingly great determination in both the free and the needy factors." Not genuine! Analog signals are constrained by an indistinguishable two issues from digital signals: clamor and data transmission (the most noteworthy frequency permitted in the signal). The commotion in an analog signal restricts the estimation of the waveform's sufficiency, similarly as quantization clamor does in a digital signal. In like manner, the capacity to separate firmly divided occasions in an analog signal relies on upon the most noteworthy frequency permitted in the waveform. To comprehend this, envision an analog signal containing two firmly dispersed heartbeats.

In the event that we put the signal through a low-pass channel (evacuating the high frequencies), the beats will obscure into a solitary blob. For example, an analog signal shaped from frequencies amongst DC and 10 kHz will have the very same determination as a digital signal examined at 20 kHz. It must, since the sampling theorem ensures that the two contain a similar data.

Time Domain

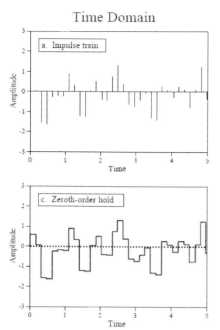

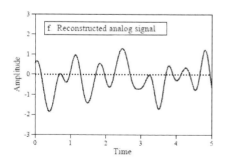

Frequency Domain

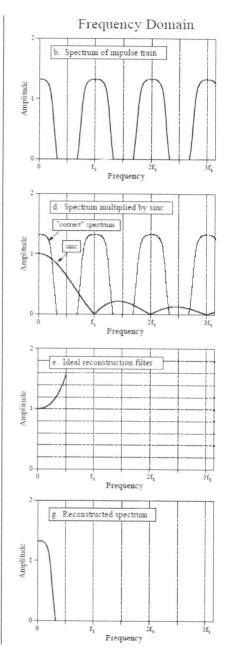

FIGURE 3-6

Analysis of digital-to-analog conversion. In (a), the digital
data are converted into an impulse train, with the spectrum
in (b). This is changed into the reconstructed signal, (f), by
using an electronic low-pass filter to remove frequencies
above one-half the sampling rate [compare (b) and (g)].
However, most electronic DACs create a zeroth-order hold
waveform, (c), instead of an impulse train. The spectrum
of the zeroth-order hold is equal to the spectrum of the
impulse train multiplied by the sinc function shown in (d).
To convert the zeroth-order hold into the reconstructed
signal, the analog filter must remove all frequencies above
the Nyquist rate, *and* correct for the sinc, as shown in (e).

ANALOG FILTERS FOR DATA CONVERSION

Figure 3-7 demonstrates a piece chart of a DSP framework, as the sampling theorem manages it ought to be. Before experiencing the analog-to-digital converter, the information signal is handled with an electronic low-pass channel to expel all frequencies over the Nyquist frequency (one-a large portion of the sampling rate).

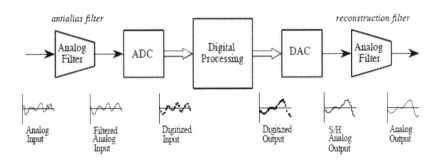

FIGURE 3-7

Analog electronic filters used to comply with the sampling theorem. The electronic filter placed before an ADC is called an *antialias filter*. It is used to remove frequency components above one-half of the sampling rate that would alias during the sampling. The electronic filter placed after a DAC is called a *reconstruction filter*. It also eliminates frequencies above the Nyquist rate, and may include a correction for the zeroth-order hold.

This is done to anticipate associating amid sampling, and is correspondingly called an antialias channel. On the flip side, the digitized signal is gone through a digital-to-analog converter and another low-pass channel set to the Nyquist frequency. This yield channel is known as a remaking channel, and may incorporate the already depicted zeroth-arrange hold frequency support. Sadly, there is a significant issue with this basic model: the confinements of electronic filters can be as awful as the issues they are attempting to forestall.

On the off chance that your principle intrigue is in programming, you are most likely suspecting that you don't have to peruse this area. Off-base! Regardless of the possibility that you have promised never to touch an oscilloscope, a comprehension of the properties of analog filters is vital for effective DSP. To start with, the attributes of each digitized signal you experience will rely on upon what sort of antialias channel was utilized when it was procured. In the event that you don't comprehend the way of the

290

antialias channel, you can't comprehend the way of the digital signal. Second, the eventual fate of DSP is to supplant equipment with programming. For instance, the multirate systems exhibited later in this article lessen the requirement for antialias and recreation filters by favor programming traps. On the off chance that you don't comprehend the equipment, you can't plan programming to supplant it. Third, a lot of DSP is identified with digital channel plan. A typical strategy is to begin with a comparable analog channel, and change over it into programming.

Three sorts of analog filters are regularly utilized: Chebyshev, Butterworth, and Bessel (additionally called a Thompson channel). Each of these is intended to enhance an alternate execution parameter. The many-sided quality of each channel can be balanced by choosing the quantity of shafts and zeros, scientific terms that will be talked about in later. The more shafts in a channel, the more gadgets it requires, and the better it performs. Each of these names portray what the channel does, not a specific game plan of resistors and capacitors. For instance, a six shaft Bessel channel can be executed by a wide range of sorts of circuits, all of which have a similar general attributes. For DSP purposes, the attributes of these filters are more critical than how they are built. In any case, we will begin with a short portion on the electronic outline of these filters to give a general system.

Figure 3-8 demonstrates a typical building obstruct for analog channel outline, the adjusted Sallen-Key circuit. This is named after the creators of a 1950s paper depicting the system. The circuit demonstrated is a two shaft low-pass channel that can be designed as any of the three essential sorts. Table 3-1 gives the fundamental data to choose the suitable resistors and capacitors. For instance, to outline a 1 kHz, 2 shaft Butterworth channel, Table 3-1 gives the parameters: k1 = 0.1592 and k2 = 0.586. Subjectively choosing R1 = 10K and C = 0.01uF (regular esteems for operation amp circuits), R and Rf can be figured as 15.95K and 5.86K, individually. Adjusting these last two esteems to the closest 1% standard resistors, brings about R = 15.8K and R = 5.90K All of the parts ought to be 1% exactness or better.

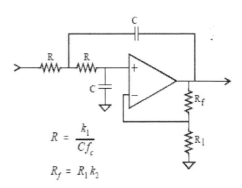

FIGURE 3-8
The modified Sallen-Key circuit, a building block for active filter design. The circuit shown implements a 2 pole low-pass filter. Higher order filters (more poles) can be formed by cascading stages. Find k_1 and k_2 from Table 3-1, arbitrarily select R_1 and C (try 10K and 0.01μF), and then calculate R and R_f from the equations in the figure. The parameter, f_c, is the cutoff frequency of the filter, in hertz.

$$R = \frac{k_1}{Cf_c}$$

$$R_f = R_1 k_2$$

TABLE 3-1
Parameters for designing Bessel, Butterworth, and Chebyshev (6% ripple) filters.

# poles		Bessel k_1	Bessel k_2	Butterworth k_1	Butterworth k_2	Chebyshev k_1	Chebyshev k_2
2	stage 1	0.1251	0.268	0.1592	0.586	0.1293	0.842
4	stage 1	0.1111	0.084	0.1592	0.152	0.2666	0.582
	stage 2	0.0991	0.759	0.1592	1.235	0.1544	1.660
6	stage 1	0.0990	0.040	0.1592	0.068	0.4019	0.537
	stage 2	0.0941	0.364	0.1592	0.586	0.2072	1.448
	stage 3	0.0834	1.023	0.1592	1.483	0.1574	1.846
8	stage 1	0.0894	0.024	0.1592	0.038	0.5359	0.522
	stage 2	0.0867	0.213	0.1592	0.337	0.2657	1.379
	stage 3	0.0814	0.593	0.1592	0.889	0.1848	1.711
	stage 4	0.0726	1.184	0.1592	1.610	0.1582	1.913

The specific operation amp utilized isn't basic, the length of the solidarity pick up frequency is more than 30 to 100 times higher than the channel's cutoff frequency. This is a simple necessity the length of the channel's cutoff frequency is underneath around 100 kHz.

Four, six, and eight post filters are framed by falling 2,3, and 4 of these circuits, separately. For instance, Fig. 3-9 demonstrates the schematic of a 6 shaft Bessel channel made by falling three phases. Each stage has diverse esteems for k1 and k2 as given by Table 3-1, bringing about various resistors and capacitors being utilized. Require a high-pass channel? Essentially swap the R and C parts in the circuits (allowing Rf and R1 to sit unbothered).

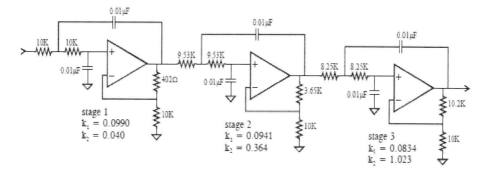

FIGURE 3-9
A six pole Bessel filter formed by cascading three Sallen-Key circuits. This is a low-pass filter with a cutoff frequency of 1 kHz.

This kind of circuit is extremely basic for the little amount assembling and R&D applications; in any case, genuine generation requires the channel to be made as an integrated circuit. The issue is, it is hard to make resistors specifically in silicon. The appropriate response is the exchanged capacitor channel. Figure 3-10 illustrates its operation by contrasting it with a basic RC organize. In the event that a stage capacity is bolstered into a RC low-pass channel, the yield rises exponentially until it coordinates the information. The voltage on the capacitor doesn't change momentarily, in light of the fact that the resistor limits the stream of electrical charge.

The exchanged capacitor channel operates by supplanting the essential resistor-capacitor connect with two capacitors and an electronic switch. The recently included capacitor is considerably littler in incentive than the effectively existing capacitor, say, 1% of its esteem. The switch then again interfaces the little capacitor between the information and the yield at a high frequency, ordinarily 100 times quicker than the cutoff frequency of the channel. At the point when the change is associated with the information, the little capacitor quickly charges to whatever voltage is directly on the info. At the point when the change is associated with the yield, the charge on the little capacitor is exchanged to the substantial capacitor. In a resistor, the rate of charge exchange is dictated by its resistance. In an exchanged capacitor circuit, the rate of charge exchange is dictated by the estimation of the little capacitor and by the exchanging frequency. This outcomes in an extremely valuable element of exchanged capacitor filters: the cutoff frequency of the channel is straightforwardly corresponding to the clock frequency used to drive the switches. This makes the exchanged capacitor channel perfect for data procurement frameworks that operate with more than one sampling rate. These are anything but difficult to-utilize gadgets; pay ten bucks and have the execution of an eight post channel inside a solitary 8 stick IC.

This sort of circuit is extremely basic for little amount assembling and R&D applications; notwithstanding, genuine generation requires the channel to be made as an integrated circuit. The issue is, it is hard to make resistors straightforwardly in silicon. The appropriate response is the exchanged capacitor channel. Figure 3-10 illustrates its operation by contrasting it with a basic RC arrange. In the event that a stage capacity is nourished into a RC low-pass channel, the yield rises exponentially until it coordinates the information. The voltage on the capacitor doesn't change promptly, in light of the fact that the resistor limits the stream of electrical charge.

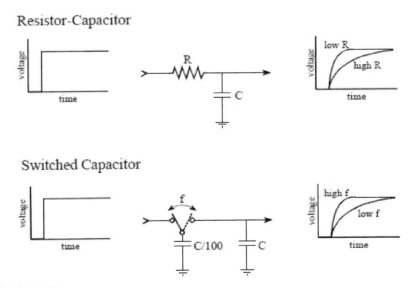

FIGURE 3-10
Switched capacitor filter operation. Switched capacitor filters use switches and capacitors to mimic resistors. As shown by the equivalent step responses, two capacitors and one switch can perform the same function as a resistor-capacitor network.

Now for the important part: the characteristics of the three classic filter types. The first performance

Parameter we need to investigate is cutoff frequency sharpness. A low-pass channel is intended to piece all frequencies over the cutoff frequency (the stopband), while passing all frequencies underneath (the passband). Figure 3-11 demonstrates the frequency reaction of these three filters on a logarithmic (dB) scale. These diagrams are appeared for filters with a one hertz cutoff frequency, yet they can be specifically scaled to whatever cutoff frequency you have to utilize. How do these filters rate? The Chebyshev is unmistakably the best, the Butterworth is more regrettable, and the Bessel is totally terrible! As you likely induced, this is the thing that the Chebyshev is intended to do, move off (drop in sufficiency) as quickly as could be allowed.

Sadly, even a 8 shaft Chebyshev isn't on a par with you might want for an antialias channel. For instance, envision a 12 bit framework sampling at 10,000 examples for each second. The sampling theorem directs that any frequency over 5 kHz will be associated, something you need to keep away from. With a little mystery, you choose that all frequencies over 5 kHz must be lessened in abundancy by an element of 100, guaranteeing that any associated frequencies will have a plentifulness of short of what one percent. Taking a gander at Fig. 3-11c, you find that a 8 shaft Chebyshev channel, with a cutoff frequency of 1 hertz, doesn't achieve a weakening (signal diminishment) of 100 until around 1.35 hertz. Scaling this to the illustration, the channel's cutoff frequency must be set to 3.7 kHz so that everything over 5 kHz will have the required lessening. This outcomes in the frequency band between 3.7 kHz and 5 kHz being squandered on the deficient move off of the analog channel.

An unpretentious point: the weakening element of 100 in this case is likely adequate despite the fact that there are 4096 stages in 12 bits. From Fig. 3-4, 5100 hertz will pseudonym to 4900 hertz, 6000 hertz will nom de plume to 4000 hertz, and so on. You couldn't care less what the amplitudes of the signals in the vicinity of 5000 and 6300 hertz are, on the grounds that they false name into the unusable district between 3700 hertz and 5000 hertz. All together for a frequency to assumed name into the channel's passband (0 to 3.7 kHz), it must be more prominent than 6300 hertz, or 1.7

times the channel's cutoff frequency of 3700 hertz. As appeared in Fig. 3-11c, the weakening given by a 8 post Chebyshev channel at 1.7 times the cutoff frequency is around 1300, substantially more satisfactory than the 100 we began the investigation with. The good to this story: In many frameworks, the frequency band between around 0.4 and 0.5 of the sampling frequency is an unusable no man's land of channel move off and associated signals. This is an immediate aftereffect of the confinements of analog filters.

The frequency reaction of the ideal low-pass channel is level over the whole passband. The majority of the filters look extraordinary in this regard in Fig. 3-11, yet simply because the vertical hub is shown on a logarithmic scale. Another story is advised when the charts are changed over to a straight vertical scale, as is appeared in Fig. 3-12. Passband swell can now be found in the Chebyshev channel (wavy varieties in the plentifulness of the passed frequencies). Actually, the Chebyshev channel gets its fantastic move off by permitting this passband swell. At the point when more passband swell is permitted in a channel, a speedier move off can be accomplished. All the Chebyshev filters outlined by utilizing Table 3-1 have a passband swell of around 6% (0.5 dB), a great bargain, and a typical decision. A comparative outline, the elliptic channel, permits swell in both the passband and the stopband. Albeit harder to outline, elliptic filters can accomplish a far superior tradeoff between move off and passband swell.

In correlation, the Butterworth channel is advanced to give the most keen move off conceivable without permitting swell in the passband. It is generally called the maximally level channel, and is indistinguishable to a Chebyshev intended for zero passband swell. The Bessel channel has no swell in the passband, however the move off far more awful than the Butterworth.

The last parameter to assess is the progression reaction, how the channel reacts when the info quickly changes starting with one esteem then onto the next. Figure 3-13 demonstrates the progression reaction of each of the three filters. The level pivot is appeared for filters with a 1 hertz cutoff frequency, however can be scaled (conversely) for higher cutoff frequencies. For instance, a 1000 hertz cutoff frequency would demonstrate a stage reaction in milliseconds, as opposed to seconds. The Butterworth and Chebyshev filters overshoot and show ringing (motions that gradually diminishing in sufficiency). In correlation, the Bessel channel has neither of these dreadful issues.

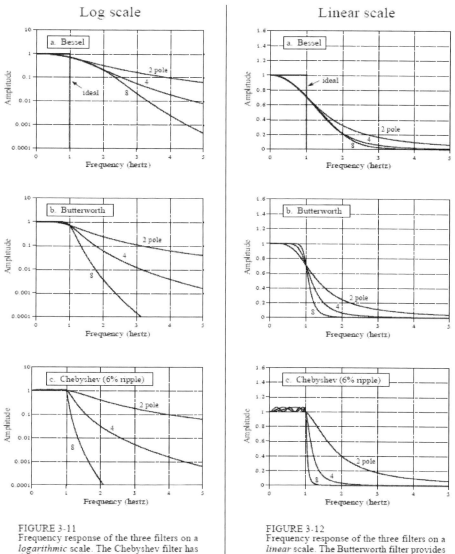

FIGURE 3-11
Frequency response of the three filters on a *logarithmic* scale. The Chebyshev filter has the sharpest roll-off.

FIGURE 3-12
Frequency response of the three filters on a *linear* scale. The Butterworth filter provides the flattest passband.

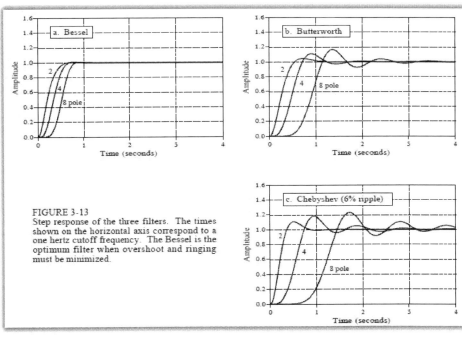

FIGURE 3-13
Step response of the three filters. The times shown on the horizontal axis correspond to a one hertz cutoff frequency. The Bessel is the optimum filter when overshoot and ringing must be minimized.

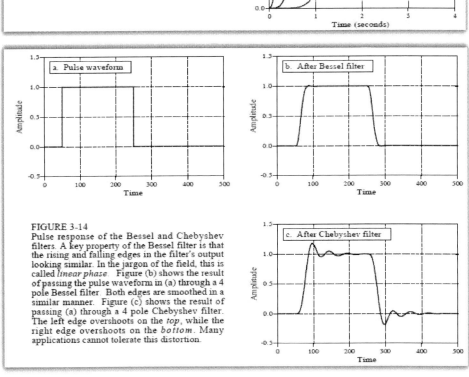

FIGURE 3-14
Pulse response of the Bessel and Chebyshev filters. A key property of the Bessel filter is that the rising and falling edges in the filter's output looking similar. In the jargon of the field, this is called *linear phase*. Figure (b) shows the result of passing the pulse waveform in (a) through a 4 pole Bessel filter. Both edges are smoothed in a similar manner. Figure (c) shows the result of passing (a) through a 4 pole Chebyshev filter. The left edge overshoots on the *top*, while the right edge overshoots on the *bottom*. Many applications cannot tolerate this distortion.

298

Figure 3-14 additionally illustrates this extremely positive normal for the Bessel channel. Figure (a) demonstrates a heartbeat waveform, which can be seen as a rising stride taken after by a falling stride. Figures (b) and (c) indicate how this waveform would show up after Bessel and Chebyshev filters, individually. In the event that this were a video signal, for example, the contortion presented by the Chebyshev channel would be wrecking! The overshoot would change the splendor of the edges of items contrasted with their focuses. More awful yet, the left half of articles would look brilliant, while the correct side of items would look dim. Numerous applications can't tolerate poor execution in the progression reaction. This is the place the Bessel channel sparkles; no overshoot and symmetrical edges.

CHOOSING THEANTIALIAS FILTER

Table 3-2 compresses the qualities of these three filters, indicating how each improves a specific parameter to the detriment of everything else. The Chebyshev enhances the move off, the Butterworth upgrades the passband evenness, and the Bessel advances the progression reaction. The choice of the antialias channel depends completely on one issue: how data is spoken to in the signals you expect to handle. While there are numerous courses for data to be encoded in an analog waveform, just two strategies are normal, time area encoding, and frequency space encoding.

	Voltage gain at DC	Step Response			Frequency Response		
		Overshoot	Time to settle to 1%	Time to settle to 0.1%	Ripple in passband	Frequency for x100 attenuation	Frequency for x1000 attenuation
Bessel							
2 pole	1.27	0.4%	0.60	1.12	0%	12.74	40.4
4 pole	1.91	0.9%	0.66	1.20	0%	4.74	8.45
6 pole	2.87	0.7%	0.74	1.18	0%	3.65	5.43
8 pole	4.32	0.4%	0.80	1.16	0%	3.35	4.53
Butterworth							
2 pole	1.59	4.3%	1.06	1.66	0%	10.0	31.6
4 pole	2.58	10.9%	1.68	2.74	0%	3.17	5.62
6 pole	4.21	14.3%	2.74	3.92	0%	2.16	3.17
8 pole	6.84	16.4%	3.50	5.12	0%	1.78	2.38
Chebyshev							
2 pole	1.84	10.8%	1.10	1.62	6%	12.33	38.9
4 pole	4.21	18.2%	3.04	5.42	6%	2.59	4.47
6 pole	10.71	21.3%	5.86	10.4	6%	1.63	2.26
8 pole	28.58	23.0%	8.34	16.4	6%	1.34	1.66

TABLE 3-2
Characteristics of the three classic filters. The Bessel filter provides the best step response, making it the choice for time domain encoded signals. The Chebyshev and Butterworth filters are used to eliminate frequencies in the stopband, making them ideal for frequency domain encoded signals. Values in this table are in the units of *seconds* and *hertz*, for a one hertz cutoff frequency.

In frequency space encoding, the data is contained in sinusoidal waves that join to shape the signal. Sound signals are an astounding case of this. At the point when a man hears discourse or music, the apparent sound relies on upon the frequencies exhibit, and not on the specific state of the waveform. This can be appeared by passing a sound signal through a circuit that progressions the period of the different sinusoids, however holds their frequency and plentifulness. The subsequent signal looks totally changed on an oscilloscope, however sounds indistinguishable. The appropriate data has been left in place, despite the fact that the waveform has been essentially adjusted. Since associating loses and covers frequency parts, it straightforwardly crushes data encoded in the frequency area. Subsequently, digitization of these signals generally includes an antialias channel with a sharp cutoff, for example, a Chebyshev, Elliptic, or Butterworth. Shouldn't something be said about the terrible stride reaction of these filters? It doesn't make a difference; the encoded data isn't influenced by this kind of bending.

Interestingly, time area encoding utilizes the state of the waveform to store data. For instance, doctors can screen the electrical action of a man's heart by joining anodes to their trunk and arms (an electrocardiogram or EKG). The state of the EKG waveform gives the data being looked for, for example, when the different chambers contract amid a pulse. Pictures are another case of this kind of signal. As opposed to a waveform that fluctuates after some time, pictures encode data in the state of a waveform that differs over separation. Pictures are framed from districts of brilliance and shading, and how they identify with different locales of shine and shading. You don't take a gander at the Mona Lisa and say, "My, what a fascinating gathering of sinusoids."

Here's the issue: The sampling theorem is an investigation of what occurs in the frequency space amid digitization. This makes it perfect to under-stand the analog-to-digital conversion of signals having their data encoded in the frequency space. Be that as it may, the sampling theorem is little help in seeing how time space encoded signals ought to be digitized. We should investigate.

Figure 3-15 illustrates the decisions for digitizing a period area encoded signal. Figure (an) is a case analog signal to be digitized. For this situation, the data we need to catch is the state of the rectangular heartbeats. A short blasted of a high frequency sine wave is likewise incorporated into this case signal. This speaks to wideband commotion, impedance, and comparative garbage that dependably shows up on analog signals. Alternate figures indicate how the digitized signal would show up with various antialias channel choices: a Chebyshev channel, a Bessel channel, and no channel.

Understand that none of these alternatives will enable the first signal to be reproduced from the tested data. This is on the grounds that the first signal naturally contains frequency parts more prominent than one-portion of the sampling rate. Since these frequencies can't exist in the digitized signal, the reproduced signal can't contain them either. These high frequencies result from two sources: (1) commotion and obstruction, which you might want to take out, and (2) sharp edges in the waveform, which presumably contain data you need to hold.

The Chebyshev channel, appeared in (b), assaults the issue by forcefully evacuating all high frequency segments. This outcomes in a separated analog signal that can be tested and later impeccably recreated. Notwithstanding, the remade analog signal is indistinguishable to the separated signal, not the first signal. Albeit nothing is lost in sampling, the waveform has been seriously contorted by the antialias channel. As appeared in (b), the cure is more terrible than the ailment! Try not to do it!

The Bessel channel, (c), is intended for quite recently this issue. Its yield nearly looks like the first waveform, with just a delicate adjusting of the edges. By changing the channel's cutoff frequency, the smoothness of the edges can be exchanged for disposal of high frequency parts in the signal. Utilizing more shafts in the channel permits a superior tradeoff between these two parameters. A typical rule is to set the cutoff frequency at around one-fourth of the sampling frequency. This outcomes in around two specimens along the rising part of each edge. See that both the Bessel and the Chebyshev channel have expelled the blasted of high frequency clamor exhibit in the first signal.

The last decision is to utilize no antialias channel by any means, as is appeared in (d). This has the solid favorable position that the estimation of each example is indistinguishable to the estimation of the first analog signal. As it were, it has consummated edge sharpness; an adjustment in the first signal is promptly reflected in the digital data. The hindrance is that associating can mutilate the signal. This takes two unique structures. To begin with, high frequency obstruction and commotion, for example, the case sinusoidal burst, will transform into futile specimens, as appeared in (d). That is, any high frequency commotion exhibit in the analog signal will show up as associated clamor in the digital signal. In a more broad sense, this is not an issue of the sampling, but rather an issue of the upstream analog hardware. It is not the ADC's motivation to lessen commotion and obstruction; this is the duty of the analog hardware before the digitization happens. It might turn out that a Bessel channel ought to be put before the digitizer to control this issue. Notwithstanding, this implies the channel ought to be seen as a major aspect of the analog handling, not something that is being accomplished for the digitizer.

The second indication of associating is more unpretentious. At the point when an occasion happens in the analog signal, (for example, an edge), the digital signal in (d) recognizes the change on the following specimen. There is no data in the digital data to show what occurs between tests. Presently, contrast utilizing no channel and utilizing a Bessel channel for this issue. For instance, envision drawing straight lines between the specimens in (c). The time when this built line crosses one-a large portion of the plentifulness of the progression gives a subsample gauge of when the edge happened in the analog signal. At the point when no channel is utilized, this subsample data is totally lost. You needn't bother with a favor theorem to assess how this will influence your specific circumstance, only a decent comprehension of what you plan to do with the data once is it procured.

MULTIRATE DATA CONVERSION

There is a solid pattern in hardware to supplant analog hardware with digital calculations. Data conversion is a magnificent case of this. Consider the plan of a digital voice recorder, a framework that will digitize a voice signal, store the data in digital shape, and later reproduce the signal for playback. To reproduce understandable discourse, the framework must catch the frequencies between around 100 and 3000 hertz. Be that as it may, the analog signal delivered by the amplifier likewise contains considerably higher frequencies, say to 40 kHz. The savage compel approach is to pass the analog signal through an eight post low-pass Chebyshev channel at 3 kHz, and after that specimen at 8 kHz. On the flip side, the DAC recreates the analog signal at 8 kHz with a zeroth request hold. Another Chebyshev channel at 3 kHz is utilized to deliver the last voice signal

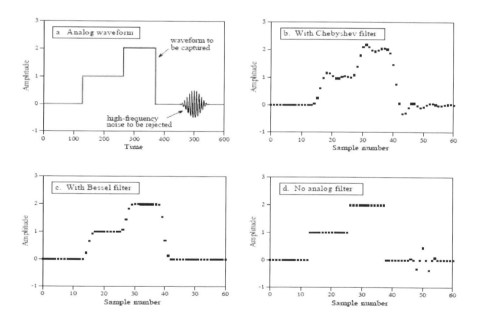

FIGURE 3-15
Three antialias filter options for time domain encoded signals. The goal is to eliminate high frequencies (that will alias during sampling), while simultaneously retaining edge sharpness (that carries information). Figure (a) shows an example analog signal containing both sharp edges and a high frequency noise burst. Figure (b) shows the digitized signal using a *Chebyshev filter*. While the high frequencies have been effectively removed, the edges have been grossly distorted. This is usually a terrible solution. The *Bessel filter*, shown in (c), provides a gentle edge smoothing while removing the high frequencies. Figure (d) shows the digitized signal using *no antialias filter*. In this case, the edges have retained perfect sharpness; however, the high frequency burst has aliased into several meaningless samples.

There are numerous helpful advantages in sampling speedier than this immediate examination. For instance, envision updating the digital voice recorder utilizing a 64 kHz sampling rate. The antialias channel now has a less demanding undertaking: pass all frequencies underneath 3 kHz, while dismissing all frequencies over 32 kHz.

A comparative rearrangements happens for the recreation channel. So, the higher sampling rate permits the eight post filters to be supplanted with basic resistor-capacitor (RC) systems. The issue is, the digital framework is currently overwhelmed with data from the higher sampling rate.

The following level of complexity includes multirate methods, utilizing more than one sampling rate in a similar framework. It works like this for the digital voice recorder illustration. In the first place, pass the voice signal through a basic RC low-pass channel and test the data at 64 kHz. The subsequent digital data contains the coveted voice band in the vicinity of 100 and 3000 hertz, additionally has an unusable band between 3 kHz and 32 kHz. Second, evacuate these unusable frequencies in programming, by utilizing a digital low-pass channel at 3 kHz. Third, resample the digital signal from 64 kHz to 8 kHz by essentially disposing of each seven out of eight examples, a system called annihilation. The subsequent digital data is proportional to that delivered by forceful analog separating and direct 8 kHz sampling.

Multirate strategies can likewise be utilized as a part of the yield bit of our case framework. The 8 kHz data is pulled from memory and changed over to a 64 kHz sampling rate, a technique called introduction. This includes setting seven specimens, with an estimation of zero, between each of the examples gotten from memory. The subsequent signal is a digital motivation prepare, containing the coveted voice band in the vicinity of 100 and 3000 hertz, in addition to unearthly duplications between 3 kHz and 32 kHz. Allude back to Figs. 3-6 a&b to comprehend why this it genuine. Everything over 3 kHz is then expelled with a digital low-pass channel. After conversion to an analog signal through a DAC, a straightforward RC system is all that is required to create the last voice signal.

Multirate data conversion is significant for two reasons: (1) it replaces analog segments with programming, an unmistakable monetary favorable position in mass-delivered items, and (2) it can accomplish more elevated amounts of execution in basic applications. For instance, minimized circle sound frameworks utilize strategies of this sort to accomplish the most ideal sound quality. This expanded execution is a consequence of supplanting analog segments (1% exactness), with digital calculations (0.0001% accuracy from round-off mistake).

SINGLE BIT DATA CONVERSION

A famous procedure in media communications and high constancy music multiplication is single piece ADC and DAC. These are multirate systems where a higher sampling rate is exchanged for a lower number of bits. In the extraordinary, just a solitary piece is required for each example. While there are a wide range of circuit setups, most depend on the utilization of delta tweak. Three illustration circuits will be displayed to give you a kind of the field. These circuits are actualized in IC's, so don't stress where the greater part of the individual transistors and operation amps ought to go. Nobody will solicit you to assemble one from these circuits from essential parts.

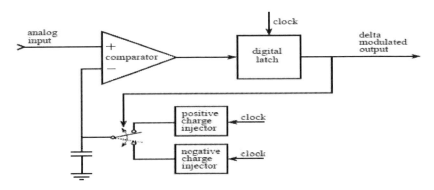

FIGURE 3-16
Block diagram of a delta modulation circuit. The input voltage is compared with the voltage stored on the capacitor, resulting in a digital zero or one being applied to the input of the latch. The output of the latch is updated in synchronization with the clock, and used in a feedback loop to cause the capacitor voltage to track the input voltage.

Figure 3-16 demonstrates the square graph of a regular delta modulator. The analog information is a voice signal with an abundancy of a couple of volts, while the yield signal is a surge of digital zeros. A comparator chooses which has the more prominent voltage, the approaching analog signal, or the voltage put away on the capacitor. This choice, as a digital one or zero, is connected to the contribution of the hook. At each clock beat, ordinarily at a couple of hundred kilohertz, the hook exchanges whatever digital state shows up on its contribution, to its yield. This lock guarantees that the yield is synchronized with the clock, in this way characterizing the sampling rate, i.e., the rate at which the 1 bit yield can refresh itself.

An input circle is shaped by taking the digital yield and utilizing it to drive an electronic switch. On the off chance that the yield is a digital one, the switch interfaces the capacitor to a positive charge injector. This is a free term for a circuit that builds the voltage on the capacitor by a settled sum, say 1 millivolt for each clock cycle. This might be simply a resistor associated with an expansive positive voltage. On the off chance that the yield is a digital zero, the change is associated with a negative charge injector. This abatements the voltage on the capacitor by the same settled sum.

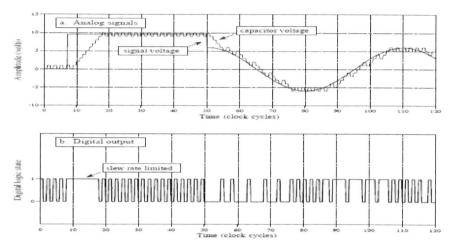

FIGURE 3-17
Example of signals produced by the delta modulator in Fig. 3-16. Figure (a) shows the analog input signal, and the corresponding voltage on the capacitor. Figure (b) shows the delta modulated output, a digital stream of ones and zeros.

Figure 3-17 illustrates the signals delivered by this circuit. At time meet zero, the analog information and the voltage on the capacitor both begin with a voltage of zero. As appeared in (a), the information signal all of a sudden increments to 9.5 volts on the eighth clock cycle. Since the information signal is currently more positive than the voltage on the capacitor, the digital yield changes to a one, as appeared in (b). This outcomes in the change being associated with the positive charge injector, and the voltage on the capacitor expanding by a little sum on each clock cycle. In spite of the fact that an augmentation of 1 volt for each check cycle is appeared in (a), this is just for delineation, and an estimation of 1 millivolt is more commonplace. This staircase increment in the capacitor voltage proceeds until it surpasses the voltage of the info

307

signal. Here the framework achieved a balance with the yield swaying between a digital one and zero, making the voltage on the capacitor waver between 9 volts and 10 volts. In this way, the criticism of the circuit drives the capacitor voltage to track the voltage of the info signal. In the event that the info signal changes quickly, the voltage on the capacitor changes at a steady rate until a match is gotten. This steady rate of progress is known as the huge number rate, similarly as in other electronic gadgets, for example, operation amps.

Presently, consider the qualities of the delta adjusted yield signal. On the off chance that the analog information is expanding in esteem, the yield signal will comprise of a bigger number of ones than zeros. Similarly, if the analog info is diminishing in esteem, the yield will comprise of a bigger number of zeros than ones. On the off chance that the analog information is steady, the digital yield will substitute in the vicinity of zero and one with an equivalent number of each. Put in more broad terms, the relative number of ones versus zeros is straightforwardly corresponding to the incline (subsidiary) of the analog information.

This circuit is a shabby technique for changing an analog signal into a serial stream of zeros for transmission or digital stockpiling. A particularly alluring element is that every one of the bits have a similar significance, dissimilar to the traditional serial organization: begin bit, LSB, ·, MSB, stop bit. The circuit at the recipient is indistinguishable to the criticism part of the transmitting circuit. Similarly as the voltage on the capacitor in the transmitting circuit takes after the analog info, so does the voltage on the capacitor in the getting circuit. That is, the capacitor voltage appeared in (an) additionally speaks to how the reproduced signal would show up.

A basic impediment of this circuit is the unavoidable tradeoff between (1) most extreme slew rate, (2) quantization size, and (3) data rate. Specifically, if the most extreme slew rate and quantization size are changed in accordance with adequate esteems for voice correspondence, the data rate winds up in the MHz go. This is too high to be of business esteem. For example, customary sampling of a voice signal requires just around 64,000 bits for each second.

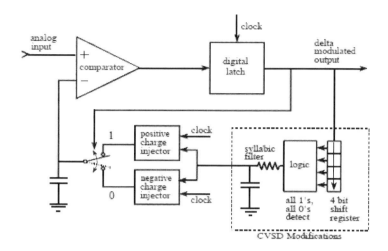

FIGURE 3-18
CVSD modulation block diagram. A logic circuit is added to the basic delta modulator to improve the slew rate.

An answer for this issue is appeared in Fig. 3-18, the Continuously Variable Slope Delta (CVSD) modulator, a strategy actualized in the Motorola MC3518 family. In this approach, the clock rate and the quantization size are set to something worthy, say 30 kHz, and 2000 levels. This outcomes in a ghastly slew rate, which you rectify with extra hardware. In operation, a move resister consistently takes a gander at the last four bits that the framework has delivered. On the off chance that the circuit is in a huge number rate restricted condition, the last four bits will be each of the ones (positive slant) or every one of the zeros (negative slant). A rationale circuit identifies this circumstance and produces an analog signal that expansion the level of charge created by the charge injectors. This lifts the huge number rate by expanding the span of the voltage steps being connected to the capacitor.

An analog channel is typically put between the rationale hardware and the charge injectors. This permits the progression size to rely on upon to what extent the circuit has been in a huge number restricted condition. For whatever length of time that the circuit is slew constrained, the progression measure continues getting bigger and bigger. This is regularly called a syllabic channel, since its qualities rely on upon the normal length of the syllables making up discourse. With legitimate improvement (from the chip maker's spec sheet, not your own work), data rates of 16 to 32 kHz deliver adequate quality discourse. The consistently changing stride measure makes the digital data hard to see, however luckily, you don't have to. At the recipient, the analog signal is recreated by consolidating a syllabic channel that is indistinguishable to the one in the transmission circuit. In the event that the two filters are coordinated, little bending outcomes from the CVSD tweak. CVSD is likely the most effortless approach to digitally transmit a voice signal.

While CVSD regulation is incredible for encoding voice signals, it can't be utilized for universally useful analog-to-digital conversion. Regardless of the possibility that you get around the way that the digital data is identified with the subordinate of the information signal, the changing stride size will befuddle things destroyed. Furthermore, the DC level of the analog signal is normally not caught in the digital data.

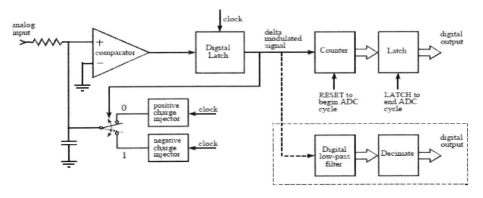

FIGURE 3-19
Block diagram of a delta-sigma analog-to-digital converter. In the simplest case, the pulses from a delta modulator are counted for a predetermined number of clock cycles. The output of the counter is then latched to complete the conversion. In a more sophisticated circuit, the pulses are passed through a digital low-pass filter and then resampled (decimated) to a lower sampling rate.

The delta-sigma converter, appeared in Fig. 3-19, wipes out these issues by cunningly joining analog hardware with DSP calculations. See that the voltage on the capacitor is currently being contrasted and ground potential. The criticism circle has additionally been altered so that the voltage on the capacitor is diminished when the circuit's yield is a digital one, and expanded when it is a digital zero. As the info signal increments and abatements in voltage, it tries to raise and lower the voltage on the capacitor. This adjustment in voltage is distinguished by the comparator, bringing about the charge injectors creating a balancing charge to keep the capacitor at zero volts.

In the event that the info voltage is certain, the digital yield will be made out of a greater number of ones than zeros. The overabundance number of ones being expected to generate the negative accuse that crosses out of the positive info signal. In like manner, if the information voltage is negative, the digital yield will be made out of a larger number of zeros than ones, giving a net positive charge infusion. On the off chance that the info signal is equivalent to zero volts, an equivalent number of zeros will be generated in the yield, giving a general charge infusion of zero.

The relative number of zeros in the yield is currently identified with the level of the info voltage, not the slant as in the past circuit. This is considerably less difficult. For example, you could shape a 12 bit ADC by nourishing the digital yield into a counter, and checking the quantity of ones more than 4096 clock cycles. A digital number of 4095 would relate to the most extreme positive info voltage. In like manner, digital number 0 would compare to the most extreme negative information voltage, and 2048 would relate to an info voltage of zero. This additionally demonstrates the starting point of the name, delta-sigma: delta balance taken after by summation (sigma).

The zeros delivered by this sort of delta modulator are anything but difficult to change once again into an analog signal. All that is required is an analog low-pass channel, which may be as straightforward as a solitary RC arrange. The high and low voltages comparing to the digital zeros normal out to shape the right analog voltage. For instance, assume that the zeros are spoken to by 5 volts and 0 volts, individually. In the event that 80% of the bits in the data stream are ones, and 20% are zeros, the yield of the low-pass channel will be 4 volts.

This technique for changing the single piece data stream once more into the first waveform is vital for a few reasons. In the first place, it depicts a smooth approach to supplant the counter in the delta-sigma ADC circuit. Rather than essentially checking the beats from the delta modulator, the double signal is gone through a digital low-pass channel, and after that obliterated to decrease the sampling rate. For instance, this methodology may begin by changing each of the zeros in the digital stream into a 12 bit test; ones turn into an estimation of 4095, while zeros turn into an estimation of 0. Utilizing a digital low-pass channel on this signal creates a digitized variant of the first waveform, similarly as an analog low-pass channel would shape an analog amusement. Destruction at that point decreases the sampling rate by disposing of the majority of the examples. This outcomes in a digital signal that is proportionate to direct sampling of the first waveform.

This approach is utilized as a part of numerous business ADC's for digitizing voice and other sound signals. A case is the National Semiconductor ADC16071, which gives 16 bit analog-to-digital conversion at sampling rates up to 192 kHz. At a sampling rate of 100 kHz, the delta modulator operates with a clock frequency of 6.4 MHz, the low-pass digital channel is a 246 point FIR. This evacuates all frequencies in the digital data over 50 kHz, ½ of the inevitable sampling rate. Thoughtfully, this can be seen as shaping a digital signal at 6.4 MHz, with each example spoken to by 16 bits. The signal is then obliterated from 6.4 MHz to 100 kHz, fulfilled by erasing each 63 out of 64 tests. In real operation, substantially more goes ahead within this gadget than portrayed by this basic talk.

Delta-sigma converters can likewise be utilized for digital-to-analog conversion of voice and sound signals. The digital signal is recovered from memory, and changed over into a delta adjusted stream of zeros. As said over, this single piece signal can undoubtedly be changed into the recreated analog signal with a straightforward low-pass analog channel. Similarly as with the antialias channel, generally just a solitary RC system is required. This is on the grounds that most of the filtration is dealt with by the superior digital filters.

Delta-sigma ADC's have a few idiosyncrasies that breaking point their utilization to particular applications. For instance, it is hard to multiplex their data sources. At the point when the information is changed starting with one signal then onto the next, legitimate operation is not set up until the digital channel can clear itself of data from the past signal. Delta-sigma converters are additionally constrained in another regard: you don't know precisely when each example was taken. Each gained test is a composite of the one piece data assumed control over a fragment of the information signal. This is not an issue for signals encoded in the frequency space, for example, sound, however it is a huge impediment for time area encoded signals. To comprehend the state of a signal's waveform, you frequently need to know the exact moment each example was taken. In conclusion, a large portion of these gadgets are particularly intended for sound applications, and their execution determinations are cited appropriately. For instance, a 16 bit ADC utilized for voice signals does not really imply that each specimen has 16 bits of exactness. A great deal more probable, the producer is expressing that voice signals can be digitized to 16 bits of dynamic range. Try not to hope to get an entire 16 bits of helpful data from this gadget for universally useful data procurement.

While these clarifications and illustrations give a prologue to single piece ADC and DAC, it must be stressed that they are improved depictions of refined DSP and integrated circuit innovation. You wouldn't anticipate that the producer will tell their rivals all the inside workings of their chips, so don't anticipate that them will let you know.

CHAPTER 15: DYNAMIC MEMORY ALLOCATION AND FRAGMENTATION

INTRODUCTION

In C and C++, it can be exceptionally helpful to assign and de-allot spaces of memory as and when required. This is standard practice in both dialects and practically unavoidable in C++. In any case, the treatment of such dynamic memory can be tricky and wasteful. For desktop applications, where memory is uninhibitedly accessible, these challenges can be overlooked. For continuous implanted frameworks, overlooking the issues is impossible.

Dynamic memory allocation has a tendency to be non-deterministic; the time taken to designate memory may not be unsurprising and the memory pool may wind up noticeably divided, bringing about sudden allocation disappointments. In this paper the issues will be laid out in detail. Offices in the Nucleus RTOS for dealing with dynamic memory are laid out and a way to deal with deterministic dynamic memory allocation nitty gritty.

C/C++ MEMORY SPACES

It might be valuable to think as far as data memory in C and C++ as being partitioned into three separate spaces:

STATIC MEMORY

This is the place variables, which are characterized outside of capacities, are found. The watchword static does not for the most part influence where such variables are found; it determines their extension to be neighborhood to the present module. Variables that are characterized within a capacity, which are expressly proclaimed static, are likewise put away in static memory. Ordinarily, static memory is situated toward the start of the RAM territory. The real allocation of locations to variables is performed by the inserted programming improvement toolbox: a coordinated effort between the compiler and the linker. Ordinarily, program segments are utilized to control situation, however more propelled procedures, similar to Fine Grain Allocation, give more control. Ordinarily, all the rest of the memory, which is not utilized for static stockpiling, is utilized to constitute the dynamic stockpiling region, which suits the other two memory spaces.

AUTOMATIC VARIABLES

Variables characterized inside a capacity, which are not proclaimed static, are automatic. There is a catchphrase to unequivocally proclaim such a variable - auto-yet it is never utilized. Automatic variables (and capacity parameters) are typically put away on the stack. The stack is regularly found utilizing the linker. The finish of the dynamic stockpiling range is regularly utilized for the stack. Compiler advancements may bring about variables being put away in registers for part or the greater part of their lifetimes; this may likewise be proposed by utilizing the watchword enroll.

THE HEAP

The rest of the dynamic stockpiling region is usually dispensed to the heap, from which application projects may dynamically designate memory, as required.

Figure 1 outlines a run of the mill memory format for the three C/C++ data memory spaces. In the event that a working framework like Nucleus is utilized, each assignment regularly has its own private stack.

DYNAMIC MEMORY IN C

In C, dynamic memory is apportioned from the heap utilizing some standard library capacities. The two key dynamic memory capacities are malloc() and free().

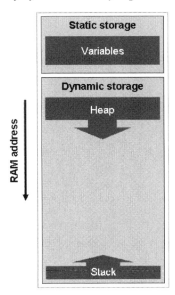

Figure 1: C/C++ data memory spaces

THE MALLOC()

The function takes a solitary parameter, which is the size of the asked for memory zone in bytes. It restores a pointer to the distributed memory. In the event that the allocation comes up short, it returns **NULL**. The prototype for the standard library function is this way:

void *malloc(size_t size);

THE FREE()

The function takes the pointer returned by malloc() and de-designates the memory. No sign of accomplishment or disappointment is returned. The function prototype is this way:

void free(void *pointer);

To delineate the utilization of these functions, here is some code to statically characterize an array and set the fourth component's esteem:

```
int my_array[10];
my_array[3] = 99;
```

The accompanying code does likewise work utilizing dynamic memory allocation:

```
int *pointer;
pointer = malloc(10 * sizeof(int));
*(pointer+3) = 99;
```

The pointer de-referencing linguistic structure is hard to peruse, so typical array referencing punctuation might be utilized, as [and] are simply administrators:

```
pointer[3] = 99;
```

At the point when the array is at no time in the future required, the memory might be de-assigned along these lines:

```
free(pointer);
pointer = NULL;
```

Doling out NULL to the pointer is not obligatory, but rather is great practice, as it will make a mistake be produced if the pointer is mistaken used after the memory has been de-designated.

The measure of heap space really allotted by malloc() is regularly single word bigger than that asked. The extra word is utilized to hold the size of the allocation and is for later use by free(). This "size word" goes before the data region to which malloc() restores a pointer.

There are two different variations of the malloc() function: calloc() and realloc().

THE CALLOC()

The function does essentially an indistinguishable occupation from malloc(), with the exception of that it takes two parameters – the quantity of array components and the size of every component – rather than a solitary parameter (which is the result of these two esteems). The designated memory is likewise instated to zeros. Here is the prototype:

```
void *calloc(size_t nelements, size_t elementSize);
```

THE REALLOC()

The function resizes a memory allocation already made by malloc(). It takes as parameters a pointer to the memory territory and the new size that is required. On the off chance that the size is decreased, data might be lost. In the event that the size is expanded and the function can't broaden the current allocation, it will automatically dispense another memory zone and duplicate data over. Regardless, it restores a pointer to the apportioned memory. Here is the prototype:

void *realloc(void *pointer, size_t size);

DYNAMIC MEMORY IN C++

Administration of dynamic memory in C++ is very like C in many regards. In spite of the fact that the library functions are probably going to be accessible, C++ has two extra administrators - new and delete-which empower code to be composed all the more plainly, briefly and adaptably, with less probability of blunders. The new administrator can be utilized as a part of three ways:

p_var = new typename;
p_var = new type(initializer);
p_array = new type [size];

In the initial two cases, space for a solitary question is distributed; the second one incorporates introduction. The third case is the component for apportioning space for an array of items.

The delete administrator can be summoned in two ways:

delete p_var;
delete[] p_array;

The first is for a solitary question; the second de-apportions the space utilized by an array. It is essential to utilize the right de-allocator for each situation.

There is no administrator that gives the functionality of the C realloc() function. Here is the code to dynamically distribute an array and instate the fourth component:

int* pointer;
pointer = new int[10];
pointer[3] = 99;

Utilizing the array get to documentation is characteristic.

De-allocation is performed in this way:

delete[] pointer;
pointer = NULL;

Once more, doling out NULL to the pointer after de-allocation is quite recently great programming rehearse.

Another alternative for overseeing dynamic memory in C++ is the utilization the Standard Template Library. This might be unwise for constant inserted frameworks.

ISSUES AND PROBLEMS

Issues we need to confront when utilizing dynamic memory allocation in C/C++ incorporate the accompanying:

SUFFICIENCY

How might we make certain that we have given adequate memory, so that a basic memory allocation will never be won't?

GARBAGE ADMINISTRATION

How might we make certain that memory that is at no time in the future required is discharged to the memory chief at precisely the correct time? In the event that we discharge memory too soon, we will have dangling pointers or twofold free blunders. On the off chance that we discharge memory past the point of no return, we will have memory spills. These sorts of issue torment advancement of vast C/C++ programs.

FRAGMENTATION

How might we stay away from the circumstance in which we need to designate N bytes of memory, yet all the accessible memory is in parts littler than N, despite the fact that the aggregate accessible is significantly bigger than N? Memory fragmentation is a torment of long-running C/C++ frameworks that utilization dynamic memory broadly.

TIMELINESS

When we have to dispense memory, what is the upper bound on the time that the memory administrator may take to benefit the demand? Memory directors for C/C++

ordinarily look freelists or more intricate structures for sections of adequate size, in this way calls to alloc or new normally show a variable and now and again long dormancy.

When in doubt, dynamic conduct is troublesome progressively implanted frameworks. The two key territories of concern are assurance of the move to be made on asset fatigue and non-deterministic execution. While considering dynamic memory use, there are two likely issue territories: stacks and the utilization of malloc().

STACKS

A stack is situated in memory, set up to be a specific size and the stack pointer introduced to point to the word taking after the designated memory. From that point, issues happen if stack operations result in data being composed outside of the distributed memory space. This might be stack flood, where more data is pushed on to the stack than it has ability to oblige. Or, on the other hand it can be stack undercurrent, where data is flown off of an unfilled stack (because of a programming mistake).

In both cases the issues can be hard to situate, as they normally show themselves later in totally inconsequential code. It might even outcome is issues in another, random errand.

UTILIZATION OF MALLOC()

There are various issues with dynamic memory allocation in an ongoing framework.

To begin with, the standard library functions (malloc() and free()) are not typically reentrant, which would be dangerous in a multithreaded application. On the off chance that the source code is accessible, this ought to be direct to amend by locking assets utilizing RTOS offices (like a semaphore).

A more obstinate issue is related with the execution of malloc(). Its conduct is eccentric, as the time it takes to apportion memory is to a great degree variable. Such non-deterministic conduct is heinous continuously frameworks.

Without awesome care, it is anything but difficult to bring memory spills into application code executed utilizing malloc() and free(). This is caused by memory being assigned and never being de-apportioned. Such mistakes tend to cause a continuous execution corruption and inevitable disappointment. This type of bug can be hard to find.

Memory allocation disappointment is a worry. Not at all like a desktop application, most installed frameworks don't have the chance to fly up a discourse and talk about alternatives with the client. Frequently, resetting is the main alternative, which is ugly. On the off chance that allocation disappointments are experienced amid testing, mind must be brought with diagnosing their cause. It might be that there is essentially lacking memory accessible – this recommends different strategies. In any case, it might be that there is adequate memory, yet not accessible in one touching piece that can fulfill the allocation ask. This circumstance is called memory fragmentation.

MEMORY FRAGMENTATION

The ideal approach to comprehend memory fragmentation is to take a gander at a case. For this illustration, it is accepted that there is a 10K heap. Initial, a region of 3K is asked for, consequently:

```
#define K (1024)
burn *p1;
p1 = malloc(3*K);
```

At that point, a further 4K is asked:

```
p2 = malloc(4*K);
```

The subsequent circumstance is appeared in Figure 2 – 3K of memory is presently free.

At some point later, the principal memory allocation, indicated by p1, is de-assigned:

```
free(p1);
```

This leaves 6K of memory free in two 3K lumps, as delineated in Figure 3.

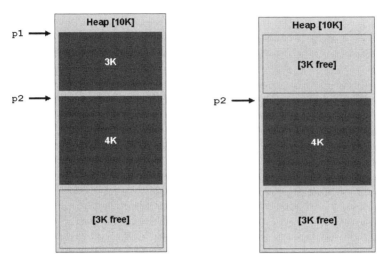

Figure 2: Two memory areas allocated   Figure 3: Non-contiguous free memory

A further request for a 4K allocation is issued:

p1 = malloc(4*K);

This outcomes in a faliure - NULL is returned into p1 - on the grounds that, despite the fact that 6K of memory is accessible, there is not a 4K adjacent square accessible. This is memory fragmentation.

No doubt an undeniable arrangement would be to de-section the memory, blending the two 3K pieces to make a solitary one of 6K. Be that as it may, this is impractical on the grounds that it would involve moving the 4K piece to which p2 focuses. Moving it would change its address, so any code that has taken a duplicate of the pointer would then be broken. In different dialects, (for example, Visual Basic, Java and C#), there are de-fragmentation (or "junk accumulation") offices. This is conceivable in light of the fact that these dialects don't bolster coordinate pointers, so moving the data has no unfavorable impact upon application code.

This de-fragmentation may happen when a memory allocation fizzles or there might be an intermittent waste gathering process that is run. In either case, this would seriously trade off ongoing execution and determinism.

MEMORY WITH A RTOS

Memory administration offices that are perfect with constant necessities – i.e. they are deterministic – are normally furnished with business ongoing working frameworks. A generally utilized plan, which distributes squares – or "partitions" – of memory under the control of the OS, is utilized by Nucleus.

CORE RTOS BLOCK/PARTITION MEMORY ALLOCATION

Piece memory allocation is performed utilizing a "partition pool", which is characterized statically or dynamically and designed to contain a predefined number of squares of a predetermined settled size. For Nucleus OS, the API call to characterize a partition pool has the accompanying prototype:

STATUS NU_Create_Partition_Pool(NU_PARTITION_POOL *pool, Burn *name, VOID *start_address, UNSIGNED pool_size, UNSIGNED partition_size, OPTION suspend_type);

This is most unmistakably comprehended by methods for an illustration:

status = NU_Create_Partition_Pool(&MyPool, "any name", (VOID *) 0xB000, 2000, 40, NU_FIFO);

This makes a partition pool with the descriptor MyPool, containing 2000 bytes of memory, loaded with partitions of size 40 bytes (i.e. there are 50 partitions). The pool is situated at address 0xB000. The pool is arranged with the end goal that, if an assignment endeavors to distribute a square, when there are none accessible, and it solicitations to be suspended on the allocation API call, suspended undertakings will be woken up in a first-in, first-out request. The other choice would have been undertaking need arrange.

Another API call is accessible to ask for allocation of a partition. Here is an illustration utilizing Nucleus RTOS:

status = NU_Allocate_Partition(&MyPool, &ptr, NU_SUSPEND);

This asks for the allocation of a partition from MyPool. Whenever effective, a pointer to the allotted piece is returned in ptr. On the off chance that no memory is accessible, the assignment is suspended, in light of the fact that NU _ SUSPEND was determined; different choices, which may have been chosen, would have been to suspend with a timeout or to just come back with a mistake.

At the point when the partition is never again required, it might be de-dispensed in this way:

status = NU_Deallocate_Partition(ptr);

On the off chance that an undertaking of higher need was suspended pending accessibility of a partition, it would now be run.

There is no plausibility for fragmentation, as just settled size squares are accessible. The main disappointment mode is genuine asset weariness, which might be controlled and contained utilizing assignment suspend, as appeared.

Extra API calls are accessible which can furnish the application code with the way to deal with and acquire data about the status of partitions:

NU _ Delete _ Partition _ Pool() – evacuates a partition pool.

NU _ Partition _ Pool _ Information() – restores an assortment of data about a partition pool.

NU _ Established _ Partition _ Pools() – restores the quantity of partition pools [currently] in the framework.

NU _ Partition _ Pool _ Pointers() – returns pointers to all the partition pools in the framework.

Care is required in allotting and de-assigning partitions, as the likelihood for the presentation of memory leaks remains.

MEMORY LEAK DETECTION

The potential for software engineer mistake bringing about a memory leak when utilizing partition pools is perceived by sellers of constant working frameworks. Commonly, a profiler device is accessible which helps with the area and amendment of such bugs. Figure 4 shows a screen shot from the Mentor Graphics EDGE Profiler, working with Nucleus RTOS. The chart demonstrates the measure of memory that has been apportioned from the pool. Each spot demonstrates an allocation or de-allocation; tapping on an allocation brings about its relating de-allocation being highlighted and the other way around. Unmatched allocations are appeared in red and may show a memory leak.

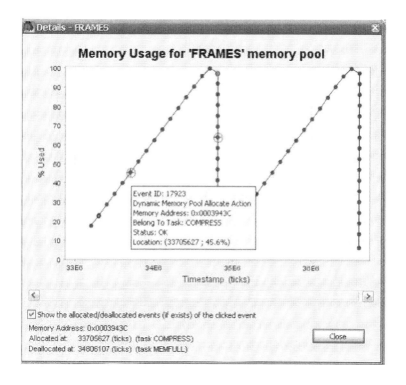

Figure 4: Mentor Graphics EDGEProfiler.

REAL-TIME MEMORY SOLUTIONS

Having recognized various issues with dynamic memory conduct continuously frameworks, some conceivable arrangements and better methodologies can be proposed.

STACKS

In spite of the fact that it could be a consequence of a programming blunder, the in all probability explanation behind stack flood is that the stack space allocation was lacking. Determining stack size is exceptionally testing. It is practically difficult to evaluate statically for generally frameworks. The least complex approach is to make estimations on a running framework. Assign a liberal measure of space for the stack, fill it with a known esteem – non-zero, odd numbers bode well, as they less inclined to be a legitimate address. Run the code for a sensible timeframe and examine the stack to decide what amount was utilized.

Core RTOS incorporates offices for stack observing – particularly an API call: **NU _ Check _ Stack().**

Faults checking in the part may likewise be designed utilizing the image **NU _ ENABLE _ STACK _ CHECK.**

To screen at run time for stack flood/undercurrent, a great strategy is to put a "guard word" at either end of the stack space, as represented in Figure 5. These might be instated to a known esteem (again a non-zero, odd number is ideal) and a foundation (low need) errand used to screen the words for changes amid execution. On the other hand, a memory administration unit might be utilizedto trap a blunder if the guard words are gotten to.

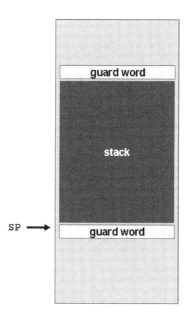

Figure 5: Stack guard words

DYNAMIC MEMORY

It is conceivable to utilize partition memory allocation to actualize malloc() in a strong and deterministic design. The thought is to characterize a progression of partition pools with square sizes in a geometric movement; e.g. 32, 64, 128, 256 bytes. A malloc() function might be composed to deterministically choose the right pool to give enough space to a given allocation ask. For instance, if 56 bytes are asked for, a 64 byte partition would be utilized; for 99 bytes, a 128 byte partition. Lamentably, a 65 byte asked for would be happy with a 128 byte partition.

This approach exploits the deterministic conduct of the partition allocation API call, the strong mistake dealing with (e.g. undertaking suspend) and the resistance from fragmentation offered by square memory. The decision of partition sizes, being forces of 2, is to encourage proficient code utilizing a bit cover.

0x0000	0x1000	0x2000	0x3000	0x4000	0x5000	Comments
						Start with all memory available for allocation.
A	B	C				Allocated three blocks A, B, and C, of size 0x1000.
A		C				Freed block B. Notice that the memory that B used cannot be included for an allocation larger than B's size.

CONCLUSION

C and C++ utilize memory in different ways, both static and dynamic. Dynamic memory incorporates stack and heap.

Dynamic conduct in installed continuous frameworks is for the most part a wellspring of worry, as it has a tendency to be non-deterministic and disappointment is hard to contain.

Utilizing the offices given by most ongoing working frameworks, including Nucleus RTOS, a dynamic memory office might be actualized which is deterministic, insusceptible from fragmentation and with great blunder taking care of.

CHAPTER 16:PROGRAMMABLE LOGIC DEVICES AND EMBEDDED SYSTEMS

INTRODUCTION

A peaceful transformation is occurring. Over the previous decade, the thickness of the normal programmable logic device has started to soar. The most extreme number of gates in a FPGA is presently around 20,000,000 and multiplying at regular intervals. Then, the cost of these chips is dropping. What the greater part of this implies is that the cost of an individual NAND or NOR is quickly moving toward zero! And the originators of embedded systems are observing. Some system originators are purchasing processor cores and incorporating them into system-on-a-chip outlines; others are wiping out the processor and software by and large, picking an option equipment just a plan.

As this pattern proceeds with, it turns out to be harder to isolate equipment from software. All things considered, both equipment and software fashioners are presently portraying logic in abnormal state terms, though in various languages, and downloading the ordered outcome to a bit of silicon. Definitely, nobody would guarantee that dialect decision alone denotes a genuine qualification between the two fields. Turing's thought of machine-level equality and the presence of dialect to-dialect translators have long back shown every one of us that that sort of thinking is stupid. There are even now items that enable fashioners to make their equipment outlines in conventional programming languages like C. Therefore, dialect contrasts alone are insufficient of a qualification.

Both equipment and software plans are arranged from a comprehensible form into a machine-lucid one. And both plans are at last stacked into some bit of silicon. Does it make a difference that one chip is a memory device and the other a bit of programmable logic? If not, by what other method would we be able to recognize equipment from software?

I am not persuaded that an unambiguous qualification amongst equipment and software can ever be found, however, I don't believe that matters all that much. Despite where the line is drawn, there will keep on being engineers like you and me who cross the limit in our work. So as opposed to attempt to nail down an exact limit amongst equipment and software plan, we should accept that there will be cover in the two fields. And we should all find out about new things. Equipment architects must figure out how to compose better programs, and software engineers must figure out how to use programmable logic.

DIFFERENT TYPES OF PROGRAMMABLE LOGIC

Many sorts of programmable logic are accessible. The present scope of offerings incorporates everything from little devices equipped for actualizing just a handful of logic conditions to gigantic FPGAs that can hold a whole processor core (in addition to peripherals!). Notwithstanding this unimaginable distinction in estimate, there is likewise much variety in engineering. In this area, I will acquaint you with the most widely recognized sorts of programmable logic and highlight the most important elements of each sort.

PLDs

At the low end of the range are the original Programmable Logic Devices (PLDs). These were the principal chips that could be utilized to execute an adaptable computerized logic plan in equipment. As it were, you could evacuate a few the 7400-arrangement TTL parts (ANDs, ORs, and NOTs) from your board and supplant them with a solitary PLD. Different names you may experience for this class of device are Programmable Logic Array (PLA), Programmable Array Logic (PAL), and Generic Array Logic (GAL).

PLDs are frequently utilized for address deciphering, where they have a few clear favorable circumstances over the 7400-arrangement TTL parts that they supplanted. To start with, obviously, is that one chip requires less board zone, power, and wiring than a few do. Another preferred standpoint is that the plan inside the chip is adaptable, so an adjustment in the logic does not require any rewiring of the board. Or maybe, the interpreting logic can be changed by just supplanting that one PLD with another part that has been programmed with the new outline.

Inside each PLD is an arrangement of completely associated macrocells. These macrocells are ordinarily involved some measure of combinatorial logic (and OR gates, for instance) and a flip-flounder. At the end of the day, a little Boolean logic condition can be worked inside each macrocell. This condition will consolidate the condition of some number of parallel contributions to a double yield and, if important, store that yield in the flip-flounder until the point that the following clock edge. Obviously, the particulars of the accessible logic gates and flip-flops are particular to every maker and item family. Be that as it may, the general thought is dependably the same.

Since these chips are truly little, they don't have much pertinence to the rest of this exchange. Be that as it may, you do need to understand the origin of programmable logic chips before we can go ahead to discuss the bigger devices. Equipment outlines for these straightforward PLDs are for the most part written in languages like ABEL or PALASM (the equipment reciprocals of getting together) or drawn with the assistance of a schematic catch device.

CPLDs

As chip densities expanded, it was normal for the PLD makers to advance their items into bigger (logically, however not really physically) parts called Complex Programmable Logic Devices (CPLDs). For most viable purposes, CPLDs can be thought of as numerous PLDs (in addition to some programmable interconnect) in a solitary chip. The bigger size of a CPLD enables you to execute either more logic conditions or a more confused outline. Truth be told, these chips are sufficiently huge to supplant many those troublesome 7400-arrangement parts.

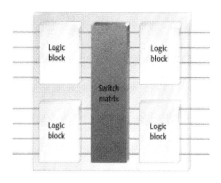

CPLD FUNCTION BLOCK AND MACROCELL

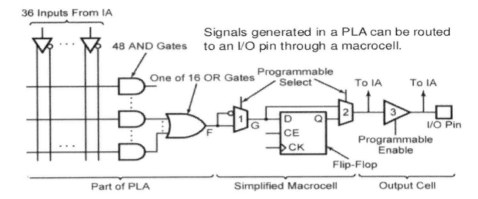

36 Inputs From IA

48 AND Gates

Signals generated in a PLA can be routed to an I/O pin through a macrocell.

One of 16 OR Gates

Programmable Select

To IA   To IA

I/O Pin

Programmable Enable

Flip-Flop

Part of PLA   Simplified Macrocell   Output Cell

Figure 1. Internal structure of a CPLD

Figure 1 contains a square outline of a theoretical CPLD. Each of the four logic squares appeared there is what might as well be called one PLD. In any case, in a genuine CPLD there might be more (or less) than four logic pieces. I have recently drawn it that route for effortlessness. Note likewise that these logic squares are themselves involved macrocells and interconnect wiring, much the same as an ordinary PLD.

Dissimilar to the programmable interconnect inside a PLD, the switch framework inside a CPLD could conceivably be completely associated. As such, a portion of the theoretically conceivable associations between logic piece yields and sources of info may not really be supported inside a given CPLD. The impact of this is frequently to make 100% use of the macrocells extremely hard to accomplish. Some equipment outlines just won't fit inside a given CPLD, despite the fact that there are adequate logic gates and flip-flops accessible.

Since CPLDs can hold bigger outlines than PLDs, their potential uses are more shifted. They are still now and then utilized for basic applications like address deciphering, however more frequently contain superior control-logic or complex limited state machines. At the top of the line (regarding quantities of gates), there is likewise a ton of cover in potential applications with FPGAs. Generally, CPLDs have been picked over FPGAs at whatever point superior logic is required. In light of its less adaptable inward engineering, the deferral through a CPLD (measured in nanoseconds) is more unsurprising and normally shorter.

FPGAs

Field Programmable Gate Arrays (FPGAs) can be utilized to actualize any equipment plan. One normal utilize is to model a piece of equipment that will in the long run discover its way into an ASIC. Nonetheless, there is nothing to state that the FPGA can't stay in the last item. Regardless of whether it will rely on upon the relative weights of improvement cost and creation taken a toll for a specific venture. (It costs fundamentally more to build up an ASIC, however the cost per chip might be bring down over the long haul. The cost tradeoff includes anticipated that number of chips would be created and the normal probability of equipment bugs and/or changes. This makes for a fairly muddled cost investigation, without a doubt.)

The improvement of the FPGA was unmistakable from the PLD/CPLD development simply portrayed. This is clear when you take a gander at the structures inside. Figure 2 delineates a normal FPGA design. There are three key parts of its structure: logic pieces, interconnect, and I/O squares. The I/O pieces form a ring around the external edge of the part. Each of these gives exclusively selectable information, yield, or bi-directional access to one of the broadly useful I/O sticks on the exterior of the FPGA bundle. Inside the ring of I/O pieces lies a rectangular array of logic squares. And interfacing logic squares to logic pieces and I/O pieces to logic pieces is the programmable interconnect wiring.

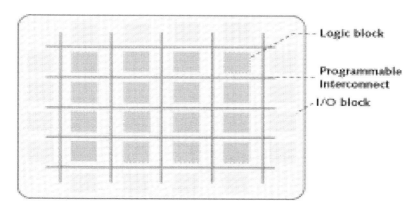

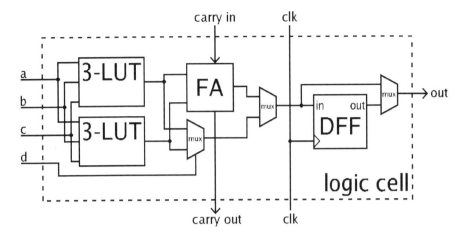

Figure 2. Internal structure of an FPGA

The logic hinders inside a FPGA can be as little and straightforward as the macrocells in a PLD (a purported fine-grained engineering) or bigger and more complex (coarse-grained). Be that as it may, they are never as huge as a whole PLD, as the logic pieces of a CPLD seem to be. Keep in mind that the logic squares of a CPLD contain numerous macrocells. Be that as it may, the logic obstructs in a FPGA are for the most part just two or three logic gates or a look-into table and a flip-slump.

As a result of all the additional flip-flounders, the engineering of a FPGA is a great deal more adaptable than that of a CPLD. This improves FPGAs in enlist overwhelming and pipelined applications. They are likewise regularly utilized as a part of place of a processor-in addition to software arrangement, especially where the preparing of info data streams must be performed at a quick pace. Also, FPGAs are normally denser (more gates in a given territory) and cost not exactly their CPLD cousins, so they are the accepted decision for bigger logic plans.

EQUIPMENT PLAN AND ADVANCEMENT

The way toward making computerized logic is much the same as the embedded software advancement, prepare you are as of now comfortable with. A portrayal of the equipment's structure and behavior is composed in an abnormal state equipment depiction dialect (normally VHDL or Verilog) and that code is then gathered and downloaded prior to execution. Obviously, schematic catch is likewise a possibility for outline passage, however it has turned out to be less prevalent as plans have turned out to be more complex and the dialect based instruments have made strides. The general procedure of equipment improvement for programmable logic is appeared in Figure 3 and portrayed in the passages that take after. Maybe the most striking distinction amongst equipment and software configuration is the way an engineer must consider the issue. Software designers tend to think consecutively, notwithstanding when they are building up a multithreaded application. The lines of source code that they compose are constantly executed in a specific order, in any event inside a given string. On the off chance that there is a working system it is utilized to make the presence of parallelism, yet there is still only one execution motor. Amid plan section, equipment planners must think-and program-in parallel. The greater part of the info signals is prepared in parallel, as they go through an arrangement of execution motors everyone a progression of macrocells and interconnections-toward their goal yield signals. Therefore, the announcements of an equipment depiction dialect make structures, all of which are "executed" at the extremely same time. (Note, in any case, that the transference from macrocell to macrocell is normally synchronized to some other flag, similar to a clock.)

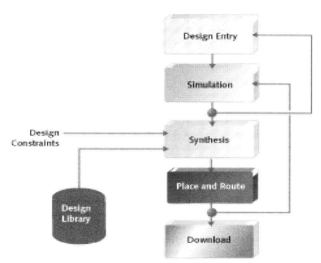

Figure 3. Programmable logic design process

335

Normally, the design section step is taken after or blended with times of useful reproduction. That is the place a simulator is utilized to execute the design and affirm that the correct yields are created for a given arrangement of test inputs. In spite of the fact that issues with the size or timing of the equipment may in any case manifest later, the designer can in any event make sure that his logic is practically correct before going ahead to the following phase of improvement.

Gathering just starts after a practically correct portrayal of the equipment exists. This equipment assemblage comprises of two particular strides. Initial, a middle of the road portrayal of the equipment design is created. This progression is called amalgamation and the outcome is a portrayal called a netlist. The netlist is device autonomous, so its substance doesn't rely on upon the particulars of the FPGA or CPLD; it is generally stored in a standard format called the Electronic Design Interchange Format (EDIF).

The second step in the interpretation procedure is called put and course. This progression includes mapping the logical structures portrayed in the netlist onto real macrocells, interconnections, and info and yield pins. This procedure is like the equal stride in the improvement of a printed circuit board, and it might take into account either programmed or manual design advancements. The consequence of the place and course handle is a bitstream. This name is utilized generically, in spite of the way that each CPLD or FPGA (or family) has its own, generally restrictive, bitstream format. Suffice it to state that the bitstream is the double data that must be stacked into the FPGA or CPLD to make that chip execute a specific equipment design.

Progressively there are likewise debuggers accessible that at any rate take into consideration single-venturing the equipment design as it executes in the programmable logic device. In any case, those exclusive supplement a recreation situation that can utilize a portion of the information created amid the place and course venture to give entryway level reproduction. Clearly, this sort of mix of device-particular information into a generic simulator requires a decent working connection between the chip and recreation instrument vendors.

DEVICE PROGRAMMING

When you have made a bitstream for a specific FPGA or CPLD, you should some way or another download it to the device. The subtle elements of this procedure are needy upon the chip's fundamental procedure innovation. Programmable logic devices resemble non-volatile memories in that there are various basic innovations. Truth be told, the very same arrangement of names is utilized: PROM (for one-time programmables), EPROM, EEPROM, and Flash.

Much the same as their memory partners, PROM and EPROM-based logic devices must be programmed with the assistance of a different bit of lab gear called a device programmer. Then again, a large number of the devices in light of EEPROM or Flash innovation are in-circuit programmable. At the end of the day, the extra hardware that is required to perform device (re)programming is given inside the FPGA or CPLD silicon also. This makes it conceivable to eradicate and reprogram the device internals by means of a JTAG interface or from an on-board embedded processor. (Note, notwithstanding, that since this extra hardware consumes up room and expands general chip costs, a couple of the programmable logic devices in view of EEPROM or Flash still require inclusion into a device programmer.)

Notwithstanding non-volatile advancements, there are additionally programmable logic devices in light of SRAM innovation. In such cases, the substance of the device is volatile. This has both points of interest and drawbacks. The undeniable drawback is that the inward logic must be reloaded after each system or chip reset. That implies you'll require an extra memory chip or something to that affect in which to hold the bitstream. Yet, it likewise implies that the substance of the logic device can be controlled on the fly. Truth be told, you could envision a situation in which the genuine bitstream is reloaded from a remote source (by means of a network or some likeness thereof), so that the equipment design c be overhauled as effectively as software.

APPLICATIONS

Since you understand the innovation, you're presumably pondering what these FPGAs and CPLDs are doing inside the embedded systems. Be that as it may, their

337

utilizations are varied to the point that it is difficult to sum up. Or maybe, I'll simply address a portion of the rising patterns. This ought to ideally answer your inquiry, however as a matter of fact in a roundabout way.

PROTOTYPING

Ordinarily a CPLD or FPGA will be utilized as a part of a model system. A little device might be available to enable the designers to change a board's paste logic more effortlessly amid item advancement and testing. Or an extensive device might be incorporated to permit prototyping of a system-on-a-chip design that will in the end discover its way into an ASIC. In any case, the essential thought is the same: enable the equipment to be adaptable amid item advancement. At the point when the item is prepared to deliver in huge amounts, the programmable device will be supplanted with a more affordable, however practically equal, hard-wired option.

EMBEDDED CORES

More and more vendors are offering or giving without end their processors and peripherals in a form that is prepared to be coordinated into a programmable logic-based design. They either perceive the potential for development in the system-on-a-chip zone and need a bit of the sovereignties or need to advance the utilization of their specific FPGA or CPLD by giving libraries of prepared to-utilize building squares. In any case, you will pick up with bring down system costs and speedier time-to-showcase. Why build up your own equipment when you can purchase a proportionate bit of virtual silicon?

The Intellectual Property (IP) advertise is developing quickly. It's normal to discover microprocessors and microcontrollers for deal in this form, and additionally complex peripherals like PCI controllers. A large number of the IP cores are even configurable. Would you like a 16-bit bus or a 32-bit bus? Do you require the drifting point portion of the processor? And, obviously, you'll discover the greater part of the standard supporting thrown of straightforward peripherals like serial controllers and clock/counter units are accessible also.

HALF BREED CHIPS

There's likewise been some development toward cross breed chips, which consolidate a devoted processor core with a territory of programmable logic. The vendors of half and half chips are wagering that a processor core embedded inside a programmable logic device will require dreadfully many gates for run of the mill applications. So they've made half breed chips that are part settled logic and part programmable logic. The settled logic contains a completely practical processor and maybe even some on-chip memory. This piece of the chip additionally interfaces to devoted address and data bus sticks outwardly of the chip. Application-particular peripherals can be embedded into the programmable logic portion of the chip, either from a library of IP cores or the client's own designs.

RECONFIGURABLE COMPUTING

As specified before, a SRAM-based programmable device can have its inside design modified on-the-fly. This training is known as reconfigurable computing. In spite of the fact that originally proposed in the late 1960's by a specialist at UCLA, this is as yet a moderately new field of study. The decades-long postponement had for the most part to do with an absence of adequate reconfigurable equipment. On-the-fly reprogrammable logic chips have just as of late achieved entryway densities making them appropriate for much else besides scholarly research. Be that as it may, the eventual fate of reconfigurable computing is splendid and it is as of now finding a specialty in top of the line interchanges, military, and insight applications.

POINTS TO KEEP IN MIND FOR PROGRAMMABLE LOGIC (PL) SELECTION

1. ENTRYWAY COUNT

The entryway count without anyone else's input is practically futile. Distinctive vendors utilize diverse measures: number of accessible gates, equal number of NAND gates, equal number of gates in a PLD, equal number of gates in an ASIC, and so forth.

You basically can't analyze these numbers crosswise over vendors. A superior examination can be made as far as quantities of registers (flip-lemon) and I/O pins.

2. NUMBER OF I/O PINS

Are there satisfactory sources of info and yields for your design? This is regularly a more restricting limitation than entryway count, and it particularly influences the cost of the chip. Subsequently, numerous producers offer a similar part with various quantities of I/O pins.

3. COST PER CHIP

Clearly, cost is a factor in the event that you will be including a CPLD or FPGA in your creation system. Would it be less expensive over the long haul to build up a settled ASIC design and create an expansive amount of them? On the off chance that you stay with the programmable device, you will need to utilize the littlest part with satisfactory assets for your design.

4. ACCESSIBLE TOOLS

The most famous Verilog and VHDL recreation and amalgamation tools are sold by outsider device vendors. These tools for the most part have support for a clothing rundown of normal FPGAs and CPLDs. This implies the tools understand the limitations of your specific chip and likewise understand the planning relating information that leaves the place and course instrument.

5. PERFORMANCE

As a rule, CPLDs are speedier and present more unsurprising postponements than FPGAs. In any case, that is on account of their inside structure is less adaptable. So you need to surrender something for the additional speed. What is normally lost is thickness. The bigger your design, the more likely it is that you should utilize a slower part. When utilizing a FPGA, the genuine performance of your design won't generally be known until the point when the last place and course handle is finished, since the directing specifics will assume a part.

6. <u>POWER CONSUMPTION</u>

Power consumption can be an important thought in any system. EEPROM and Flash-based devices as a rule require more power than those in view of PROM, EPROM, or SRAM innovations.

7. <u>PACKAGING</u>

Programmable logic devices are accessible in a wide range of bundles. Your decision of a bundle will in all probability be driven by your need to lessen power consumption, warm dissemination, measure, and/or cost.

USING PROGRAMMABLE LOGICDEVICES

Everydigital logic design is capable of using PLDs. If you usuallystartyour designby:

- By means of AND & ORfunctions
- Rational of 7400 seriescomponents
- Consuming truth tables
- Statediagrams

You are nowon the path to using PLDs.

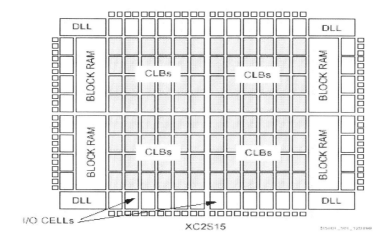

341

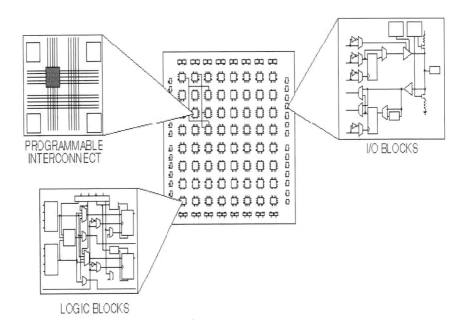

PROGRAMMABLE
INTERCONNECT

I/O BLOCKS

LOGIC BLOCKS

Arranging a microprocessor-based system, with memory and I/O? What about all that "paste" logic you use to interface with the bus, give chip chooses, and any strange signs required by exceptional chips? The greater part of these capacities are at present finished with 7400 arrangement TTL. What about utilizing a PLD?

Designing a stand-alone PC board which utilizes a state machine to control different yield signals? Utilizing locks to synchronize signals? Utilizing counters to partition down ace clock frequencies? Changing over parallel-to-serial and back once more? These capacities fit effortlessly in present day PLDs. *Most anything found in your TTL Databook can be replaced with your own, PERSONALIZED, programmable logicdevice.*

342

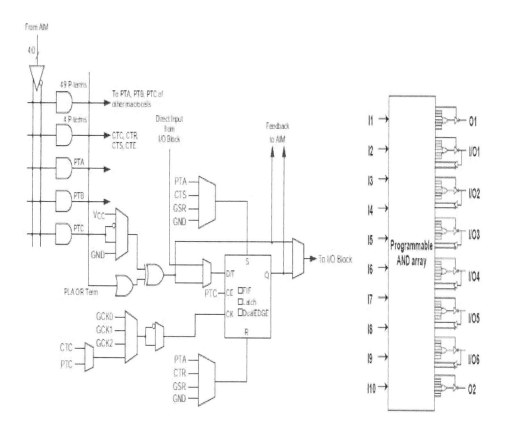

PLDAPPLICATIONS

- GlueLogic
- State Machines
- Synchronization
- Decoders
- Counters
- BusInterfaces
- Parallel-to-Serial
- Serial-to-Parallel
- Subsystems
- and ManyOthers

343

WHYPLDs ?

Perhaps you have effectively heard all the superb purposes behind utilizing PLDs. All things considered, they are valid! In the first place, we should audit a portion of the more important ones:

INCREASED INTEGRATION

You can lessen the bundle count of your designs while all the while expanding the components offered by your item.

LOWER POWER

CMOS and less bundles consolidate to lessen power consumption.

IMPROVED RELIABILITY

Lower power in addition to less interconnections and bundles convert into significantly enhanced system unwavering quality. Lower Cost. PLDs lessen inventory costs, as well.

EASIER TO USE!

Yes, trust it or not, once you move beyond the underlying learning time frame, PLDs are simpler to use than discrete logic capacities.

EASIER TO CHANGE

Oh no! Need to roll out an improvement? You won't require "blue wire" when you utilize a PLD – all progressions are inward, and should be possible rapidly. ECNs are a snap – and system dependability is kept up!

Figure 1 depicts the PLD design handle. In the wake of having perused the initial segment of this application note, you now have the ideal application for a PLD, isn't that so? So here you go!

How would you make an interpretation of your thought into a working model? In the first place, you require a computer with an editor or some likeness thereof. On the off chance that you have a workstation with a schematic editor, you may input your design utilizing commonplace logic squares. Something else, a line or full screen content tool, utilized as a part of the non-record mode will do. A case of an ABEL™ content record is on the following page.

Next, turn the logic compiler free on your design. To start with it will check for typographical errors and any irregularities in your detail. Most compilers at that point endeavor to lessen your logic utilizing standard logic diminishment theory. At that point, a simulator will check the test vectors you input, looking at your logic depiction against the anticipated reactions. This is an astounding approach to confirm your design. Check with the suitable software manuals for more information.

Toward the finish of the arrangement procedure, a JEDEC document is out-put. This document is a standard format acknowledged by most programming equipment. Next download this document to your picked programmer.

Now you are prepared to "assemble" your model. Ensure the programmer has the correct information to expert gram the device you have picked (an Atmel PLD, obviously), connect to your device, and go! Most programmers will even practically test your model for you in the event that you incorporate test vectors in your JEDEC record.

Take your arranged PLD, and connect it to your system. In the event that you discover any errors, simply utilize your editor to roll out the important improvements, and rehash the procedure. It's simple!

ILLUSTRATION DESIGN

The accompanying design is a basic case utilizing ABEL™ to handle the logic depiction document and an AT22V10 as the objective device. The conditions are on the following page, and are an immediate propagation of the real ABEL input record.

Each of the three admissible input formats are appeared. A fact table is utilized to portray a straightforward 2-to-4 decoder, as is regularly used to decipher chip chooses in a microprocessor system. Next, the state machine format is utilized to portray a partition by-4 counter. And at long last, Boolean conditions are utilized to depict some random logic.

Note the test vectors used to test the device. The "c" terminology implies that this stick has a low-to-high-to-low arrangement of moves for this vector. Each time this happens, the counter should increase. Likewise take note of that the counter begins in the reset condition, which is both outputs "1" for a dynamic low output.

Figure 1. PLD DesignProcess

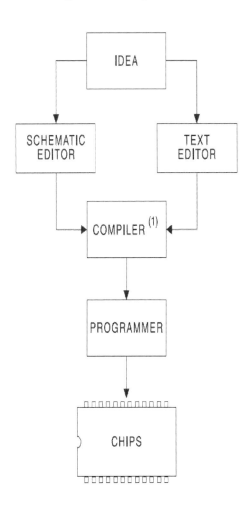

Note: 1. Samples of compilers are ABEL, CUPL™, PLdesigner XL™, and LOG/iC. Every one of these producescomprisesunits which allow recreation of your design. They also diminish your logic calculations, which stretches you elasticity in relating yourdesign.

EXAMPLE ABEL-HDL DESCRIPTIONFILE

```
module X3;
title 'Example using 22V10 - KHG 1/6/88'; X310 device 'P22V10'; "
Clk,A12,A13 pin1,2,3;
CE0,CE1,CE2,CE3 pin20,21,22,23;
Q1,Q2,CarOut pin17,18,14;
CarEn,A,B,C,D pin6,7,8,9,10;
Out1,Out2          pin15,16; "
X,Z,c          = .X. , .Z. , .C.; "
"Counter States
State1 = ^b00; State2 = ^b01;
State3          = ^b10;   State4  = ^b11; "
```

"The truth table shows the 2 to 4 decoder, which decodes " $A13$ and $A12$ into CE0, CE1,

CE2, and CE3.

```
truth_table ([A13,A12] -> [CE0,CE1,CE2,CE3]) [ 0, 0 ] -> [ 0, 1, 1, 1 ];
[ 0, 1 ] -> [ 1, 0, 1, 1 ];
[ 1, 0 ] -> [ 1, 1, 0, 1 ];
[ 1, 1 ] -> [ 1, 1, 1, 0 ];
```

"The following state description defines the divide by 4 counter state_diagram [Q2,Q1]

```
State State1: GOTO State2; State State2: GOTO State3; State State3: GOTO
State4;
State State4: GOTO State1;
```

"The following equations are general in nature to illustrate Boolean input

"format. The CarOut equation uses state 4 above to produce a carry.

Equations

```
CarOut = Q2 & Q1 & CarEn; "& = AND

Out1 = A & B + C & D; "+ = OR, AND takes precedence

Out2          = A & C + B & D;
```

"The following are the appropriate test vectors test_vectors"

```
([Clk, CarEn,A13,A12,A, B,C, D]- >[CE0,CE1,CE2,CE3,Q2,Q1,CarOut,Out1,Out2]);

[ 0, 0, 0, 0, 0, 0, 0, 0 ] - >[ 0, 1, 1, 1, 1, 1, 0, 0, 0 ];

[ c, 0, 0, 1, 1, 1, 0, 0 ] - >[ 1, 0, 1, 1, 0, 0, 0, 1, 0 ];

[ c, 0, 1, 0, 1, 0, 1, 0 ] - >[ 1, 1, 0, 1, 0, 1, 0, 0, 1 ];

[ c, 0, 1, 1, 0, 0, 1, 1 ] - >[ 1, 1, 1, 0, 1, 0, 0, 1, 0 ];

[ c, 0, 0, 0, 0, 1, 0, 1 ] - >[ 0, 1, 1, 1, 1, 1, 0, 0, 1 ];

[ 0, 1, 0, 1, 1, 1, 1, 1 ] - >[ 1, 0, 1, 1, 1, 1, 1, 1, 1 ];

end X3;
```

EXAMPLE VHDL DESCRIPTION FILE

```
library ieee;
use ieee.std_logic_1164.all;
-------------------------------------------------

entity AND_Gate is
port( x: in std_logic;
y: in std_logic;
F: out std_logic
);
end AND_ent;
-------------------------------------------------

architecture AND_arch of AND_Gate is
begin
F <= x AND y;
end AND_arch;
-------------------------------------------------
```

EXAMPLE VERILOG DESCRIPTION FILE

```
module some_logic_component (c, a, b);
// declare port signals
output c;
input a, b;
// declare internal wire
wire d;
//instantiate structural logic gates
and a1(d, a, b); //d is output, a and b are inputs
not n1(c, d); //c is output, d is input

        endmodule
```

CHAPTER 17: THE DATA CENTER EVOLUTION FROM MAINFRAME TO CLOUD

Cloud figuring did not murder the mainframe. The problematic innovation did, in any case, it made the mainframe advance. The Cloud is not a Mainframe however. Also, the Mainframe is not a Super Computer as well.

MAINFRAME

The mainframe computer is a deep rooted legend. They have been around since the begin of figuring, and they keep on existing in overhauled frame today. Be that as it may, even with cloud figuring, mainframes appear as though they will completely subside to the very specialty advertise they lived in amid the age of the beginning of processing. The greatest preferred standpoint of mainframes at the present time is that you effectively possess one. On the off chance that you don't officially claim one, there is no motivation to put into one, as the arrangements given by cloud registering are frequently considerably more practical in practically every circumstance.

One advantage expansive organization appreciate about mainframes is the 100% finish control over their own data. When utilizing cloud administrations, you believe an outsider organization to not touch your data. With mainframes, you never need to stress over them snooping or touching your data. In any case, most substantial cloud organizations are very reliable and the odds of them accomplishing something you don't need them to be very little.

In any case, on the off chance that you as of now do possess one, there are unquestionably motivations to keep it. The cost of getting countless lines of code exchanged over would most likely alone exceed the advantages of changing to cloud. Likewise, mainframes have the capacity to be modified and concentrated more than cloud administrations can, as the hardware itself is responsible for the client. Mainframe computers can have nothing to do with your web association, which is great since it diminishes transmission capacity being utilized and takes into consideration simple utilize notwithstanding when the web is down.

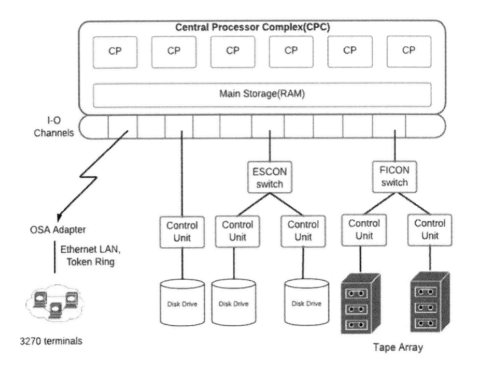

DIFFERENCES FROM SUPERCOMPUTERS

A supercomputer is a computer that is at the bleeding edge of the current handling limit, especially the speed of figuring. Supercomputers are utilized for logical and building issues (superior registering) which are data crunching and calculating, while mainframes are utilized for exchange preparing. The distinctions are as per the following:

Mainframes are frequently around measured in a huge number of instructions per second (MIPS), however supercomputers are measured in floating point operations per second (FLOPS) and all the more as of late by traversed edges per second or TEPS. Cases of whole number operations incorporate moving data around in memory or checking esteems. Floating-point operations are generally expansion, subtraction, and duplication with enough digits of exactness to demonstrate ceaseless marvels, for

350

example, climate forecast and atomic reproductions. As far as computational capacity, supercomputers are all the more intense.

Mainframes are worked to be solid for exchange handling, as it is ordinarily comprehended in the business world: a business trade of merchandise, administrations, or cash. A commonplace exchange, as characterized by the Transaction Processing Performance Council, would incorporate the refreshing to a database framework for such things as stock control (merchandise), carrier reservations (administrations), or managing an account (cash). An exchange could allude to an arrangement of operations including disk read/composes, operating framework calls, or any type of data exchange starting with one subsystem then onto the next. This operation does not tally toward the preparing energy of a computer. Exchange preparing is not selected to mainframes but rather additionally utilized as a part of the performance of microprocessor-based servers and online systems.

In 2007, an amalgamation of the distinctive innovations and structures for supercomputers and mainframes has prompted the alleged Gameframe.

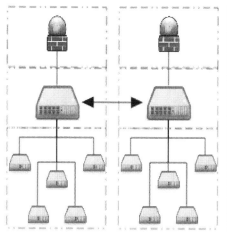

Year	Supercomputer	Peak speed (Rmax)	Location
2013	NUDT Tianhe-2	33.86 PFLOPS	Guangzhou, China
2012	Cray Titan	17.59 PFLOPS	Oak Ridge, U.S.
2012	IBM Sequoia	17.17 PFLOPS	Livermore, U.S.
2011	Fujitsu K computer	10.51 PFLOPS	Kobe, Japan
2010	Tianhe-IA	2.566 PFLOPS	Tianjin, China
2009	Cray Jaguar	1.759 PFLOPS	Oak Ridge, U.S.
2008	IBM Roadrunner	1.026 PFLOPS / 1.105 PFLOPS	Los Alamos, U.S.

Example architecture of a geographically disperse computing system connecting many nodes over a network

CLOUD

The cloud is an interesting new innovation. For one thing, it tends to cost not as much as a mainframe, particularly for introductory obtaining. It likewise takes into consideration moderately innocuous redesigns, as the organizations who are contending with each other for your cloud space will probably update just to keep their clients. Cloud innovation likewise enables you to maintain a strategic distance from support costs and the migraines that may originate from a mainframe computer: the organization you are utilizing should do it to keep its clients. Cloud figuring likewise takes into account practically interminable compactness: access to your work is just restricted by your capacity to get to the web.

One issue with cloud processing is its reliance on a genuinely capable web association, one that will ideally never go down or go down as meager as conceivable to be satisfactory to legitimize the costs an association blackout would cost. In the event that that is incomprehensible, at that point a mainframe is most likely vital. In any case, this ought to be an uncommon issue, as most organizations today have great associations for different reasons in any case.

Despite the fact that the decision amongst mainframe and cloud advances may be an extreme one to make for the individuals who have as of now put resources into mainframe before, I can propose going to cloud on the off chance that it bodes well, as I trust that what's to come is traveling toward that path.

The cloud world acquired a few ideas from the mainframe world that preceded it. The utilization based evaluating model, Linux virtual machines, and multi-occupancy originated from that past mainframe era. NASA disposed of its mainframes, however these gigantic machines can at present be found in numerous expansive associations.

WHAT IS A MAINFRAME COMPUTER?

A mainframe computer is a sort of enormous, capable, costly, and dependable computer that has been around for a considerable length of time—IBM declared the System/360 50 years prior. A large portion of the applications running on these machines were composed in COBOL, a programming dialect that is similarly as old as the mainframes.

A few merchants offer mainframes today, yet "mainframe condition" basically implies IBM zSeries machines. The old set up mainframe condition operating framework is called z/OS. The greater part of the noteworthy money related handling is on z/OS.

This is not a machine worked for conventional workloads—a mainframe runs difficult tasks, for example, the dealing with the databases of an insurance agency, the logical research of a national government, and the charge card exchanges of a bank. Many individuals have never at any point seen a mainframe.

IS THE MAINFRAME DIED?

Who needs to work with mainframes? Without a doubt, coders need to overcome the world with Python, APIs, and web administrations. They would prefer not to work with old CICS RPG programs. Framework directors need to fabricate appropriated registering frameworks with cloud building hinders that are blame tolerant and very versatile. Back officers need to lease shoddy product hardware, not douse up their financial plan with a top of the line costly unit.

Truth be told, the mainframe is as of now dead, a few times over. Its passing has been accounted for as the result of each new problematic innovation to clear the IT world. The mainframe was executed off by the desktop PC upset. Furthermore, again by the customer server upset. What's more, now by the cloud figuring upset, where enormous amounts of CPU, storage, and memory are right away accessible for anybody to lease. On the off chance that mainframes are old innovation and fundamentally dead, at that point why are they still so central to such a variety of ventures.

THE MAINFRAME IS' N DEAD

The mainframe is as yet enormous in the business. In spite of the expectations and bits of gossip, it is truly not leaving. While a portion of the littler clients have dropped off, the majority of the greater clients are developing their workloads on the mainframe.

There are two sides to why the mainframe showcase is as yet going solid. One is secure—an old business-basic application running on a mainframe, with numerous times of business rationale incorporated with it, costs a fortune to move somewhere else.

The other is the mainframe's importance in a present day cross breed cloud design, running VMs on-commence and putting away petabytes of data. The mainframe has developed a considerable measure throughout the years. You can run Linux on the mainframe.

A ton of what these huge suppliers are doing is truly attempting to reproduce the mainframe by hashing together a great deal of servers. A private cloud produced using numerous product boxes—one that can give, say, 5,000 virtual machines—has things just the same as a mainframe.

- Both contain tremendous pools of CPU and memory for virtual machines, and monstrous measures of storage for articles and pictures.
- Both run an OS that virtualizes workloads to expand effectiveness.
- Both can manage high volumes of exchanges. A large number of the scaling issues being experienced in the cloud were comprehended long prior by mainframe experts.

A venture that runs Java on-start may discover a mainframe valuable. Z/OS is presumably the most effective place to run Java. You put the code where the data is, and you get the chance to evacuate any system inactivity for the exchanges.

THE MAINFRAME'S PLACE IN THE CUTTING EDGE CLOUD WORLD

Can a mainframe convey the nimbleness, effectiveness, and quality that cloud processing gives? One burly mainframe can be more helpful than an armada of item boxes, however just for specific sorts of work. Nobody will purchase another IBM z10 for little workloads—that would resemble purchasing a major truck for the school run—however on a huge scale it can be a superior decision. Regardless of the high cost, mainframe utilize might be cheaper than ware hardware use for big business scale workloads.

"The web did not slaughter print, MP3s did not murder the record business, the cell phone did not execute the desktop, and cloud figuring has not executed off the

mainframe. These troublesome advances have caused exceptional moves in their business sectors."

In the event that past is genuinely introduction, at that point it shouldn't come as a shock to any individual who has considered the historical backdrop of data framework that virtualization, propelled cloud designs and open, conveyed registering models are beginning to look a ton like the mainframe of old—yet on a bigger scale.

Wherever you look, actually, individuals are discussing pooled assets, higher usage rates, incorporated frameworks and a rash of other mainframe-like components planned to enable the undertaking to adapt to the rising tide of digital data. Put another way: If the system is the new PC, at that point the data center is the new "mainframe."

Obviously, this new mainframe data center will contrast from the old in various ways, most quite in the expertise sets and improvement situations expected to run it. At the current OCP Summit, for example, there was no lack of speakers highlighting the requirement for associations to increase their insight into cutting edge virtual and cloud innovations that will pull workaday foundation administration assignments from physical layer framework to more adaptable software-characterized builds. It is significant, in any case, that the virtualization and asset usage systems that introduced the cloud were not made out of entire material amid the customer server period, yet were in actuality extended from before mainframe situations.

This reality isn't lost on large portions of the main cloud developers, for example, Equinix' Raouf Abdel, who as of late expressed straight to Forbes: "what's to come is foundation. We are nearly relocating back to the mainframe show." Almost, yet not exactly. The key distinction is that once upon a time, the mainframe was a solitary processing substance sustaining any number of neighborhood terminals. Nowadays, different data foundation is shared over extraordinary separations, here and there a large portion of a world away, and frequently claimed and overseen by various associations. Yet, the final product is to a great extent the same: a solid framework that can bereconfigured and repurposed to a great extent in software with almost no adjustment on the hardware side, spare the intermittent move up to new, more intense gear.

This must create a lot of fulfillment among mainframe-utilizing CIOs who has needed to bear the disdain of partners for staying with "old innovation" amid the 20-year customer server run. In any case, the inquiry remains, is customary huge iron equipped for supporting present day scale-out data situations? Assuredly, says CA Technologies' Denise Dubie. Truth be told, why try tearing out long-serving mainframes when they can give all the power, security and dependability required for Big Data stacks and thriving value-based situations? It won't not bode well to construct Greenfield arrangements in light of the mainframe, however this is one region in which inheritance framework can give a noteworthy go to extensive associations hoping to pull out all the stops on the cloud.

To do that, however, you'll require another administration that can bring the mainframe into the developing API economy. SOA Software, for example, offers another Lifecycle Manager suite that basically makes a "RESTful Mainframe" that can give REST-based API administration to zOS-based Web administrations. This ought to give a prepared answer for versatile applications specifically as they chase for quick and adaptable access to backend endeavor frameworks, while in the meantime furnishing data center administrators with cutting edge benefit revelation and effect examination over all mainframe, appropriated and outsider foundation.

History, at that point, does in truth rehash itself, albeit never in the very same way. The present development toward cloud figuring and framework union is going on at a scale that early mainframe improvements would never have thought about. Be that as it may, on the off chance that we take after this pattern to its definitive decision, we could end up getting to an open, unified data condition that truly extends the world over.

In the event that that is the situation, is it too soon to begin discussing the world as the new mainframe? In the event that undertakings need the readiness of open cloud suppliers, for example, Amazon, Facebook and Google, they should totally reconsider their IT framework and operation.

CLOUD COMPUTING

Additionally on-request computing, is a sort of Internet-based computing that gives shared preparing assets and data to computers and different gadgets on request. It is a model for empowering omnipresent, on-request access to a common pool of configurable computing assets. Cloud computing and storage arrangements give clients and undertakings different capacities to store and process their data in outsider data centers. It depends on sharing of assets to accomplish rationality and economies of scale, like an utility (like the power framework) over a system. At the establishment of cloud computing is the more extensive idea of focalized framework and shared administrations.

Cloud computing is a model for empowering universal, helpful, on-request arrange access to a common pool of configurable computing assets (e.g., systems, servers, storage, applications and administrations) that can be quickly provisioned and discharged with insignificant administration exertion.

Defenders guarantee that cloud computing enables organizations to maintain a strategic distance from forthright framework expenses, and concentrate on ventures that separate their organizations rather than on foundation. Defenders additionally guarantee that cloud computing enables ventures to get their applications up and running quicker, with enhanced reasonability and less support, and empowers IT to all the more quickly modify assets to meet fluctuating and flighty business request. Cloud suppliers commonly utilize a "pay as you go" display. This can prompt out of the blue high charges if chairmen don't adjust to the cloud valuing model.

The present accessibility of high-limit systems, ease computers and storage gadgets and also the across the board appropriation of hardware virtualization, benefit arranged engineering, and autonomic and utility computing have prompted a development in cloud computing. Organizations can scale up as computing needs increment and after that scale down again as requests diminish.

Cloud computing has turned into a profoundly requested administration or utility because of the upsides of high computing power, modest cost of administrations, elite, versatility, openness and in addition accessibility. Some cloud sellers are experiencing development rates of half per annum, however due to being in a phase of outset, despite everything it has entanglements that need proper thoughtfulness regarding make cloud computing administrations more dependable and easy to understand.

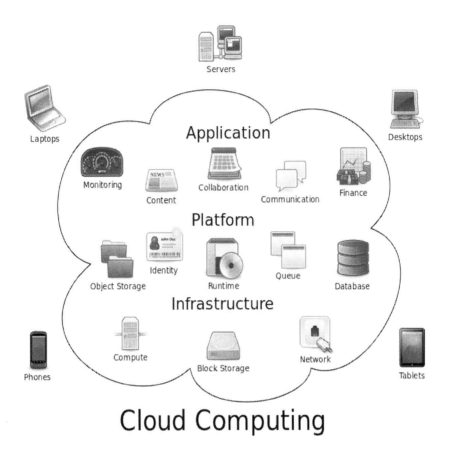

Cloud computing metaphor: For a user, the network elements representing the provider-rendered services are invisible, as if obscured by a cloud.

Since 2000, cloud computing has appeared. In mid 2008, NASA's OpenNebula, improved in the RESERVOIR European Commission-subsidized venture, turned into the main open-source software for conveying private and crossover clouds, and for the federation of clouds. Around the same time, endeavors were centered around giving quality of service ensures (as required by ongoing intuitive applications) to cloud-based foundations, in the structure of the IRMOS European Commission-subsidized venture, bringing about a continuous cloud environment. By mid-2008, Gartner saw an open door for cloud computing "to shape the relationship among consumers of IT services, the individuals who utilize IT services and the individuals who offer them" and watched that "organizations are changing from organization claimed hardware and software resources for per-utilize service-based models" so that the "anticipated move to computing ... will bring about sensational development in IT items in a few territories and critical reductions in different zones."

Microsoft Azure was declared as "Purplish blue" in October 2008 and discharged on 1 February 2010 as Windows Azure, before being renamed to Microsoft Azure on 25 March 2014. For a period, Azure was on the TOP500 supercomputer list, before it dropped off it.

In July 2010, Rackspace Hosting and NASA together propelled an open-source cloud-software activity known as OpenStack. The OpenStack extend proposed to enable organizations to offer cloud-computing services running on standard hardware. The early code originated from NASA's Nebula stage and from Rackspace's Cloud Files stage.

On March 1, 2011, IBM declared the IBM SmartCloud system to bolster Smarter Planet. Among the different components of the Smarter Computing foundation, cloud computing is a basic piece.

On June 7, 2012, Oracle declared the Oracle Cloud. While parts of the Oracle Cloud are still being developed, this cloud offering is ready to be the first to furnish clients with access to an incorporated arrangement of IT solutions, including the Applications (SaaS), Platform (PaaS), and Infrastructure (IaaS) layers.

RELATIVE CONCEPTS

Cloud computing is the consequence of the evolution and adoption of existing advancements and ideal models. The objective of cloud computing is to enable clients to take benefit from these advancements, without the requirement for profound information about or expertise with every one of them. The cloud means to cut expenses, and enables the clients to concentrate on their center business as opposed to being blocked by IT hindrances.

The fundamental empowering innovation for cloud computing is virtualization. Virtualization software isolates a physical computing gadget into at least one "virtual" gadgets, each of which can be effortlessly utilized and figured out how to perform computing undertakings. With operating system–level virtualization basically making a versatile arrangement of numerous free computing gadgets, sit without moving computing assets can be allotted and utilized all the more effectively. Virtualization gives the nimbleness required to accelerate IT operations, and lessens taken a toll by expanding framework utilization. Autonomic computing robotizes the procedure through which the client can provision assets on-demand. By limiting client inclusion, automation accelerates the procedure, diminishes work costs and decreases the likelihood of human mistakes.

Clients routinely confront troublesome business issues. Cloud computing receives concepts from Service-oriented Architecture (SOA) that can enable the client to break these issues into services that can be coordinated to give a solution. Cloud computing gives the greater part of its assets as services, and makes utilization of the entrenched benchmarks and best practices picked up in the area of SOA to enable worldwide and simple access to cloud services standardizedly.

Cloud computing additionally use concepts from utility computing to give measurements to the services utilized. Such measurements are at the center of general society cloud pay-per-utilize models. In addition, measured services are a fundamental piece of the criticism circle in autonomic computing, enabling services to scale on-demand and to perform programmed disappointment recuperation.

Cloud computing is a sort of framework computing; it has advanced by tending to the QoS (quality of service) and dependability issues. Cloud computing gives the devices and advances to fabricate data/process escalated parallel applications with considerably more moderate costs contrasted with traditional parallel computing systems.

MODE, CLIENT–SERVER

Client–server computing alludes extensively to any appropriated application that recognizes service suppliers (servers) and service requestors (customers).

FRAMEWORK COMPUTING

"A type of dispersed and parallel computing, whereby a 'super and virtual computer' is made out of a group of organized, inexactly coupled computers acting in concert to perform vast errands."

HAZE COMPUTING

Distributed computing worldview that gives data, process, storage and application services nearer to customer or close client edge gadgets, for example, organize switches. Moreover, haze computing handles data at the system level, on savvy gadgets and on the end-client customer side (e.g. cell phones), rather than sending data to a remote location for handling.

DEW COMPUTING

In the current computing progressive system, the Dew computing is positioned as the ground level for the cloud and mist computing ideal models. Contrasted with mist computing, which underpins developing IoT applications that demand continuous and unsurprising idleness and the dynamic system reconfigurability, Dew computing pushes the frontiers to computing applications, data, and low level services far from centralized virtual hubs to the end clients.

MAINFRAME COMPUTER

Powerful computers utilized for the most part by vast organizations for basic applications, normally mass data preparing, for example, enumeration; industry and consumer insights; police and mystery knowledge services; undertaking asset arranging; and budgetary transaction handling.

UTILITY COMPUTING

The "bundling of computing assets, for example, computation and storage, as a metered service like a traditional open utility, for example, power."

SHARED

A circulated architecture without the requirement for central coordination. Members are both providers and consumers of assets (in contrast to the traditional client–server demonstrate).

ATTRIBUTES

Spryness enhances with clients' capacity to re-provision mechanical framework assets. Cost reductions asserted by cloud suppliers. An open cloud conveyance demonstrate converts capital consumption to operational use. This purportedly brings boundaries down to section, as framework is regularly given by an outsider and need not be bought for one-time or occasional escalated computing undertakings. Evaluating on an utility computing premise is fine-grained, with utilization based options and less IT aptitudes are required for implementation (in-house). The e-FISCAL venture's best in class storehouse contains a few articles investigating cost perspectives in more detail, a large portion of them concluding that costs reserve funds rely on upon the sort of exercises bolstered and the kind of foundation accessible in-house.

Gadget and location freedom empower clients to get to frameworks utilizing a web program paying little respect to their location or what gadget they utilize (e.g., PC, cell phone). As framework is off-webpage (ordinarily given by an outsider) and got to by means of the Internet, clients can connect from anyplace.

Upkeep of cloud computing applications is simpler, in light of the fact that they don't should be introduced on every client's computer and can be gotten to from better places.

Multitenancy empowers sharing of assets and expenses over a substantial pool of clients taking into consideration:

- centralization of framework in locations with bring down costs, (for example, land, power, and so forth.)
- peak-stack limit builds (clients require not design for most noteworthy conceivable load-levels)
- utilization and effectiveness changes for frameworks that are frequently only 10–20% used.

PERFORMANCE

Monitored, and consistent and approximately coupled architectures are constructed utilizing web services as the framework interface.

EFFICIENCY

It might be expanded when different clients can chip away at similar data at the same time, instead of sitting tight for it to be spared and messaged. Time might be spared, as information does not should be re-entered when fields are coordinated, nor do clients need to introduce application software moves up to their computer.

RELIABILITY

Unwavering quality enhances with the utilization of different repetitive destinations, which makes very much planned cloud computing appropriate for business continuity and debacle recuperation.

SCALABILITY AND ELASTICITY

Versatility and flexibility by means of dynamic ("on-demand") provisioning of assets on a fine-grained, self-service premise in close ongoing (Note, the VM startup time changes by VM sort, location, OS and cloud suppliers), without clients engineering for top burdens. This gives the capacity to scale up when the utilization require increments or down if assets are not being utilized.

SECURITY

Security can enhance because of centralization of data, expanded security-centered assets, and so forth., however concerns can persist about loss of control over certain touchy data, and the absence of security for put away parts. Security is regularly in the same class as or superior to other traditional frameworks, to a limited extent since suppliers can commit assets to unraveling security issues that numerous clients can't bear to handle. Be that as it may, the complexity of security is significantly expanded when data is appropriated over a more extensive territory or over a more prominent number of gadgets, and also in multi-occupant frameworks shared by inconsequential clients. In addition, client access to security review logs might be troublesome or inconceivable. Private cloud installations are to a limited extent inspired by clients' craving to hold control over the framework and abstain from losing control of information security.

FIVE FUNDAMENTAL ATTRIBUTES

The National Institute of Standards and Technology's definition of cloud computing distinguishes "five fundamental attributes":

ON-DEMAND SELF-SERVICE

A consumer can singularly provision computing capacities, for example, server time and system storage, as required naturally without requiring human interaction with each service supplier.

BROAD NETWORK ACCESS

Capacities are accessible over the system and gotten to through standard instruments that advance use by heterogeneous thin or thick customer stages (e.g., cell phones, tablets, portable PCs, and workstations).

ASSET POOLING

The supplier's computing assets are pooled to serve numerous consumers utilizing a multi-inhabitant display, with various physical and virtual assets progressively allocated and reassigned by consumer demand.

QUICK VERSATILITY

Capacities can be flexibly provisioned and discharged, at times naturally, proportional quickly outward and internal comparable with demand. To the consumer, the abilities accessible for provisioning frequently seem boundless and can be appropriated in any amount whenever.

MEASURED SERVICE

Cloud frameworks naturally control and enhance asset use by utilizing a metering ability at some level of abstraction proper to the kind of service (e.g., storage, preparing, data transfer capacity, and dynamic client accounts). Asset utilization can be monitored, controlled, and announced, giving straightforwardness to both the supplier and consumer of the used service.

SERVICE MODELS

In spite of the fact that service-oriented architecture advocates "everything as a service" (with the acronyms EaaS or XaaS or basically aas), cloud-computing suppliers offer their "services" as indicated by various models, which happen to shape a stack: foundation , stage and software-as-a-service.

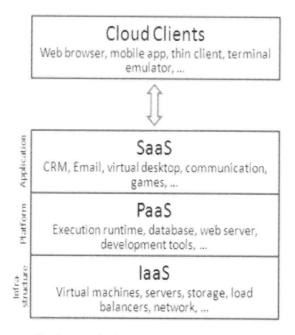

Cloud-computing layers accessible within a stack

INFRASTRUCTURE AS A SERVICE (IAAS)

In the most fundamental cloud-service demonstrate—and as indicated by the IETF (Internet Engineering Task Force)— suppliers of IaaS offer computers—physical or (all the more frequently) virtual machines—and different assets. IaaS alludes to online services that dynamic the client from the subtle elements of foundation like physical computing assets, location, data partitioning, scaling, security, reinforcement and so on. A hypervisor, for example, Xen, Oracle VirtualBox, KVM, VMware ESX/ESXi, or Hyper-V runs the virtual machines as visitors. Pools of hypervisors inside the cloud operational framework can bolster extensive quantities of virtual machines and the capacity to scale services all over as indicated by clients' differing necessities. IaaS clouds regularly offer additional assets, for example, a virtual-machine disk-picture library, crude square storage, record or protest storage, firewalls, stack balancers, IP addresses, virtual local area networks (VLANs), and software packs. IaaS-cloud suppliers supply these assets on-demand from their vast pools of hardware introduced in data centers. For wide-area connectivity, clients can utilize either the Internet or bearer clouds (devoted virtual private networks).

To convey their applications, cloud clients introduce operating-framework pictures and their application software on the cloud foundation. In this model, the cloud client fixes and keeps up the operating frameworks and the application software. Cloud suppliers commonly charge IaaS services on an utility computing premise: cost mirrors the measure of assets dispensed and consumed.

PLATFORM AS A SERVICE (PAAS)

PaaS merchants offer an advancement environment to application developers. The supplier ordinarily creates toolbox and gauges for advancement and channels for distribution and installment. In the PaaS models, cloud suppliers convey a computing platform, normally including operating framework, programming-dialect execution environment, database, and web server. Application developers can create and run their software solutions on a cloud platform without the cost and complexity of purchasing and dealing with the hidden hardware and software layers. With some PaaS offers like Microsoft Azure and Google App Engine, the hidden computer and storage assets scale consequently to coordinate application demand so that the cloud client does not need to allot assets physically. The last has likewise been proposed by an architecture expecting to encourage continuous in cloud environments. Significantly more particular application sorts can be given through PaaS, for example, media encoding as given by services like bitcodin.com or media.io.

Some integration and data administration suppliers have likewise grasped particular applications of PaaS as conveyance models for data solutions. Illustrations incorporate iPaaS and dPaaS. iPaaS (Integration Platform as a Service) empowers clients to create, execute and represent integration streams. Under the iPaaS integration show, clients drive the improvement and organization of integrations without introducing or dealing with any hardware or middleware. dPaaS (Data Platform as a Service) conveys integration—and data-administration—items as a completely oversaw service. Under the dPaaS display, the PaaS supplier, not the client, deals with the improvement and execution of data solutions by building custom-made data applications for the client. dPaaS clients hold straightforwardness and control over data through data-visualization apparatuses.

Platform as a Service (PaaS) consumers don't oversee or control the fundamental cloud foundation including network, servers, operating frameworks, or storage, yet have control over the sent applications and potentially configuration settings for the application-facilitating environment.

SOFTWARE AS A SERVICE (SAAS)

In the software as a service (SaaS) display, clients access application software and databases. Cloud suppliers deal with the framework and platforms that run the applications. SaaS is some of the time alluded to as "on-demand software" and is generally estimated on a compensation per-utilize premise or utilizing a subscription charge.

In the SaaS demonstrate, cloud suppliers introduce and operate application software in the cloud and cloud clients get to the software from cloud customers. Cloud clients don't deal with the cloud foundation and platform where the application runs. This wipes out the need to introduce and run the application on the cloud client's own computers, which improves upkeep and support. Cloud applications contrast from different applications in their versatility—which can be accomplished by cloning tasks onto numerous virtual machines at run-time to take care of changing work demand. Load balancers circulate the work over the arrangement of virtual machines. This procedure is straightforward to the cloud client, who sees only a solitary get to point. To suit countless clients, cloud applications can be multitenant, implying that any machine may serve more than one cloud-client organization.

The valuing model for SaaS applications is ordinarily a monthly or yearly level expense per client, so costs wind up noticeably adaptable and flexible if clients are included or expelled anytime.

Proponents guarantee that SaaS gives a business the possibility to lessen IT operational expenses by outsourcing hardware and software upkeep and support to the cloud supplier. This empowers the business to reallocate IT operations costs far from hardware/software spending and from personnel costs, towards meeting different objectives. In addition, with applications facilitated centrally, updates can be discharged without the requirement for clients to put in new software. One disadvantage of SaaS accompanies putting away the clients' data on the cloud supplier's server. Subsequently, there could be unapproved access to the data. Hence, clients are progressively embracing insightful outsider key-administration frameworks to help secure their data.

CLOUD CUSTOMERS

Clients get to cloud computing utilizing networked customer gadgets, for example, desktop computers, portable workstations, tablets and smartphones and any Ethernet empowered gadget, for example, Home Automation Gadgets. Some of these gadgets—cloud customers—depend on cloud computing for all or a lion's share of their applications in order to be basically pointless without it. Illustrations are thin customers and the program based Chromebook. Many cloud applications don't require particular software on the customer and rather utilize a web program to connect with the cloud application. With Ajax and HTML5 these Web UIs can accomplish a comparative, or surprisingly better, look and feel to local applications. Some cloud applications, nonetheless, bolster particular customer software devoted to these applications (e.g., virtual desktop customers and most email customers). Some heritage applications (line of business applications that as of not long ago have been pervasive in thin customer computing) are conveyed through a screen-sharing innovation.

DEPLOYMENT MODELS

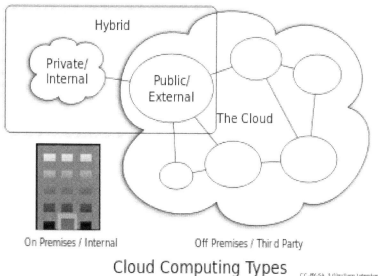

Cloud computing types

PRIVATE CLOUD

Private cloud will be cloud foundation operated exclusively for a solitary organization, regardless of whether oversaw inside or by an outsider, and facilitated either inside or remotely. Undertaking a private cloud extend requires a critical level and level of engagement to virtualize the business environment, and requires the organization to rethink decisions about existing assets. At the point when done right, it can enhance business, yet every progression in the venture raises security issues that must be routed to counteract genuine vulnerabilities. Self-run data centers are for the most part capital escalated. They have a noteworthy physical impression, requiring allocations of space, hardware, and environmental controls. These advantages must be invigorated

369

periodically, bringing about additional capital uses. They have pulled in feedback since clients "still need to purchase, fabricate, and oversee them "and along these lines don't profit by less active administration, basically" the economic model that makes cloud computing such an interesting concept".

PUBLIC CLOUD

A cloud is known as a "public cloud" when the services are rendered over a network that is open for public utilize. Public cloud services might be free. In fact there might be next to zero distinction amongst public and private cloud architecture, nonetheless, security consideration might be significantly extraordinary for services (applications, storage, and different assets) that are made accessible by a service supplier for a public group of onlookers and when communication is affected over a non-put stock in network. For the most part, public cloud service suppliers like Amazon AWS, Microsoft and Google claim and operate the framework at their data center and get to is for the most part by means of the Internet. AWS and Microsoft offer direct connect services called "AWS Direct Connect" and "Sky blue ExpressRoute" separately, such connections oblige clients to buy or rent a private connection to a peering point offered by the cloud supplier.

HYBRID CLOUD

Hybrid cloud is a composition of at least two clouds (private, community or public) that stay particular elements yet are bound together, offering the advantages of different arrangement models. Hybrid cloud can likewise mean the capacity to connect collocation, oversaw as well as devoted services with cloud assets.

Gartner, Inc. characterizes a hybrid cloud service as a cloud computing service that is made out of some combination of private, public and community cloud services, from various service suppliers. A hybrid cloud service crosses isolation and supplier limits with the goal that it can't be just placed in one classification of private, public, or community cloud service. It enables one to augment either the limit or the capacity of a cloud service, by aggregation, integration or customization with another cloud service.

Changed utilize cases for hybrid cloud composition exist. For instance, an organization may store delicate customer data in house on a private cloud application, however interconnect that application to a business knowledge application given on a public cloud as a software service. This case of hybrid cloud develops the capacities of the venture to convey a particular business service through the addition of remotely accessible public cloud services. Hybrid cloud adoption relies on upon various elements, for example, data security and consistence necessities, level of control required over data, and the applications an organization employments.

Another case of hybrid cloud is one where IT organizations utilize public cloud computing assets to meet impermanent limit needs that can't be met by the private cloud. This capacity empowers hybrid clouds to utilize cloud blasting for scaling crosswise over clouds. Cloud blasting is an application arrangement demonstrate in which an application keeps running in a private cloud or data center and "blasts" to a public cloud when the demand for computing limit increments. An essential favorable position of cloud blasting and a hybrid cloud show is that an organization only pays for additional process assets when they are required. Cloud blasting empowers data centers to make an in-house IT foundation that backings normal workloads, and utilize cloud assets from public or private clouds, amid spikes in handling demands.

The particular model of hybrid cloud, which is worked on heterogeneous hardware, is called "Cross-platform Hybrid Cloud". A cross-platform hybrid cloud is normally controlled by various CPU architectures, for instance, x86-64 and ARM, underneath. Clients can straightforwardly send and scale applications without information of the cloud's hardware assorted qualities. This sort of cloud rises up out of the raise of ARM-construct framework with respect to chip for server-class computing.

OTHERS

COMMUNITY CLOUD

Community cloud shares framework between a few organizations from a particular community with common concerns (security, consistence, jurisdiction, and so on.), regardless of whether oversaw inside or by an outsider, and either facilitated inside or remotely. The expenses are spread over less clients than a public cloud (yet more than a private cloud), so only a portion of the cost investment funds capability of cloud computing are figured it out.

DISTRIBUTED CLOUD

A cloud computing platform can be collected from a distributed arrangement of machines in various locations, connected to a solitary network or center point service. It is conceivable to recognize two sorts of distributed clouds: public-asset computing and volunteer cloud.

Public-asset computing—This sort of distributed cloud comes about because of a broad definition of cloud computing, since they are more similar to distributed computing than cloud computing. Nonetheless, it is considered a sub-class of cloud computing, and a few illustrations incorporate distributed computing platforms, for example, BOINC and Folding@Home.

Volunteer cloud—Volunteer cloud computing is described as the intersection of public-asset computing and cloud computing, where a cloud computing foundation is fabricated utilizing volunteered assets. Many difficulties emerge from this kind of foundation, in view of the unpredictability of the assets used to assemble it and the dynamic environment it operates in. It can likewise be called shared clouds, or specially appointed clouds. An interesting exertion in such direction is Cloud@Home, it plans to actualize a cloud computing framework utilizing volunteered assets giving a plan of action to boost contributions through money related restitution.

INTERCLOUD

The Intercloud is an interconnected worldwide "cloud of clouds" and an extension of the Internet "network of networks" on which it is based. The attention is on coordinate interoperability between public cloud service suppliers, more so than amongst suppliers and consumers (similar to the case for hybrid-and multi-cloud).

MULTICLOUD

Multicloud is the utilization of different cloud computing services in a solitary heterogeneous architecture to diminish dependence on single sellers, increment adaptability through decision, moderate against debacles, and so forth. It varies from hybrid cloud in that it alludes to numerous cloud services, instead of various arrangement modes (public, private, heritage).

ARCHITECTURE

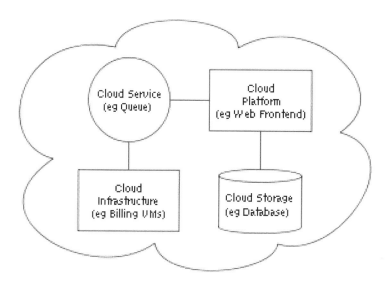

Cloud computing sample architecture

Cloud architecture, the frameworks architecture of the software frameworks required in the conveyance of cloud computing, normally includes different cloud components speaking with each other over a free coupling instrument, for example, an informing line. Versatile provision infers insight in the utilization of tight or free coupling as connected to systems, for example, these and others.

CLOUD ENGINEERING

Cloud engineering is the application of engineering controls to cloud computing. It conveys an orderly way to deal with the abnormal state concerns of commercialization, standardization, and administration in conceiving, creating, operating and keeping up cloud computing frameworks. It is a multidisciplinary technique enveloping contributions from various areas, for example, frameworks, software, web, performance, information, security, platform, hazard, and quality engineering.

SECURITY AND PROTECTION

Cloud computing postures security concerns on the grounds that the service supplier can get to the data that is in the cloud whenever. It could coincidentally or intentionally modify or even erase information. Many cloud suppliers can impart information to outsiders if fundamental for reasons for peace even without a warrant. That is permitted in their protection approaches, which clients must consent to before they begin utilizing cloud services. Solutions to security incorporate strategy and legislation and also end clients' decisions for how data is put away. Clients can encode data that is prepared or put away inside the cloud to avert unapproved get to.

As indicated by the Cloud Security Alliance, the main three dangers in the cloud are Insecure Interfaces and API's, Data Loss and Leakage, and Hardware Failure—which represented 29%, 25% and 10% of all cloud security blackouts separately. Together, these shape shared innovation vulnerabilities. In a cloud supplier platform being shared by various clients there might be a plausibility that information belonging to various clients lives on same data server. In this manner, Information spillage may emerge by confuse when information for one client is given to other. Additionally, Eugene Schultz, chief innovation officer at Emagined Security, said that programmers are investing generous energy and exertion searching for approaches to enter the cloud. "There are some genuine Achilles' heels in the cloud framework that are making huge gaps for the terrible folks to get into". Since data from hundreds or thousands of organizations can be put away on expansive cloud servers, programmers can hypothetically pick up control of enormous stores of information through a solitary assault—a procedure he called "hyperjacking". A few cases of this incorporate the Dropbox security break, and iCloud 2014 hole. Dropbox had been ruptured in October 2014, having more than 7 million of its clients passwords stolen by programmers with an end goal to get monetary incentive from it by Bitcoins (BTC). By having these passwords, they can read private data and in addition have this data be recorded via web crawlers (making the information public).

There is the issue of legitimate responsibility for data (If a client stores a few data in the cloud, can the cloud supplier benefit from it?). Many Terms of Service assentions are quiet on the question of possession. Physical control of the computer gear (private cloud) is more secure than having the hardware off site and under someone else's control (public cloud). This conveys incredible impetus to public cloud computing service suppliers to organize assembling and keeping up strong administration of secure services. Some private ventures that don't have expertise in IT security could find that it is more secure for them to utilize a public cloud. There is the hazard that end clients don't comprehend the issues included when marking on to a cloud service (persons now and again don't read the many pages of the terms of service understanding, and simply click "Acknowledge" without perusing). This is essential now that cloud computing is getting to be noticeably mainstream and required for a few services to work, for instance for a clever personal right hand (Apple's Siri or Google Now).

On a very basic level private cloud is viewed as more secure with larger amounts of control for the proprietor, however public cloud apparently is more adaptable and requires less time and money venture from the client.

LIMITATIONS

As indicated by Bruce Schneier, "The drawback is that you will have restricted customization options. Cloud computing is cheaper as a result of economics of scale, and like any outsourced task, you have a tendency to get what you get. A restaurant with a constrained menu is cheaper than a personal culinary specialist who can cook anything you need. Less options at a significantly cheaper value: it is a component, not a bug and the cloud supplier won't not meet your legitimate needs. As a business, you have to measure the advantages against the dangers."

WHAT'S TO COME

Cloud computing is in this manner still as much an exploration point, as it is a market advertising. What is clear through the evolution of cloud computing services is that the chief specialized officer (CTO) is a noteworthy main thrust behind cloud adoption. The real cloud innovation developers continue to put billions a year in cloud R&D; for instance: in 2011 Microsoft submitted 90% of its US$9.6bn R&D spending plan to its cloud. Centaur Partners additionally foresee that SaaS income will develop from US$13.5B in 2011 to $32.8B in 2016. This expansion likewise incorporates Finance and Accounting SaaS. Additionally, more ventures are swinging to cloud innovation as a productive approach to enhance quality services because of its capacities to decrease overhead costs, downtime, and computerize framework organization.

CONCLUSION

The mainframe/terminal model was established on a principal shortage of figure assets. At the time, computers were large to the point that they required exceptionally particular rooms, HVAC, operators-the works. On the off chance that you needed to utilize them, you frequently remained in line, put forth your defense, and were in the long run remunerated with a portion of the rare and profoundly significant cycles through a terminal.

The cloud computing revolution, an incredible inverse, is established on a key wealth of intense yet disconnected computing. There are such a variety of servers sitting on networks everywhere throughout the world that they are presently viewing for your attention. The trap is amassing the software, procedures, and applications appropriate for restraining the millions of public web connected server hubs into something strong.

Mainframes are planned at both the hardware and software level to keep up a high level of state-completion and transactional ability; the present flood of cloud computing is being worked around task lining and all the more inexactly coupled arrangements of services. This is an undeniable contrast. I as of late sat in a cloud computing breakout session at Zendcon where a senior developer was desperately requesting assistance from alternate participants, saying: "We've been taking a gander at this hard, and porting our frameworks to non-relational databases in the cloud will be hard... we require offer assistance."

Dissimilar to the mainframe period, the distributed frameworks of the public cloud won't not be the comfortable the greater part of your workloads right now. Cloud computing is not a methodical catch-all; rather it is a troublesome 'and'.

The only genuine connection is the one of 'remote trust'- – utilizing a non-proximal asset. Precisely the same speculation now has even the cracking Register calling the Nokia SideKick episode a disappointment of the cloud storage supplier.

"**Believing**" the mainframe operators was not a decision; it was a need. You couldn't bear to have your own computer, plain and basic. What's more, let us not overlook the straightforwardness of networking, security, and so on in those days– there was no such thing as BGP, on the grounds that for a large portion of the mainframe period, "switch" was not even a word yet. So regardless of the possibility that you push the 'trust model' and remote get to similarity, I will counter that there was no decision however to put stock in, only need; and by remote I trust you are remembering the relatively basic network topology connecting the client to the asset.

SHORTAGE VERSUS WEALTH, RATIONAL VERSUS COUPLED ARE SIMILARLY AS CRITICAL

How could we arrive at any rate? It is no mischance Google and Amazon were early players in the cloud computing market. They rode an unfathomable move in consumer practices, from disconnected buys and decision making to progressively online buys and decision making. To understand their gigantic, parallel demand builds, they needed to procure a huge number of servers. They needed to concentrate on the SW and operational procedures to take care of a wave of demand. Like the terminal get to driven period of the 70's, they at that point presented a cut of this bound together uber-asset for people to consume – I get that part–but the distinctions in the why (wealth) and the how (inexactly coupled and stateless) are more key to the eventual fate of the market than the comparability.

THE TRIUMPH OF SW OVER HW

The mainframe model of writing computer programs was not so dreamy as our current model for a straightforward reason–you just couldn't squander a MIP. HW was above all else, and in this way the faction of the all-compelling server was conceived. We endured unbelievably long obtainment cycles for servers due to this "all-compelling server" heritage, we acquired from the past. The present the truth is the inverse. In our future servers will be obtained in minutes or less–the love of rare HW is over, and everyone's eyes are on the procedures and software that enables us to utilize the bounteous humming swarm of register.

We now have such a large number of capable computers that we are eager to incredibly give up crude performance for sensibility. You have such a great amount of process out there; it is not about crude performance but rather effortlessness and convenience.

CHAPTER 18: COMPUTER SECURITY AND MOBILE SECURITY CHALLENGES

PREFACE

Computer security, otherwise called cybersecurity or IT security is the assurance of data systems from robbery or harm to the hardware, the product, and to the data on them, and additionally from interruption or confusion of the services they give. It incorporates controlling physical access to the hardware, and in addition ensuring against hurt that may come by means of system get to, data and code infusion, and because of negligence by administrators, regardless of whether purposeful, inadvertent, or because of them being deceived into veering off from secure methodology.

The field is of developing significance because of the expanding dependence on computer systems in many social orders. Computer systems now incorporate a wide assortment of "smart" devices, including smartphones, TVs and small devices as a component of the Internet of Things – and systems incorporate the Internet and private data systems, as well as Bluetooth, Wi-Fi and different remote systems.

VULNERABILITIES AND ATTACKS

A powerlessness is a system helplessness or blemish, and numerous vulnerabilities are archived in the Common Vulnerabilities and Exposures (CVE) database and weakness administration is the repetitive routine with regards to distinguishing, ordering, remediating, and relieving vulnerabilities as they are found. An exploitable helplessness is one for which no less than one working attack or "adventure" exists. To secure a computer system, it is essential to comprehend the attacks that can be made against it, and these dangers can commonly be grouped into one of the classes underneath:

BACKDOORS

A secondary passage in a computer system, a cryptosystem or a calculation, is any mystery technique for bypassing typical validation or security controls. They may exist for various reasons, including by unique plan or from poor arrangement. They may likewise have been included later by an approved gathering to permit some real get to, or by an attacker for malignant reasons; yet paying little heed to the thought processes in their reality, they make powerlessness.

DISSENT OF-SERVICE ATTACK

Dissent of service attacks are intended to make a machine or system asset inaccessible to its proposed clients. Attackers can refuse assistance to singular casualties, for example, by intentionally entering a wrong secret sufficiently key back to back circumstances to cause the casualty record to be bolted, or they may over-burden the capacities of a machine or system and square all clients without a moment's delay. While a system attack from a solitary IP address can be hindered by including another firewall govern, many types of Distributed disavowal of service (DDoS) attacks are conceivable, where the attack originates from an extensive number of focuses – and safeguarding is a great deal more troublesome. Such attacks can begin from the zombie computers of a botnet, however a scope of different strategies are conceivable including reflection and enhancement attacks, where honest systems are tricked into sending movement to the casualty.

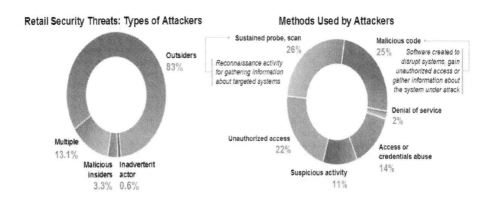

Source. 2013 IBM Cyber Security Intelligence Index for Retail

380

DIRECT-ACCESS ATTACKS

An unapproved user increasing physical access to a computer is probably ready to specifically download data from it. They may likewise bargain security by making working system changes, introducing programming worms, keyloggers, or secret listening devices. Notwithstanding when the system is ensured by standard security measures, these might have the capacity to be circumvent by booting another working system or instrument from a CD-ROM or other bootable media. Disk encryption and Trusted Platform Module are intended to keep these attacks.

EAVESDROPPING

Eavesdropping is the demonstration of surreptitiously tuning in to a private discussion, regularly between has on a system. For example, projects, for example, Carnivore and NarusInsight have been utilized by the FBI and NSA to listen in on the systems of internet service suppliers. Indeed, even machines that work as a shut system (i.e., with no contact to the outside world) can be listened stealthily upon through observing the swoon electro-attractive transmissions created by the hardware; TEMPEST is a detail by the NSA alluding to these attacks.

SPOOFING

Spoofing of user character portrays a circumstance in which one individual or program effectively takes on the appearance of another by distorting data.

TAMPERING

Tampering portrays a malignant change of items. Purported "Abhorrent Maid" attacks and security services planting of reconnaissance capacity into switches are illustrations.

PRIVILEGE ESCALATION

Privilege escalation depicts a circumstance where an attacker with some level of confined access can, without approval, hoist their privileges or access level. So for instance, a standard computer user might have the capacity to trick the system into giving them access to confined data; or even to "wind up root" and have full unhindered access to a system.

PHISHING

Phishing is the endeavor to secure delicate data, for example, usernames, passwords, and charge card subtle elements straightforwardly from users. Phishing is regularly done by email spoofing or texting, and it frequently guides users to enter points of interest at a fake site whose look and feel are practically indistinguishable to the honest to goodness one. Going after a casualty's trusting, phishing can be named a type of social designing.

CLICKJACKING

Clickjacking, otherwise called "UI review attack or User Interface change attack", is a malevolent procedure in which an attacker traps a user into tapping on a catch or connection on another website page while the user planned to tap on the top level page. This is finished utilizing numerous straightforward or obscure layers. The attacker is essentially "seizing" the snaps implied for the top level page and directing them to some other unimportant page, doubtlessly possessed by another person. A comparable system can be utilized to seize keystrokes. Deliberately drafting a mix of templates, iframes, catches and message boxes, a user can be driven into trusting that they are writing the secret word or other data on some true website page while it is being directed into an imperceptible casing controlled by the attacker.

SOCIAL BUILDING AND TROJANS

Social building intends to persuade a user to unveil privileged insights, for example, passwords, card numbers, and so forth by, for instance, imitating a bank, a contractual worker, or a client.

SYSTEMS AT HAZARD

Computer security is basic in any industry which utilizes computers.

BUDGETARY SYSTEMS

Sites that acknowledge or store Mastercard numbers and ledger data are noticeable hacking targets, in view of the potential for prompt monetary benefit from exchanging cash, making buys, or offering the data on the underground market. In-store installment systems and ATMs have likewise been altered with a specific end goal to assemble client account data and PINs.

UTILITIES AND MECHANICAL HARDWARE

Computers control capacities at numerous utilities, including coordination of media communications, the power lattice, atomic power plants, and valve opening and shutting in water and gas systems. The Internet is a potential attack vector for such machines if associated, however the Stuxnet worm exhibited that even gear controlled by computers not associated with the Internet can be helpless against physical harm caused by noxious orders sent to mechanical hardware (all things considered uranium improvement rotators) which are tainted through removable media. In 2014, the Computer Emergency Readiness Team, a division of the Department of Homeland Security, explored 79 hacking episodes at vitality organizations.

AVIONICS

The avionics business is extremely dependent on a progression of complex system which could be attacked. A straightforward power blackout at one air terminal can cause repercussions around the world, a great part of the system depends on radio transmissions which could be disturbed, and controlling air ship over seas is particularly perilous in light of the fact that radar reconnaissance just stretches out 175 to 225 miles seaward. There is additionally potential for attack from inside an airplane.

The outcomes of an effective attack extend from loss of privacy to loss of system trustworthiness, which may prompt more genuine concerns, for example, exfiltration of data, system and aviation authority blackouts, which thusly can prompt airplane terminal terminations, loss of air ship, loss of traveler life, harms on the ground and to transportation framework. A fruitful attack on a military aeronautics system that controls weapons could have significantly more genuine results.

PURCHASER DEVICES

Desktop computers and portable workstations are commonly tainted with malware either to assemble passwords or money related record data, or to build a botnet to attack another objective. Smart telephones, tablet computers, smart watches, and other mobile devices, for example, Quantified Self devices like movement trackers have likewise progressed toward becoming targets and a considerable lot of these have sensors, for example, cameras, amplifiers, GPS recipients, compasses, and accelerometers which could be misused, and may gather individual data, including delicate wellbeing data. Wi-Fi, Bluetooth, and PDA arrange on any of these devices could be utilized as attack vectors, and sensors may be remotely initiated after a fruitful break. Home mechanization devices, for example, the Nest indoor regulator are likewise potential targets.

SUBSTANTIAL ENTERPRISES

Substantial enterprises are common targets. Much of the time this is gone for monetary benefit through wholesale fraud and includes data ruptures, for example, the loss of a huge number of customers' charge card points of interest by Home Depot, Staples, and Target Corporation.

Not all attacks are monetarily persuaded be that as it may; for instance security firm HBGary Federal endured a genuine arrangement of attacks in 2011 from hacktivist assemble Anonymous in countering for the association's CEO guaranteeing to have invaded their gathering, and Sony Pictures was attacked in 2014 where the intention seems to have been to humiliate with data holes, and challenged person the organization by wiping workstations and servers.

AUTOMOBILES

In the event that access is picked up to an auto's inner controller territory organize, it is conceivable to handicap the brakes and turn the guiding wheel. Computerized motor planning, voyage control, non-freezing stopping devices, safety belt tensioners, entryway locks, airbags and propelled driver help systems make these disturbances conceivable, and self-driving autos go considerably further. Associated autos may utilize Wi-Fi and Bluetooth to speak with locally available customer devices, and the mobile phone system to contact attendant and crisis help services or get navigational or diversion data; each of these systems is a potential section point for malware or an attacker. Analysts in 2011 were even ready to utilize a noxious conservative disk in an auto's stereo system as a fruitful attack vector, and autos with worked in voice acknowledgment or remote help highlights have locally available mouthpieces which could be utilized for eavesdropping.

A 2015 report by U.S. Congressperson Edward Markey scrutinized producers' security measures as lacking, and furthermore highlighted protection worries about driving, area, and analytic data being gathered, which is powerless against manhandle by both makers and hackers.

GOVERNMENT

Government and military computer systems are commonly attacked by activists and outside forces. Neighborhood and provincial government foundation, for example, activity light controls, police and knowledge organization interchanges, work force records and money related systems are likewise potential focuses as they are presently all to a great extent computerized.

EFFECT OF SECURITY RUPTURES

Genuine budgetary harm has been caused by security ruptures, but since there is no standard model for evaluating the cost of an episode, the main data accessible is what is made open by the associations included. "A few computer security counseling firms create evaluations of aggregate overall misfortunes owing to infection and worm attacks and to threatening advanced acts by and large. The 2003 misfortune evaluates by these organizations run from $13 billion (worms and infections just) to $226 billion (for all types of undercover attacks). The unwavering quality of these evaluations is frequently tested; the hidden approach is essentially episodic."

In any case, sensible appraisals of the monetary cost of security breaks can really enable associations to settle on balanced venture choices. As indicated by the great Gordon-Loeb Model dissecting the ideal venture level in data security, one can presume that the sum a firm spends to ensure data ought to for the most part be just a little division of the normal misfortune (i.e., the normal estimation of the misfortune coming about because of a cyber/data security break).

ATTACKER INSPIRATION

Likewise with physical security, the inspirations for breaks of computer security shift between attackers. Some are adrenaline junkies or vandals, others are activists or offenders searching for monetary benefit. State-supported attackers are presently common and very much resourced, yet begun with novices, for example, Markus Hess who hacked for the KGB, as related by Clifford Stoll, in The Cuckoo's Egg.

A standard piece of risk demonstrating for a specific system is to distinguish what may spur an attack on that system, and who may be propelled to break it. The level and detail of safety measures will change contingent upon the system to be secured. A home PC, bank, and arranged military system confront altogether different dangers, notwithstanding when the basic advances being used are comparable.

COMPUTER INSURANCE (COUNTERMEASURES)

In computer security a countermeasure is an activity, gadget, system, or strategy that diminishes a risk, a weakness, or an attack by disposing of or anticipating it, by limiting the damage it can cause, or by finding and revealing it so restorative move can be made.

SECURITY MEASURES

A condition of computer "security" is the applied perfect, accomplished by the utilization of the three procedures: danger counteractive action, detection, and reaction. These procedures depend on different arrangements and system parts, which incorporate the accompanying:

➢ User account access controls and cryptography can secure systems records and data, individually.

➢ Firewalls are by a wide margin the most common avoidance systems from a system security point of view as they can (if appropriately designed) shield access to interior system services, and piece certain sorts of attacks through parcel sifting. Firewalls can be both hardware-or programming based.

➢ Interruption Detection System (IDS) items are intended to identify arrange attacks in-advance and aid post-attack legal sciences, while review trails and logs serve a comparative capacity for singular systems.

➢ **"Reaction"** is fundamentally characterized by the evaluated security prerequisites of an individual system and may cover the range from basic update of insurances to notice of legitimate experts, counter-attacks, and so forth. In some unique cases, a total decimation of the traded off system is favored, as it might happen that not all the bargained assets are distinguished.

Today, computer security contains basically "preventive" measures, similar to firewalls or a leave technique. A firewall can be characterized as a method for sifting system data between a host or a system and another system, for example, the Internet, and can be executed as programming running on the machine, guiding into the system stack (or, on account of most UNIX-based working systems, for example, Linux, incorporated with the working system piece) to give continuous separating and blocking. Another usage is a supposed physical firewall which comprises of a different machine sifting system activity. Firewalls are common among machines that are forever associated with the Internet.

In any case, moderately couples of associations keep up computer systems with successful detection systems, less still have composed reaction mechaniSMS set up. As result, as Reuters brings up: "Organizations interestingly report they are losing more through electronic robbery of data than physical taking of advantages". The essential hindrance to compelling destruction of cybercrime could be followed to over the top dependence on firewalls and other computerized "detection" systems. However, it is essential confirmation assembling by utilizing parcel catch machines that puts culprits in a correctional facility.

LESSENING VULNERABILITIES

While formal check of the rightness of computer systems is conceivable, it is not yet common. Working systems formally confirmed incorporate seL4, and SYSGO's PikeOS – however these make up a little rate of the market.

Cryptography legitimately actualized is currently virtually difficult to straightforwardly break. Breaking them requires some non-cryptographic information, for example, a stolen key, stolen plaintext (at either end of the transmission), or some other additional cryptanalytic data.

Two component confirmation is a technique for alleviating unapproved access to a system or touchy data. It requires "something you know"; a secret key or PIN, and "something you have"; a card, dongle, cellphone, or other bit of hardware. This expands security as an unapproved individual needs both of these to obtain entrance.

Social designing and direct computer access (physical) attacks must be forestalled by non-computer implies, which can be hard to authorize, in respect to the affectability of the data. Indeed, even in an exceedingly trained condition, for example, in military associations, social building attacks can in any case be hard to anticipate and counteract.

It is conceivable to lessen an attacker's odds by staying up with the latest with security fixes and refreshes, utilizing a security scanner or/and procuring equipped individuals in charge of security. The impacts of data misfortune/harm can be lessened via cautious going down and protection.

SECURITY BY OUTLINE

Security by plan, or on the other hand secure by configuration, implies that the product has been composed from the beginning to be secure. For this situation, security is considered as a principle include.

A portion of the procedures in this approach include:

> The rule of minimum privilege, where each piece of the system has just the privileges that are required for its capacity. That way regardless of the

possibility that an attacker accesses that part, they have just restricted access to the entire system.

➤ Mechanized hypothesis demonstrating to demonstrate the rightness of essential programming subsystems.

➤ Code surveys and unit testing, ways to deal with make modules more secure where formal accuracy proofs are unrealistic.

➤ Resistance top to bottom, where the outline is with the end goal that more than one subsystem should be abused to trade off the trustworthiness of the system and the data it holds.

➤ Default secure settings, and configuration to "fizzle secure" as opposed to "come up short unreliable". In a perfect world, a safe system ought to require a ponder, cognizant, learned and free choice with respect to true blue experts to make it shaky.

➤ Review trails following system action, so that when a security break happens, the instrument and degree of the rupture can be resolved. Putting away review trails remotely, where they must be annexed to, can shield interlopers from covering their tracks.

➤ Full exposure of all vulnerabilities, to guarantee that the "window of powerlessness" is kept as short as conceivable when bugs are found.

SECURITY ENGINEERING

The Open Security Architecture association characterizes IT security engineering as "the plan ancient rarities that depict how the security controls (security countermeasures) are situated, and how they identify with the general data innovation design. These controls fill the need to keep up the system's quality traits: privacy, respectability, accessibility, responsibility and confirmation services".

Techopedia characterizes security engineering as "a brought together security plan that addresses the necessities and potential dangers required in a specific situation or condition. It likewise determines when and where to apply security controls. The plan procedure is for the most part reproducible." The key characteristics of security design are:

389

- the relationship of various parts and how they rely on upon each other.
- the assurance of controls in light of hazard evaluation, great practice, accounts, and lawful matters.
- the standardization of controls.

HARDWARE INSURANCE MECHANISMS

While hardware might be a wellspring of insecurity, for example, with microchip vulnerabilities perniciously presented amid the assembling procedure, hardware-based or helped computer security likewise offers a contrasting option to programming just computer security. Utilizing devices and techniques, for example, dongles, trusted platform modules, interruption mindful cases, drive locks, impairing USB ports, and mobile-empowered access might be viewed as more secure because of the physical access (or advanced secondary passage access) required so as to be bargained. Each of these is canvassed in more detail beneath.

USB DONGLES

USB dongles are ordinarily utilized as a part of programming permitting plans to open programming capacities, however they can likewise be viewed as an approach to avoid unapproved access to a computer or other gadget's product. The dongle, or key, basically makes a protected scrambled passage between the product application and the key. The guideline is that an encryption conspire on the dongle, for example, Advanced Encryption Standard (AES) gives a more grounded measure of security, since it is harder to hack and repeat the dongle than to just duplicate the local programming to another machine and utilize it. Another security application for dongles is to utilize them for accessing electronic substance, for example, cloud programming or Virtual Private Networks (VPNs). Likewise, a USB dongle can be arranged to bolt or open a computer.

TPMs

Trusted platform modules (TPMs) secure devices by incorporating cryptographic abilities onto access devices, using microchips, or supposed computers-on-a-chip. TPMs utilized as a part of conjunction with server-side programming offer an approach to distinguish and verify hardware devices, anticipating unapproved system and data access.

COMPUTER CASE INTERRUPTION DETECTION

Computer case interruption detection alludes to a push-catch switch which is activated when a computer case is opened. The firmware or BIOS is modified to demonstrate an alarm to the administrator when the computer is booted up whenever.

DRIVE LOCKS

Drive locks are basically programming instruments to scramble hard drives, making them inaccessible to cheats. Devices exist particularly to encrypt outer drives too.

INCAPACITATING USB PORTS

Incapacitating USB ports is a security alternative for counteracting unapproved and pernicious access to a generally secure computer. Contaminated USB dongles associated with a system from a computer inside the firewall are considered by the magazine Network World as the most common hardware risk confronting computer networks.

MOBILE-EMPOWERED ACCESS DEVICES

Mobile-empowered access devices are developing in prominence because of the pervasive idea of PDAs. Worked in abilities, for example, Bluetooth, the more current Bluetooth low energy (LE), Near field communication (NFC) on non-iOS devices and biometric approval, for example, thumb print per users, and additionally QR code per user programming intended for mobile devices, offer new, secure courses for mobile telephones to interface with access control systems. These control systems give computer security and can likewise be utilized for controlling access to secure structures.

SECURE WORKING SYSTEMS

One utilization of the expression "computer security" alludes to innovation that is utilized to execute secure working systems. In the 1980s the United States Department of Defense (DoD) utilized the "Orange Book" standards, yet the present global standard

ISO/IEC 15408, "Common Criteria" characterizes various continuously more stringent Evaluation Assurance Levels. Numerous common working systems meet the EAL4 standard of being "Deliberately Designed, Tested and Reviewed", yet the formal check required for the most elevated amounts implies that they are uncommon. A case of an EAL6 ("Semiformally Verified Design and Tested") system is Integrity-178B, which is utilized as a part of the Airbus A380 and a few military planes.

SECURE CODING

In programming designing, secure coding means to prepare for the unplanned presentation of security vulnerabilities. It is additionally conceivable to make programming planned from the beginning to be secure. Such systems are "secure by plan". Past this, formal check intends to demonstrate the rightness of the calculations basic a system; vital for cryptographic conventions for instance.

ABILITIES AND ACCESS CONTROL LISTS

Inside computer systems, two of numerous security models fit for authorizing privilege partition are access control lists (ACLs) and capacity based security. Utilizing ACLs to limit programs has been ended up being uncertain much of the time, for example, if the host computer can be deceived into by implication allowing confined record access, an issue known as the befuddled agent issue. It has likewise been demonstrated that the guarantee of ACLs of offering access to a question just a single individual can never be ensured by and by. Both of these issues are settled by abilities. This does not mean commonsense defects exist in all ACL-based systems, however just that the planners of specific utilities must assume liability to guarantee that they don't present imperfections.

Capacities have been for the most part limited to explore working systems, while business OSs still utilize ACLs. Abilities can, be that as it may, likewise be actualized at the dialect level, prompting a style of programming that is basically a refinement of standard protest arranged outline. An open source extend in the range is the E dialect.

The most secure computers are those not associated with the Internet and protected from any obstruction. In this present reality, the most secure systems are working systems where security is not an extra.

REACTION TO RUPTURES

Reacting powerfully to endeavored security breaks (in the way that one would for endeavored physical security ruptures) is frequently exceptionally troublesome for an assortment of reasons:

IDENTIFYING ATTACKERS

Distinguishing attackers is troublesome, as they are frequently in an alternate purview to the systems they endeavor to break, and work through intermediaries, impermanent mysterious dial-up accounts, remote associations, and other anonymizing techniques which make backtracking troublesome and are regularly situated in yet another locale. In the event that they effectively break security, they are regularly ready to erase logs to cover their tracks.

PURSUING EACH ATTACKER

The sheer number of endeavored attacks is large to the point that associations can't invest energy seeking after every attacker (a regular home user with a changeless (e.g., link modem) association will be attacked no less than a few times each day, so more appealing targets could be dared to see some more). Note notwithstanding, that the majority of the sheer greater part of these attacks are made via mechanized defenselessness scanners and computer worms.

LAW ENFORCEMENT OFFICERS

Law requirement officers are regularly new to data innovation, thus do not have what it takes and enthusiasm for seeking after attackers. There are likewise budgetary limitations. It has been contended that the high cost of innovation, for example, DNA testing, and enhanced criminology mean less cash for different sorts of law implementation, so the general rate of culprits not getting managed goes up as the cost of the innovation increments. What's more, the ID of attackers over a system may require logs from different focuses in the system and in numerous nations, the arrival of these records to law implementation (except for being deliberately surrendered by a system head or a system manager) requires a court order and, contingent upon the conditions, the lawful procedures required can be attracted out to the point where the records are either consistently demolished, or the data is never again significant.

PROMINENT COMPUTER SECURITY ATTACKS AND RUPTURES

ROBERT MORRIS AND THE PRINCIPAL COMPUTER WORM

In 1988, just 60,000 computers were associated with the Internet, and most were centralized servers, minicomputers and expert workstations. On November 2, 1988, many begun to slow down, on the grounds that they were running a malevolent code that requested processor time and that spread itself to different computers – the primary internet "computer worm". The product was followed back to 23-year-old Cornell University graduate understudy Robert Tappan Morris, Jr. who said 'he needed to tally what number of machines were associated with the Internet'.

ROME LABORATORY

In 1994, over a hundred interruptions were made by unidentified saltines into the Rome Laboratory, the US Air Force's fundamental order and research office. Utilizing Trojan stallions, hackers could acquire unlimited access to Rome's organizing systems and expel hints of their exercises. The gatecrashers could get grouped records, for example, air entrusting request systems data and besides ready to enter associated networks of NASA's Goddard Space Flight Center, Wright-Patterson Air Force Base, some Defense temporary workers, and other private division associations, by acting like a trusted Rome focus user.

TJX LOSES 45.7M CLIENT VISA SUBTLE ELEMENTS

In mid 2007, American attire and home products organization TJX declared that it was the casualty of an unapproved computer systems interruption and that the hackers had accessed a system that put away data on charge card, plastic, check, and stock return exchanges.

STUXNET ATTACK

The computer worm known as Stuxnet allegedly demolished very nearly one-fifth of Iran's atomic rotators by disturbing modern programmable logic controllers (PLCs) in a focused on attack for the most part accepted to have been propelled by Israel and the United States albeit neither has openly recognized this.

WORLDWIDE OBSERVATION REVELATIONS

In mid 2013, huge ruptures of computer security by the NSA were uncovered, including intentionally embeddings a secondary passage in a NIST standard for encryption and tapping the connections between Google's data focuses. These were uncovered by NSA contractual worker Edward Snowden.

TARGET AND HOME DEPOT BREAKS

In 2013 and 2014, a Russian/Ukrainian hacking ring known as "Rescator" softened into Target Corporation computers up 2013, taking approximately 40 million Mastercards, and after that Home Depot computers in 2014, taking in the vicinity of 53 and 56 million Mastercard numbers. Notices were conveyed at both companies, yet disregarded; physical security breaks utilizing self-checkout machines are accepted to have assumed an extensive part. "The malware used is totally unsophisticated and uninteresting," says Jim Walter, executive of risk insight operations at security innovation organization McAfee – implying that the heists could have effectively been halted by existing antivirus programming had directors reacted to the notices. The span of the burglaries has brought about significant consideration from state and Federal United States experts and the examination is progressing.

ASHLEY MADISON RUPTURE

In July of 2015, a hacker bunch known as "The Impact Team" effectively ruptured the extramarital relationship site Ashley Madison. The gathering guaranteed that they had taken organization data as well as user data also. After the break, The Impact Team dumped messages from the organization's CEO, to demonstrate their point, and debilitated to dump client data unless the site was brought down forever. With this underlying data discharge, the gathering expressed "Eager Life Media has been told to take Ashley Madison and Established Men disconnected forever in all structures, or we will discharge all client records, incorporating profiles with every one of the clients' mystery sexual dreams and coordinating charge card exchanges, genuine names and addresses, and representative reports and messages. Alternate sites may remain on the web." When Avid Life Media, the parent organization that made the Ashley Madison site, did not take the webpage disconnected, The Impact Group discharged two more packed records, one 9.7GB and the second 20GB. After the second data dump, Avid Life Media CEO Noel Biderman surrendered, yet the site stayed utilitarian.

LEGAL ISSUES AND GLOBAL REGULATION

Struggle of laws in cyberspace has turned into a noteworthy reason for worry for computer security group. A portion of the principle difficulties and objections about the antivirus business are the absence of worldwide web controls, a worldwide base of common guidelines to judge, and inevitably rebuff, cyber crimes and cyber offenders. There is no worldwide cyber law and cybersecurity arrangement that can be conjured for implementing worldwide cybersecurity issues.

International legitimate issues of cyber attacks are convoluted in nature. Regardless of the possibility that an antivirus firm finds the cyber criminal behind the production of a specific infection or bit of malware or type of cyber attack, frequently the neighborhood specialists can't make a move because of absence of laws under which to arraign. Origin attribution for cyber crimes and cyber attacks is a noteworthy issue for all law requirement offices.

"Computer infections change starting with one nation then onto the next, starting with one purview then onto the next — moving far and wide, utilizing the way that we don't have the capacity to all inclusive police operations like this. So the Internet is as though somebody had given free plane tickets to all the online lawbreakers of the world." Use of dynamic DNS, quick flux and slug verification servers have added claim complexities to this circumstance.

GOVERNMENT

The part of the administration is to make directions to constrain organizations and associations to secure their systems, foundation and data from any cyber attacks, additionally to ensure its own national framework, for example, the national power-lattice.

The topic of whether the legislature ought to intercede or not in the direction of the cyberspace is an extremely polemical one. In fact, for whatever length of time that it has existed and by definition, the cyberspace is a virtual space free of any administration mediation. Where everybody concur that a change on cybersecurity is more than crucial, is the administration the best on-screen character to fathom this issue? Numerous administration authorities and specialists surmise that the legislature should venture in and that there is a significant requirement for direction, basically because of the disappointment of the private division to take care of productively the cybersecurity issue. R. Clarke said amid a board discourse at the RSA Security Conference in San Francisco, he trusts that the "business just reacts when you debilitate control. In the event that industry doesn't react (to the danger), you need to follow through." On the other hand, officials from the private area concur that enhancements are vital, yet surmise that the administration mediation would influence their capacity to enhance proficiently.

ACTIONS AND TEAMS IN THE US

ENACTMENT

The 1986 18 U.S.C. § 1030, all the more commonly known as the Computer Fraud and Abuse Act is the key enactment. It denies unapproved access or harm of "ensured computers" as characterized in 18 U.S.C. § 1030(e)(2).

Albeit different measures have been proposed, for example, the "Cybersecurity Act of 2010 – S. 773" in 2009, the "International Cybercrime Reporting and Cooperation Act – H.R.4962" and "Ensuring Cyberspace as a National Asset Act of 2010 – S.3480" in 2010 – none of these has succeeded.

Official request 13636 Improving Critical Infrastructure Cybersecurity was marked February 12, 2013.

AGENCIES

NATION SECURITY

The Department of Homeland Security has a devoted division in charge of the reaction system, hazard administration program and necessities for cybersecurity in the United States called the National Cyber Security Division. The division is home to US-CERT operations and the National Cyber Alert System. The National Cybersecurity and Communications Integration Center unites government associations in charge of securing computer networks and organized foundation.

FEDERAL BUREAU OF INVESTIGATION

The third need of the Federal Bureau of Investigation (FBI) is to: "Ensure the United States against cyber-based attacks and high-innovation crimes", and they, alongside the National White Collar Crime Center (NW3C), and the Bureau of Justice Assistance (BJA) are a piece of the multi-agency team, The Internet Crime Complaint Center, otherwise called IC3.

Notwithstanding its own particular obligations, the FBI partakes close by non-benefit associations, for example, InfraGard.

DIVISION OF JUSTICE

In the criminal division of the United States Department of Justice works a segment called the Computer Crime and Intellectual Property Section. The CCIPS is responsible for researching computer crime and protected innovation crime and is had some expertise in the inquiry and seizure of computerized prove in computers and networks.

USCYBERCOM

The United States Cyber Command, otherwise called USCYBERCOM, is entrusted with the barrier of determined Department of Defense data networks and "guarantee US/Allied flexibility of activity in cyberspace and deny the same to our enemies." It has no part in the assurance of regular citizen networks.

ROLE OF FCC

The U.S. Federal Communications Commission's part in cybersecurity is to fortify the insurance of basic communications framework, to help with keeping up the unwavering quality of networks amid fiascos, to help in quick recuperation after, and to guarantee that people on call approach powerful communications services.

COMPUTER EMERGENCY READINESS TEAM

Computer Emergency Response Team is a name given to master groups that handle computer security occurrences. In the US, two unmistakable association exist, in spite of the fact that they do work firmly together.

US-CERT: some portion of the National Cyber Security Division of the United States Department of Homeland Security.

CERT/CC: made by the Defense Advanced Research Projects Agency (DARPA) and keep running by the Software Engineering Institute (SEI).

INTERNATIONAL ACTIVITIES

A wide range of groups and associations exist, including:

FIRST

The Forum of Incident Response and Security Teams (FIRST) is the worldwide relationship of CSIRTs. The US-CERT, AT&T, Apple, Cisco, McAfee, Microsoft are all individuals from this international group.

COUNCIL OF EUROPE

The Council of Europe shields social orders worldwide from the danger of cybercrime through the Convention on Cybercrime.

The reason for the Messaging Anti-Abuse Working Group (MAAWG) is to unite the messaging business to work cooperatively and to effectively address the different types of messaging abuse, for example, spam, infections, foreswearing of-service attacks and other messaging misuses. France Telecom, Facebook, AT&T, Apple, Cisco, Sprint are a portion of the individuals from the MAAWG.

ENISA : The European Network and Information Security Agency (ENISA) is an agency of the European Union with the target to enhance system and data security in the European Union

EUROPE

CSIRTs in Europe team up in the TERENA team TF-CSIRT. TERENA's Trusted Introducer service gives an accreditation and affirmation conspire for CSIRTs in Europe. A full rundown of known CSIRTs in Europe is accessible from the Trusted Introducer site.

NATIONAL GROUPS

Here are the principle computer crisis reaction groups the world over. Most nations have their own group to ensure arrange security.

CANADA

On October 3, 2010, Public Safety Canada revealed Canada's Cyber Security Strategy, following a Speech from the Throne sense of duty regarding support the security of Canadian cyberspace. The point of the technique is to reinforce Canada's "cyber systems and basic framework segments, bolster monetary development and ensure Canadians as they associate with each other and to the world." Three primary columns characterize the methodology: securing government systems, collaborating to secure imperative cyber systems outside the federal government, and helping Canadians to be secure on the web. The methodology includes different offices and organizations over the Government of Canada. The Cyber Incident Management Framework for Canada diagrams these duties, and gives an arrangement to facilitated reaction amongst government and different accomplices in case of a cyber occurrence. The Action Plan 2010–2015 for Canada's Cyber Security Strategy diagrams the progressing execution of the methodology.

Open Safety Canada's Canadian Cyber Incident Response Center (CCIRC) is in charge of alleviating and reacting to dangers to Canada's basic framework and cyber systems. The CCIRC offers help to moderate cyber dangers, specialized help to react and recoup from focused cyber attacks, and gives online devices to individuals from

Canada's basic foundation areas. The CCIRC posts normal cyber security notices on the Public Safety Canada site. The CCIRC additionally works a web based announcing instrument where people and associations can report a cyber episode. Canada's Cyber Security Strategy is a piece of a bigger, coordinated way to deal with basic foundation assurance, and capacities as a partner report to the National Strategy and Action Plan for Critical Infrastructure.

On September 27, 2010, Public Safety Canada cooperated with STOP.THINK.CONNECT, a coalition of non-benefit, private part, and government associations committed to illuminating the overall population on the most proficient method to secure themselves on the web. On February 4, 2014, the Government of Canada propelled the Cyber Security Cooperation Program. The program is a $1.5 million five-year activity gone for enhancing Canada's cyber systems through gifts and commitments to ventures in help of this target. Open Safety Canada expects to start an assessment of Canada's Cyber Security Strategy in mid 2015. Open Safety Canada regulates and routinely refreshes the GetCyberSafe entry for Canadian residents, and does Cyber Security Awareness Month amid October.

CHINA

China's system security and data innovation authority group was set up February 27, 2014. The authority group is entrusted with national security and long haul improvement and co-appointment of significant issues identified with arrange security and data innovation. Financial, political, social, social and military fields as identified with arrange security and data innovation procedure, arranging and major macroeconomic strategy are being looked into. The advancement of national system security and data innovation law are continually under investigation for upgraded national security capacities.

GERMANY

Berlin begins National Cyber Defense Initiative: On June 16, 2011, the German Minister for Home Affairs, authoritatively opened the new German NCAZ (National Center for Cyber Defense) Nationales Cyber-Abwehrzentrum situated in Bonn. The NCAZ nearly coordinates with BSI (Federal Office for Information Security) Bundesamt für Sicherheit in der Informationstechnik, BKA (Federal Police Organization) Bundeskriminalamt (Deutschland), BND (Federal Intelligence Service) Bundesnachrichtendienst, MAD (Military Intelligence Service) Amt für nook Militärischen Abschirmdienst and other national associations in Germany dealing with national security viewpoints. As per the Minister the essential assignment of the new association established on February 23, 2011, is to identify and avoid attacks against the national framework and specified occurrences like Stuxnet.

INDIA

A few arrangements for cybersecurity have been fused into rules confined under the Information Technology Act 2000.

The National Cyber Security Policy 2013 is an approach system by Department of Electronics and Information Technology (DeitY) which expects to shield the general population and private framework from cyber attacks, and defend "data, for example, individual data (of web users), money related and saving money data and sovereign data".

The Indian Companies Act 2013 has likewise presented cyber law and cyber security commitments with respect to Indian executives.

PAKISTAN

Cyber-crime has risen quickly in Pakistan. There are around 30 million internet users with 15 million mobile supporters in Pakistan. As indicated by Cyber Crime Unit (CCU), a branch of Federal Investigation Agency, just 62 cases were accounted for to the unit in 2007, 287 cases in 2008, proportion dropped in 2009 however in 2010, more than 312 cases were enrolled. Yet, unreported episodes of cyber-crime are immense in numbers.

The principal ever appropriate law, i.e. "Pakistan's Cyber Crime Bill 2007", which concentrates on electronic crimes, i.e. cyber psychological warfare, criminal access, electronic system misrepresentation, electronic fraud, abuse of encryption and so forth has been there.

National Response Center for Cyber Crime (NR3C) - FIA is a law requirement agency devoted to battle cyber crime. Initiation of this Hi-Tech crime battling unit unfolded in 2007 to distinguish and control the marvel of technological abuse in the public arena. However alongside that specific private firms are likewise working in attachment with Govt to work towards cyber security and check cyber attacks.

SOUTH KOREA

Following cyberattacks in the main portion of 2013, when government, news-media, TV slot, and bank sites were traded off, the national government focused on the preparation of 5,000 new cybersecurity specialists by 2017. The South Korean government rebuked its northern partner for these attacks, and in addition occurrences that happened in 2009, 2011, and 2012, however Pyongyang denies the allegations.

DIFFERENT NATIONS

- CERT Brazil, individual from FIRST (Forum for Incident Response and Security Teams)
- CARNet CERT, Croatia, individual from FIRST
- AE CERT, United Arab Emirates
- SingCERT, Singapore
- CERT-LEXSI, France, Canada, Singapore

NEW ERA OF WARFARE

Cybersecurity is ending up noticeably progressively imperative as more data and innovation is being made accessible on cyberspace. There is developing worry among governments that cyberspace will turn into the following theater of fighting. As Mark Clayton from the Christian Science Monitor portrayed in an article titled "The New Cyber Arms Race":

Later on, wars won't simply be battled by troopers with weapons or with planes that drop bombs. They will likewise be battled with the snap of a mouse an a large portion of a world away that unleashes painstakingly weaponized computer programs that upset or demolish basic businesses like utilities, transportation, communications, and energy. Such attacks could likewise incapacitate military networks that control the development of troops, the way of fly warriors, the order and control of warships.

This has prompted new terms, for example, cyberwarfare and cyberterrorism. More basic framework is being controlled by means of computer programs that, while expanding effectiveness, uncovered new vulnerabilities. The test will be to check whether governments and companies that control basic systems, for example, energy, communications and other data will have the capacity to anticipate attacks before they happen. As Jay Cross, the main researcher of the Internet Time Group, commented, "Connectedness sires weakness."

THE CYBER SECURITY WORK SHOWCASE

Cyber Security is a quickly developing field of IT worried with lessening associations' danger of hack or data rupture. Business, government and non-legislative associations all utilize cybersecurity experts. In any case, the utilization of the expression "cybersecurity" is more pervasive in government sets of responsibilities.

Run of the mill cybersecurity work titles and depictions include:

SECURITY ANALYST

Breaks down and evaluates vulnerabilities in the framework (programming, hardware, networks), explores accessible instruments and countermeasures to cure the distinguished vulnerabilities, and suggests arrangements and best practices. Breaks down and evaluates harm to the data/foundation because of security episodes, looks at accessible recuperation devices and forms, and suggests arrangements. Tests for consistence with security approaches and methods. May aid the creation, usage, and additionally administration of security arrangements.

SECURITY ENGINEER

Performs security observing, security and data/logs investigation, and criminological examination, to recognize security episodes, and mounts occurrence reaction. Examines and uses new innovations and procedures to upgrade security abilities and execute enhancements. May likewise survey code or perform other security designing strategies.

SECURITY ARCHITECT

Outlines a security system or real parts of a security system, and may head a security configuration group fabricating another security system.

SECURITY ADMINISTRATOR

Introduces and oversees association wide security systems. May likewise go up against a portion of the errands of a security examiner in littler associations.

BOSS INFORMATION SECURITY OFFICER (CISO)

An abnormal state administration position in charge of the whole data security division/staff. The position may incorporate hands-on specialized work.

BOSS SECURITY OFFICER (CSO)

An abnormal state administration position in charge of the whole security division/staff. A more up to date position now esteemed required as security dangers develop.

SECURITY CONSULTANT/SPECIALIST/INTELLIGENCE

Wide titles that incorporate any one or the majority of alternate parts/titles, entrusted with securing computers, networks, programming, data, or potentially data systems against infections, worms, spyware, malware, interruption detection, unapproved access, disavowal of-service attacks, and a steadily expanding rundown of attacks by hackers going about as people or as a major aspect of composed crime or remote governments.

Understudy programs are additionally accessible to individuals keen on starting a profession in cybersecurity. In the interim, an adaptable and compelling alternative for data security experts of all experience levels to continue examining is online security preparing, including webcasts.

PHRASING

The following terms utilized with respect to building secure systems are clarified below.

AUTHORIZATION

Access approval confines access to a computer to group of users using confirmation systems. These systems can secure either the entire computer –, for example, through an intuitive login screen – or singular services, for example, a FTP server. There are numerous techniques for distinguishing and verifying users, for example, passwords, recognizable proof cards, and, all the more as of late, smart cards and biometric systems.

ANTI-VIRUS SOFTWARE

Hostile to infection programming comprises of computer programs that endeavor to distinguish, ruin and take out computer infections and different malignant programming (malware).

APPLICATIONS

Applications with known security blemishes ought not be run. Either abandon it killed until the point when it can be fixed or generally settled, or erase it and supplant it with some other application. Openly known defects are the primary section utilized by worms to consequently break into a system and after that spread to different systems associated with it. The security site Secunia gives a pursuit apparatus to unpatched known blemishes in well known items.

VERIFICATION SYSTEMS

Verification systems can be utilized to guarantee that communication end-focuses are who they say they are.

ROBOTIZED HYPOTHESIS DEMONSTRATING

Robotized hypothesis demonstrating and other confirmation devices can empower basic calculations and code utilized as a part of secure systems to be numerically demonstrated to meet their determinations.

BACKUPS

Backups are a method for securing data; they are another duplicate of all the essential computer documents kept in another area. These records are continued hard disks, CD-Rs, CD-RWs, tapes and all the more as of late on the cloud. Proposed areas for backups are a flame resistant, waterproof, and warmth verification safe, or in a different, offsite area than that in which the first documents are contained. A few people and organizations additionally protect their backups in store boxes inside bank vaults. There is likewise a fourth alternative, which includes utilizing one of the document facilitating services that moves down records over the Internet for both business and people, known as the cloud.

Backups are likewise essential for reasons other than security. Catastrophic events, for example, seismic tremors, tropical storms, or tornadoes, may strike the building where the computer is found. The building can be ablaze, or a blast may happen. There should be a current reinforcement at another secure area, in the event of such sort of calamity. Further, it is suggested that the substitute area be set where a similar fiasco would not influence both areas. Cases of exchange debacle recuperation locales being bargained by a similar calamity that influenced the essential site incorporate having had an essential site in World Trade Center I and the recuperation site in 7 World Trade Center, both of which were decimated in the 9/11 attack, and having one's essential site and recuperation site in the same beach front area, which prompts both being helpless against sea tempest harm (for instance, essential site in New Orleans and recuperation site in Jefferson Parish, both of which were hit by Hurricane Katrina in 2005). The reinforcement media ought to be moved between the geographic locales in a safe way, with a specific end goal to keep them from being stolen.

ACCESS CONTROL LIST

Capacity and access control list systems can be utilized to guarantee privilege detachment and required access control. This area talks about their utilization.

CHAIN OF TRUST

Chain of trust strategies can be utilized to endeavor to guarantee that all product stacked has been ensured as valid by the system's fashioners.

SECRECY

Secrecy is the nondisclosure of data but to another approved individual.

CRYPTOGRAPHIC

Cryptographic methods can be utilized to protect data in travel between systems, decreasing the likelihood that data traded between systems can be blocked or changed.

CYBERWARFARE

Cyberwarfare is an Internet-based clash that includes politically persuaded attacks on data and data systems. Such attacks can, for instance, incapacitate official sites and networks, disturb or handicap basic services, take or adjust grouped data and challenged person money related systems.

DATA INTEGRITY

Data respectability is the precision and consistency of put away data, shown by a nonattendance of any change in data between two updates of a data record.

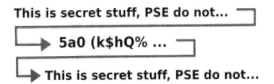

CRYPTOGRAPHIC SYSTEMS

Cryptographic systems include changing data, scrambling it so it ends up noticeably garbled amid transmission. The expected beneficiary can unscramble the message; in a perfect world, busybodies can't.

Encryption is utilized to shield the message from the eyes of others. Cryptographically secure figures are intended to make any pragmatic endeavor of breaking infeasible. Symmetric-key figures are appropriate for mass encryption utilizing shared keys, and open key encryption utilizing computerized endorsements can give a viable answer for the issue of safely imparting when no key is partaken ahead of time.

Endpoint security programming causes networks to forestall exfiltration (data burglary) and infection contamination at arrange section focuses made helpless by the commonness of possibly tainted compact figuring devices, for example, portable PCs and mobile devices, and outer storage devices, for example, USB drives.

Firewalls are a critical strategy for control and security on the Internet and different networks. A system firewall can be a communications processor, regularly a switch, or a devoted server, alongside firewall programming. A firewall fills in as a guardian system that secures an organization's intranets and other computer networks from interruption by giving a channel and safe exchange point for access to and from the Internet and different networks. It screens all system movement for legitimate passwords or other security codes and just allows approved transmission all through the system. Firewalls can discourage, however not totally anticipate, unapproved access (hacking) into computer networks; they can likewise give some assurance from online interruption.

Honey pots are computers that are either deliberately or unexpectedly left helpless against attack by saltines. They can be utilized to get wafers or fix vulnerabilities.

Interruption-detection systems can filter a system for individuals that are on the system yet who ought not be there or are doing things that they ought not be doing, for instance attempting a considerable measure of passwords to access the system.

A **microkernel** is the near-least measure of programming that can give the mechaniSMS to execute a working system. It is utilized exclusively to give low-level, accurately characterized machine code whereupon a working system can be produced. A straightforward illustration is the mid '90s GEMSOS (Gemini Computers), which gave greatly low-level machine code, for example, "section" administration, on which a working system could be manufactured. The hypothesis (on account of "fragments") was that—as opposed to have the working system itself stress over compulsory access division by methods for military-style marking—it is more secure if a low-level, freely investigated module can be accused exclusively of the administration of independently named portions, be they memory "sections" or document system "sections" or executable content "fragments." If programming below the perceivability of the working system is (as for this situation) accused of naming, there is no hypothetically reasonable means for a shrewd hacker to subvert the naming plan, since the working system in essence does not give mechaniSMS for meddling naming: the working system is, basically, a customer (an "application," ostensibly) on the microkernel and, thusly, subject to its confinements.

Pinging The ping application can be utilized by potential wafers to discover if an IP address is reachable. On the off chance that a wafer finds a computer, they can attempt a port sweep to recognize and attack services on that computer.

Social designing mindfulness keeps representatives mindful of the perils of social building as well as having a strategy set up to avert social designing can decrease fruitful breaks of the system and servers.

MOBILE SECURITY

Mobile security or mobile telephone security has turned out to be progressively vital in mobile registering. Of specific concern is the security of individual and business data now put away on smartphones.

An ever increasing number of users and organizations utilize smartphones as communication instruments, additionally as a methods for arranging and sorting out their work and private life. Inside organizations, these advancements are causing significant changes in the association of data systems and thusly they have turned into the wellspring of new dangers. In fact, smartphones gather and accumulate an expanding measure of touchy data to which access must be controlled to ensure the protection of the user and the licensed innovation of the organization.

All smartphones, as computers, are favored focuses of attacks. These attacks abuse shortcomings identified with smartphones that can originate from methods for communication like Short Message Service (SMS, otherwise known as content messaging), Multimedia Messaging Service (MMS), Wi-Fi networks, Bluetooth and GSM, the accepted worldwide standard for mobile communications. There are additionally attacks that endeavor programming vulnerabilities from both the web program and working system. At long last, there are types of noxious programming that depend on the feeble information of normal users.

Diverse security counter-measures are being produced and connected to smartphones, from security in various layers of programming to the spread of data to end users. There are great practices to be seen at all levels, from configuration to use, through the improvement of working systems, programming layers, and downloadable applications.

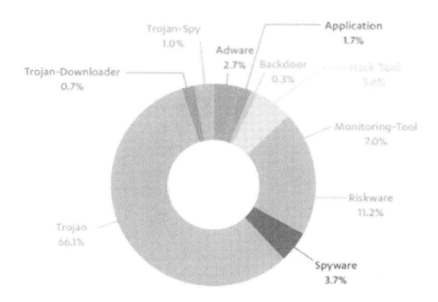

CHALLENGES OF MOBILE SECURITY

THREATS

A smartphone user is presented to different dangers when they utilize their telephone. In simply the last two fourth of 2012, the quantity of exceptional mobile dangers developed by 261%, as indicated by ABI Research. These dangers can disturb the operation of the smartphone, and transmit or change user data. Therefore, the applications conveyed there must ensure protection and honesty of the data they handle. Moreover, since some applications could themselves be malware, their usefulness and exercises ought to be constrained (for instance, confining the applications from accessing area data by means of GPS, blocking access to the user's address book, keeping the transmission of data on the system, sending SMS messages that are charged to the user, and so forth.).

There are three prime focuses for attackers:

1. **Data:** smartphones are devices for data administration, in this manner they may contain touchy data like charge card numbers, confirmation data, private data, movement logs (schedule, call logs);
2. **Identity:** smartphones are profoundly adjustable, so the gadget or its substance are related with a particular individual. For instance, each mobile gadget can transmit data identified with the proprietor of the mobile telephone contract, and an attacker might need to take the identity of the proprietor of a smartphone to submit different offenses;
3. **Accessibility:** by attacking a smartphone one can constrain access to it and deny the proprietor of the service. The wellspring of these attacks are similar performing artists found in the non-mobile processing space:
4. **Experts**, regardless of whether business or military, who concentrate on the three targets specified previously. They take delicate data from the overall population, and in addition embrace mechanical undercover work. They will likewise utilize the identity of those attacked to accomplish different attacks;
5. Hoodlums who need to pick up pay through data or characters they have stolen. The cheats will attack many individuals to build their potential salary;
6. Dark cap hackers who particularly attack accessibility. They will likely create infections, and make harm the gadget. Sometimes, hackers have an enthusiasm for taking data on devices.
7. Dim cap hackers who uncover vulnerabilities. They will likely uncover vulnerabilities of the gadget. Dark cap hackers don't plan on harming the gadget or taking data.

OUTCOMES

At the point when a smartphone is contaminated by an attacker, the attacker can endeavor a few things:

➢ The attacker can control the smartphone as a zombie machine, in other words, a machine with which the attacker can convey and send orders which will be utilized to send spontaneous messages (spam) by means of SMS or email;

➢ The attacker can without much of a stretch constrain the smartphone to make telephone calls. For instance, one can utilize the API (library that contains the essential capacities not present in the smartphone) PhoneMakeCall by Microsoft, which gathers phone numbers from any source, for example, business repository, and afterward call them. Be that as it may, the attacker can likewise utilize this technique to call paid services, bringing about a charge to the proprietor of the smartphone. It is likewise extremely unsafe in light of the fact that the smartphone could call crisis services and along these lines upset those services;

➢ A traded off smartphone can record discussions between the user and others and send them to an outsider. This can cause user protection and modern security issues;

➢ An attacker can likewise take a user's identity, usurp their identity (with a duplicate of the user's sim card or even the phone itself), and in this manner imitate the proprietor. This brings security worries up in nations where smartphones can be utilized to put orders, see ledgers or are utilized as an identity card;

➢ The attacker can lessen the utility of the smartphone, by releasing the battery. For instance, they can dispatch an application that will run constantly on the smartphone processor, requiring a great deal of vitality and depleting the battery. One variable that recognizes mobile processing from conventional desktop PCs is their constrained execution. Blunt Stajano and Ross Anderson initially portrayed this type of attack, calling it an attack of "battery fatigue" or "lack of sleep torment";

➢ The attacker can keep the operation and additionally beginning of the smartphone by making it unusable. This attack can either erase the boot scripts,

413

bringing about a telephone without a working OS, or alter certain records to make it unusable (e.g. a script that dispatches at startup that strengths the smartphone to restart) or even insert a startup application that would exhaust the battery;

> The attacker can expel the individual (photographs, music, recordings, and so forth.) or expert data (contacts, logbooks, notes) of the user.

ATTACKS IN LIGHT OF CORRESPONDENCE

ATTACK IN LIGHT OF SMS AND MMS

A few attacks get from defects in the administration of SMS and MMS.

Some mobile telephone models have issues in overseeing double SMS messages. It is conceivable, by sending a not well shaped square, to make the telephone restart, prompting disavowal of service attacks. In the event that a user with a Siemens S55 got an instant message containing a Chinese character, it would prompt a refusal of service. For another situation, while the standard requires that the greatest size of a Nokia Mail address is 32 characters, some Nokia telephones did not confirm this standard, so if a user enters an email address more than 32 characters, that prompts finish brokenness of the email handler and puts it down and out. This attack is called "revile of hush". An investigation on the security of the SMS framework uncovered that SMS messages sent from the Internet can be utilized to play out a conveyed disavowal of service (DDoS) attack against the mobile broadcast communications foundation of a major city. The attack misuses the deferrals in the conveyance of messages to over-burden the system.

Another potential attack could start with a telephone that sends a MMS to different telephones, with a connection. This connection is contaminated with an infection. Endless supply of the MMS, the user can open the connection. On the off chance that it is opened, the telephone is contaminated, and the infection sends a MMS with a tainted connection to every one of the contacts in the address book. There is a genuine case of this attack: the infection Commwarrior utilizes the address book and sends MMS messages including a contaminated document to beneficiaries. A user introduces the product, as got by means of MMS message. At that point, the infection started to send messages to beneficiaries taken from the address book.

ATTACKS IN LIGHT OF CORRESPONDENCE NETWORKS

ATTACKS IN LIGHT OF THE GSM NETWORKS

The attacker may attempt to break the encryption of the mobile system. The GSM organize encryption calculations have a place with the group of calculations called A5. Because of the strategy of security through lack of clarity it has not been conceivable to transparently test the power of these calculations.

There were initially two variations of the calculation: A5/1 and A5/2 (stream figures), where the previous was intended to be generally solid, and the last was intended to be powerless deliberately to permit simple cryptanalysis and listening in. ETSI constrained a few nations (regularly outside Europe) to utilize A5/2. Since the encryption calculation was made open, it was demonstrated it was conceivable to break the encryption: A5/2 could be broken on the fly, and A5/1 in around 6 hours . In July 2007, the 3GPP affirmed a change demand to disallow the usage of A5/2 in any new mobile telephones, which implies that is has been decommissioned and is never again actualized in mobile telephones. More grounded open calculations have been added to the GSM standard, the A5/3 and A5/4 (Block figures), also called KASUMI or UEA1 distributed by the ETSI. On the off chance that the system does not bolster A5/1, or whatever other A5 calculation actualized by the telephone, at that point the base station can determine A5/0 which is the invalid calculation, whereby the radio movement is sent decoded. Indeed, even in the event that mobile telephones can utilize 3G or 4G which have considerably more grounded encryption than 2G GSM, the base station can minimize the radio correspondence to 2G GSM and indicate A5/0 (no encryption) . This is the reason for listening in attacks on mobile radio networks utilizing a fake base station regularly called an IMSI catcher.

What's more, following of mobile terminals is troublesome since each time the mobile terminal is accessing or being accessed by the system, another impermanent identity (TMSI) is apportioned to the mobile terminal. The TSMI is utilized as identity of the mobile terminal whenever it accesses the system. The TMSI is sent to the mobile terminal in scrambled messages.

Once the encryption calculation of GSM is broken, the attacker can block all decoded correspondences made by the casualty's smartphone.

Attacks based on Wi-Fi

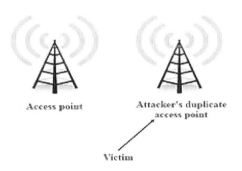

Access point

Attacker's duplicate access point

Victim

ACCESS POINT SPOOFING

An attacker can attempt to listen in on Wi-Fi interchanges to infer data (e.g. username, secret key). This sort of attack is not extraordinary to smartphones, but rather they are extremely helpless against these attacks in light of the fact that all the time the Wi-Fi is the main methods for correspondence they need to access the internet. The security of wireless networks (WLAN) is along these lines an imperative subject. At first wireless networks were secured by WEP keys. The shortcoming of WEP is a short encryption key which is the same for every associated customer. What's more, a few diminishments in the inquiry space of the keys have been found by scientists. Presently, most wireless networks are ensured by the WPA security convention. WPA depends on the "Transient Key Integrity Protocol (TKIP)" which was intended to enable relocation from WEP to WPA on the gear as of now sent. The real upgrades in security are the dynamic encryption keys. For little networks, the WPA is a "pre-shared key" which depends on a common key. Encryption can be helpless if the length of the mutual key is short. With restricted open doors for input (i.e. just the numeric keypad) mobile telephone users may characterize short encryption keys that contain just numbers. This improves the probability that an attacker prevails with a beast drive attack. The successor to WPA, called WPA2, should be sufficiently protected to withstand a savage constrain attack.

Likewise with GSM, if the attacker prevails with regards to breaking the distinguishing proof key, it will be conceivable to attack the telephone as well as the whole system it is associated with.

Numerous smartphones for wireless LANs recollect that they are as of now associated, and this instrument keeps the user from having to re-relate to every association. Be that as it may, an attacker could make a WIFI access point twin with an indistinguishable parameters and qualities from the genuine system. Utilizing the way that some smartphones recall the networks, they could confound the two networks and associate with the system of the attacker who can capture data on the off chance that it doesn't transmit its data in encoded shape.

Lasco is a worm that at first taints a remote gadget utilizing the SIS record organize. Sister record organize (Software Installation Script) is a script document that can be executed by the system without user collaboration. The smartphone in this way trusts the document to originate from a trusted source and downloads it, contaminating the machine.

RULE OF BLUETOOTH-BASED ATTACKS

Security issues identified with Bluetooth on mobile devices have been contemplated and have demonstrated various issues on various telephones. One simple to misuse helplessness: unregistered services don't require verification, and powerless applications have a virtual serial port used to control the telephone. An attacker just expected to interface with the port to take full control of the gadget. Another case: a telephone must be inside reach and Bluetooth in revelation mode. The attacker sends a record by means of Bluetooth. In the event that the beneficiary acknowledges, an nfection is transmitted. For instance: Cabir is a worm that spreads through Bluetooth association. The worm looks for close-by telephones with Bluetooth in discoverable mode and sends itself to the objective gadget. The user must acknowledge the approaching document and introduce the program. In the wake of introducing, the worm contaminates the machine.

ATTACKS IN VIEW OF VULNERABILITIES IN SOFTWARE APPLICATIONS

Different attacks depend on imperfections in the OS or applications on the telephone.

The mobile web browser is a developing attack vector for mobile devices. Similarly as regular Web browsers, mobile web browsers are reached out from immaculate web route with gadgets and modules, or are totally local mobile browsers.

Jailbreaking the iPhone with firmware 1.1.1 was construct totally in light of vulnerabilities on the web browser. Thus, the abuse of the powerlessness depicted here underlines the significance of the Web browser as an attack vector for mobile devices. For this situation, there was a helplessness in light of a stack-based cushion flood in a library utilized by the web browser (Libtiff).

A weakness in the web browser for Android was found in October 2008. As the iPhone defenselessness above, it was expected to an out of date and helpless library. A noteworthy distinction with the iPhone defenselessness was Android's sandboxing design which restricted the impacts of this powerlessness to the Web browser handle.

Smartphones are likewise casualties of exemplary theft identified with the web: phishing, malevolent websites, and so forth. The huge distinction is that smartphones don't yet have solid antivirus software accessible.

WORKING SYSTEM

In some cases it is conceivable to conquer the security protects by altering the working system itself. As true illustrations, this area covers the control of firmware and malignant mark declarations. These attacks are troublesome.

In 2004, vulnerabilities in virtual machines running on specific devices were uncovered. It was conceivable to sidestep the bytecode verifier and access the local hidden working system. The consequences of this examination were not distributed in detail. The firmware security of Nokia's Symbian Platform Security Architecture (PSA) depends on a focal design document called SWIPolicy. In 2008 it was conceivable to control the Nokia firmware before it is introduced, and in truth in some downloadable forms of it, this document was intelligible, so it was conceivable to alter and change the picture of the firmware. This defenselessness has been tackled by a refresh from Nokia.

In principle smartphones have preference over hard drives since the OS records are in ROM, and can't be changed by malware. In any case, in a few systems it was conceivable to go around this: in the Symbian OS it was conceivable to overwrite a document with a record of a similar name. On the Windows OS, it was conceivable to change a pointer from a general setup record to an editable document.

At the point when an application is introduced, the marking of this application is confirmed by a progression of testaments. One can make a legitimate mark without utilizing a substantial authentication and add it to the rundown. In the Symbian OS all declarations are in the registry: c:\resource\swicertstore\dat. With firmware changes clarified above it is anything but difficult to embed an apparently substantial yet malignant endorsement.

ATTACKS IN LIGHT OF HARDWARE VULNERABILITIES

1. Electromagnetic Waveforms

In 2015, scientists at the French government organization ANSSI exhibited the ability to trigger the voice interface of certain smartphones remotely by utilizing "particular electromagnetic waveforms". The endeavor exploited recieving wire properties of earphone wires while connected to the sound yield jacks of the helpless smartphones and adequately ridiculed sound contribution to infuse summons by means of the sound interface.

2. Juice Jacking

Juice Jacking is a technique for physical or a hardware helplessness particular to mobile stages. Using the double reason for the USB charge port, numerous devices have been vulnerable to having data ex-filtrated from, or malware introduced on to a mobile gadget by using malevolent energizing booths set out in the open places, or covered up in typical charge connectors.

3. Secret word breaking

In 2010, scientist from the University of Pennsylvania examined the likelihood of breaking a gadget's secret word through a smirch attack (actually imaging the finger smircesh on the screen to recognize the user's watchword). The scientists could perceive the gadget watchword up to 68% of the time under specific conditions.

4. Noxious software (malware)

As smartphones are a lasting purpose of access to the internet (for the most part on), they can be traded off as effectively as computers with malware. A malware is a computer program that plans to hurt the system in which it lives. Trojans, worms and infections are altogether considered malware. A Trojan is a program that is on the smartphone and enables outer users to associate tactfully. A worm is a program that replicates on numerous computers over a system. An infection is malevolent software intended to spread to different computers by embeddings itself into genuine projects and running projects in parallel. Notwithstanding, it must be said that the malware are far less various and vital to smartphones as they are to computers.

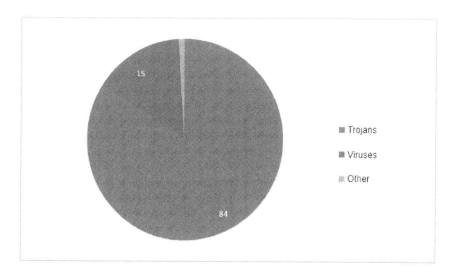

In any case, late examinations demonstrate that the advancement of malware in smartphones have soared over the most recent couple of years representing a risk to investigation and recognition.

5. The three periods of malware attacks

Ordinarily an attack on a smartphone made by malware happens in 3 stages: the infection of a host, the achievement of its objective, and the spread of the malware to different systems. Malware regularly utilize the assets offered by the tainted smartphones. It will utilize the yield devices, for example, Bluetooth or infrared, however it might likewise utilize the address book or email deliver of the individual to taint the user's colleagues. The malware misuses the assume that is given to data sent by an associate.

6. Infection

Infection is the methods utilized by the malware to get into the smartphone, it can either utilize one of the issues beforehand introduced or may utilize the artlessness of the user. Infections are arranged into four classes as indicated by their level of user collaboration:

7. Unequivocal authorization

The most considerate association is to inquire as to whether it is permitted to taint the machine, plainly showing its potential malignant conduct. This is normal conduct of a proof of idea malware.

8. Inferred authorization

This infection is on the grounds that the user has a propensity for introducing software. Most Trojans attempt to tempt the user into introducing alluring applications (diversions, helpful applications and so on.) that really contain malware.

9. Normal communication

This infection is identified with a typical conduct, for example, opening a MMS or email.

10. No collaboration

The last class of infection is the most perilous. For sure, a worm that could contaminate a smartphone and could taint different smartphones with no connection would be disastrous.

11. Achievement of its objective

Once the malware has contaminated a telephone it will likewise look to fulfill its objective, which is typically one of the accompanying: money related harm, harm data or potentially gadget, and hid harm:

12. Money related harms

The attacker can take user data and either pitch them to a similar user, or pitch to an outsider.

13. Harm

Malware can incompletely harm the gadget, or erase or alter data on the gadget.

14. Hidden harm

The two previously mentioned sorts of harm are perceivable, however the malware can likewise leave a secondary passage for future attacks or even direct wiretaps.

15. Spread to different systems

Once the malware has contaminated a smartphone, it generally means to spread somehow:

- ➢ It can spread through proximate devices utilizing Wi-Fi, Bluetooth and infrared;
- ➢ It can likewise spread utilizing remote networks, for example, phone calls or SMS or messages.

CASES OF MALWARE

Here are different malware that exist in the realm of smartphones with a short portrayal of each.

1. Infections and Trojans

Cabir (otherwise called Caribe, SybmOS/Cabir, Symbian/Cabir and EPOC.cabir) is the name of a computer worm created in 2004 that is intended to contaminate mobile telephones running Symbian OS. It is accepted to be the principal computer worm that can taint mobile telephones

Commwarrior, discovered March 7, 2005, is the principal worm that can taint many machines from MMS. It is sent as a file document COMMWARRIOR.ZIP that contains a record COMMWARRIOR.SIS. At the point when this record is executed, Commwarrior endeavors to interface with close-by devices by Bluetooth or infrared under an arbitrary name. It at that point endeavors to send MMS message to the contacts in the smartphone with various header messages for every individual, who get the MMS and regularly open them without assist confirmation.

Phage is the principal Palm OS infection that was found. It exchanges to the Palm from a PC by means of synchronization. It contaminates all applications that are in the smartphone and it installs its own particular code to work without the user and the system recognizing it. All that the system will identify is that its standard applications are working.

RedBrowser is a Trojan which depends on java. The Trojan takes on the appearance of a program called "RedBrowser" which enables the user to visit WAP destinations without a WAP association. Amid application establishment, the user sees a demand on their telephone that the application needs authorization to send messages. In this way, if the user acknowledges, RedBrowser can send SMS to paid call focuses. This program utilizes the smartphone's association with interpersonal organizations (Facebook, Twitter, and so on.) to get the contact data for the user's colleagues (given the required authorizations have been given) and will send them messages.

WinCE.PmCryptic.A is a noxious software on Windows Mobile which plans to acquire cash for its creators. It utilizes the pervasion of memory cards that are embedded in the smartphone to spread all the more successfully.

CardTrap is an infection that is accessible on various sorts of smartphone, which plans to deactivate the system and outsider applications. It works by supplanting the documents used to begin the smartphone and applications to keep them from executing. There are distinctive variations of this infection, for example, Cardtrap.A for SymbOS devices. It likewise taints the memory card with malware fit for contaminating Windows.

Apparition Push is vindictive software on Android OS which naturally root the android gadget and introduces noxious applications specifically to system segment then unroots the gadget to keep users from expelling the risk by ace reset (The danger can be evacuated just by reflashing). It disables the system assets, executes rapidly, and harder to identify.

RANSOMWARE

Mobile ransomware is a sort of malware that keeps users out of their mobile devices in a compensation to-open your-gadget ploy, it has developed significantly as a danger class since 2014. Particular to mobile registering stages, users are frequently less security-cognizant, especially in accordance with examining applications and web joins believing the local insurance ability of the mobile gadget working system. Mobile ransomware represents a huge risk to organizations dependent on moment access and accessibility of their restrictive data and contacts. The probability of a voyaging agent paying a payoff to open their gadget is fundamentally higher since they are off guard given bothers, for example, convenience and more outlandish direct access to IT staff.

SPYWARE

Flexispy is an application that can be considered as a Trojan, in light of Symbian. The program sends all data got and sent from the smartphone to a Flexispy server. It was initially made to secure kids and keep an eye on two-timing life partners.

NUMBER OF MALWARE

The following is a chart which stacks the distinctive practices of smartphone malware regarding their impacts on smartphones:

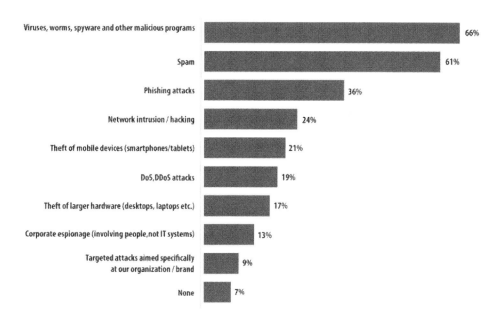

EFFECTS OF MALWARE

We can see from the chart that no less than 66% malwares are the lion's share that shows no negative conduct, with the exception of their capacity to spread.

CONVEYABILITY OF MALWARE CROSSWISE OVER STAGES

There is a large number of malware. This is somewhat because of the assortment of operating systems on smartphones. Be that as it may, attackers can likewise make their malware focus on various stages, and malware can be discovered which attacks an OS yet can spread to various systems.

In any case, malware can utilize runtime conditions like Java virtual machine or the .NET Framework. They can likewise utilize different libraries display in many operating systems. Other malware convey a few executable files so as to keep running in numerous situations and they use these amid the spread procedure. Practically speaking, this sort of malware requires an association between the two operating systems to use as an attack vector. Memory cards can be utilized for this reason, or synchronization software can be utilized to engender the infection.

COUNTERMEASURES

The security mechaniSMS set up to counter the dangers portrayed above are exhibited in this area. They are separated into various classes, as all don't demonstration at a similar level, and they run from the administration of security by the operating system to the behavioral instruction of the user. The dangers avoided by the different measures are not the same relying upon the case. Considering the two cases specified above, in the primary case one would shield the system from debasement by an application, and in the second case the establishment of a suspicious software would be counteracted.

SECURITY IN OPERATING SYSTEMS

The main layer of security inside a smartphone is at the level of the operating system (OS). Past the standard parts of an operating system (e.g. asset administration, booking forms) on a smartphone, it should likewise build up the conventions for presenting outside applications and data without presenting hazard.

A focal thought found in the mobile operating systems is the possibility of a sandbox. Since smartphones are as of now being intended to suit numerous applications, they should set up mechaniSMS to guarantee these offices are alright for themselves, for different applications and data on the system, and the user. In the event that a malevolent program figures out how to achieve a gadget, it is vital that the defenseless region introduced by the system be as little as could reasonably be expected. Sandboxing extends this thought to compartmentalize distinctive procedures, keeping them from communicating and harming each other. In light of the historical backdrop of operating systems, sandboxing has diverse usage. For instance, where iOS will concentrate on constraining access to its open API for applications from the App Store as a matter of course, Managed Open In enables you to confine which applications can access which sorts of data. Android constructs its sandboxing with respect to its inheritance of Linux and TrustedBSD.

ROOTKIT DETECTORS

The interruption of a rootkit in the system is an extraordinary peril in an indistinguishable route from on a computer. It is vital to forestall such interruptions, and to have the capacity to identify them as frequently as could be expected under the circumstances. Without a doubt, there is worry that with this sort of malevolent program, the outcome could be an incomplete or finish sidestep of the gadget security, and the obtaining of executive rights by the attacker. In the event that this happens, at that point nothing keeps the attacker from contemplating or handicapping the wellbeing highlights that were bypassed, sending the applications they need, or scattering a technique for interruption by a rootkit to a more extensive crowd. We can refer to, as a protection instrument, the Chain of trust in iOS. This component depends on the mark of the diverse applications required to begin the operating system, and a testament marked by Apple. If the mark checks are uncertain, the gadget distinguishes this and stops the boot-up. In the event that the Operating System is bargained because of Jailbreaking, root pack recognition may not work on the off chance that it is crippled by the Jailbreak strategy or software is stacked after Jailbreak incapacitates Rootkit Detection.

PROCESS DETACHMENT

Android utilizes mechaniSMS of user handle separation acquired from Linux. Every application has a user related with it, and a tuple (UID, GID). This approach fills in as a sandbox: while applications can be malignant, they can't escape the sandbox held for them by their identifiers, and along these lines can't meddle with the correct working of the system. For instance, since it is outlandish for a procedure to end the procedure of another user, an application would thus be able to not stop the execution of another.

FILE AUTHORIZATIONS

From the heritage of Linux, there are likewise filesystem authorizations mechaniSMS. They help with sandboxing: a procedure can't alter any files it needs. It is in this manner unrealistic to uninhibitedly degenerate files fundamental for the operation of another application or system. Besides, in Android there is the technique for locking memory authorizations. It is impractical to change the authorizations of files introduced on the SD card from the telephone, and thus it is difficult to introduce applications.

MEMORY PROTECTION

In an indistinguishable route from on a computer, memory security averts benefit heightening. Without a doubt, if a procedure figured out how to achieve the region assigned to different procedures, it could write in the memory of a procedure with rights better than their own, with root in the most pessimistic scenario, and perform activities which are past its consents on the system. It would suffice to embed work calls are approved by the benefits of the malevolent application.

IMPROVEMENT THROUGH RUNTIME SITUATIONS

Software is frequently created in abnormal state dialects, which can control what is being finished by a running project. For instance, Java Virtual Machines ceaselessly screen the activities of the execution strings they oversee, screen and allocate assets, and forestall malevolent activities. Cushion floods can be counteracted by these controls.

428

SECURITY SOFTWARE

Over the operating system security, there is a layer of security software. This layer is made out of individual segments to fortify different vulnerabilities: counteract malware, interruptions, the distinguishing proof of a user as a human, and user confirmation. It contains software parts that have gained from their involvement with computer security; notwithstanding, on smartphones, this software must manage more noteworthy imperatives.

ANTIVIRUS AND FIREWALL

An antivirus software can be sent on a gadget to confirm that it is not contaminated by a known danger, for the most part by signature location software that identifies noxious executable files. A firewall, then, can watch over the current activity on the system and guarantee that a vindictive application does not try to convey through it. It might similarly confirm that an introduced application does not try to build up suspicious correspondence, which may keep an interruption endeavor.

VISUAL NOTIFICATIONS

Keeping in mind the end goal to make the user mindful of any unusual activities, for example, a call they didn't start, one can interface a few capacities to a visual notice that is difficult to bypass. For instance, when a call is set off, the called number ought to dependably be shown. In this way, if a call is activated by a malevolent application, the user can see, and make proper move

TURING TEST

In an indistinguishable vein from above, it is vital to affirm certain activities by a user choice. The Turing test is utilized to recognize a human and a virtual user, and it frequently comes as a captcha.

BIOMETRIC RECOGNIZABLE PROOF

Another technique to utilize is biometrics. Biometrics is a method of distinguishing a man by methods for their morphology (by acknowledgment of the eye or face, for instance) or their conduct (their mark or method for composing for instance). One favorable position of utilizing biometric security is that users can abstain from remembering a watchword or other mystery mix to validate and keep pernicious users from accessing their gadget. In a system with solid biometric security, just the essential user can access the smartphone.

ASSET OBSERVING IN THE SMARTPHONE

At the point when an application passes the different security boundaries, it can take the activities for which it was composed. At the point when such activities are set off, the action of a malevolent application can be in some cases recognized on the off chance that one screens the different assets utilized on the telephone. Contingent upon the objectives of the malware, the outcomes of infection are not generally the same; every pernicious application are not expected to hurt the devices on which they are sent. The accompanying areas portray diverse approaches to distinguish suspicious movement.

BATTERY

Some malware is gone for depleting the vitality assets of the telephone. Observing the vitality utilization of the telephone can be an approach to identify certain malware applications.

MEMORY USE

Memory use is characteristic in any application. Notwithstanding, in the event that one finds that a significant extent of memory is utilized by an application, it might be hailed as suspicious.

SYSTEM ACTIVITY

On a smartphone, numerous applications will undoubtedly interface by means of the system, as a feature of their typical operation. Be that as it may, an application utilizing a ton of transfer speed can be firmly associated with endeavoring to convey a considerable measure of data, and disperse data to numerous different devices. This perception just permits a doubt, since some genuine applications can be exceptionally asset serious as far as system interchanges, the best illustration being spilling video.

SERVICES

One can screen the movement of different services of a smartphone. Amid specific minutes, a few services ought not be dynamic, and on the off chance that one is recognized, the application ought to be suspected. For instance, the sending of a SMS when the user is shooting video: this correspondence does not bode well and is suspicious; malware may endeavor to send SMS while its action is covered. The different focuses specified above are just signs and don't give conviction about the authenticity of the movement of an application. Be that as it may, these criteria can help target suspicious applications, particularly if a few criteria are joined.

SYSTEM RECONNAISSANCE

System movement traded by telephones can be checked. One can put shields in arrange directing focuses keeping in mind the end goal to distinguish irregular conduct. As the mobile's utilization of system conventions is a great deal more obliged than that of a computer, expected system data streams can be anticipated (e.g. the convention for sending a SMS), which licenses identification of irregularities in mobile networks.

SPAM CHANNELS

Similar to the case with email trades, we can identify a spam battle through methods for mobile interchanges (SMS, MMS). It is accordingly conceivable to recognize and limit this sort of endeavor by channels conveyed on organize framework that is handing-off these messages.

ENCRYPTION OF PUT AWAY OR TRANSMITTED DATA

Since it is constantly conceivable that data traded can be caught, interchanges, or even data storage, can depend on encryption to keep a noxious element from utilizing any data acquired amid correspondences. Be that as it may, this represents the issue of key trade for encryption calculations, which requires a protected channel.

TELECOM ARRANGE OBSERVING

The networks for SMS and MMS show unsurprising conduct, and there is not as much freedom contrasted and what one can do with conventions, for example, TCP or UDP. This infers one can't foresee the utilization made of the basic conventions of the web; one may produce almost no activity by counseling basic pages, once in a while, or create overwhelming movement by utilizing video gushing. Then again, messages traded by means of mobile telephone have a system and a particular model, and the user does not, in a typical case, have the opportunity to mediate in the points of interest of these interchanges. In this way, if a variation from the norm is found in the flux of system data in the mobile networks, the potential risk can be immediately recognized.

MAKER OBSERVATION

In the creation and appropriation chain for mobile devices, it is the duty of producers to guarantee that devices are conveyed in a fundamental design without vulnerabilities. Most users are not specialists and a large portion of them don't know about the presence of security vulnerabilities, so the gadget setup as given by makers will be held by numerous users. The following are recorded a few focuses which makers ought to consider.

EVACUATE INVESTIGATE MODE

Telephones are infrequently set in an investigate mode amid assembling, however this mode must be debilitated before the telephone is sold. This mode enables access to various elements, not expected for routine use by a user. Because of the speed of advancement and generation, diversions happen and a few devices are sold in troubleshoot mode. This sort of organization opens mobile devices to abuses that use this oversight.

DEFAULT SETTINGS

At the point when a smartphone is sold, its default settings must be right, and not leave security crevices. The default arrangement is not generally changed, so a decent introductory setup is fundamental for users. There are, for instance, default designs that are powerless against refusal of service attacks.

SECURITY REVIEW OF APPLICATIONS

Alongside smart telephones, appstores have risen. A user ends up confronting an enormous scope of applications. This is particularly valid for suppliers who oversee appstores on the grounds that they are entrusted with looking at the applications gave, from various perspectives (e.g. security, content). The security review ought to be especially wary, in light of the fact that if a blame is not identified, the application can spread rapidly inside a couple of days, and contaminate countless.

IDENTIFY SUSPICIOUS APPLICATIONS REQUESTING RIGHTS

When introducing applications, it regards caution the user against sets of authorizations that, gathered together, appear to be possibly risky, or if nothing else suspicious. Systems like, for example, Kirin, on Android, endeavor to distinguish and disallow certain arrangements of authorizations.

DISAVOWAL METHODOLOGY

Alongside appstores showed up another component for mobile applications: remote denial. To begin with created by Android, this technique can remotely and all around uninstall an application, on any gadget that has it. This implies the spread of a noxious application that figured out how to dodge security checks can be quickly halted when the danger is found.

MAINTAIN A STRATEGIC DISTANCE FROM INTENSELY ALTERED SYSTEMS

Makers are enticed to overlay custom layers on existing operating systems, with the double motivation behind offering altered choices and incapacitating or charging for

433

specific elements. This has the double impact of taking a chance with the presentation of new bugs in the system, combined with a motivation for users to adjust the systems to evade the maker's confinements. These systems are once in a while as steady and dependable as the first, and may experience the ill effects of phishing endeavors or different adventures.

ENHANCE SOFTWARE FIX FORMS

New forms of different software parts of a smartphone, including operating systems, are routinely distributed. They remedy many imperfections after some time. By the by, makers frequently don't send these updates to their devices in an opportune manner, and at times not in the slightest degree. In this manner, vulnerabilities endure when they could be amended, and on the off chance that they are not, since they are known, they are effortlessly exploitable.

USER MINDFULNESS

Much pernicious conduct is permitted by the indiscretion of the user. From essentially not leaving the gadget without a secret key, to exact control of authorizations allowed to applications added to the smartphone, the user has an extensive obligation in the cycle of security: to not be the vector of interruption. This safety measure is particularly essential if the user is a worker of an organization that stores business data on the gadget. Itemized beneath are a few precautionary measures that a user can take to oversee security on a smartphone.

A current review by internet security specialists BullGuard demonstrated an absence of understanding into the rising number of vindictive dangers influencing mobile telephones, with 53% of users guaranteeing that they are unconscious of security software for Smartphones. A further 21% contended that such insurance was pointless, and 42% let it be known hadn't entered their thoughts ("Using APA," 2011). These measurements demonstrate customers are not worried about security dangers since they trust it is not a major issue. The key here is to recall forget smartphones are successfully handheld computers and are similarly as helpless.

BEING DOUBTFUL

A user ought not think everything that might be introduced, as some data might be phishing or endeavoring to appropriate a malevolent application. It is consequently prudent to check the notoriety of the application that they need to purchase before really introducing it.

AUTHORIZATIONS GIVEN TO APPLICATIONS

The mass dispersion of applications is joined by the foundation of various consents mechaniSMS for each operating system. It is important to illuminate these consents mechaniSMS to users, as they vary starting with one system then onto the next, and are not generally straightforward. What's more, it is once in a while conceivable to change an arrangement of authorizations asked for by an application if the quantity of consents is excessively extraordinary. In any case, this last point is a wellspring of hazard in light of the fact that a user can allow rights to an application, a long ways past the rights it needs. For instance, a note taking application does not oblige access to the geolocation service. The user must guarantee the benefits required by an application amid establishment and ought not acknowledge the establishment if asked for rights are conflicting.

BE WATCHFUL

Insurance of a user's telephone through basic signals and safeguards, for example, bolting the smartphone when it is not being used, not leaving their gadget unattended, not putting stock in applications, not putting away touchy data, or scrambling delicate data that can't be isolated from the gadget.

ENSURE DATA

Smartphones have a huge memory and can convey a few gigabytes of data. The user must be cautious about what data it conveys and whether they ought to be secured. While it is generally not sensational if a melody is replicated, a file containing bank data or business data can be more dangerous. The user must have the judiciousness to maintain a strategic distance from the transmission of touchy data on a smartphone, which can be effectively stolen. Moreover, when a user disposes of a gadget, they should make certain to expel every individual data first.

These insurances are measures that leave no simple answer for the interruption of individuals or pernicious applications in a smartphone. In the event that users are watchful, many attacks can be crushed, particularly phishing and applications looking for just to get rights on a gadget.

INCORPORATED STORAGE OF INSTANT MESSAGES

One type of mobile assurance enables organizations to control the conveyance and storage of instant messages, by facilitating the messages on an organization server, instead of on the sender or beneficiary's telephone. At the point when certain conditions are met, for example, a lapse date, the messages are erased.

RESTRICTIONS OF CERTAIN SECURITY MEASURES

The security mechaniSMS specified in this article are to a huge degree acquired from learning and involvement with computer security. The elements forming the two gadget sorts are comparative, and there are basic measures that can be utilized, for example, antivirus and firewall. In any case, the usage of these arrangements is not really conceivable or possibly profoundly obliged inside a mobile gadget. The purpose behind this distinction is the specialized assets offered by computers and mobile devices: despite the fact that the registering energy of smartphones is winding up noticeably speedier, they have different restrictions than their processing power.

SINGLE-ASSIGNMENT SYSTEM

Some operating systems, including some still ordinarily utilized, are single-entrusting. Just the frontal area errand is executed. It is hard to present applications, for example, antivirus and firewall on such systems, since they couldn't play out their observing while the user is operating the gadget, when there would be most need of such checking.

VITALITY SELF-GOVERNANCE

A basic one for the utilization of a smartphone is vitality self-governance. It is essential that the security mechaniSMS not expend battery assets, without which the self-sufficiency of devices will be influenced significantly, undermining the powerful utilization of the smartphone.

SYSTEM DIRECTLY

System Directly identified with battery life, organize use ought not be too high. It is in reality a standout amongst the most costly assets, from the perspective of vitality utilization. In any case, a few computations may should be migrated to remote servers keeping in mind the end goal to save the battery. This adjust can make usage of certain concentrated calculation mechaniSMS a sensitive recommendation.

Moreover, it ought to be noticed that it is regular to find that updates exist, or can be created or sent, yet this is not generally done. One can, for instance, discover a user who does not realize that there is a more current rendition of the operating system good with the smartphone, or a user may find known vulnerabilities that are not redressed until the point when the finish of a long improvement cycle, which enables time to abuse the provisos.

UP AND COMING GENERATION OF MOBILE SECURITY

There is relied upon to be four mobile environments that will make up the security structure:

RICH OPERATING SYSTEM

In this class will fall conventional Mobile OS like Android, iOS, Symbian OS or Windows Phone. They will give the conventional usefulness and security of an OS to the applications.

SECURE OPERATING SYSTEM (SECURE OS)

A secure piece which will keep running in parallel with a completely included Rich OS, on a similar processor center. It will incorporate drivers for the Rich OS ("ordinary world") to speak with the secure portion ("secure world"). The trusted foundation could incorporate interfaces like the show or keypad to areas of PCI-E address space and recollections.

TRUSTED EXECUTION ENVIRONMENT (TEE)

Comprised of hardware and software. It helps in the control of access rights and houses touchy applications, which should be disengaged from the Rich OS. It viably goes about as a firewall between the "ordinary world" and "secure world".

SECURE ELEMENT (SE)

The SE comprises of alter safe hardware and related software. It can give elevated amounts of security and work pair with the TEE. The SE will be obligatory for facilitating vicinity installment applications or authority electronic marks.

Made in the USA
San Bernardino, CA
09 May 2020